FRIENDLY
TAKEOVER

James B. Lieber

FRIENDLY
TAKEOVER

How an Employee Buyout
Saved a Steel Town

VIKING

VIKING
Published by the Penguin Group
Penguin Books USA Inc., 375 Hudson Street,
New York, New York 10014, U.S.A.
Penguin Books Ltd, 27 Wrights Lane,
London W8 5TZ, England
Penguin Books Australia Ltd, Ringwood,
Victoria, Australia
Penguin Books Canada Ltd, 10 Alcorn Avenue,
Toronto, Ontario, Canada M4V 3B2
Penguin Books (N.Z.) Ltd, 182–190 Wairau Road,
Auckland 10, New Zealand

Penguin Books Ltd, Registered Offices:
Harmondsworth, Middlesex, England

First published in 1995 by Viking Penguin,
a division of Penguin Books USA Inc.

10   9   8   7   6   5   4   3   2   1

LIBRARY OF CONGRESS CATALOGING IN PUBLICATION DATA
Leiber, James B.
Friendly takeover : how an employee buyout saved a steel town / James B. Lieber.
p.   cm.
Includes bibliographical references and index.
ISBN 0-670-82075-X
1. Weirton Steel Corporation.   2. Employee ownership—West Virginia—Weirton.
3. Steel industry and trade—West Virginia—Weirton.   I. Title.
HD5658.I52W414   1995
338.7'669142'0975412—dc20   94-45179

This book is printed on acid-free paper.
∞

Printed in the United States of America
Set in Adobe Sabon
Designed by Kathryn Parise

To my wife, Margie,
who believed

Acknowledgments

Many people helped with this project. In particular, I would like to thank Paul Altomare, Gary Anderson, Jane Anderson, Jim Andreozzi, Richard "Red" Arango, John Balzano, Ronald Bancroft, Warren Bartell, Steve Bauman, Walter Bish, Irving Bluestone, Bill Breneissen, Traci Bright, Sam Cadile, Bill Carroll, John Chernenko, Michael Chesick, Sharon Coleman, Ed Conley, Michael Connery, Carol Copenhaver, Joe Copenhaver, Charles Cronin, Jack Curtis, Robert D'Anniballe, Robert Daum, Miles Dean, William Doepken, George Doty, Ike Eisnaugle, Herbert Elish, Dave Elo, Dick Emens, Thomas Evans, Lou Fakaris, Ben Fisher, Richard Garan, Tom Gaudio, Joshua Gotbaum, Elliott Goldstein, Alan Gould, David Gould, Luis Granados, Chris Graziani, Victor Greco, James Haas, Ralph Heise, Duke Horstenmyer, Michael Hrabovsky, Kenneth

Hunt, Ken Jacobs, Mike Jacobs, Anthony Julian, Eugene Keilin, Louis Kelso, John Kirkwood, Louis Kondus, Norman Kurland, Charles Lafferty, William Lee, Bob Lewis, Delbert Littleton, Russell Long, James Longacre, Robert Loughhead, Howard Love, Allan Lowenstein, Alice Lynd, Staughton Lynd, John Madigan, Joe Mayernik, Jess McHenry, Willie McKenzie, Darlene McKinley, James McNamara, Edward Mixon, Emil Morelli, Richard Mort, Randy Paulin, Bob Pearce, Michael Pearson, Craig Petrella, Jim Petrovich, John Phillips, Jack Redline, David Robertson, Jay Rockefeller, William Saunders, Richard Schubert, David Shuler, John "Skip" Spadafora, Father Charles Schneider, Rick Smith, Tina Smith, Harvey Sperry, Reverend Terry Stoops, Tom Sturges, Lee Sweat, Larry Sweiger, Jim Testa, Virgil Thompson, Frank Tluchowski, Dominic Tonacchio, George Vacheresse, Carl Valdiserri, J. J. Varlas, Pete Visnic, Ben Wade, John Walker, and Mike Zatezalo.

Further, I would like to thank the Board of Directors of Weirton Steel and the Executive Committee of the Independent Steel Workers Union for their cooperation. The *Weirton Daily Times* was helpful in providing me with clippings, and the Mary Weir Public Library also was extremely accommodating in supplying me with historical materials. The Weirton Chamber of Commerce furnished me with an office, at an absurdly low rate, for conducting interviews.

Also, I would like to thank Ruth Hart, John Kimmell, Amy Pope, and Karen Eriksen for help with research and the preparation of the manuscript. My editor, David Stanford, supplied solid judgment, and my children, Sara, Molly, and Anne, remained remarkably patient throughout.

"We are misfits when we
have to fit ourselves to a new
situation. And misfits live and
breathe in an atmosphere
of passion."

—Eric Hoffer
THE TEMPER OF OUR TIME

Preface

"Your reputation has gone way beyond West Virginia . . ."
—BILL CLINTON

As children growing up in Pittsburgh in the 1950s and 1960s, we took air-raid drills seriously. According to local legend, our city was the Soviet Union's number two nuclear target, behind Washington and ahead of New York. After all, we were America's steel center, the foundry of the free world.

In high school we learned to equate steel with prosperity. My friends, whose parents worked in the sprawling, spewing factories lining the rivers, wore stylish clothes, carried discretionary cash, and sometimes owned cars. The only hard times occurred during infrequent but lengthy strikes in the industry. Many of these kids had other career goals besides becoming "millhunks." But in the back of their minds was the notion that well-paying positions awaited them at U.S. Steel or Jones & Laughlin Steel, alongside their fathers, uncles, and perhaps even grandfathers. Steel was stability, the anchor of a vast blue-collar middle class.

It's over now: the jobs, the money, the distinctive muscular pride that defined local culture. Now, mills have been razed. One is a mall, another a water theme park. Main streets in the mill towns are boarded up. Once there were more than a hundred thousand steelworkers in the Pittsburgh area. Now there are about four thousand. Overall population is in steep decline. None of us realistically can expect our children to stay here.

It ended with food banks and finger pointing. Management and labor blamed each other. Politicians whined about foreign competition and the hardness of the dollar. Critics in the media bashed banks for making bad loans to Latin America instead of investing in domestic industry and infrastructure. Militant steelworkers put rotten fish in their safe-deposit boxes at Mellon Bank, disrupted services at wealthy churches, and dumped twisted scrap on the altars. In Clairton, radicals packing guns occupied the Lutheran church. During a two-week armed standoff, which I mediated unsuccessfully, the notion of performing a feasibility study to determine whether an industrial facility could be sold to its employees—something that had happened at Weirton Steel—was on the table briefly.

Fortunately, the siege ended without bloodshed. Afterwards, one of the leaders, a Lutheran minister who declared himself a Trotskyite, did hard time. Later, one of the labor dissidents whom I represented became a born-again Christian, and went free.

In the late 1980s, I began visiting Weirton, a West Virginia town thirty miles downriver on the Ohio. Entering Weirton gave me the feeling of driving into the past, into postwar Pittsburgh, Gary, or Birmingham during the heyday of big steel. The community did not have the ramshackle, ghost town feel of others in the Ohio Valley. Snaking from one end of town to the other, the enormous mill, which specialized in tinplate steel, used mainly in canning, was a bustling hub into which trains, trucks, and full shifts of employees—eight thousand in all—came and went. Blue-collar families sustained merchants, paid taxes, painted their homes, and generally upheld a middle-class lifestyle. Community spirit was palpable. During a period of unbridled corporate raiding and looting, Weirton seemed to stand alone as a positive, even uplifting, national economic story. Obvious questions arose: How had they done it? Could they make it last?

When Bill Clinton brought his presidential campaign to Weirton in the summer of 1992, he told steelworkers:

> Of course your reputation has gone way beyond West Virginia, so I had heard about Weirton and followed the activities here over the last several years.
>
> I think the involvement of the employees, the production process, the way the employees participate in the ownership and contribute to the stock value and pay themselves based on the profitability of the company—it's all very, very impressive.
>
> There are a lot of things here I think the American people could learn a lot from, and I think we could rebuild the manufacturing sector in America more quickly if more companies learned more of the lessons that you practice here.

For years I searched to find the key to the Weirton story—its survival and its success, which at times seemed as improbable as that of a horse-and-buggy company making it in the automotive age. How could a big unionized mill compete against newer Japanese, German, and Korean facilities, nonunion cowboy capitalist minimills such as those at Nucor? How could it compete against aluminum and plastics?

This is a book about politics in the private sector. Most Americans have a glancing, sporadic, and vicarious relation to electoral politics, as our low voter turnout figures attest. But political participation at home and on the job where we struggle for power, make decisions, and divide wealth, is daily, direct, and all but compulsory.

The private sector is by definition private, and company towns may be among the most private places of all. Writers entering this arena find no tradition of openness or Freedom of Information Act to help them. Even the best companies tend to be guarded about information, and what they release often has the sweet smell of public relations.

This is not an "authorized" book about a corporation. In general I had to rely on the voluntary cooperation of individuals, which came slowly, and was asked to play by rules. The company wanted me to clear with it all employee interviews in advance. I agreed to the limitation regarding management personnel, but not labor. As it turned out, however, the people who chose to talk to me seemed less studied and far more candid than those in public political life, who are usually so concerned with images and public opinion.

Many Americans will find that the Weirton story is relevant to their own lives. In many businesses and industries the brutal reality of the postmodern economy can hit in a hurry, accompanied by friendly sounding buzzwords like "right-sizing," "employee participation," and "total quality." Sometimes change comes in the form of a major structural shift, such as a spin-off, or as an employee stock ownership plan (ESOP). In a troubled business, the latter means that you must decide whether to buy out your employer, and, in a real sense, buy your own job.

What happened at Weirton suggests most of the issues that can arise, in such a situation, how to cope or not to cope with them, and who wins and who loses when an employee-owned start-up strains to survive. This narrative focuses on the early years, when the situation was not confusing, and on those who played major roles in the unfolding drama.

There were no larger-than-life figures in Weirton—no Martin Luther Kings, Lech Wałęsas, or Mother Teresas—just a succession of ordinary people, sometimes in bitter conflict with each other, wrestling relentlessly with problems. Along the way, it became clear that Weirton was as much a cauldron for the major ideas and trends of the late twentieth century as it was for iron, coke, tin, and zinc.

Pittsburgh, Pennsylvania
February 1, 1995

Contents

PART TWO: GAIN

PART ONE

Pain

1   Black Tuesday

"You've always hated Weirton, haven't you, Pete?"
—RICHARD "RED" ARANGO

On February 22, 1982, Denise Youngstedt, a paralegal in a poverty law office in Steubenville, Ohio, a hard-bitten steel town, wrote an impassioned letter to Staughton Lynd, a lawyer whom she knew only by reputation in Youngstown, a hundred miles to the north. Both worked for the Legal Services Corporation, a federally chartered nonprofit corporation that grew out of the Johnson administration's "war on poverty." In keeping with its conservative mood, Washington in recent years had heaped red tape on the corporation to keep it from lobbying, organizing its low-income clients, and engaging in high-impact law-reform cases.

Youngstedt and Lynd were among the corporation's employees who found it hard to accept such limitations. She and her then husband, Jim McNamara, a Legal Services lawyer, had represented the Committee for Justice, a small racially integrated group of activists who had fought successful court battles against police brutality in Steubenville in the late 1970s but now focused on local layoffs and deindustrialization.

In Youngstown, Lynd had filed heroic but losing suits to block steel mill shutdowns, while spearheading a failed worker and community drive to buy the facilities. Youngstedt arranged that Lynd would speak at a conference on plant closings at the hall of United Steelworkers Local 1190 in Steubenville. "It means," she wrote, "that you will be talking to the folks who will lose everything when they close the plants down." Sponsors included the USW Local, the Committee for Justice, and Legal Services. Four days later the paralegal alerted Lynd that the USW had backed out of sponsoring him but would still allow the event to be held at its hall.

Brilliant, low-key, and provocative, Lynd, fifty-two, had led a life of conviction. After receiving his doctorate in 1960, he taught American history at Spelman, a black college in Atlanta, and at Yale. In 1964 he spent the summer in the civil rights movement in Mississippi. The following year, he chaired the first peace march on Washington against the Vietnam War, following a mission to Hanoi with Tom Hayden, after which the State Department stripped Lynd of his passport. Despite writing highly regarded histories of radicalism, slavery, and nonviolence, Lynd suddenly found it impossible to land college teaching jobs and believed himself blacklisted because of his New Left activities.

With his wife, Alice, a frequent coauthor, he moved to Chicago in 1968. After five years of community organizing, he applied to the law school at the University of Chicago, which triggered a debate among faculty, at least one of whom threatened to resign but then backed down when Lynd won admission. As a student, Lynd excelled and made the law review. After graduation he took a job with the Youngstown, Ohio, firm of Green, Schiavoni, Murphy, Haines and Sgambati, which represented Ohio's major unions. Quickly making a name for himself by counseling dissident Teamsters, Lynd also published a slim book, *Labor Law for the Rank and Filer*, which stressed self-help: "Whenever a problem can be solved without the help of lawyers do it. Lawyers, like doctors, make their profession seem more mysterious than it really is." His views clashed with those of his managing partner, Eugene Green, who fired him in 1978. Lynd joined Legal Services, and he began offering free representation to truckers accused of wildcat striking. But Green, Lynd's former partner, filed a successful brief against Legal Services to disqualify it from serving the truckers. "All I want to do," said Green, "is to get Legal Services to live up to its enabling statute, and not become the legal arm of those who attack the labor movement from within."

The United Steelworkers union leadership felt much as the Teamsters bosses had about Lynd. During the Youngstown steel shutdown Lynd had taken the USW and its president, Lloyd McBride, to task for failing to support the proposed community buyout of the mills until it was too late. In 1975, Lynd was among those who had challenged the union's Experimental Negotiating Agreement (ENA) with the Big Eight steel companies. The most lucrative pact in the union's history, the ENA included automatic cost-of-living increases, which made steelworkers the best-paid industrial workers in America. The union, however, gave up the right to strike, which enraged dissidents backed by Lynd. Perhaps most threatening to organized labor, Lynd had begun to write and speak in favor of creating a new power center, which he called the "rank and file group," among workers in factories, apart from their union. He defined it as "an organization that acts differently, a group that you can turn to when you have a problem, a group that creates change."

Lynd also set corporate teeth on edge. In court he had log-jammed United States Steel's "Greenfield" plan in the late seventies to build a new mill in rural Conneaut, Ohio, rather than first modernizing the "brownfield mills" in older urban centers. When USS announced the closing of the Youngstown works, he planned and participated in sit-ins at the corporation's tower in Pittsburgh, at its office building in Youngstown, as well as at the executives' Ohio country club. During the searing court battle over the Youngstown shutdown, Lynd subpoenaed USS chairman David Roderick to come to the federal court proceedings in Youngstown, and forced him to explain to hundreds of working people in the gallery why corporate strategy dictated their community's demise.

In early 1980, a federal judge issued a rare injunction blocking U.S. Steel from closing its Youngstown works pending the outcome of the case. Ultimately, the court decided against Lynd and his clients. In early 1982, U.S. Steel took the highly public step of dynamiting its Youngstown blast furnaces, which ensured that local people would never be able to work in a large full-scale steel operation again.

In late February, the Committee for Justice publicized Lynd's upcoming speech with leaflets in nearby Toronto, Ohio, at the plant gates of Timet Corporation, which machined nuclear warheads, in Steubenville at Wheeling-Pittsburgh Steel, and in Weirton, West Virginia, at the huge Weirton division of National Steel, the largest mill complex between the East Coast and Gary. In Weirton, one potent rumor circulated that operations would shut down, while another held that a Japanese firm, possibly Honda, would take over the mills.

Joined by a span across the Ohio River, Steubenville and Weirton both had populations of roughly twenty-five thousand, but no one ever called them the Twin Cities. Alike in one respect—their vices— both towns housed thriving illegal gambling rooms, numbers lotteries, and bookie joints tolerated for the most part by law enforcement. It was not unusual for laid-off steelworkers to "run" numbers during hard times, or even take work in Las Vegas as dealers or croupiers. While Steubenville had a historic brothel district, Weirton contented itself with a row of seedy stripper bars.

Otherwise, the towns had entirely different atmospheres. In Steubenville, the mills were relegated to uninhabited flats. The shabby but pleasant downtown afforded a sweeping view of the Ohio River waterfront. In Weirton, the steel plants bellied up to the sidewalk on Main Street. One facility, the colossal twenty-two-story basic oxygen furnace whose roof ventilators extended up from its sides like arms, looked like the Jolly Green Giant, which in fact was its nickname, beseeching heaven. In most places, the mills blocked any view of the river. To see it, you had to climb one of the hills ringing the town. Movies such as *The Deer Hunter* and *Reckless* that wanted to make a point about the gritty, claustral quality of steel town life used Weirton as a backdrop.

Another difference between Steubenville and Weirton was race. In Steubenville, which was about 14 percent black, blacks relaxed, strolled, bet, and hit the bars downtown. In Weirton, about 4 percent black, they drove past the downtown, a preserve of white male workers—many laid off, between shifts, or retired—who hung out in bars, at the bus station lunch counter, or on corners.

The two towns also had different unions. While the United Steelworkers represented hourly employees at Wheeling-Pittsburgh's plants in Steubenville, it had failed to organize Weirton Steel, the largest mill not under its jurisdiction in the United States. Weirton workers belonged to the Independent Steel Workers (ISU), which the USW regarded as company-dominated. Relations between the two unions were chilly for many reasons, not the least of which was because the Weirton workers happily worked and lined their pockets at times when the rest of the industry was out on strike.

In 1954 Walter Adams, a noted steel economist, wrote: "America's Steel Industry is the most powerful in the world. . . . Its product is the basic ingredient of our industrial civilization. . . . Our economy for many years will undoubtedly be founded on Steel." Because steel was central to prosperity and security, trouble in the industry was treated as a national issue and dealt with at the highest levels. In 1952, during the Korean War, President Truman caused a constitutional crisis by seizing and running strike-stalled steel mills. Ten years later President Kennedy, confronting United States Steel chairman Roger Blough in much the same way as he had faced down Soviet leader Nikita Khrushchev during the Cuban missile crisis, forced the industry to retract a price hike.

In 1978 Roger Brown, chairman of the Republic Steel Corporation, which would be blended with Jones & Laughlin to create LTV, accurately depicted steel as "a sick industry and neither the public nor the government wants to recognize that." Steel's fall had many fathers. The large integrated producers, which smelted iron from ore, cooled it with coke and manganese to make steel, and finished it in various shapes and coatings, had insufficiently capitalized their operations. As mills moldered, product quality suffered. The companies, which had bloated managements and work crews, also relied excessively on vertical integration, choosing to own and maintain ore and coal reserves plus barge and rail lines rather than buying or leasing only what was needed. Sales slipped as Detroit made smaller, lighter cars, and container makers shifted to plastics, aluminum, composites, and paper. Foreign producers with leading-edge technologies, lower labor costs, government protection and subsidies permitted slower returns on investment than their American counterparts and made deep inroads into domestic markets. During an inflationary period that featured a hard dollar relative to foreign currencies, American capital flew from basic industries to other ventures, and often overseas. However, neither Republican administrations nor the Carter White House, which had crafted a package of more than a billion dollars in loan guarantees to save Chrysler, chose to intervene in steel, where key decisions were left in private hands.

During the last week in February 1982, National Steel, the nation's fifth-largest producer, indicated that its chairman, Howard M. "Pete" Love, would make a statement on March 2 regarding its Weirton division. It was a horrible time for an announcement in the recession-mired industry where employment had sunk to its lowest ebb since 1933, and more than two hundred thousand jobs had been lost since 1978. At Weirton, about twenty-six hundred of eight thousand employees already were laid off.

In the previous three years, five major producers, Washburton Wire, McLouth Steel, Penn Dixie, Alan-Wood Steel, and Wisconsin Steel, had gone into bankruptcy, and the shakeout was expected to continue. Soon two other giants, LTV and Wheeling-Pittsburgh Steel, the nation's second- and seventh-largest steel companies, would seek protection from creditors and reorganization through the bankruptcy courts. In 1982, steel's plague year, the industry would lose $90 per ton, more than $3 billion in all. At National, the red ink would climb to $462 million, amounting to 37 percent of its shareholders' equity.

In the days before Love's announcement, rumors continued to swirl through Weirton that National would shut down the mill or sell it to the Japanese. Others held that the corporation planned wider layoffs or would seek to reopen the labor contract in order to wring concessions from the workforce.

During a break in a routine arbitration of a worker's grievance on

Thursday, February 25, Bill Doepken, Weirton Steel's industrial relations counsel, approached his opponent, David Robertson, the Independent Steel Workers Union's attorney, and asked him to meet with management the next morning at eight. It was important.

Longtime friends in their late thirties, after law school both had started careers in Weirton's industrial relations department. Slim, mustachioed, and well tailored, Doepken, though management's attorney, was seen as straight-talking and fair-minded by workers, some of whom over the course of a year had told him that they would be willing to make economic concessions if management would use the savings to upgrade the mill. Doepken relayed the information to divisional management who conveyed it to National. Because Weirton was a highly insular town, some people held it against Doepken that he chose to live in a suburb of Pittsburgh rather than "in the Valley."

The son of a chief chemist at Weirton Steel who had died of brain cancer, David Robertson had lived his whole life in Weirton (except for the years away at college and law school), a situation about which he appeared ambivalent. He particularly admired his brother, a doctor, who had escaped to California. Before saying something difficult, he often weighed the consequences to himself and others by sighing: "I still have to live in this town."

Robertson left industrial relations in 1973 to become the union's attorney at the urging of National Steel's Machiavellian labor lawyer, Donald Ebbert, who held out the promise to the young lawyer of a subsequent major job in management. After a few years of representing the ISU, Robertson reapproached Ebbert, who failed to come through with a company job.

Feeling betrayed, Robertson committed himself to union work with a vengeance. He also married the daughter of a local union official. By the standards of American Federation of Labor founder Samuel Gompers, who when asked the purpose of unions simply answered "more," Robertson, a confessed workaholic, became the most successful labor lawyer in the industry, where his clients' wages and pensions topped those won by the USW. In fact, Weirton's hourly employees had become the best-paid industrial workers in the world.

A rotund, balding man with a roughly trimmed fringe of hair, intelligent but weak eyes behind glasses, the beginnings of a double chin, and a few tricks up his sleeve, Robertson, whose appearance reminded some union members of Benjamin Franklin, also had prospered. He and his law partner, a trial attorney named Martin Bogarad, also had represented many of the six thousand union members in their car accidents, divorces, and real estate transactions. When George Sisshon, the president of Weirton Steel, left in 1977, Robertson and his family bought his handsome home.

The fact that Robertson had chosen a Jewish partner probably said something about his breadth and sensitivity. The town had a slight but palpable undercurrent of anti-Semitism. Jews did not rise high at Weirton Steel. When the local newspaper profiled a citizen who had a name that might be Jewish, it was quick to point out his church affiliation whether or not it was relevant. Like most blacks, most Jews in the upper Ohio Valley chose to live in Steubenville rather than Weirton.

On Friday at 8:00 A.M., Robertson reported to the General Office, a modern low-slung complex on a hill above the mills, to meet with Bill Doepken, Weirton Steel president Jack Redline, executive vice president Carl Valdiserri, vice president of industrial relations John Madigan, and comptroller Gene West, who had known of National's plans for months, and told them to Robertson, with the understanding that he would not reveal them to his clients before Love made his announcement. Robertson felt that he "was being brought into the inner circle." He was asked how to handle the situation; they didn't want emotional outbursts or violence. It was agreed that after Love spoke, National's boardroom would be made available to the Weirton delegation so they could deal with the shock and blow off steam. Also, plans were made to convene a meeting of all the union's stewards following the announcement so that they could take the information into every part of the plant.

On Monday, March 1, National chairman Love flew into Charleston, West Virginia, for a private meeting with then Governor John D. Rockefeller IV. The scion of a family synonymous with wealth, Jay

Rockefeller presided over a state that ranked forty-seventh in annual median family income ($7,400). Only 10 percent of its families took home more than $15,000, while 17 percent earned less than $3,000.

Even without money, Rockefeller would have been unusual in West Virginia. In the 1950s he took a year's leave of absence from Harvard to live in a Japanese village. Discovering that a year was not sufficient time to learn the language or "be there with any meaning," he stayed for three.

After returning to college for his final year, he joined the VISTA federal antipoverty program, taking an assignment in Emmons, West Virginia, a village of fifty-six families, where economic life focused on tiny "punch" mines that paid workers eight to ten dollars per day. During a first isolated, awkward year, he felt as if his communications problems in Japan were being repeated. Becoming better acclimated over the next two years, he worked on getting the town a school bus, library, preschool program, and elementary school, which he helped to build by hand.

Breaking his family tradition by becoming a Democrat, he won a seat in the state legislature as a Democrat in 1966 and was elected West Virginia secretary of state in 1968. In 1972, he ran unsuccessfully for governor, then sat out politics for four years as president of West Virginia Wesleyan College. He won the governorship in 1976 and reelection in 1980.

In fact, much of his attractiveness to the West Virginia electorate derived from his family's money. On one hand voters hoped that Rockefeller's family connections and influence would rain dollars and jobs on West Virginia. On the other, in a state notorious for bribery, people expected that a Rockefeller would not be tempted. In this, they were right. The tall, horn-rimmed, scholarly, slightly dreamy governor, who looked like the professor of East Asian history he might have become, exuded rectitude.

Not surprisingly, his administration had not been able to reverse the decline of West Virginia. The state sat atop enough coal to power America for hundreds of years, but Americans wanted to burn cleaner fuels. Moreover, the coal industry sought to reduce its labor intensity by strip mining rather than deep mining. The state's population had been declining for over a decade. With a poor educational system and a jagged topography that made construction tricky and roads hellish, West Virginia had trouble drawing new business. The most completely unionized workforce in the United States and the notoriety of local wildcat strikes also discouraged entrepreneurs.

Unlike the rest of the state, the Northern Panhandle, which contained Weirton, was hilly rather than mountainous. A center of manufacturing, especially of glass and steel rather than mining, its median family income was a thousand dollars higher than the state average. The Panhandle's educational average of 11.6 years bested the West Virginia figure by a full grade. As the most economically stable part of the state, and the most distant from the capital at Charleston, the region historically had received the least attention from state government.

On March 1, Love and Rockefeller had a short and difficult meeting. The chairman previewed his announcement to the Weirton employees.

When other companies recently had closed large coal mines, Rockefeller had received no notice, and had to read about the shutdowns in the newspapers. Now, he respected Love for giving advance warning that National would pull out of Weirton, wondering if the unusual courtesy had something to do with the fact that their sisters had been college roommates. Regardless, the news about Weirton Steel, the largest employer, taxpayer, and user of electricity in West Virginia, gave Rockefeller "an immediate sense of fear for the future of the state." He felt "crushed by the feeling that we in West Virginia were being done in by the decisions of others."

For the governor, National's news was the worst since the Buffalo Creek dam break in 1972, which had killed 125 people. That, he recalled, "was death in the literal sense. I remember driving all night from Morgantown to get down there at sunrise to that valley of death. There is no experience that can ever equate to seeing arms and legs sticking out of piles of wood and things. But if there was an industrial equivalent to it, an emotional hard hit, the feeling that Weirton would probably close was as close as you could come in West Virginia."

The forty-minute drive between Weirton and Pittsburgh spans Appalachia and a modern corporate center. As the highway winds out of the West Virginia Panhandle and through rolling forest, farms, and coal camps, one sees the pickups and vans of bow hunters parked on the berm. Finally the road tunnels through a mountain that opens suddenly to reveal the vista of a business skyline. For the better part of a century, National had not entered the local skyscraper competition. But as the Weirton delegation motored across the Monongahela on the Fort Pitt Bridge on "Black Tuesday," March 2, 1982, the first structure that came into view was National's new riverfront headquarters. Unlike Alcoa's aluminum tower or U.S. Steel's maroon steel colossus, National's headquarters did not have a metallic skin, but was faced instead with creamy white concrete, which signaled the transition from a steel firm to a holding company of diverse properties including pharmaceuticals, petrochemicals, savings and loans, and discount stores as well as steel. Because the new offices weren't ready, the Weirton group, which included twenty-one members of the ISU's executive committee, five members of the Independent Guards Union (IGU), a tiny organization of mill cops, and eight members of management, took seats around a conference table at National's old and traditionally modest headquarters in a law building adjacent to the Allegheny County Courthouse.

A tall, finely featured man with a massive bald head that seemed appropriate to his reputation as an analytical manager, Pete Love, chairman of National since 1979, had spearheaded the diversification strategy. At precisely 9:10 he entered the room with vice-chairman George Angevine. In soft, measured, almost emotionless tones, Love began by offering that what he had to say was "difficult." Some of the unionists grumbled. "They're thinking: 'the prick,' " Love said to himself. But it is fair to say that neither side in Weirton cared for the CEO.

The managers, mainly engineers, feared Love, a graduate of Harvard Business School, as an "M.B.A. type" who lacked any allegiance to steel. Jack Redline, the Weirton division's president within the corporation and once Love's boss, believed that Love's "silver spoon" connections as the son of a former Chrysler chairman had propelled him to the peak of National, Chrysler's main steel supplier. He detested Love's strategy of buying unrelated companies as the antics of a "business playboy" who also liked to fly the corporate jet to major golf tournaments while urging austerity on subordinates. But for the moment, Redline and Love had buried the hatchet and were working together. Also, Redline and his staff knew what Love was going to say, and saw it as an opportunity. Labor, however, expected the worst. Before becoming chairman, Love had worked at the corporation's other mills: Great Lakes Steel in Detroit, Midwest Steel outside Chicago, and Granite City Steel near Saint Louis, all of which were organized by the United Steelworkers. But Weirton's ISU workers had had no direct dealings with the chairman and feared that if he had to make a tough choice between workers belonging to their relatively small independent union or the large powerful international, he would choose the latter.

Historically, two types of steel masters have come out of Pittsburgh: the paternal, philanthropic, community-oriented leaders like Andrew Carnegie, and the rapacious, cold-blooded tyrants such as Charles Schwab. During the industry's painful shakeout in the late 1970s and early 1980s when Wall Street urged getting rid of "overcapacity" in the face of weakened demand, the hard-nosed latter-day Schwab types, who abounded, closed down operations and walked away from the chaos without a second look.

Like some of his predecessors at National, Love, who involved himself in every community and charitable activity from the Boy Scouts to the ballet and chose to live near the center of Pittsburgh rather than in a walled-off suburban estate, had a sense of social obligation that coated his business judgments.

In addition, while National's board looked like a typical assemblage of prosperous white males, it included some members likely to be receptive to the human as well as fiscal factors in a business decision. For example, Jean Mayer, president of Tufts University, had been a leader in the fight against hunger and for world nutritional reform. Sigo Falk was the scion of a Jewish philanthropic family that had invested in National Steel from the first and also devoted itself to community health care and reform-minded educational projects. During World War II, Falk's father had set up a kibbutz near Santo Domingo for Jews who had fled Nazi Germany. George Stimson, the previous chairman and a former president of Weirton, had deep roots in Weirton, having married the daughter of Tom Millsopp, an early president of the division and mayor of the town. Henry Hillman, a moderate-to-liberal billionaire, had built bridges between the black and business communities in Pittsburgh, where he acted as a counterweight to the decidedly conservative influence of the Mellons and Scaifes. His wife, Elsie, a Republican National Committee member, championed moderates such as Richard Thornburgh while supporting the Equal Rights Amendment (ERA), taking a pro-choice line on abortion, and generally advocating women's issues within the party.

Love and his board knew that National, a troubled, cash-short business, could not attract adequate capital. Its stock sold at a third of book value. Its management consultant, Bain & Company of Boston, recommended slashing employee costs.

Historically, National had paid the high "labor premium" at Weirton in order to keep out the United Steelworkers. In addition, the division, once National's flagship, had a narrow mill. At forty-eight inches it could not serve the car industry as well as the other National facilities, which rolled steel sheets more than twice as wide.

Weirton focused on tin plate for canning, which National and its consultant saw as a mature and declining market. Love, the son of a automaker, was betting that Detroit would rebound and buy more steel than would the canneries, which packaged consumer goods.

He and his board wanted Weirton, its labor costs, and product lines off the books, but there were no buyers for huge aging American steelworks in the early 1980s. For over a year, National had searched for a way to shed Weirton without traumatizing the West Virginia community, which depended almost totally on the mill. Now the corporation was ready to take a step that no other steelmaker had taken.

Standing uncomfortably, Love explained that National would not continue to invest in Weirton, which had been only marginally profitable over the past five years. The corporation required a 15 percent return on investment (ROI). At Weirton, ROI hovered around 1 percent. National would direct capital funds "to other projects throughout the corporation which have the potential for substantially higher returns." In the present economy there was no possibility of selling the mill to an outside buyer. Alternatives included shutting it down, "harvesting" it—in other words, running it into the ground without repairs or new equipment—or operating it for a time as a much smaller scale finishing facility with a total employment of about fifteen hundred. Love said that he and National's board favored a different course: "a sale of the entire division to its employees" through a mechanism called an employee stock ownership plan, or ESOP, a term that few from Weirton besides top management and David Robertson, the union's attorney, had heard.

Under an ESOP, Love explained, a trust is created and banks make loans to it, which allows the trust to buy the company's stock. The company makes payments out of pretax earnings to the trust to retire the debt. As the banks are repaid, the trust allocates stock to employees. As eyes glazed over in the room, Love indicated that National would fly New Jersey attorney Allan Lowenstein, an ESOP expert with whom it had conferred, to Weirton the following day to advise the division's union and management. Further, National would be willing to end its relationship with Lowenstein in order to allow him to represent Weirton in upcoming buyout negotiations with the corporation. Then the chairman took three questions.

The first was a plant. Jack Redline, Weirton's president, asked Love whether National would reconsider its decision if the employees at Weirton would take deep cuts in wages and benefits, say five dollars an hour. Love said no, the decision was irrevocable.

Redline had arranged the question in advance with Love. Its purpose was to show that the proposed spin-off of the division was not simply a ruse to get the employees in a concessionary mood. A basically straightforward man, Redline was a poor actor. Not fooled by his performance, the union officials in the room continued to believe that National had ulterior motives.

Then David Robertson, the union's attorney, raised his hand. Since learning of National's plan, he had crammed ESOP materials and sensed their complexity. Unlike the general counsel of major unions,

Robertson had no staff of economists or tax and pension experts to assist him. For eleven years he had had to be master of the big picture as well as the minutiae for the ISU. Feeling burned out, he had hoped to leave the union in 1982. The crisis put his plans on hold. Now, he asked Love, how long did National feel that the negotiations to sever Weirton would take. The chairman hoped matters could be wrapped up by the end of the year. In fact, the transaction would take twenty-two months.

Finally, the ISU president, Richard "Red" Arango, forty-six, a 250-pound former fullback, groaned, "You've always hated Weirton, haven't you, Pete?"

"No, Red," said Love, "that's not true." The separation, he explained, simply had made sense from a business standpoint. Then the chairman left the room. "No one," he recalls, "applauded when I left."

The Weirton management team seemed remarkably upbeat in the wake of the announcement. No longer would Weirton be shackled by National's corporate strategy. As a stand-alone company, they insisted that the division would thrive.

Angry and confused, the labor delegation wondered why Weirton's employees should buy a mill that National didn't want. Some of these union leaders, who served the highest paid industrial workers in the world, saw a way of life coming to an end and themselves saddled with a failure.

Hulking, goateed Mike Hrabovsky, a crane man in the blooming mill, who looked like a pro-wrestling villain, accused Jack Redline of knowing in advance what Love was going to do, a serious charge in an era when labor demanded as much notice as possible of plant shutdowns in order to plan for dislocation and minimize the impact. Redline, who disliked Hrabovsky for being "negative" and "radical," vigorously denied the charge while in fact he and Carl Valdiserri, the executive vice president of the division, had known of National's plans and Bain & Company's recommendations the previous fall, and at the corporation's urging both had gone to New Jersey to consult with Allan Lowenstein, the ESOP lawyer.

To ease the mood Hrabovsky tried a joke. "At least," he said, "an ESOP is better than a henway."

"What the hell's a henway?" snapped Redline.

"About eight pounds," said Hrabovsky. The joke fell flat. The men made their way back to Weirton in stony silence. "It was like a funeral procession," recalled Hrabovsky.

2   Weir's World

"I believe I am warranted in the assumption that I am one of the men whom Mr. Roosevelt calls economic royalists."

—ERNEST T. WEIR

Weirton, Weirton Steel, and National Steel all began with Ernest Tener Weir, who was born in Pittsburgh in 1875. His parents, Northern Irish immigrants, chose the middle name to honor the Teners, their wealthy relatives—a Tener later would become Pennsylvania's governor. The Weirs, however, eked out a marginal living from a riding stable in a Pittsburgh park, which his father ran until his death in 1890. At fifteen, the son quit school to become an office boy

19

in a factory where a Tener was an official. The boy's weekly wage, three dollars, was the sole support of his mother and younger brother. In later life Weir would recall his mother as a saint and dismiss his father as a horse-fancier lacking ambition.

Himself driven to succeed, Weir quickly rose to a salesman's job and often traveled as far as Texas to sell barbed wire. On one of his trips, his pocket was picked and Weir charged his hundred-dollar loss to his expense account. After the company refused the item in order "to teach the young man a lesson," Weir looked for another job.

Still in his early twenties, he landed one as chief clerk at the Oliver Tin Plate Company on Pittsburgh's South Side, which soon suffered a strike. The disruption, violence, vandalism, and loss of customers, according to a longtime associate, "left a permanent scar on the mind of Ernest Weir. It became his adamant conviction that a strike held no real benefits for anyone; and that there was no valid excuse for one. . . ."

In 1901, Weir moved to the American Sheet and Tin Plate Company, which three years earlier had been gobbled up by the Tin Plate Trust organized by Daniel Gray "Czar" Reid and William B. "Tinplate" Leeds, who took $20,000,000 worth of stock as promoters' fees. The trust controlled 90 percent of the nation's tinplate productive capacity. Reid and Leeds swapped their holdings for stock in the new United States Steel Corporation, which made Weir an employee of the world's largest corporation. Promoted in 1903 to general manager of the company's plant at Monessen, Pennsylvania, at a salary of $5,000 per year, Weir nonetheless perceived no career path to the top of USS, which had absorbed almost two hundred engineers and battalions of executives. Consequently, he and his friend James Phillips, a sales manager for U.S. Steel six years his senior, searched for a steel mill to buy.

The Jackson Sheet and Tin Plate Company in Clarksburg, West Virginia, which had gone into bankruptcy before opening, became available for $190,000. Despite their large salaries, Weir and Phillips lacked holdings sufficient to secure a note. According to legend, Weir offered his father-in-law, who likewise lacked collateral, as a cosigner. Impressed by the father-in-law's faith in the young man, the banker extended ample credit. In 1905, Weir and Phillips closed on the Clarksburg facility, which they renamed the Phillips Tin Plate Company.

As Weir readied the plant, Phillips, the chief executive, went on the road to gather orders. He died a month later, the victim of a train wreck caused, ironically, by shifting steel, which tipped a passing freight train. Weir took over for Phillips as chief executive and went on the road in his place. In the plant, he relied increasingly on John C. Williams, twenty-five, who had been general superintendent at Monessen. A Welsh native later described as "blue-eyed, slow-spoken [and] hard-fisted," Williams had run a steel mill in Italy at age twenty-one, then contemplated joining the British South African Police, but decided to migrate to America, which he foresaw becoming the world's leading tinplate market. Known for being able to do every job in the plant, Williams also handled discipline.

In those early days if a worker quit in midweek, he drew pay only for the hours he had worked. But if fired, he could take a whole week's wage. Generally, the best way to get fired was to hit the boss. Instead of firing the man, Williams would slug back. The employee either went back to his job or quit voluntarily.

Because of the Clarksburg plant's poor design, Weir and Williams faced more daunting problems. One day the twenty-ton wheel, which drove the wringerlike rolls through which hot steel was passed and squeezed to the proper gauge, suddenly exploded, hurtling fragments through the roof and a quarter mile beyond the plant.

Later, a steam engine began rocking dangerously in a foundation that had been dug too shallowly. The normal course would have involved stopping operations for a lengthy period in order to dig a new foundation. But the fledgling company was flooded with orders that Weir hated to lose. Somehow, while slowing the engine, company crews managed to dig around and partially under the old foundation to reach bedrock, from which a new foundation was poured upward.

The plant also had a poor water supply. Pickling, a key step in making tinplate, involves passing steel sheets through an acid bath to remove oil and dirt, and produce a mirrorlike surface. At Clarksburg, the limited water supply had to be recycled continuously, which caused the solution called "pickle liquor" to become too acidic, resulting in etched, unsalable metal. Weir's solution to the water problem was to surreptitiously buy land on the side of a chemical company's reservoir and start to drain it. Outraged, the chemical firm retained celebrity lawyer John W. Davis, a former West Virginian and eventual presidential candidate in 1924, who exacted a promise from Weir not to use the pond, and suggested instead that the mill be moved. Despite drought, design flaws, and the sharp depression of 1906, Weir always made money.

Unlike many steel masters, Weir believed in investing in modern equipment, which he tried to buy during down cycles in the industry when tool prices dipped. By 1909, Weir had expanded operations at the Clarksburg mills, and began paying dividends to investors, a practice that would be unbroken for seven decades. Nonetheless, Weir knew that his company, which bought sheet bars for rolling and finishing, could be snuffed out by his suppliers, who also competed with him in finished steel markets. Weir arranged an interview with Judge Elbert H. Gary, the chairman of U.S. Steel, which dominated all phases of raw steel production as well as the tinplate business and supplied Weir with bars. Gary told Weir that USS had never stopped the supply of bars to a competitor, and had "no intention of doing it now," but would give "no guarantee" regarding the future.

Weir began to crave integration—the ability to process from ore to finished goods—as his only way to ensure survival. He wanted iron and coal mines, blast furnaces to smelt iron, and open hearths to mix the iron with coke and manganese to make steel. Such operations required new economies of scale. First, he would have to expand the tinplate operations. The Clarksburg site would not support growth.

In 1909, Weir began searching for new ground. He found a patch of orchards and wheat fields called Crawford's Crossing on the east border of the Ohio River outside the village of Holliday's Cove, West Virginia. The river would solve the company's water problems and bring down its freight rates. Also located near a great reserve of metallurgical coal called the Pittsburgh basin, the site seemed ideal for full-scale steel making.

The Weir legend is a blend of Horatio Alger, who pulled himself up by his bootstraps; Brigham Young, who found a spot in the wilderness and said, "This is the place," and thrived; and Daddy Warbucks, a reactionary potentate who coveted control of his domain and brooked no interference from labor unions. The Alger stereotype fits. Despite modest roots and an eighth grade education, Weir relentlessly bettered and readied himself for opportunity. He devoured books in and out of his field and especially loved *David Copperfield*, which he claimed to have read fifty times. In later life he stacked copies at his five homes and passed them out to guests. A fair-haired, plain-faced man with rimless glasses and lively eyes, who resembled Harry Truman, another Middle American commoner, Weir developed a muscular, literate writing style. But even after great success he remained a halting speaker.

The wilderness motif is a bit overdone. In some of the more mythological materials about Weir and his company, the 250 or so people around Crawford's Crossing are even called settlers, though Holliday's Cove had been continuously inhabited since the 1790s. During the Civil War its woolen mill provided uniforms to the Union army. By the time of Weir's arrival, the village had long had links by rail to the outside, electricity, and had a variety of churches, shoe shops, and a drugstore.

While Weir chose a rural setting because he believed cities bred unions, it does not appear that he initially intended to dominate all aspects of economic life. He tried, for example, to interest real estate firms in creating housing for his employees, but failing to convince them that the new steelworks would succeed, he had no choice but to start a home-building division in his company.

After clearing wheat fields and uprooting apple trees, the company built ten mills in the area it called Weirton, which when added to Clarksburg's twelve made a total of twenty-two. In 1910, it constructed ten more mills in Weirton and a year later acquired the twelve mills of the Pope Tin Plate Company across the river in Steubenville, Ohio, which had signed a contract with the Amalgamated Association of Iron and Steel Workers, a decaying, moderately led union, which had been defeated by the Carnegie Steel Company in the murderous Homestead Strike of 1892. When Weir refused to sign a new union contract, the Steubenville workers walked off their jobs and tried to spread the strike to Weirton. The company responded as if under siege: it mounted searchlights on the mills, hired armed thugs who beat workers indiscriminately, and put sentries on trolleys to keep all strangers out of town. Submitting to the company's demands in 1914, the Steubenville workers disbanded their Amalgamated Association local and went back to work.

During the next two years the company added two more mills, bought coal mines, began building a blast furnace capable of making 600 tons of iron, and installed open hearths and equipment to heat and pour new steel ingots for rolling. With fifty mills at three locations, the Phillips Company trailed only mammoth U.S. Steel in tinplate production. Three years later, in August 1918, the company changed its name to Weirton Steel in honor of its founder's forty-third birthday.

The following year, a new union, the National Committee for Organizing Iron and Steel Workers, swept through the Ohio Valley. In addition to the armed guards, Weirton reacted with a heavy anticommunist propaganda campaign. Weir personally paid the local newspaper editor $500 to plant red flags at the local Finnish Hall, a mecca for unionists. The police, who were in the company's employ, raided the hall, charged the Finns with Bolshevik subversion, and hauled them before a magistrate, who fined them ten dollars a piece, forced them to kiss the American flag, and ordered them out of town. The Weirton works closed for only a week.

During the 1920s, Weirton Steel expanded blast furnace and open-hearth capacity, and became a licensee of machinery invented, but not yet commercially utilized, by the American Rolling Mill Company of Ashland, Kentucky. The new technology, which did away with the tedious manual feeding of metal into mills by workers who wielded huge tongs, represented the most important stride in steel making in the first half of the twentieth century. At the head of the new rolling mill, a power-driven feeder drove an inch-thick slab of red-hot steel through a series of roll stands that compressed it into a strip, flung it onto a run-out table, and wound it into a coil. Once an all-day job, primary rolling now took three minutes.

In order to take full advantage of automation, Weir's engineers blueprinted a new plant designed for fully continuous rolling from the blooming mill, where the popsicle-shaped ingots were reheated, liquified, and molded into slabs, through the rolling mills, and all the way to the coilers. Implementation required $7 million, which Weir sought from New York banks. After he unfurled the plans, two banks extended the credit without requiring collateral. Weir seemed energized by debt, as he explained later in life:

> Debt is a good thing for a company—extremely good when used with judgement. Of course we withheld money from earnings but bank loans were our major source of funds. Through our early years, we were constantly in and out of debt on an increasing scale. Loans provided the means for rapid growth. And, with the constant threat of the sheriff knocking on our door, there was a powerful stimulus to pay them off as soon as we could; then go on from there.

Throughout the twenties, Weirton Steel invested aggressively in a host of new factories, including a sinter plant, which collected blast furnace flue dirt into iron clumps that could be charged back into the furnace, state-of-the-art coke ovens, and a network of docks and material-handling equipment on the Ohio River. By 1926 Weirton was earning $9 per ingot, which outpaced all integrated producers including United States Steel at $6 and Bethlehem at $5.25.

Profits exploded by 128 percent in 1928 and jumped another 37.3 percent in 1929, when less than a month before the stock market crash Weir literally scribbled on the back of an envelope an agreement to put together National Steel. His cosigners were George Fink, whose expanding Great Lakes Steel was the only other steel producer in Detroit besides Henry Ford's Rouge River Company, and George Humphrey, president of the M. A. Hanna Furnace Company formed by Marc Hanna, the Ohio industrialist who had engineered President McKinley's election. The Hanna Company owned 150,000,000 tons of choice Mesabi Iron Range iron ore eighty miles west of Duluth, a fleet of lake freighters, coal mines in Pennsylvania and West Virginia, and blast furnaces in Ohio, Buffalo, and Detroit. Weir, who had suffered through U.S. Steel's stranglehold on iron mines, particularly coveted the ore. Also, one of Humphrey's blast furnaces was located on the Detroit River within miles of Ford's mill, and the two jigsawed nicely. Not all of Hanna's assets went into the merger, which was tightly woven to avoid redundance. Weirton had enough coal, so National did not take the Hanna mines. Weir controlled 51 percent of the new company. Neither outside financing nor a broker's fees was required to put the deal together.

As the Depression deepened, the strength of National became clear. The mix of Weirton, Great Lakes Steel, and Hanna was sound. Management was lean (the corporate headquarters staff in Pittsburgh including Weir numbered ten), and decentralized with Fink and Humphrey still in charge of their works. Corporate production focused on tinplate for canning rather than for structural materials. People, reasoned Weir, had to eat. Can stock seemed almost immune to cycles in the economy. As the only steel producer to make money throughout the Depression, the company merited a feature in *Fortune* entitled: "National Steel: A Phenomenon."

During the Depression the Weirton community, according to a boosterish 1936 history, "suffered less than any one city or town in the country." At no point did unemployment exceed "approximately one percent of the population." Not only was there work in Weirton, but the modern plants—though hot and hazardous—were relatively safe compared to the rest of the industry. In a 1930 safety contest involving nineteen rolling, finishing, and fabricating mills, two of Weirton Steel's facilities finished first and second. In 1941, Weirton Steel reported the lowest accident figures among eight major producers, and in June of that year was less than half as dangerous as was the overall industry.

Not surprisingly, people flocked to Weirton, which, by the mid-thirties, had ten thousand jobs, about four thousand homes, and between thirty thousand and forty thousand residents. No one knew for sure because the community, which in aerial photographs looked like a dense smoking maze, had no municipal government or records. Reputedly the largest unincorporated city in America, it was provided with police, fire protection, a hospital, water, gas, sewage, and paving by the Weirton Improvement Association, a subsidiary of the steel company, which also built the stadium, golf course, and a mammoth public pool named for Weir's mother.

The mill jobs attracted eastern and southern European immigrants as well as droves of "hoopies," so called because some had worked as barrel makers in southern West Virginia. Hoopies, it was said, learned the "Three R's" in their schools: Readin', Ritin', and Route 2 to Weirton."

Blacks, mainly from the Deep South, also migrated to Weirton, but did not concentrate as heavily in the community as they did in northern urban centers such as Cleveland, Chicago, and Detroit. Not advanced in its racial approach, Weirton Steel set aside rest rooms and water fountains for "colored," and slotted most of its black employees into "bull work"—hard physical labor. Housing was segregated, with blacks restricted to sections in the low-lying flats hard against the mills, while white managers as well as white hourly workers could aspire to homes on the more pleasant hills ringing the valley. By 1936, blacks had established two Baptist churches and one African Methodist Episcopal church whose congregations totaled about four hundred members. Whites belonged to thirteen congregations, including two Roman Catholic parishes (huge Saint Paul's had three thousand members), two Eastern Orthodox churches, eight Protestant churches, and an Orthodox Jewish congregation with seventy members.

Father Charles Schneider of Saint Joseph the Worker Roman Catholic Church, the successor to Saint Paul's (it now counts four thousand members), suggests that one reason Weirton thrived was that it was a new community in which no ethnic group had a leg up on any other. Weirton escaped the common pattern of Anglo-Saxon neighborhoods being handed down to the Irish and later turned over to Slavs and blacks. Among whites, at least, the absence of generational elites translated into feelings of equality.

At the height of the Depression, Weirton Steel wages supported three hundred retail establishments including six bakeries, twenty-six barbershops, forty-two "beer parlors," four cigar stores, seven cleaners, ten clothing stores, eight department stores, seven drugstores, seven furniture stores, sixty groceries, four hardware stores, four jewelers, nine car dealerships, thirteen restaurants, eighteen gas stations, six shoe stores, six cobblers, four tailors, four A & Ps, two G. C. Murphy's, a variety of newsstands including one specializing in Italian papers, a mineral bath, several pool halls, a dozen liquor stores, and a novelty shop. The town also supported six attorneys, eight dentists, twenty-four physicians, and three funeral homes.

Weir himself chose never to live in the town, preferring Pittsburgh, where he was regarded as the last of the great steel barons and was accorded a private dining room at the Duquesne Club, the exclusive haunt of the region's industrialists. Weir presided over daily lunches with visiting dignitaries and the inner circle at National, where only one informal rule was observed: business would not be discussed. Topics to Weir's liking included world affairs, sports, music, theater, and politics.

A lifelong Republican, who in time would rise to chairmanship of the Republican National Finance Committee and whose family would be among the handful of leading contributors to the party, Weir nonetheless often took maverick stands in business and politics. Newly in office, Roosevelt summoned his friend "Ernie" to Washington for several private meetings; Weir strongly supported the New Deal as a needed shot of federal power to end the Depression. However, during the summer of 1933, Weir turned on the administration as "defeatist," claiming that it viewed the American economy as "mature," and in the absence of future growth intended to redistribute wealth. Passage of the National Industrial Recovery Act (NIRA) particularly stung the industrialist. While the act relaxed antitrust enforcement against business, its famous Section 7a gave workers the clear right to organize unions. Called "labor's Magna Carta" by Mike Tighe, the ancient president of the Amalgamated Association of Iron and Steel Workers, Section 7a stimulated the greatest surge of organizing in steel since the strike of 1919.

In some ways, Weirton would not have seemed a likely target for labor unrest. In July of 1933, none of its 14,689 employees was laid off, versus 15 percent across the industry. And at Weirton, employees worked an average of 47.6-hour weeks versus 41.9 elsewhere in steel, which resulted in higher earnings.

But wounds still festered from the 1919 strike. Unlike most steel companies, Weirton blacklisted the pro-union activists of 1919. Though lost by labor, that strike had netted for other steelworkers outside of Weirton pension plans and an end to the twelve-hour day—which, during grueling swing shifts, kept workers at their posts around the clock.

Anticipating problems, Weir consulted Eugene Grace, president of Bethlehem Steel who had created company-dominated unions called employee representation plans (ERPs). Weir ordered his operations chief, John C. Williams, to form an organization for workers along the lines of those at Bethlehem. William's execution was quick and ham-handed. On June 22, 1933, notices were posted that the company would adopt an ERP on July 1, and hold a nominating convention and election of officers in the interim. The announcement, not even seen by many employees, was poorly understood by others, especially the non-English speakers who were common in a workforce that was about 40 percent foreign-born. United States secretary of labor Frances Perkins received protests, and the Amalgamated Association, which sensed an opportunity, sent organizers to Weirton, recruited local leadership, including an articulate mill roller named William Jennings Bryan Long, and announced it had a list of eight thousand workers who wanted Amalgamated representation rather than that of the company union. In August, the tin mill workers, dissatisfied with the handling of their grievances by the ERP, walked out. When management hired truckloads of "colored replacements," tensions spread to other mills. The company removed the black scabs, and the tin mill employees returned to work.

Dissatisfaction continued to build over the ERP's handling (or lack of handling) of grievances and disputes. In late September, the men in the cold rolling department complained of burns from being forced to handle metal that was not given the usual opportunity to cool. William Long warned a superintendent that unless management settled the problem within twenty-four hours the company would face a general strike. The superintendent responded that the company did not deal with "outside" unions. The next day about six thousand workers went on strike.

There was great confusion in Weirton among both workers and management over the cause of the strike. Almost immediately, a group of three hundred electricians voted to go back to work. Notoriously conservative, the national office of the Amalgamated Association declared the strike a "wildcat that violated all the rules and laws of the union." Nonetheless, about three thousand workers voted to continue the strike, which turned violent. After a picket was hit by a car, other strikers turned over another car, pinning men underneath. Stone throwing was met with tear gas and clubbing.

The new National Labor Board (the NLB, not to be confused with the later NLRB) attempted to mediate, and eventually obtained an agreement signed by Weir and Long, providing that the strikers would go back to work, and that the company would hold an election between the Amalgamated Association and the ERP to determine which would represent the workers. Subsequently management gave representatives of the ERP the money to campaign, buy workers' AA cards, and hold beer parties. Even so, on the election's eve, Weir called off the vote, claiming that the government had altered agreed-upon procedures. Infuriated, top Roosevelt aide General Hugh Johnson of the National Recovery Administration called Weir, lashed at him for bad faith, and warned: "If this election is not held as scheduled you will go to jail."

"What you mean, General," countered Weir, well aware that the NLB had no teeth, "is that we will go to court. That's fine with me. I have complete confidence in the courts. If I am wrong, I'll go to jail."

The matter landed before a federal judge in Delaware, the state of National's incorporation. In Weirton, strike activists were fired. Others were kidnapped and beaten by mysterious vigilante committees that also burned crosses. Someone bombed a platform in a grove where the Amalgamated held dances, and also blew up one of the union's lodges. According to local legend, off-season Chicago Bears also were used as guards and thumpers. The intimidated union cancelled the charters of its lodges in the Weirton-Steubenville area.

Weir won in Weirton. He also triumphed in court, where a conservative Republican judge ruled Section 7a of the NIRA "unconstitutional and void," because he viewed the steel company as principally engaged in manufacturing rather than interstate commerce. A key plank of the New Deal had been defeated.

Guided by Senator Robert Wagner, Washington passed the new National Labor Relations Act (NLRA) in 1935, which allowed unions to organize in industries such as steel, and gave clear enforcement powers to the National Labor Relations Board (NLRB). Weir's attorney, Earl Reed, formed a committee of corporate lawyers who counseled their clients to ignore the new law pending tests in the courts. The penchant for settling labor crises in lawsuits rather than on the picket line became a Weirton trademark.

Weir also became vociferous in opposition to a third term for Roosevelt. After the president made his famous 1936 acceptance speech at the Democratic Convention, castigating "economic royalists," a group of business leaders whom he accused of using wealth to obstruct the "era of social pioneering," Weir took to the pages of *Fortune* to reply:

> I believe I am warranted in the assumption that I am one of the men whom Mr. Roosevelt calls economic royalists. I have personal means; I am the chief executive of a large corporation; and I have been and am opposed to the policies and actions of the Administration. I deny that these things, in themselves, make me an antisocial force, or that I have ever used them in an antisocial manner.

Weir also recounted his own rags-to-riches story and pronounced it typical in American business.

> Walter P. Chrysler started as an engine repairman in a roundhouse. Henry Ford started as a machinist in Detroit. Thomas Edison started as a news butcher on trains. Charles F. Kettering began life on a small farm. Charles M. Schwab began as an unskilled worker in the steel industry. John D. Rockefeller was a grocery clerk. These are only a few of the many thousands of men who founded entirely new enterprises or gave radically new directions to industries; made thousands of jobs where none existed before; created new conveniences and brought them within reach of all the people; added tremendously to the national wealth. Yet they are the kind of men Mr. Roosevelt now calls economic royalists. Isn't it a logical question to ask whether men such as these, who came from the common people and during their entire careers worked with and through the common people, have a more genuine and practical interest in the common people than a man like Mr. Roosevelt, whose whole experience in the creation of jobs has been limited to the expansion of governmental payrolls?

In 1936, Roosevelt trounced Alfred M. Landon, the Republican nominee, who won only two states; and John L. Lewis, president of the United Mine Workers and the Congress of Industrial Organizations (CIO), started the Steel Workers Organizing Committee (SWOC), which absorbed the corpse of the Amalgamated Association of Iron and Steel Workers. SWOC, later the United Steelworkers, stunned the nation by quickly winning recognition at U.S. Steel in 1937. The CIO union then set its sights on the second tier of major mills collectively known as Little Steel.

At Weirton, Lewis's efforts won a cool reception. In May 1937 the company and its ERP held a parade rally against the CIO, which the Associated Press estimated that more than ten thousand employees attended. Men carried signs reading: "We Don't Want a Dictator," "We'll Take Weir Not Lewis," "No Labor Racketeers," and "Comical Industrial Outlaws."

SWOC called for strikes at Bethlehem Steel, Inland Steel, Republic Steel, and Youngstown Sheet and Tube, but not at Weirton, which escaped the bloodiest industrial violence since the Homestead Strike of 1892. At the South Chicago plant of Republic Steel, ten marchers were killed. Four other union members died in Youngstown, Ohio, and Beaver Falls, Pennsylvania. While the rest of Little Steel came to terms with the United Steelworkers in 1941, Weirton remained independent.

Though negotiations between the United Steelworkers and United States Steel set wage patterns for the industry, Weir went his own way. In 1941 when U.S. Steel offered a seven cents per hour raise, Weir offered his workers a dime, saying: "It isn't enough—seven cents. When profit reports come later they'll make poor mouth claims look ridiculous. And it will cost a lot of labor confidence."

During World War II, Weirton again bucked the industry, which, led by U.S. Steel, wanted a price hike. Weir, by then president of the American Iron and Steel Institute (AISI), the industry's trade association and lobby group, favored a freeze. At a wartime board meeting of the AISI in New York, Bethlehem's Eugene Grace snickered that it was "presumptuous" for a smaller company such as National to resist the industry's trends. During a heated exchange, Weir resigned the presidency of the association, revoked National Steel's membership, and then marched out of the banquet. In time, the matter was smoothed over and Weir was induced to finish out his term, though he refused to accept a traditional second term.

Prior to the war, Weir opposed much of big business by urging strict adherence to the Neutrality Acts as well as to limiting the exports of key materials such as scrap, which was shipped to Germany and Japan, and armaments, which went to the Allies. Weir feared that if the economy became tied to the overseas fighting, "hysteria" would build for America's entrée into the hostilities.

However, after Pearl Harbor, Weir set aside his isolationist views, made peace with the New Deal, and like the other major steelmakers committed the company to wartime production. National along with Jones & Laughlin Steel furnished the great bulk of howitzer shells for the campaign against the Germans at Monte Cassino. Because of its technological proficiency and flexibility, Weirton was asked to roll magnesium and bronze as well as steel for weaponry. In addition, after several other steel companies had failed, the Manhattan Project presented Weirton with a high-precision metal-finishing problem, the successful application of which was used in the atomic bomb. The government even offered to pay for and hold title to the ordnance facilities at Weirton Steel, which would have increased the company's earnings. But, Weir, who neither wanted to be a profiteer nor have government property in his plant, rejected the offer.

He also continued to strive to keep the United Steelworkers out of Weirton. In 1941, based on charges filed by the USW, the National Labor Relations Board found Weirton Steel guilty of promoting a company-dominated union. The continuing situation led the board to issue a cease and desist order in 1942, which brought about the demise of the employee representation plan.

However, some of the officials of the ERP promptly formed a new organization called the Weirton Independent Union (WIU). In 1949 the NLRB entertained a petition to have Weirton Steel found in contempt for refusing to obey the decree of 1942 by interfering with "genuine self-organization." The board's master received testimony over the course of three years and in 1950 declared that:

> 1. That while the WIU was formed by action of some of the workers, the Weirton Steel Company "steadily increased its interference in WIU affairs, which culminated in paying its officers, stewards, and other officials overtime in February, 1944, and thereafter,

to take countermeasures against CIO attempts to organize Weirton employees."

2. As part of the same interference, Weirton Steel discharged nearly a score of members of the United Steelworkers of America.

The United States Court of Appeals for the Third Circuit, not only upheld these findings, but additionally held the company and some of its officers, including George Fink, president of National Steel, and Thomas K. Millsopp, president of the Weirton division, in contempt. The court directed the company to pay to the NLRB $48,000 for costs and to make whole eighteen Weirton employees who had been discharged for pro-union (USW) activities. The order involved reinstatement plus back pay awards totaling $195,773, a staggering sum for the time. In order to purge itself of contempt, the company had to withdraw recognition from the WIU, which disbanded within hours of the court decision.

Two groups, the United Steelworkers of America, which in those days called itself the USA-CIO, and the newly formed Independent Steel Workers Union (ISU), contended to represent the membership. Both utilized heavy Cold War imagery. Philip Murray, the president of the USW, began making personal appearances "behind the iron curtain of Weirton." Dripping acid, the ISU's new newspaper caricatured an addled Philip Murray giving a speech to an empty hall in Weirton, defined the CIO as the "Communist Inspired Organization," and accused the USW of treason for fomenting labor strife during the Korean War. The ISU won the election by a three-to-one margin. Though red-baiting figured in the victory, it was probably more important to voters that Weirton workers traditionally had received higher pay than their USW counterparts, a practice that they knew would continue if their union remained nonaligned, and never went on strike.

Throughout the 1950s, the USW attempted to organize in Weirton, but without success. Unable to draw the signatures of 30 percent of the eleven thousand workers necessary to trigger an election, it finally withdrew, to the great derision of the ISU.

National, however, recognized the USW without a fight at Great Lakes Steel in Detroit in 1942, which was the only reasonable choice in a labor market dominated by the CIO's autoworkers. The corporation also allowed its mills outside Chicago and in Saint Louis to fall into the CIO fold. During steel strikes called by the USW, such as the 116-day stoppage in 1959, Weirton worked around the clock picking up business from stilled steel companies and honored commitments from National's shutdown divisions. Among steelworkers belonging to the USW, the ISU had the reputation as a complacent "scab" union.

Donald Ebbert, a close associate of Weir's and a brilliant labor lawyer at Thorp, Reed & Armstrong in Pittsburgh, designed the ISU to be ineffective, compromised, and self-lacerating. In some ways it became all of these things. But, if the ISU simply had been a lickspittle company union as its critics contended, the USW would have made more headway among the workers who, after all, were overwhelmingly Democrats and from the same ethnic backgrounds found in the region's other mills.

At Weirton Steel, the labor force and its union were organized into six divisions. Steel Works One involved primary iron and steel making and included workers assigned to the blast furnaces, open hearths, blooming mills, coke plants, sinter plant (which reclaimed iron from flue ducts), and support services such as the electricians and masons who repaired the refractories lining the furnaces and the "torpedo" cars that ferried the hot metal.

Steel Works Two covered maintenance and crafts employees posted throughout the company, such as pipefitters, electrical workers, diesel engineers, brakemen, welders, painters, carpenters, lab workers, truck drivers, and bulldozer operators.

The Strip Steel division included workers who processed the bloom or slab through the hot mill and annealed, pickled, or bonded it. The remaining three divisions included the tin mill, sheet mill, and the Steubenville plant, all of which applied various finishes to the steel before shipping.

Each division was further divided into departments of about 175 workers each, who elected a steward to handle their grievances. The divisions also held a second election to name three of these stewards respectively as a chairman, vice-chairman, and secretary, and to place them on the union's executive committee. Finally, a plant-wide vote was held among union members to pick the ISU president. All officials served three-year terms.

Perhaps the most controversial aspect of the ISU framework, and the one that the USW always seized upon in criticizing the Weirton Union, was the company's practice of paying stewards for "a sixth day" when they were supposed to handle union business. The eighteen members of the executive committee also received a full week's pay directly from the company, but did not labor in the mill at all.

The executive committee—or simply "committee," as it was known—met in full session at least once a week. Its principal function was to negotiate the labor contract. But the committeemen, each of whom had offices in the squat brick ISU building between the tiny Orthodox Jewish shul and the Tin Mill on West Street, daily involved themselves in company and labor practices disputes.

The committee was, as David Robertson, the union's longtime lawyer, put it, a "flat organization" without a hierarchical structure. Each member, whether a chairman, vice-chairman, or secretary, had one vote. The president, who conducted meetings and acted as a spokesman, voted only to break ties. According to Bill Doepken, Don Ebbert's protégé, who became Weirton's counsel and later vice president of industrial relations, the structure was intended to keep a powerful labor leader from developing in Weirton.

Historically, the company manipulated the union in two ways. First, according to Doepken, if a steward or committeeman did its bidding, it would grant his grievances at contract time. Grievances ordinarily were dollarized. If the company conceded that it had unjustly given a worker a period of "time off" without pay or dismissed him, money would flow back into the mill, making the steward appear effective and electable. On the other hand, if the steward consistently stood up to management, it would fight his grievances tooth and nail.

The company also had a number of jobs that it could place in a variety of spots. For example, highly paid scarfers, who torched impurities off the slabs, could work in either Steel Works One or the Strip Steel division. The stewards of the unit that landed the jobs looked better to their constituents than those who came up empty.

Though compromising at times, the additional pay for the sixth day created a competitive political atmosphere. New faces always emerged to challenge stewards and committee members perceived as sellouts. Rapid turnover in these positions, as well as in the union presidency, was the rule. Contrary to the experience of larger national unions, few labor "dinosaurs" developed. Many ISU officials even won reputations for responsiveness and service.

The executive committee, despite its origin, was a unique institution. Having eighteen full-time officials on-site rather than in a remote headquarters meant that leadership was constantly in touch with grassroots sentiments. As problems appeared between negotiations, the committee evolved a process of fine-tuning the contract. Moreover, many committee members became sensitive to the financial and strategic workings of the company: management found them hard to fool.

The union hall was a power center with an open door. Workers went there often to communicate with the top leadership—they didn't have to go to Pittsburgh as did steelworkers in Birmingham, Wheeling, or Gary.

During the 1954 certification contest from which the USW withdrew, the ISU distributed a flier criticizing the USW union by pointing out that "ninety-eight percent of the membership voted in the last ISU election. That's the best voting record ever set by any major union. And there was competition for every steward's post in the ISU! No steward or officer ever got his job in a controlled election!!"

What about the CIO???
Who ran against McDonald for Steelworkers President?
   NOBODY!!!
Who ran against Rusen for District Director?
   NOBODY!!!
Who ran against Stalin for Premier of Russia?
   NOBODY!!!
Do you know any CIO member who ever talked to Murray or McDonald???

Bucky Buchanan [the ISU president] lives right here in Weirton. He spends his days talking to members of the ISU and fighting for the things these members want and deserve. Every other ISU Officer lives with the workers he represents.

National's executives, such as divisional president Jack Redline, who had worked at other operations in the National system, invariably said that the ISU, contrary to the popular view, was a "tougher" union than the USW. Mainly, the ISU had to be dealt with constantly, not just at contract time.

■

While E. T. Weir could be called antiunion, it made less sense to term him antilabor. He paid well. He consciously created a world where workers and managers lived side by side, participated together in an array of sports leagues, and vacationed together on company-sponsored charters. The company took great public pride in workmanship and safety, and frequently promoted hourly employees into salary ranks. Even General Hugh Johnson, who threatened to jail Weir, conceded that before his hassles with the administration began: "Weir was considered by it the most liberal and progressive employer in the industry."

Weir's management style also was enlightened. He encouraged subordinates to think for themselves and to disagree with him. He decentralized decision making and delegated authority and responsibility as far downward as possible. While developing a logical, lifetime plan for the business, and attempting to anticipate its shape and needs as far forward as fifty years, he remained highly flexible. His tremendous and ever-accumulating fund of technical knowledge allowed him to take progressive but prudent positions on modernization. Playing no favorites, he judged middle managers based on individualized profit-and-loss statements. He kept his inner circle small and himself accessible.

After World War II, Weir declined an offer of a million dollars per year to head U.S. Steel, a position whose apparent elusiveness had sparked him to build an empire. He chose to stay with National, but his focus changed.

Weir, who died in 1957 at eighty-two, shocked many by devoting much of the last ten years of his life to studying and opposing the Cold War, which he viewed as irrational. He insisted that

> what we are actually doing in the Cold War is waging a religious war against Communism. If there has been some good in wars for other reasons, there has been none in religious wars. All have been futile. The deaths, suffering, and destruction resulted only in more rigid attitudes on both sides and continuing hatreds. The truth is we are fighting a myth. The Russian system is not communistic, it is another form of state capitalism. Our position will have no effect on the Russian people even if they are able to learn its true purpose. Some of them doubtless believe in their system and support it with a religious fervor. While most accept and even welcome it for the practical reason that to them it has brought improvement over life under the Czars. For various reasons, most underdeveloped countries do not share our hostility toward Communism and some see benefits in it. There is no strong support for us in any of the less advanced countries.

While detesting communism, Weir viewed Soviet foreign policy as fearful and defensive. He felt that America had an obligation to better understand Russia and its leaders, and to engage them in a process of constant negotiations, rather than in political and military confrontations that could lead to a third world war. The Russian people in time could evolve into seekers of wider democratic and economic freedoms. Though not trustworthy, the Soviet government would have to adopt a less belligerent stance.

Weir's views, which paralleled those of George Kennan and Senator J. William Fulbright, received wide coverage including a long, almost unedited piece he contributed to *Izvestia*. At the end of his life, he won praise from American liberals and radicals who had detested his New Deal opposition, and received criticism from his natural conservative allies. In the fifties Weir received plenty of hate mail accusing him of being soft on communism, of being pro-communist, and even a traitor. He shrugged it off. He knew exactly what he was doing, thought it should be done, and lost no sleep. By no means the cranky whim of later life, Weir's anti–Cold War crusade flowed naturally from his long-held views that international tensions and armaments formed the pretext for governmental interference into daily life, which eroded economic and political freedom.

While always making money, National Steel went through a period of drift in the fifties as Weir aged. George M. Humphrey, his cofounder and chief financial adviser, went to Washington to serve as President Eisenhower's secretary of the treasury. In failing health, the other cofounder, George Fink, who had kept a large measure of autonomy in running Great Lakes Steel, seriously overestimated the car industry's demand for steel, which saddled his division with huge inventories.

A key Weir strategy also backfired. The chairman believed in focusing on the development of finishing equipment while building relatively few facilities for basic iron and steel making. In the regular cyclical downturns of the industry, the policy proved wise, because the corporation avoided the high cost of maintaining unused blast furnaces. In times of high demand, the company's relative lack of pig iron did not matter because it was able to substitute scrap for iron in its steel-making furnaces. During the Korean War, however, scrap became scarce. Lacking steel-making capacity to meet orders, the company was forced to buy steel from other companies for processing. Earnings dropped substantially.

In 1957, after Weir became fatally ill, George Humphrey returned from Washington to become National's chairman. The Detroit operation was reorganized. George Fink had already been retired. Weirton president Tom Millsopp became president of National under Humphrey and succeeded him as chairman and chief executive officer three years later.

A high school graduate and former open-hearth furnaceman in Sharon, Pennsylvania, who became a flying ace in World War I and barnstormer afterwards, Millsopp took a sales job at Weirton Steel in 1927 and became president at age thirty-seven. Despite an overwhelming Democratic majority, when the city of Weirton finally incorporated in 1947, it elected the brush-cut, cigar-chomping Millsopp, a Republican, as its first mayor. Running city hall like a business, he kept the payroll lean and taxes low by competitively bidding out services and repair contracts. His own salary was twenty-five cents per year. Overwhelmingly reelected to a second term, he turned a budget surplus over to his successor. During Millsopp's eight years, the city added a new hospital, a community center named after him, and a library that Ernest Weir donated in honor of his wife.

3 The Mill of the Future

"Every mill that closed in Youngstown made steel with open-hearth furnaces."

—STAUGHTON LYND

In the post-Weir years, National corrected its conservatism regarding primary iron and steel making. Weirton in the 1960s spent $400 million to build its widely publicized "Mill of the Future." Bearing no resemblance to typical long and low-slung black hangars that house rows of boxy hearths, the green windowless twenty-two-story skyscraper, which contained only two globular basic oxygen furnaces (BOFs), loomed over Main Street in downtown Weirton.

Inside the building, the two blimp-sized BOFs nested in a lattice of girders. Atop each vessel, nightmarish tangles of pipes conveyed their

42

extraordinary excess heat to other mills. Developed in Austria in 1952, the BOF process utilized controlled injections of pure oxygen at the speed of sound, triggering a violent reaction that yielded a three-hundred-ton "heat" of steel in one hour. It marked a decided improvement over prevailing open-hearth technology, which used air in its mix and took twelve hours to finish a heat.

The BOFs were aligned with a new four-strand continuous caster. While other companies had constructed experimental casters, Weirton became the first in America to deploy the radically new device commercially.

Casting was the most important stride in steel making since continuous rolling, which Weirton also had pioneered. When not continuously cast, newly made steel must be poured, or "teemed," into ingot molds and cooled. Once the steel solidifies, stripper cranes pull the molds off. Because the steel must be reshaped, it is then reheated in a brick-lined soaking pit. Finally, it is compressed into a slab in the blooming mill, which readies it for running through a high-speed hot strip mill. In continuous casting, the liquid steel is poured from a tower through a pocked oscillating mold that looks like a rectangular colander, and is sprayed in car wash fashion by jets of water. As the steel passes through the mold it solidifies, but stays soft enough to be compressed, shaped, and smoothed by passing it through opposing automatic "pinch rolls." Emerging from the caster, the slab, which still has a liquid center, is cut like taffy to specified lengths. The caster eliminates ingots, stripper cranes, materials-handling equipment, soaking pits, blooming mills, and substantial numbers of employees, and reduces scrap loss. Savings over the conventional blooming process exceeds 50 percent.

Following Weirton, National put casters in all of its primary plants, while the rest of the domestic industry lagged behind. Under the chairmanship of Tom Millsopp in the mid-sixties, National again outperformed the rest of the Big Eight steel producers.

But not all signs augured well. Japanese steel had achieved a toe-hold on the West Coast and was being bought, albeit in small quantities, by Detroit auto makers. Starting to compete with steel for the container business, aluminum quickly won the frozen orange juice and quart oil can markets.

In the 1970s, Detroit, which rapidly lost market share to imports, built smaller, lighter cars using less steel. Foreign steel, made in modern plants by relatively low priced labor, took ever bigger bites out of other markets. In order to prevent work stoppages during which American buyers would look offshore for supplies, the major steelmakers, in their 1973 contract with the USW, won a no-strike clause, known as the Experimental Negotiating Agreement. In exchange for giving up the right to strike, labor received annualized 3 percent raises plus cost-of-living (COLA) increases. During the double-digit inflation years of the 1970s, USW steelworkers' wages and fringes climbed to an average of $24 per hour, creating a wide and dangerous gap between themselves and offshore labor. The Weirton Steel workers, who no longer had the no-strike advantage, nonetheless received a $2 premium over the USW at the negotiating table, keeping them the highest-paid industrial workers in the world.

For a time, as in the Depression, it appeared that Weirton's focus on tinplate for canning would see the company through. After all, people still had to eat and Weirton's customers included household names such as Campbell Soup, Del Monte, and Heinz. In fact, in 1973 under the presidency of Jack Redline the division had a big year, shipping a record 3,533,519 tons and earning $50,415,000 before taxes.

Following Redline's success, National sent him to Great Lakes Steel as president. By 1975, pretax Weirton profits plummeted to $5 million before collapsing altogether in 1976 and 1977 when the division recorded respective losses of $6 million and $32.5 million. Some, including Redline, blamed the lax management under his successor George Sisshon. A clearer culprit, aluminum suddenly grabbed the bulk of the beer and beverage can market away from steel.

In 1979, when National announced Redline's reinstallation as president of Weirton, the community rejoiced. During his first term he had been a popular leader known for a mastery of plant details, an easy-going, tobacco-chewing style, and a sure money-making touch. Upon his return, hopeful banners and placards sprouted around town declaring that "Jack Is Back to Lead the Attack."

In general, the industry was in crisis and Weirton was no exception. Redline returned to a plant that he viewed as being "run by the union." He lamented that safety had loosened and that men were sleeping, drinking, and holding "steak fries," hot-plate barbecues, in the mill during work.

Redline resolved to take on the union. He imposed harsh discipline for failure to wear safety shoes and eye gear. He refused to negotiate any grievances, forcing the ISU to take them all to end-stage arbitration. He trimmed the workforce, especially hourly labor, which sank from 9,371 in 1977 to 5,397 in 1982. He returned the division to the black, though barely, in 1978 when it showed a profit of $1.6 million, which dropped to $1.1 million in 1981. It wasn't enough.

In the early 1980s, the industry's strategy was to shed unproductive assets while diversifying into new fields. U.S. Steel's $6.4 billion leveraged buyout of Marathon Oil in March 1982 symbolized the new era. As a diversified rather than steel-focused company, U.S. Steel changed its name to USX.

National Steel was reorganizing into a holding company whose name would be changed to National Intergroup and whose holdings would include oil, pharmaceuticals, and a leaner steel group with about a third less capacity. Between 1978 and 1988, American producers reduced their potential steel yields from 137.6 million tons to 89.2 million tons, a drop of 35 percent. The secure blue-collar way of life that had existed since World War II now came to an end.

Between 1979 and 1981, National, which had invested $150 million in Weirton, became reluctant to add the additional capital required in light of the division's high labor costs and the "maturity" of the tinplate industry. Nor could the corporation imagine that Weirton employees would grant it major concessions.

National closed the venerable Hanna Furnace Company, sold the assets of its Steel Products subsidiary, a fabricator of Quonset huts, grain bins, windows, and doors, shut down half of Great Lakes Steel, and looked for something to do with Weirton. National's management consultant, Bain & Company of Boston, suggested that the corporation sell the division to workers and managers, who would take over a new, stand-alone company as an employee stock ownership plan (ESOP). Bain believed that Weirton's employees might be willing to make concessions to themselves.

News of Pete Love's announcement of the closing of Weirton Steel returned to Weirton before the delegation and spread at lightning speed through the other mill towns in the Ohio Valley. Later, people would say that as had happened with President Kennedy's assassination they remembered precisely what they were doing when they heard the news. It was inconceivable to imagine Weirton without National Steel, much as it had been impossible to imagine Homestead, McKeesport, or Youngstown without U.S. Steel, or Johnstown or Lackawanna without Bethlehem Steel.

The social effects of deindustrialization were becoming well known. In the economically nondiversified steel towns, there were not enough jobs to absorb the unemployed. In many cases workers had to leave. Sociologists called the blue-collar flight "outmigration" as if one could migrate anywhere else. The mills were not salable, though occasionally small nonunion job shops would rent space and perhaps a crane in the cavernous husks and provide work to handfuls of men under dangerous conditions. Mainly the mills sat empty, though occasionally, as in Youngstown, they were razed. The vast manufacturing zone from Pittsburgh to Chicago became known as the rust belt. With their tax base eroded, towns cut back or eliminated the most basic services, including police and fire. As populations shrank and aged, merchants failed. For the first time since the Depression, hunger and homelessness became regional phenomena. Towns became sleepy shells of their former selves. People in Weirton wondered if the same thing would happen to them.

Officially Weirton put a good face on Love's announcement. Jack Redline and ISU president Red Arango pledged cooperation between management and the union, and Mayor Don Mentzer, a retired steel mill railroad worker declared: "Unity is our strength. Weirton Steel is all our lives and our children and grandchildren. Without Weirton Steel there would be no Weirton. . . . Everyone is optimistic."

In truth, local reaction to the separation from National was nervous and pessimistic. With an average age of forty-four in the mill, a question arose as to whether the new company would be able to honor pensions. Perhaps it would be better simply to retire now? Experienced engineers and workers began taking other jobs. To prevent a skill drain, management and the union, which swore to disseminate accurate information during the transition process, began publicly asserting that pensions were protected. However, on March 5, 1982, the U.S. Department of Labor clarified that while retirement benefits earned under National were "vested," a new stand-alone company would not necessarily have to provide pensions. Anxiety mounted over the pension issue.

In a company-dominated town, many sense a lack of control over their lives, which can breed fatalism. When Arango returned from Pittsburgh on March 2 to meet with the ISU stewards, they teased him about wearing a suit and tie. "It's what you wear," he responded, "when you're going to a funeral." Later, when asked about National's ESOP plan, he said sadly: "It doesn't look like we have much of a choice. . . . They just don't want us anymore. They're divorcing us."

Conspiracy theories also set in. According to one clung to by Mike Hrabovsky and widely held by others, National would sell the mill to the employees, wait for it to fail, then buy it out of bankruptcy court at a fraction of the original sale price. The thought that National was somehow orchestrating moves to its advantage gained currency when it delivered attorney Allan Lowenstein to Weirton to advise employees, who wondered why the corporation they would have to negotiate against was picking their negotiator. "Sending Lowenstein," said Bill Doepken, the labor relations attorney, "set the deal back six months."

A successful banking and corporate lawyer who had built his New Jersey partnership from four to a hundred lawyers, Lowenstein, sixty-eight, like many ESOP specialists, originally had been a socialist. The possibility of a classless company where adversarial lines between management and labor faded away and all employee owners would adopt a spirit of cooperation appealed to him. He believed that Weirton's middle-class workers, many of whom earned between forty and sixty thousand per year, would welcome a change in workplace relations.

Lowenstein's early ESOP experience involved small- to medium-sized family-owned businesses. When these companies ran out of family members to head them, the attorney structured sales of the firms to employees as reorganized ESOPs. In 1976, he made a quantum leap when retained by Okonite, a century-old New Jersey steel wire and bar producer, which during the conglomerate craze of the period had been bought and sold repeatedly and wound up as a profitable division of the Omega Alpha Corporation, which later went bankrupt. Lowenstein recast Okonite as a stand-alone ESOP and ingeniously financed its successful resurrection from bankruptcy court by catalyzing a $13 million U.S. Economic Development Administration (EDA) loan to the state of New Jersey that converted into a twenty-year loan to Okonite at 2 percent, which then served as collateral for $44 million in credit from banks.

In 1981, Lowenstein steered the Hyatt Clark division of General Motors, a roller bearing plant that employed about twelve hundred autoworkers, to independent status as an ESOP. Again, the financing was creative. Not only did Lowenstein assemble bank and EDA loans, but he also induced GM to buy about 85 percent of the new company's output during its start-up years. At the time, Hyatt Clark was the largest hundred-percent-employee-owned entity in America. It initially performed well, and Lowenstein, who became chairman of its board, won a national reputation as an ESOP designer.

Similarities existed between Hyatt Clark and the proposed Weirton ESOP. Both had powerful corporate parents who appeared to favor healthy separations. Both spin-offs would try to make it despite mature product lines. Hyatt produced bearings for rear-wheel-drive cars at a time when the auto industry was shifting to front-wheel and four-wheel drive. Weirton would rise or fall on tinplate. While unions represented hourly workers at both sites, Lowenstein's presence gave Weirton, with its supposedly pliant independent union, an edge over Hyatt, which had a militant United Auto Workers local that battled from the start with him and his management team. Being the largest steel mill in North America without workers under the United Steelworkers umbrella clearly was fortunate for Weirton, since the USW at that time opposed ESOPs. Although the ISU had never taken a position on employee ownership, it seemed open to it.

While Bain & Company had come up with the idea of an ESOP for Weirton, National Steel had consulted for well over a year with Lowenstein about an employee buyout as well as its own makeover into a holding company. Now Lowenstein wanted to represent Weirton and told National: "I would have to put on a different hat and fight them for maximum benefits on the contract. National Steel said fine, we want to see this accomplished, we're big boys, we can defend ourselves and we're perfectly happy for you to go over and represent Weirton and do the best job you know how."

While National not only waived any conflict of interest objections to Lowenstein's serving Weirton, it thought so highly of the New Jersey lawyer that it allowed him to pick its negotiator, his rival for the upcoming negotiations. Lowenstein chose Elliott Goldstein, a respected Atlanta attorney who had headed the American Bar Association's corporate section. By hiring Goldstein, National broke a tradition begun by Ernest Weir of using counsel from Thorp, Reed and Armstrong in Pittsburgh, which for seventy years literally had been the firm down the hall. Though National gave Lowenstein the green light to switch clients, he met resentment and suspicion, as he put it, that "National was pulling a dirty trick on the Weirton community," and that he was a part of it.

Lowenstein began meeting labor at the union hall and management at the General Office "on the hill" on March 3, 1982. While avuncular in appearance, he spoke in a rapid, assertive East Coast patter that opened a cultural chasm between him and the spartan West Virginians. Moreover, what he had to say shocked them.

The attorney spelled out to employees that they would have to take a substantial pay cut to attract capital in order to modernize their new stand-alone company and to keep it competitive. When asked how much of a pay cut, Lowenstein said that the problem could be answered only through a detailed feasibility study conducted by an outside management consultant.

Lowenstein also insisted that the operation would have to buy high-quality steel slabs from automated mills in Germany. And while Lowenstein's instincts were right—the German slabs were cheaper than those processed through Weirton's blooming mill—the idea of buying foreign steel rankled American steelworkers who already saw themselves losing their livelihoods to offshore producers.

While Lowenstein believed that the joint labor-management team should be assembled to effect the transition, he felt that as soon as possible an independent group of prestigious business leaders with strong ties to the banking community should become the controlling element of a new corporate board of directors. The idea made

Weirtonians, who already saw themselves in the hands of a remote corporation in Pittsburgh, swallow hard; and the fear arose that Lowenstein, an outsider, would use the board in an attempt to take control of the new company, perhaps becoming chairman, as he had at Hyatt Clark.

Leadership of the emerging company, a media darling that would rank around the middle of the Fortune 500, would be a significant plum. While Lowenstein disavowed any intention of heading the ESOP, he allowed that he did not regard Weirton divisional president Jack Redline as a capable candidate for the job. Redline, the hero of local management and bane of the union, deeply wanted the position. Signs began to sprout around town reading: "Let's Back Jack."

Lowenstein also believed that the company's coke-making batteries on Brown's Island in the Ohio River, which had employed about five hundred workers but had been closed due to lack of environmental compliance, should remain shut. Again, it was cheaper to buy coke than to produce it. The message proved unpopular with the union that represented the laid-off coke workers.

Brown's Island had had a tragic history. Shortly after Jack Redline opened the state-of-the-art facility in 1972, it had had a terrible explosion and fire that claimed eighteen lives. Now, Redline differed with Lowenstein and voiced the hope that the proposed ESOP could restart the island ovens. But during the first week in March, he was forced to announce a new round of layoffs throughout the mill.

Redline followed Lowenstein's suggestion for assembling a joint labor-management committee and initially headed it. The group, which also included Arango, the six chairmen of the ISU's hourly divisions, the chairman of its salaried clerical division, and John Chernenko, the president of the plant guards' union, initially had the narrow purpose of retaining consultants to make a detailed feasibility study of the proposed ESOP.

During early March, professionals deluged management and the union with proposals to negotiate (in lieu of Lowenstein) on behalf of the embryonic entity and/or to assess future feasibility. Local state and federal politicians came to town to analyze the apparently leaderless situation. "They're walking around up there like Pearl Harbor Day," said West Virginia state senator Patrick McCune. "We've got to instill a sense of optimism and alleviate their fears and concerns whether they believe it or not." Senate majority leader Robert Byrd arrived and offered to set up a meeting with President Reagan, a known ESOP supporter, but the West Virginia lawmaker cautioned employees not to expect a bailout or much economic support from the Reagan White House.

On Friday morning March 5, Governor Jay Rockefeller flew to Weirton on the state plane with his key aide and troubleshooter, Miles Dean. A prematurely white-haired CPA in his early forties, Dean, the West Virginia director of economic development, had smashed graft in the state's liquor monopoly and motor vehicle pool, negotiated leases to computerize the bureaucracy, and supervised building the new stadium at West Virginia University. Neither man knew what to expect or came with an agenda.

In the low-ceilinged union hall dense with smoke, Rockefeller wanted to offer support, but could not get order from the grumbling crowd. The local grapevine had twisted the college connection between Love's and Rockefeller's sisters into a rumor that the governor and the National CEO were former Harvard roommates and close friends. It was even said that Love planned to sell Weirton Steel to Rockefeller family interests.

Unable to get attention, Rockefeller turned to Miles Dean, who said, "Put some money on the table." Rockefeller wondered where the money would come from. "I don't know," said Dean. "We'll pull it out of our ass." The governor suggested $250,000.

Bill Doepken, local management's attorney, who was within earshot and knew both men well from his dealings on behalf of the mill in Charleston, urged cutting the figure in half. Doepken, who was emerging as a leader in the transitional process, believed that if the workers in the paternalistic plant were given too much support at the outset, they foolishly would expect a free ride until the new company was off the ground.

When Rockefeller began speaking again, this time about money, the crowd listened. The governor said he would write a check for $125,000 to help defray the costs of the feasibility study. He expected the employees to match the figure. He also stated that he was "assigning Miles Dean to Weirton." Only afterward did he and Dean determine that the amount could be drawn from the state's contingency fund. Real money on the table had a calming effect, both on the union and the community. The process was under way.

After Pete Love's announcement, the title of Youngstown attorney Staughton Lynd's March 9 speech in Steubenville was changed from "Plant Closings" to "The ESOP Option Facing Weirton Workers." A newly formed group called the Weirton Rank and File Committee, whose name derived from Lynd's ideal of a third employee force in the plant apart from and purer than the union or management, became a sponsor of the event.

The Rank and File Committee, which had about twenty members, set up shop in the Steubenville Legal Services Office, a cramped former house near the river. Most of the members came from Steubenville, where Weirton Steel was the second-largest employer, and most were black and had been involved with the Committee for Justice. Tony Gilliam, thirty, a part-time law student, also had chaired the town's Human Relations Commission, and had won a major police brutality suit. A laborer in the blooming mill, and leader among black employees, Gilliam was well known for having slugged a foreman for making a racist remark. More surprisingly, at least to some of his coworkers, Gilliam had not been disciplined by the company.

Edward "Skip" Mixon, a black former tank commander, had returned from Vietnam to work in assorted jobs in the mill, including inspector and clerk. Before being diagnosed as having sleep apnea, and having surgery to correct the condition, Mixon had had trouble with drowsiness on the job and been taunted with accusations of "shiftlessness." Twice, the Equal Employment Opportunity Commission (EEOC) had had to reinstate him at Weirton.

A former president of the Weirton-Steubenville NAACP, Willie McKenzie, fifty-five, a twenty-year employee presently serving as a machine shop supervisor, had been the lead plaintiff in a landmark class action against the Weirton division's discriminatory seniority system. In the 1950s, McKenzie's house stood in the black neighborhood where the company already owned some of the land needed to build its new basic oxygen furnace. McKenzie was the first black to say no to the relatively low price Weirton Steel was offering for his house. McKenzie insisted upon and got enough money from the company to buy a comparable home in Steubenville.

Steve Bauman, thirty, was a white former student at Kent State, where he had been in the Young Communist Student League before dropping out of school to go to work in Weirton's basic oxygen furnace. While retaining his ideology, he ceased to be an activist until the late seventies, when he had supported Gilliam and other blacks in their stand against the Steubenville police. A husky, quiet man with a flair for written rhetoric, Bauman took charge of producing the Rank and File Committee's leaflets. Bauman's flier promoting Lynd's speech stressed that Weirton workers had choices.

> Contrary to what National Steel executives would like us to believe there are a number of alternatives Weirton Steel employees have. Redline and Co. want us to think that we have to accept the company's E.S.O.P. or Weirton Steel will be shut down.
>
> Though the company and its executives would like to limit discussions of alternatives as much as possible, there exists a number of alternatives Weirton Steel employees have.
>
> The alternatives for Weirton Steel employees are many. We now have a chance to take control of our community.

The leaflet closed with a flourish:

First, they came for Campbell Sheet and Tube in
Youngstown.

But I didn't live in Youngstown, so I didn't
stand up.

Then, they came for Patco.

But, I wasn't an air controller, so I didn't stand up.

Are they going for Weirton Steel now?

If so, will we stand up????

The Rank and File Committee showed a sensitivity to Weirton's history and culture by listing the location of the event as the "CIO" hall rather than the headquarters of a USW local, since the term "United Steelworkers" had virtually been stricken from local speech. Nonetheless, the location probably kept Weirton workers away. The audience for Lynd on March 9 numbered only about a hundred.

A fair-haired, wiry soft-spoken man with craggy features, wearing a suit off the rack, Lynd long had been concerned about "problems with a radical movement or a socialist movement attempting to speak to American working people . . . it's as if we haven't found the language." As an intellectual and "the son of two college professors, who grew up on the eighth floor of an apartment house in New York City," Lynd also had reservations about his own ability to bridge the language gap. But the two professors were Robert and Mary Lynd, whose classic work, *Middletown*, involved extensive interviewing in a heartland town; and Lynd, himself, seemed most comfortable in industrial Middle America.

Lynd had no trouble putting his points across on the evening of March 9, and made the clearest public presentation to date in the region on the elements of a basic ESOP plan. He told the audience that ESOPs differed in terms of governance. In some, the employees had no voice in decisions, while other ESOPs were more democratic. "The workers," said Lynd, "should control how ESOP shares are voted," as well as "make decisions as to how the trust will make investments."

He cautioned that employees going into ESOP situations had been too quick to take cuts in wages and benefits, and had even given up their pensions. "That's a mistake that compels workers for the new company to bet their pension security on the fortunes of a single firm. If the ESOP substitutes for pensions and it fails, the workers lose all their pension security. You need an ESOP with a pension, not an ESOP instead of a pension."

Lynd injected an optimistic note by telling the crowd that "compared with the situation in Youngstown, I think you've got a real good shot. For one thing, the company apparently is willing to sell the mill to you. Nobody knows why, what's behind it, but it would be hard for them to back off that position. And you have relatively new facilities. Every mill that closed in Youngstown made steel with open-hearth furnaces."

Since Love's announcement, management and union representatives at Weirton and their lawyers had met almost continuously in closed session, which distressed Lynd, since their discussions "would affect the whole community. I think maybe you'll find the need for something broader than the union to set it up." He advised that the Rank and File Committee as well as the workforce, management, and community should be able to send representatives into meetings. In the reborn company, he believed that the governing board of directors should be selected by plant-wide voting in which each department would pick its own board members. Among many models, Lynd was advocating the most radically democratic type of ESOP.

4　　New Age Economics

"Labor Unions will obviously not be needed as an instrument of power to effect a laboristic distribution of wealth."

—LOUIS KELSO, *THE CAPITALIST MANIFESTO*

Hardly a new idea, employee ownership received a boost from Congress in 1921 in the form of tax-free status for stock bonus plans, whose popularity soared in the roaring twenties but dropped after the market crash in 1929. Like John Maynard Keynes, organized labor came to regard the stock market as a casino and preferred payment of wages and benefits in fixed dollar amounts rather than in securities.

While the American Federation of Labor (AFL) under Samuel Gompers was cool to employee ownership, its nineteenth-century predecessors such as the National Labor Union and the Knights of Labor experimented with worker cooperatives. The Knights, whose flamboyant leader Terrence Powderly viewed these as a step toward a utopian "Cooperative Commonwealth," established about a hundred co-ops with equal wages and voting power in grocery stores, shoe factories, newspapers, and a bank. Most failed, according to Powderly, due to a "lack of business qualifications, lack of confidence in each other, hostility of those engaged in a similar line of business, the boycotting of the wares of the cooperative, and a lack of necessary funds."

Some cooperative foundries attempted to survive by issuing stock. In his titanic history of the American labor movement, Philip Foner notes that these firms "had to abandon cooperative principles. Stock holders demanded more and more profits, and to meet these demands, the co-operatives were forced to reduce wages, lengthen working hours, and abolish union standards. Instead of becoming yardsticks for private capitalists to follow, many co-operatives served as models for employer offensives against labor." Wholly unimpressed with the cooperative movement, Karl Marx termed it "dwarfish."

Coming of age in Colorado during the Depression, Louis Kelso noticed empty passenger trains cross the countryside while freights brimmed with human life. He saw unpicked fruit rot while people went hungry. Something clearly was wrong with the system. As a naval intelligence officer during World War II, Kelso carted *Das Kapital* to the Canal Zone, where he had time on his hands. An inexhaustible student, who had completed law school at the University of Colorado in a year and edited the law review, Kelso admired Marx for his extensive studies of factory life, use of official data on child labor, wages, manufacturing, and nutrition, as well as the German's vivid arguments in favor of social change, and perhaps above all for his choice of the term "capitalism" to describe the previously unnamed economic system of Great Britain.

But Kelso balked at Marx's "labor theory of value"—the notion that work alone creates wealth by adding value to raw materials.

While conceding that the theory "must have been approximately correct in primitive times, and to a lesser degree in pre-industrial times," Kelso sensed that riches in modern societies also flowed from "capital instruments," including machines, land, structures, and "intangibles."

Marx, according to Kelso, had come "within a hair's breadth" of making the same discovery while looking into the phenomenon of automated equipment, which operated productively without labor. Eventually Marx concluded that these tools worked "gratuitously" much as the sun ripens grapes. Kelso recognized a critical difference. Capital goods, unlike the sun, could be bought by capitalists, often with credit à la Ernest Weir.

Banks favored this class by permitting it to pay off debt with the future proceeds from the capital goods. In a productive venture, Kelso saw that capital often paid for itself in three to five years, after which it produced profits. Labor, on the other hand was "capital-less." It rarely saved enough to buy any capital goods of significance. Banks only helped laborers with financing for nonproductive purchases—car loans and mortgages—which had to be paid off with other earnings.

As capital goods became more concentrated, so did wealth. In postwar America, about 1 percent of the population owned half of the wealth. Kelso looked for ways to democratize capital and capital credit, and to make everyone a "capital worker."

In 1945, he completed a manuscript on his "two factor" theory of economics called "The Fallacy of the Full Employment Economy." It was out of step at a time when Congress debated a "Full Employment Act," which passed as the National Economic Policy in 1946 and focused upon work and welfare to earn income for consumers rather than on widening capital's availability. Kelso, who had become a lawyer in San Francisco, put the manuscript away for ten years while waiting for the moment to put his plan into action. In particular, he watched the Internal Revenue Service.

In 1953, the IRS issued a ruling allowing corporations to use stock bonuses or profit-sharing plans to borrow money in order to buy company stock. It was the opening Kelso had awaited.

The owner of a small but successful newspaper chain in California wanted to sell out to his employees, but could not find financing. Kelso structured a way for the employees to use their bonus plan to get a loan to buy 72 percent of the company's stock. The transaction, which took five months, required no funds from the employees. Proceeds from the new enterprise retired the debt twice as fast as scheduled, and the employee owners prospered. In enabling the birth of Peninsula Newspapers, Kelso created two staples of modern financial life: the leveraged buyout (LBO) and the employee stock ownership plan (ESOP).

Kelso's ESOP work especially impressed one of his clients, Mortimer Adler, a philosopher and popularizer of ideas who had been a great instigator of "great books" programs in colleges, as home editions, and in adult education. Together they reshaped Kelso's wartime manuscript and coauthored *The Capitalist Manifesto*. The book, which became a 1958 best-seller, outlined the two-factor theory, methods for reorganizing production, and tax incentives to spread equity and employee ownership.

Kelso's vision of a reformed, nonelitist capitalism won him a core of devotees who believed he had discovered "economics' missing link" and deserved a place in the discipline's pantheon with Adam Smith, David Ricardo, and Karl Marx, or at least a Nobel Prize. His devotees did not include organized labor, which saw itself reduced to a cheerleading role in factories. In the future outlined by *The Capitalist Manifesto*, Kelso insisted:

Labor unions will obviously not be needed as an instrument of power to effect a laboristic distribution of wealth. This was the function it performed in the transition from primitive to mixed capitalism, and is still performing. But to say that the labor union will not be needed to perform this function in a justly organized economy, with diffused ownership of capital and a capitalistic distribution of wealth, is not to say that there will then be no socially useful service for it to undertake. Voluntary associations of capitalist workers, operating through democratic processes of self-government, may serve their own members and the whole society by functioning as agencies for the economic education of the newly-made capitalists, and as instruments for the protection of their property rights.

While Kelso wanted to broaden capital ownership he told Congress he saw no reason to rearrange power in the workplace.

> Manager-employees should manage, and non-manager employees should be beneficial owners, but should not interfere with management. Amateur management is the last thing such a concern needs.

A bow-tied professorial figure known for saying "I'm right and the whole world is wrong," Kelso is often perceived as arrogant and has put off some adherents. Moreover, his relentless lobbying and publicizing efforts, though funded out of his own pocket, created resentment at his law firm. In 1970, he left it to form Kelso & Company, an investment bank that structured financing for several hundred ESOPs, mainly in small- and medium-sized businesses.

In 1973, Kelso and an exuberant young associate, Norman Kurland, a former civil rights activist who saw employee ownership as an engine of social change, met with Senator Russell Long of Louisiana, who chaired the Senate Finance Committee. Over the course of an evening, Kelso and Kurland explained ESOPs as well as an array of still-untried capital-spreading inventions including RECOPs (residential capital ownership plans), which would allow a taxpayer to call his home a capital instrument, thus reducing its price; CSOPs (consumer stock ownership plans), which would furnish stock in public utilities to consumers; ICOPs (individual capital ownership plans); PUBCOPs (public capital ownership plans); and COMCOPs (commercial capital ownership plans).

Then in his late sixties, Russell Long had been fifteen when an assassin shot his father, Huey Long, the populist governor of Louisiana. While Huey's "spread the wealth" philosophy and concern for the little person as set forth in his autobiography, *Every Man a King*, made a deep impression on him, Russell, a wily, cordial, bearish engineer and lawyer with a deep drawl, preferred legislative tinkering and arm-twisting to Depression-era haranguing. Also, unlike Huey, Russell held no antipathy for big business, often taking up the cudgels for the oil interests that had warred with his father.

A practical man, Russell Long paid little attention to any of Kelso's proposed devices except ESOPs, which had a track record.

Long quickly attempted to place an ESOP into the Regional Rail Reorganization Act of 1973, Congress's effort to salvage train service from the financial wreck of the Penn Central and other eastern lines. While Long failed to get employee ownership into the bill, which as a compromise included an ESOP study, Conrail, the reorganized line, later utilized an ESOP, though the study recommended against it.

Increasingly successful, Long, who eventually shepherded eighteen pieces of legislation promoting ESOPs though Congress, scored the major breakthrough in the Employee Retirement Income Security Act (ERISA). That pension bill not only explicitly legitimized ESOPs' key mechanism, using credit to buy employee stock, it also gave the plans a whopping tax advantage. While other types of businesses could take deductions for interest on loans, ERISA allowed ESOPs to deduct payments of *principal* as well on debt used to buy company stock.

Congress also freed ESOPs from ERISA's red tape. Unlike other plans, ESOPs were allowed to invest more than 10 percent of their assets in the employees' stock without demonstrating the soundness of the choice. Nor did Congress require ESOPs to diversify their holdings in order to avoid risk.

In Washington, ESOPs became a "white hat" issue with bipartisan appeal. Before taking office, Ronald Reagan declared his support in a radio commentary:

> Our Founding Fathers well understood that concentrated power is the enemy of liberty and the rights of man. They knew that the American experiment in individual liberty, free enterprise and republican self-government could succeed only if power was widely distributed. And since in any society social and political power flow from economic power, they saw that wealth and property would have to be widely distributed among the people of the country. The truth of this insight is immediately apparent. Could there be anything resembling a free enterprise economy, if wealth and property were concentrated in the hands of a few, while the greatest majority owned little more than the shirts on their backs? Could there be anything but widespread misery, where a privileged few controlled a nation's wealth, while millions labored for a pittance, and millions

more were desperate for want of employment? It should be clear to everyone that the nation's steadfast policy should afford every American of working age a realistic opportunity to acquire the ownership and control of some meaningful form of property in a growing national economy.

During the Reagan administration, Congress passed the Economic Recovery Tax Act (ERTA), which gave ESOPs a special tax credit equal to .5 percent of payroll. In other legislation, commercial creditors such as banks and insurance companies won a special 50 percent deduction on interest income from loans to ESOPs. Congress likewise handed a 50 percent exclusion on estate taxes on stock sold to ESOPs. While tax breaks overcame qualms about shop floor ownership, some studies also showed that equity among employees led to jumps in productivity as well as in morale.

The number of employee owners shot from 500,000 in 1975 to 10,000,000 in 1985 as the United States moved more rapidly in this direction than every country except Sweden. By the turn of the century, one-fourth of American workers will own a piece of their companies, and employee owners will outnumber union members.

Dubbed "new age economics" by Louis Kelso, ESOPs began cropping up in high-tech operations like W. L. Gore, the maker of Gore-Tex, a breathable but waterproof synthetic fiber, and ComSonics, which revamped and resold satellites. But ESOPs also appealed to workers in older industries hoping to avert the flight of plants to the Sun Belt or abroad.

ESOPs still had detractors. Internal Revenue Service bureaucrats lashed ESOP tax breaks, which cost the Treasury $2–3 billion per year. Pension purists viewed harshly ERISA's inclusion of an investment vehicle aimed at corporate restructuring rather than at retirement security. In some instances employees swapped their pensions and future well-being for new ESOPs.

Nor did ESOPs always crystallize in order to give workers a piece of the capital pie. As corporate takeover activity increased, target company managers viewed ESOPs as a way to save their jobs. For example, when Dan River, Inc., a Virginia-based textile company, used an ESOP to fend off raider Carl Icahn, management remained, but the unionized workforce lost its pension, paid ten times as much for its stock as did management, and gained no influence over corporate policy.

Even so, sometimes the raiders won. In the early eighties, Continental Air employees sought to form an ESOP to stay clear of Texas Air and Frank Lorenzo. A consortium of banks promised the ESOP enough credit to purchase 51 percent of Continental stock. But lawsuits by Lorenzo and the requirements of the Securities and Exchange Commission created delay. Time ran out and Texas Air took over.

Free market proponents also questioned the use of ESOPs in declining industries. The only result often was to put off the inevitable for a few traumatic years. Facing a shutdown in 1975, South Bend Lathe, a five-hundred-employee machine tool division of Amsted, formed an ESOP. Stock was held in a trust controlled by management, which eliminated the pension plan, swiftly exported two-thirds of the jobs to South Korea, and tried to induce the employees to give up their union, the United Steelworkers. During a bitter dispute in 1980, the workers went on strike against the company they owned, eventually causing its collapse.

Even the most democratic model of worker control could not save Rath Meats of Waterloo, Iowa, whose union, the United Food and Commercial Workers (UFCW), organized a buyout in 1980. Despite taking cuts in wages and benefits, the new owners, who installed the union president, Lyle Taylor, as CEO, could not turn around the hopelessly outdated facility. In its death throes, Taylor, who by all accounts had been a dedicated and effective labor leader, took the company into bankruptcy, where it refused to honor its grievance procedure, terminated its pension plan, and cancelled its union contract.

In the early 1980s, major union skepticism about ESOPs ran strong in basic industries. "In most cases," said Jack Sheehan, legislative director of the United Steelworkers, "a change in ownership isn't going to change the viability of the company." To many observers, Weirton, with its focus on tinplate, a mature industry, and its high-priced workforce, looked like a losing venture with or without an ESOP. But Weirton had two key advantages: its plant was relatively modern; and its union, the ISU, was not married to the standard anti-ESOP line of the United Steelworkers.

5   The Joint Study Committee

"I had never negotiated for the assets of a billion-dollar corporation."

—DAVID ROBERTSON

"Everybody who could spell ESOP approached us."

—BILL DOEPKEN

In March and April 1982, the Joint Study Committee of Weirton's management and labor met almost daily, and reconstituted itself. On March 9, Weirton president Jack Redline, an infrequent attendee at sessions, stepped down from the cochairmanship of the committee.

Redline preferred to run the plant and involve himself closely with customers, assuring them that the quality would hold and that nothing too radical was afoot. "I told them that an ESOP wasn't socialism; it wasn't communism; it was survival." For the most part, his personal touch worked and buyers kept their accounts with Weirton.

Redline also became the main booster in the community for the ESOP. In the morning before work, he'd talk up the idea to anyone who would listen at the downtown bus station's coffee counter. In the late afternoon he'd do the same thing at the Dairy Queen near the General Office. In the evening he'd make speeches to fraternal groups, and on Sunday, he'd lecture from the pulpit.

It was important work, which would soon be duplicated by other company and union leaders and certain members of the Joint Study Committee. In other rust belt towns facing corporate flight, after a flurry of activism, people had become defeatist, divided, and silent, which made it easier for distant corporate headquarters to forget them. Weirton's goal was to keep the heat on National's directors and top management in order to make it tough for them to turn their backs on the community or to rape the division in the deal. Jack Redline also hoped to convince employees and others in the upper Ohio Valley that, regardless of the opinion of Allan Lowenstein or any other outsider, that he (Redline) was the inevitable choice for chairman of the company once it became independent.

Redline relished the idea of running the facility without Pete Love and the rest of National's staff looking over his shoulder and without paying National Weirton's annual $26 million corporate fee. While an effective galvanizer of the community, he made the typical campaign mistake of offering something beyond his ability to deliver—the reopening of the coke plant. Also, he offhandedly trampled a sacred cow by conveying that the ESOP could be designed without a pension plan.

Silver-haired and square-jawed, Jack Redline looked like a CEO. Initially, however, Redline had intended to be a doctor, but World War II interrupted his premedical course at Penn. After the war, he transferred to Lehigh University, studied industrial engineering, and upon graduating took a job at Bethlehem Steel. As a trainee in Bethlehem's famous loop course, he was exposed to all phases of steel plant management.

Bethlehem assigned Redline to its monstrous mill at Johnstown, Pennsylvania, which at the time had seventeen thousand employees and churned out railroad axles, wheels, and hopper cars, as well as rod and wire products. Assigned to maintenance engineering, Redline specialized in rebuilding machinery and masonry. The plainspoken Redline regarded Johnstown, which had a sulfurous coke-making plant at each end of a narrow valley and always smelled like rotten eggs, as "the asshole of the world." Worse, as a man who came from moderate roots and had no corporate connections, Redline bridled under Bethlehem's rigid caste system.

After seven years, he joined U.S. Steel, where he spent a year on the road as a troubleshooter, and then became involved with tinplate production for canning. His exceptionally low weld-breakage rate caught the attention of National Steel, which hired him in 1951.

Since 1928, National had owned a large parcel of land on the shore of Lake Michigan at Portage, Indiana. In the 1950s, the Chicago market for steel became the hottest in the country, and the corporation decided to build a plant called Midwest Steel on the nearby site. National tapped Redline to be assistant superintendent of the project. It was a career-making opportunity. When the superintendent died a month later, Redline replaced him to become the youngest superintendent in the corporation at the age of thirty-five. Building a mill from the "cellars to the cranes" gave Redline an unparalleled view of steel making.

In 1966, National offered Redline the vice presidency of Weirton. "It was the worst lookin' goddam dirtiest town you ever saw. People had to have their headlights on in the daytime. And it was a very provincial town. Nobody from the outside lasted long at Weirton."

Yet the labor situation intrigued him. "Weirton was kind of a maverick. You didn't have the threat of strike every three years."

From the first, Redline cultivated good relations with the union. Before National released his biography to the press, he judiciously omitted any reference to Masonic activities in order not to offend the heavily Catholic blue-collar workforce. "At the time, Tom Millsopp

[National's chairman] had spies in the union," and Redline carefully read their letters in order to monitor his reception. "They said good things about me."

In 1967 the death of another boss again boosted Redline's career. When Weirton president Charles Tournay succumbed to cancer, Redline filled his job.

In the late 1960s Weirton was in its heyday. The new continuous caster and basic oxygen plant drew visitors from all over the world, and Redline, as chief officer of the Mill of the Future, won national honors from the industry. In his office, he set up a chart using automatic recording pins, which endlessly graphed the processes of the mill. The effect was like a constant polygraph of production. Redline knew by the sound of the scratching if and where something was amiss. Every day he went into the plant. Once a problem had been solved and all was functioning again, he liked to chew tobacco with the employees. In the community, he involved himself with the Salvation Army and Boy Scouts, presided over United Way, was named citizen of the year, and probably was as popular as any mill boss in America.

In 1972, the corporation assigned Redline to Great Lakes Steel. Quality and customer service improved, and Great Lakes went from being the least profitable division of National to "the biggest money maker in the corporation."

While in Detroit, Redline missed Weirton. Though it was easier to deal with the USW than with the ISU "which went by the book," Redline recalled having more difficulties with the Great Lakes workforce, which was 25 percent black and had serious absenteeism. As a result, Redline instituted a "buddy system" in which one worker would go to the house of another and wake him if necessary to get him to work on time. Redline could not get out of his mind the time a black worker shot the buddy who came to get him out of bed.

All the while Redline was at Great Lakes, he stayed in touch with friends in Weirton, and never forgot to send a get-well or condolence card. When National offered him the chance to go back to Weirton in 1977, he jumped at it. The Panhandle community welcomed him back with a banquet and an ode:

Jack Redline is a man of steel
Gives each man a good fair deal
Came to town when the mill was down
Picked up the pieces and turned it around

Weirton Steel was in quite a fix
Called for Redline in '66
National found what they heard was true
Tapped Jack Redline for something new

Great Lakes Steel sent an S.O.S.
Called for Redline and nothing less
Redline came and made it pay
Lifted the tonnage and saved the day

Things went crazy at the Weirton mill
Steel production took a Jack and Jill
Japanese imports made the market worse
Officers panicked with an empty purse

Things came around with Jack in town
Stout-hearted men all gathered 'round
Jack took charge and the town had hope
Times still bad but we now can cope

Listen to the river on a frosty night
Talking to the sky when the stars are bright
"Mill is working and we all feel fine
Things go right for Jack Redline!"

Redline's perception was that the power relationship in the plant had changed in his absence. "The union was running the place. They were doing the hiring and firing." While quickly eliminating more than two thousand hourly workers, he added 350 supervisors whom he regarded as "pairs of eyes on the floor to look out for shenanigans," including "drugs, drinking, leaving the plant, and pilfering." To stop stealing and false invoicing, which he estimated cost $10 million annually, his regime instituted gate checks. More than fifty employees were fired.

Not surprisingly, Redline had "real tussles" with the ISU. He remembered then ISU president Sam Bakich in 1979 saying: "Meet me in the alley and I'll beat the hell out of you." Nonetheless, Redline respected Bakich's intelligence and dedication as a union leader. Now he disdained Red Arango, Bakich's handpicked successor as ISU president, as "a good guy, but not too intelligent. He wouldn't know when to come out of the rain."

■

While Redline quickly committed to the concept of employee ownership, initially upon learning of National's intent to pull out, he had favored setting up a traditional non-ESOP company in Weirton. With George Stimson, the retired chairman of National who was also Tom Millsopp's son-in-law, and William Saunders, a Weirton vice president, Redline had explored attempting to raise the money to buy the division.

In most large companies, it is difficult to locate an indispensable person. But, if Weirton had one, it was Saunders, who was chief of a small plant called the Materials Utilization Division (MUD) in the Half Moon industrial park about two miles west of the major production units. The twenty-five-year-old facility made and tested cans, but not for commercial distribution. In American steel mills, floating brown grit coats the floor and machinery, but MUD, like a Japanese mill, was immaculate.

The prevailing philosophy of MUD and of Saunders was that Weirton's buyers of packaging materials could not be trusted to stick with steel over other materials. So MUD developed and patented cost-effective steel cans, containers, and closures that were superior to plastics, paper, aluminum, and ceramics, and licensed them to can makers. An aberration in the American steel industry, which had lost the will to innovate, MUD often went so far as to construct an experimental working replica of a packager's production facility in order to improve the customer's manufacturing process and products.

Saunders, a short, slim, leprechaunish man, was the Edison of American canning. A chemist, after World War II he had gone to work for the Department of Agriculture, where he investigated the bacteriological cleanliness of packaged food, but became more interested in the structural aspects of packaging. Later he spent fifteen years with the American Can Company in design engineering before joining National Steel.

At MUD, Saunders's tiny office was a museum of cans—cans of

snake soup from China, cans that looked like porcelain, cans that he had made of dull boron carbide, the hardest material in nature after the diamond, aerosol cans, and microwavable cans coated with a material similar to that which "hides" stealth bombers from radar. "I'm the best in the world at what I do," he would say. "I can make a can out of wet toilet paper."

In twenty years at MUD, Saunders had pioneered the development of three-piece cans without soldered seams; two-piece cans made by a "draw re-draw" technology that cupped the can body before adding a top; pull-top ends for steel cans; and new organic inner coatings, all the while lightening, thinning, and coating steel to make it competitive with aluminum. His processes and products had earned more than ninety patents.

An iconoclast, Saunders embodied the same jumble of right and left political views that had characterized E. T. Weir. Some of Saunders's seminal memories as a scientist were of his college professor and mentor who was dying of radiation poisoning from working on the Manhattan Project. On the day the atomic bomb fell on Hiroshima, the professor wrote key classified formulas for the weapon on the blackboard in class, a gesture of protest that Saunders admired, but which many at the time would have called treason. Later, Saunders became a supporter of J. Robert Oppenheimer, the physicist who lost his security clearance over Cold War questions of his patriotism, and whom Saunders believed "was no communist."

Saunders saw enormous potential for a stand-alone company in Weirton. He perceived vast markets for new products such as microwavable steel. He also knew that China was producing food cheaply but making poor containers. An independent company that could form a joint venture with the Chinese and tap that market "could be a goddam money factory."

Saunders believed that the best way to organize the new Weirton was as a "benevolent dictatorship." Redline, Stimson, and Saunders (whose talent was eminently bankable) preliminarily found that they could raise the money for the buyout, but eventually rejected the idea of shouldering the massive responsibilities of ownership. Poor health played a part in Saunders's decision. Stimson had some sensitivity about allegations of self-dealing, since he was on National's board, and Redline, without the other two, felt comfortable with simply attempting to run rather than own the mills. Redline knew that Saunders's involvement in the ESOP would be an important selling point to customers.

Redline appointed Carl Valdiserri, Weirton's executive vice president, in his place as management's cochair of the Joint Study Committee (JSC). Valdiserri, a mechanical engineer, had been at Great Lakes Steel with Redline in the 1970s, and had been in charge of installing the 104-inch continuous caster, at the time the widest in the United States. A ruddy, compact man with jet black hair, Valdiserri had come to Weirton with Redline in 1977. To some extent Valdiserri suffered in the employees' eyes from a "carpetbagger" image, but he had an open manner, related well to workers, and, unlike Redline, was not seen as the union's adversary.

Redline rounded out the management caucus on the JSC by appointing John Madigan, the vice president of industrial relations, Gene West, the division's comptroller, and Bill Doepken, the general counsel.

Red Arango, the ISU president, also had to modify his initial appointments. Initially, Arango had chosen the chairmen of the mill's seven divisions to sit on the JSC. However, excluding each division's vice chairman and secretary, who had power equal to the chairman on the union's executive committee, had bred resentment, so Arango appointed them all to the JSC, whose ISU component now swelled to twenty-one. When the ISU expanded, the Independent Guards Union (IGU) felt justified in adding two members of its executive committee along with its president to the JSC, which now lurched forward with twenty-nine members, plus Miles Dean from the governor's office. In general, Bill Doepken, the division's counsel who officially was a member of the JSC, and David Robertson, the union's attorney who was not, would formulate the agenda for the meetings, which were conducted behind closed doors in the General Office auditorium. The fact that the sessions took place "up on the hill" at the "G.O." as opposed to down in the mill in a common area raised worries from the first among some workers that their needs would be forgotten.

Large as it was, the JSC attempted to work by consensus. As a cochair, the hulking Arango was outshone by the crisp, effective Valdiserri, who at the outset developed a multicolored "critical path study" chronologically charting more than two hundred tasks that would have to be accomplished in order to launch the ESOP. According to Valdiserri's hopeful and logical scenario, in April the JSC would appoint consultants on ESOP design, pensions, and the feasibility of the spun-off company. In May, it would conduct market surveys, investigate pension options, and evaluate patents and properties. In June and July, it would resolve customer and legal claims, estimate working capital, determine overhead, get extensions on environmental compliance from the Environmental Protection Agency, find sources of raw materials, and develop a new corporate structure. In August, it would produce a business plan and set inventory levels. In the fall, it would negotiate a purchase price, finalize the ESOP structure, and obtain financing contracts in anticipation of an end-of-the-year closing. The management caucus under Valdiserri was disciplined, organized, and outwardly harmonious. It was not trusted by labor, which wondered whether the five executives were prepared to negotiate hard against National or to do its bidding.

Labor showed less cohesion. Red Arango was neither a strong nor able leader, especially on financial issues. Miles Dean was distressed to see that the union president had a tendency to let the most negative voices in the ISU, such as Mike Hrabovsky, Glenn Ohler of the tin mill, and John Pastoric of the sheet mill, grab the floor early and darken the mood.

As the union's counsel, David Robertson predigested all information for Arango and wrote his speeches. Because Arango was not a commanding president in these complex times, the thoroughly prepared and articulate Robertson, who technically was not a member of the JSC, became its key leader from the labor side. As Bill Doepken put it: "Dave Robertson was the Union."

In some respects, Robertson's role at Weirton as labor's guide and protector in a crumbling corporate labyrinth paralleled Staughton Lynd's in the Youngstown crisis three years earlier. Robertson, who represented a pariah union, like Lynd, could not expect to benefit from the substantial financial and political resources of major organized labor or to draw from its expertise on wages, pensions, contracts, and economics.

While himself an outsider to the steel belt, Lynd avoided high-priced outside talent and had a special disdain for anyone from Wall Street. He tended to make himself the focus for solving complex problems especially when they touched on law, and for advice he called upon trusted local figures or radical academics.

Throughout his career with the ISU, David Robertson had had to be "a one-man general counsel without a staff," and through relentless research and enormous powers of concentration had succeeded. Robertson was among the few labor lawyers in the region mentally on a par with Lynd, though their intellects differed. Lynd was a brilliant idealist, while Robertson was a chess player.

The fear of outsiders, especially experts, characterized Weirton, but did not extend to Robertson. Unlike Lynd, Robertson was quick to assert his own limitations—"I had never negotiated for the assets of a billion-dollar corporation"—and to urge his client to hire the best available talent regardless of price. He had no aversion to Wall Street—at times in fact he seemed smitten with it—but simply wanted the JSC to have fire power equal to National's.

Robertson did accept the consensus prejudice of the JSC against retaining key advisers from Pittsburgh. Such people, it was believed, would be among the Duquesne Club circle, therefore friendly with National's leaders, and thus could be easily compromised. "The paranoia," recalled Robertson, "was incredible."

The JSC agreed on the need to hire specialists to study the feasibility of Weirton's becoming a successful company, to design the new ESOP, and to negotiate against National. For months the committee did little but interview and investigate consultants. The process seemed to occur in reverse order, as finding a negotiator and an ESOP designer was tackled before the JSC engaged someone to determine in the first place whether the project was feasible.

The backwards nature of the process owed in part to National's dropping of Allan Lowenstein on the committee's doorstep. Lowenstein unsettled the committee, which did not know whether to regard the New Jersey lawyer, who clearly was skilled and experienced enough to slug it out with National, as a gift horse or a Trojan horse.

The JSC decided to investigate Lowenstein while calling in other candidates. Union members were dispatched to Okonite and Hyatt Clark, the major ESOPs credited to the lawyer. Managers and local United Auto Workers officials from these companies appeared in Weirton before the committee. Both ESOPs had rocky labor relations. Okonite had had a series of strikes. Leaders of the UAW local at Hyatt Clark viewed Lowenstein as antiunion. Under his chairmanship, the Hyatt board had allowed some management raises while the company exacted 25 percent pay cuts from labor. In exchange for the concessions, workers had received stock, which was held in trust. But, in accordance with Lowenstein's views against "pass-through voting," the employees would not be able to vote their shares held in trust during the first ten years of operations. Also, the local union had gotten three of thirteen seats on the board, which it regarded as token representation. On the other hand, the Weirton employees were impressed that Lowenstein had preserved Hyatt Clark pensions in his negotiations with General Motors.

The next natural step for the JSC was to attempt to interview Louis Kelso, who not only had invented the ESOP but probably had negotiated more employee buyouts than anyone. Unfortunately, by 1982, Kelso, then sixty-eight, favored working on the theoretical aspects of ESOPs rather than on intense time-eating projects. His company, however, sent its chairman and chief executive officer, Joseph Schuchert, a lawyer and investment banker, to meet with the committee.

Schuchert, unlike Lowenstein, took a strong position in favor of pass-through voting while the designated shares were still in trust. "Real economic power is in the right to vote those shares," he mentioned. "The role of management is to manage, but the role of those shareholders is to monitor and dismiss."

Schuchert put a hot potato in the process, where it would remain, when he began speaking about equal versus unequal stock allocation to employees. At that stage, most union members thought that stock would be distributed equally regardless of pay or position, because the employees expected the same percentage cuts in wages and benefits (which in fact would fall harder on lower-paid hourly employees than on upper management). But Schuchert argued that equal stock distribution amounted to "a total turnoff to productive employees."

Kelso & Company had an admirable record based on putting together about seven hundred employee-owned companies, but the firm worked on some disappointing industrial ESOPs, too, including South Bend Lathe and the fast-declining Kaiser Steel in California, where Kelso had been retained by the USW local. Schuchert also concerned the committee by indicating that he preferred not to jointly represent labor and management, which he termed "a very sensitive position."

Contrary to popular belief, management and the union at Weirton were not in bed together. In 1982, they did not especially like, respect, or trust each other. But, if both sides had engaged high-priced financial professionals, not only would the costs have doubled, the time for doing the deal with National could have lapsed, as executives and the ISU both presented positions. The union had grave doubts not only about the true loyalty of management but also about its quality. In other words, labor wondered: If the divisional management team was so good, then why was National leaving it in Weirton as opposed to deploying it elsewhere in the corporation? On the other hand, the management team saw the union as spoiled by wages and bloated crew sizes, and wondered if high labor costs could be borne by the new corporation. Nonetheless, both sides preferred being locked together in the JSC rather than going off in separate directions.

When the JSC members asked about pay cuts, Schuchert responded that they would have to shave $3.50 per hour to succeed domestically and $5.00 per hour to compete with the Japanese. He also assumed that the mill's purchase price would be about $360 million, but thought National would take back $100–150 million "in paper." Kelso & Company would have to raise the rest, and its fee would be in the vicinity of 1 percent of that sum—in other words, about $2 million. Such fees were totally outside the experience of the West Virginians.

After Schuchert, the JSC interviewed Norman Kurland. Once Kelso's protégé, Kurland had split amicably from the master, and now headed a consulting firm in Washington, D.C. Perhaps even more than Kelso, Kurland had messianic ideas about ESOPs. In Washington, he also ran a separate nonprofit institution that promoted ESOPs internationally and sent its representatives to trouble spots, including Guatemala, Northern Ireland, and Egypt, to help set up worker-owned enterprises.

A feisty, animated man, Kurland presented several mold-breaking ideas. Instead of raising funds through conventional financing, he favored attempting to change the law through lobbying in order to allow the Federal Reserve Bank to lend the necessary funds to Weirton at 1 percent interest. He believed that Weirton was such a sympathetic and important case that the White House and Congress would be moved to cooperate. Moreover, if successful, Weirton could be used as a precedent for the Fed to rehabilitate the rest of industrial America.

Even more controversially, Kurland criticized the American system of paying employees through fixed wages. "Under a wage system your choices are a layoff or a plant closing in a bad time." In Weirton, where the union had achieved the highest wages in American industry, the idea sank like a stone.

During March and April, many other would-be deal "quarterbacks" contacted the JSC. "Everybody who could spell ESOP approached us," recalled Bill Doepken. Some were from Pittsburgh, which also ruled them out, though David Robertson politely met or corresponded with them, and picked their brains.

On the last day of April, the JSC settled, albeit uncomfortably, on Allan Lowenstein as its counsel for the deal. However, to counter Lowenstein's perceived management bias, and as a hedge against his taking over the new company, the JSC also appointed another lawyer, Jack Curtis, a member of a small San Francisco firm that specialized in putting together employee-owned companies. Curtis, a former chief counsel to the Senate Finance Committee under Russell Long, was a tax specialist, who had drafted all or part of thirteen laws favoring ESOPs. After entering private practice in 1980, he generally had entered buyouts on the side of labor. He had represented the union at the Rath Packing Company (the most democratic of all ESOPS to date), the Continental Air Lines employees' committee, the Pan American unions, and the Western Airlines pilots in their negotiations. He saw himself as a lawyer who had "developed sensitivity to what organized labor felt and what employees felt about putting these deals together."

As corporate counsel, Lowenstein was still in the lead. He would handle the negotiations and the details of the acquisition. As the prospective architect of the new company, Curtis's essential task was to plan the ESOP in terms of governance, and to produce a design document.

From the first, the men could not get along. Curtis found Lowenstein autocratic. Lowenstein thought Curtis a lightweight.

In May, a handful of JSC members attended the annual ESOP Association Conference in Washington, a gathering of the burgeoning army of ESOP attorneys, analysts, accountants, actuaries, financiers, lobbyists, and pension specialists. Besides the ESOP Association there were two major trade groups of employee-owned companies: the National Center for Employee Ownership (NCEO) now of Oakland, California, but then of Arlington, Virginia, and the Industrial Cooperative Association (ICA) of Cambridge, Massachusetts.

There is a good deal of cross-pollination between the groups, but they have distinct identities. The ESOP Association, which focuses on finance and lobbying, appeals most to traditionally managed companies. Somewhat more employee-oriented, the NCEO specializes in scholarship on ESOPs. More to the left, the ICA promotes worker democracy in both co-ops and ESOPs.

In its formative period, and later as an independent company, Weirton would become closest to the ESOP Association. Not surprisingly, Staughton Lynd and the Rank and File Committee struck an early alliance with the ICA.

However, the well-tailored financial professionals who flocked to the ESOP Association meeting in Washington were not simple Wall Street "greed heads." For the most part, they subscribed to the notion that employee ownership produced happier, more enlightened employees, and led to stable work sites and communities. Significantly, the spate of insider trading scandals of the 1980s involved no ESOP professionals.

In essence, the ESOP Association convention was something of a love-fest among people who saw themselves as both doing well economically and doing good socially. The association also brought in a range of inspiring speakers from abroad who were attempting to get the employee-ownership idea off the ground in their own countries, especially in the third world and the Eastern bloc. Kelso and Kurland made major addresses conveying that those assembled were in the vanguard of an unstoppable world movement.

The Weirton delegates were celebrities at the conference. Theirs was the deal that could create the biggest totally employee-owned company in the United States, and make ESOP a household word. They were sought after for receptions and photo opportunities with politicians such as Senator Robert Byrd. While the conference featured a gamut of how-to sessions on ESOP finance and administration, Robertson's and Doepken's purpose in attending was to see if Lowenstein and Curtis could at least get along in this generally positive atmosphere.

During a panel discussion on stock voting rights, Lowenstein and Curtis clashed. Afterwards Doepken and Robertson walked the streets in Washington, trying to figure out what to do. Two days later, Lowenstein was scheduled to meet with the JSC in Weirton. Robertson picked him up at the Pittsburgh airport, along with Jack Curtis and Miles Dean, Rockefeller's aide, who was working on a grant application for a federal Urban Development Action Grant (UDAG) that would provide money to the city of Weirton, which it in turn could lend to the ESOP for plant modernization. In the car, Lowenstein and Dean had a dispute over the capital projects that had to be identified in the application. Dean wanted to list upgrading the coke plant. Lowenstein argued against the coke plant, since buying coke was cheaper. Robertson worried that he heard National's policies echoing through Lowenstein. Lowenstein and Curtis then opposed each other combatively, even angrily. Lowenstein called the ten-year deferral on pass-through voting at Hyatt Clark "exemplary." To Curtis, there was "no alternative to pass-through voting."

Afterwards, Lowenstein indicated that he did not ever want Curtis in Weirton with the JSC, but back in San Francisco drafting the ESOP documents. Also, Lowenstein insisted that a board of directors comprised of mainly independent business people should be put in place.

At the JSC meeting, Lowenstein talked for one hour and left abruptly after delivering an ultimatum. He would quit unless the independent board and pass-through voting issues were resolved his way.

6 The Rank and File Committee

> "If you are shareholders, you want to be sure you are in control."
>
> —STAUGHTON LYND

While the JSC was dealing behind closed doors with consultants, the Rank and File Committee (RFC) took advantage of the situation. On March 17, the Rank and File Committee held a meeting in Steubenville that drew about three hundred workers from the mill. In the crowd were many who were laid off (the Rank and File was attempting to be their political voice) and some key ISU leaders, including Red Arango. At the time the Rank and File and ISU were still feeling each other out, and no official breach had yet developed.

At the meeting, the Rank and File speakers insisted that all employees, including those laid off, should be represented in the process. Tony Gilliam, the young Steubenville black leader who had became the Rank and File cochairman, attacked the Joint Study Committee: "If they are negotiating for our benefit, why are they keeping it a secret?" Willie McKenzie, the older black supervisor who had led the discrimination suit, picked up on the theme: "We want to have a voice in these meetings. We don't want union and management to carry the ball and have us left with the shorter end of the stick." An ISU steward rose and shot back, "Don't accuse people of something when you don't know what you're talking about." Red Arango attempted to restore calm by pledging that "information will flow."

Steve Bauman, the young white radical from the basic oxygen shop who had become cochairman of the Rank and File and did much of its writing, also took a conciliatory note. The purpose of the meeting was not "to impugn the integrity" of Arango or the ISU. "The general consensus is that the union has done a fair job of representing us. But they have too often been outmaneuvered or outflanked by management. There are too many meetings now going on behind closed doors."

Despite Lynd's theories about the Rank and File as a "third force," and Bauman's efforts to placate Arango, most people probably believed that the group hoped to take over the ISU. Nationally, dissident rank-and-file groups had challenged traditional union bosses in a host of major industries, eventually supplanted leaders in the United Mine Workers and International Brotherhood of Teamsters, and nearly toppled the USW leadership in 1976, during the reformist presidential run of Chicagoan Ed Sadlowski. Dissidents typically won support in the eighties by challenging the long-accepted wisdom of "pattern" bargaining throughout an industry as well as their officials' resigned acceptance of management's calls for cutbacks, work rule changes, and plant closings. By defying their leaders, these rank-and-file groups caused disruptions in various industries, including canning, electrical goods, and meatpacking. They effected shifts in power from the headquarters of some unions to the locals. They also contributed to major reforms. The steel industry, for instance, gave up pattern bargaining, which had imposed artificially uniform wage conditions on vastly different companies. The United Steelworkers also stopped the odious practice of ratifying contracts by submitting them only to local presidents, and instead began holding referenda involving all rank-and-file union members.

Bauman articulated the Rank and File's ambivalent position on Weirton Steel becoming an independent ESOP. A spin-off enterprise, he offered, could lose access to the conglomerate's base of raw materials and would have trouble competing with major integrated steel companies. On the other hand, "if we're a local company we'll no longer have that hierarchy of huge corporate salaries to pay."

But Bauman also ratcheted up the pressure on the union. He defined the Rank and File's goal of gaining a seat at the bargaining table against National. And he announced that the group hoped to hold its next meeting at the ISU hall in Weirton.

The Rank and File's request to use the union hall was rejected by the ISU, which insisted that it allowed functions in the building only when its own leadership was in charge. Steve Bauman, who felt that his group had "incurred a certain amount of wrath" from the ISU and divisional management, penned a leaflet for distribution at the mill's gates that announced that the meeting would be held at the Weirton Knights of Columbus hall and questioned the adequacy of the standard two-party (management-union) system in the plant for dealing with the present crisis.

"Us Weirton Steel Workers," he wrote, "are smarter than our leaders have given us credit for. We believe it is wrong for management and the union hierarchy to do all the thinking for us. In fact it's frightening how much thinking we are not permitted to do."

The event on Monday evening, March 22, drew about two hundred to the Knights' hall in Weirton. Staughton Lynd spoke in favor of a "democratic ESOP" where everyone would be equal and no one could control a block of stock. "If you are shareholders," Lynd told the audience, "you want to be sure you are in control. You should have a voice in the investment decisions in order to prevent the same things from happening again." Tony Gilliam pressed for a seat for the Rank and File at the negotiating table. If granted, the demand would have amounted to taking over some of the union's traditional turf. Staughton Lynd explained how he thought Rank and File representation would work during the negotiations, yet attempted not to threaten the ISU. "It's not to cut the union out. You have the right to have representatives and have your committee represented at the table and have them report back and get instructions on what to demand at the table for you."

Another speaker, Ed Man, who had headed a now-defunct USW local, was one of Staughton Lynd's compatriots in the Youngstown shutdown crisis. He suggested that the Rank and File could assume a grievance-processing function, which of course would usurp another of the ISU's key roles.

Lynd discussed an obscure but critical section of the union's labor contract with National Steel. The provision provided that if the mill shut down, then National pensions would be paid out to all employees, plus each would receive a $400 monthly supplement. Lynd thought aloud about the advantages of declaring a shutdown on Monday, and working toward an ESOP on Tuesday, in a reopened independent plant. David Robertson also had spotted the contract section and had noted it at a JSC meeting. National Steel, as it happened, knew the provision well, and feared it. It was aware that a shutdown would trigger almost a billion dollars in liabilities and bankrupt the corporation.

In its lead editorial of March 25, 1982, the *Steubenville Herald-Star* ripped the Rank and File Committee's "potential to throw a monkey wrench into the sensitive work that is so vital to the process." The newspaper noted that "more than anything else, the committee has implanted a measure of fear into the average worker at Weirton Steel, a fear of placing trust in the company management and the union. The result of seating the committee, a group of twenty members, at the bargaining table would create chaos. Were one group of 25 employees given a seat at the bargaining table, what would prevent another group of 25 from being formed and making similar demands. There's potential for more that 350 such groups."

The Rank and File Committee set its next meeting for April 12, at Madonna High School, a Catholic institution in Weirton. Shortly before the date, the school's administration cancelled the event, but then relented and allowed it. Perhaps because of the waffling or the heavily negative press that the RFC was receiving or both, the program drew only forty to fifty people. Nevertheless, the Rank and File group went out of its way to seem nonthreatening, even appealing in the Catholic milieu. The committee passed out a position paper that stressed that the ESOP would be governed locally in accordance with "Christian morality" as opposed to by "absentee landlords" in "corporate board rooms." Above all, the new enterprise should follow the "principle of the priority of labor over capital as Pope John Paul II termed it in his encyclical, *Laborem Exercens.*"

Ed Mixon, the black worker who had suffered taunts of "shiftlessness" due to his illness, delivered the Rank and File's ten-point platform, including the workers' rights to be kept informed, to participate in decisions, to vote on the takeover plan, to vote one's stock as soon as the buyout is complete, to vote on a one-person-one-vote basis regardless of the number of shares held, to have an ESOP with a pension plan, to insist that National must honor its prior pension commitments, to bargain collectively under the ESOP, to have a strong democratic union, and finally, to enable presently out of work employees to have recall rights with the new company.

The Rank and File Committee made it clear that it did not necessarily accept the long-term jurisdiction of the ISU. Speaking after Mixon, Staughton Lynd announced that after the buyout, another vote should be held to select a union. He had thrown down the gauntlet.

While the Rank and File made demands, the ISU seemed sluggish and bumbling. A well-intentioned but uncomfortable public speaker, Red Arango was thrust increasingly into the limelight. Despite being scripted extensively by David Robertson, Arango had difficulty speaking about, much less mastering, the complexities of ESOPs. In April, the *Varlas Newsletter*, a mimeographed sheet written and distributed to employees by J. J. Varlas, an irreverent four-hundred-pound clerical worker, lampooned the Arango-Robertson relationship:

> I know management will understand this but, that ISU leadership—amusingly known as the WHERE? AND HOW HIGH DO YOU WANT IT GANG," leaves something to be desired when it comes to using their thinking ability. The real stinker OOPS,

THINKER is Dave Robertson, the ISU legal advisor, who like most attorneys, is an expert at compressing *no answers* in the most words of any man I've ever met. He has a near impossible task facing him of trying to make President Red Arango appear to the members of the ISU as though he actually knows what the HELL is going on at WSX today.

President Red Arango has become the idol of the ISU family—He's been IDLE since he became president of the ISU.

The *ISU LEADERSHIP* headed up by President Red Arango intends to run for re-election on their past record—OH LORDY!!—If they can stand the smell of their record then their sense of smell must be faulty—because I think if we could grind up their record in office, put it into a spray can, we could revolutionize chemical warfare. President Red Arango has become the pet of the WSX management, he appears litter trained and obedient in public and will pose for pictures with any politician trying to use our problems at WSX to get re-elected to PUBLIC OFFICE.

GETTING SERIOUS—We, the ISU members, must vote to release $500,000 from the strike fund—This will give us a chance for survival!! We must give the ISU an increase in dues for it to survive, for without the union, workers will be at the mercy of unscrupulous managers.

Arango, in fact, had been attempting to have the union release a half-million dollars from its strike fund, which contained almost $1.6 million. In addition to Governor Rockefeller, Brooke and Hancock counties, West Virginia (both of which contained parts of Weirton), and the Independent Guards Union (IGU) all had voted to contribute to the feasibility study (which alone would cost $500,000) and to the fees of the other consultants, which were expected to be enormous.

On April 20, in a referendum for which only half of the ISU members turned out, the proposal to release money from the strike fund was defeated by 1,550 to 1,406. In part, the surprising defeat was due to the confusing presence on the ballot of a second item, involving the collection of union dues. Regardless, the negative vote confirmed in some minds the stereotype of Weirton steelworkers as selfish and uncooperative, and pointed out problems with Arango's leadership.

In fairness to Arango, the executive committee of the union did not seem capable or inclined to exert leadership in the crisis. Dick Mort, the grizzled chairman of the tin mill division and the one member of the executive committee who had served since the ISU was founded, noted that "Red was in over his head, but it was the worst executive committee I was ever on. There were a lot of trouble makers, very adversarial. They only knew how to say no. A lot of them thought the ESOP was a ploy. They considered it a union breaker."

Weighed down by the Lowenstein imbroglio and the unfunded feasibility study, the buyout process stalled. On a late spring afternoon, John Madigan, the vice president of industrial relations, and one of his underlings, Chuck Lafferty, a middle manager, found themselves at adjacent urinals and began to chat. The two men, both in their late forties, didn't care for each other. Lafferty, free-spirited and loquacious, had a mane of thick white hair and a career somewhat under a cloud since a department under his aegis had had a sex scandal (in which he had not been involved). In 1982, he was foundering as an administrator of a suggestion program in the industrial engineering department.

His father, Lou Lafferty, had been the first president of the Weirton Independent Union (WIU), the company-dominated organization that the National Labor Relations Board had scuttled in 1950. In 1957, the son was hired at Weirton in a low-level salaried job.

During the 1960s, Lafferty had been active in the peace movement, helping to operate an antiwar coffee shop in Steubenville. A natural writer of prose and songs, he also had attracted notice with a column called "Blacklash" on social relations in the weekly Catholic diocesan newspaper.

Madigan knew of Lafferty's strong communications skills. The two agreed that the "right message" about the buyout was not getting out to the employees. Madigan asked Lafferty to develop a communications plan to put the idea across.

Lafferty thought in multimedia terms: younger workers were most comfortable with electronic media; older employees favored print. Communications should be two-way: Information and propaganda would have to be disseminated, but questions, fears, rumors, and shop floor intelligence also should be gathered and processed.

Lafferty's first idea was to begin conducting what he called "in-plant meetings," sessions in which a management member of the JSC and a union counterpart would engage in dialogue with small groups of employees in every corner of the mill. Lafferty had hoped to involve Weirton president Jack Redline, but Madigan nixed the idea. Madigan insisted on keeping Jack Redline out of the mill to allow him to remain above the contentious process. "I thought," recalls Lafferty, "that that was the worst thing we could have done. Ultimately it turned out to be the worst thing for Redline, because he did not get the presidency."

Other top managers and union officers, including Red Arango, started going into the mill. According to Lafferty, "the first round of in-plant meetings dealt with a lot of generalities, and letting people express their anger, frustration, bitch about National, ask questions about their own circumstances, whatever." National Steel had an audio lab group in Weirton and Lafferty prevailed upon them to show him how to make radio commercials. The early batch emphasized that an ESOP was the community's only chance for survival. Then he arranged access to local billboards and put up signs that depicted a Weirton Steel worker in 1909 beside one in 1982, which stressed continuity and tradition. Lafferty, who for years had felt unchallenged but now was energized, began exploring fund-raising ideas. Daydreaming in his office one day, he was twisting a strip of tinplate and found he could tie it in a bow. Painted green and mounted on plaques, the "Go Bows" each fetched $500 in the local business community. But their impact far exceeded their income when the townspeople started tying green ribbons to every utility pole, auto antenna, tree, and door knocker.

Lafferty also believed that it was necessary to get accurate information into local homes. He understood that while the husbands who worked in the plant might be grumbling about upcoming pay cuts, wives, who often served as household financial managers, would make the decision about whether an ESOP could help keep a family going. Lafferty argued successfully in favor of beginning a series of spouses' breakfasts so that they would hear the story unfiltered by their husbands. "It was a very successful endeavor because we ultimately got the wives on the side of the Joint Study Committee." Lafferty, who felt that every element of the community had to be organized, also helped put together a group of retirees in favor of the buyout.

On May 21, 1982, the ISU again voted on whether to release $500,000 from the union's strike fund to pay for a feasibility study by McKinsey & Company, a management consultant. This time 70 percent turned out, and by a five-to-one margin the union voted in favor of funding the study. To some extent, the dramatic shift, which occurred in five weeks, can be attributed to a less clumsily drafted ballot, but the new high-energy communications drive also was beginning to click.

7   Wall Street and Washington

"It seemed like here were these people not just laying back and complaining about what the world was doing to them."

—HARVEY SPERRY

On March 9, 1982, President Reagan stopped in the office of Senate minority leader Robert Byrd of West Virginia to discuss the defense budget and the situation in El Salvador. Byrd, however, spoke about Weirton and the president agreed to see a group from the mill. Byrd scheduled the meeting. The *Weirton Daily Times* headlined: "Reagan to Meet Local Delegation."

From the first, Weirton looked to Washington for support. Allan

Lowenstein had explained to members of the JSC, the union, and management how he had put together industrial ESOPs backed by U.S. Department of Commerce's Economic Development Administration loans. Norman Kurland believed that the White House would free the Federal Reserve Board to make low-interest financing available. Perhaps above all, Weirtonians knew that just two years before, the Carter administration had provided more than a billion dollars in loan guarantees in order to bail out Chrysler.

The members of the JSC also discovered that National Steel had taken no steps to meet the conditions of a 1981 federal court–ordered consent decree under the Clean Air Act. Antipollution measures would cost the corporation up to $200 million. Failure would result in fines up to $7,500 per day beginning January 1, 1983, or shutdowns of polluting equipment. Expected to start up operations around that time, the new ESOP would be in the difficult position of not being able to afford either compliance or noncompliance with the law.

On March 11, Weirton president Jack Redline led a group into the White House that included Bill Doepken, Red Arango, David Robertson, John Chernenko, president of the Guards, and several other JSC members. President Reagan did not attend. Instead, the five-minute meeting was convened by Craig Fuller, a member of Domestic Policy Advisor Edwin Meese's staff. The Weirton group asked for financial support and for a substantial "stretch-out" on time to comply with the Clean Air Act, which the administration had the ability to grant. Fuller was pleasant, but noncommittal. Arango and others emerged from the White House believing that the president would see them within days.

When more than a month had elapsed, David Robertson drafted a long "position paper" over Red Arango's signature, which attempted to tweak the president's conscience.

On Tuesday, October 8, 1980, then Presidential candidate, Ronald Reagan appeared in Steubenville, Ohio at the invitation of the local Save Our Steel Committee. The President's advance group had requested the local coal, steel, and labor representatives "lay their woes at the feet of Ronald Reagan." The United Steelworkers of America and other labor representatives declined to participate in the forum discussion with the Presidential candidate.

Attorney David L. Robertson, Legal Counsel for the Independent Steelworkers Union at Weirton Steel, told Mr. Reagan that his client was calling for the next administration to pursue a review of tax and depreciation loss. He also called for a balance between further environmental clean up and the cost of technology for the sake of job security.

An International Brotherhood of Teamsters' position was put forth by a local truck owner as a result of the Teamsters' declining to participate publicly with the Presidential candidate. It was obvious that the Independent Steelworkers Union has made a strategic public commitment of associating with the Presidential candidate at a critical time in the 1980 election campaign.

The then Presidential candidate Reagan pledged to put laid off steelworkers back on the job, calling for "reasonable environmental standards and a reinforcement of the belief in coal's vitality to the Nation." He further told the participants that the Carter Administration had "neglected and ignored the people of Steubenville," promising, "the GOP would remain interested in the Ohio Valley after the November 4 election."

Nevertheless, the president continued to resist meeting with the Weirton delegation. His failure to play a supporting role was consistent with an ideological aversion to propping up declining basic industries, and preferring to let free market forces have their way.

The JSC did not give up on government. But with Miles Dean and Doepken taking the lead, it focused pressure on the region's congressional delegation and local officials.

Dissatisfaction on the JSC with its proposed negotiator persisted. Miles Dean would say that "Lowenstein was day one dead." In fact, when the New Jersey lawyer first came to Weirton, Bill Doepken ran a Dun & Bradstreet check of Lowenstein's holdings and found that he owned a substantial share of a steel warehousing operation controlled by Walter Haas, brother of Jim Haas, the president of National Steel. Doepken understood that Weirton was a close-knit community where generations of the same families worked together in the mill. In that environment, he knew that Lowenstein's role as the negotiator against National and business partner with the Haas family would be seen as a conflict. Doepken quietly filed away the information.

Two months later, when the takeover process seemed to be stalled over the negotiator issue, Doepken passed the information to Robertson. While the JSC did not count ballots, Doepken knew that the power in the body rested with the union, which had the numbers if an issue ever came to a vote.

Robertson presented the issue to the JSC as a possible conflict of interest. Also, he questioned Lowenstein's motives for failing to disclose the business relationship with Haas.

Lowenstein had never been able to overcome a suspicion that he was, as Robertson put it, "a management plant." Now the new information about his business dealings finally tipped the scale against him and he was fired. The JSC tried to put a good or at least bland face on the matter, noting "philosophical differences" in its press release about the incident and presenting the matter not as a firing but as a "mutual parting of ways."

In *Iron Age*, Lowenstein insisted that he did not think that the union was prepared to take "upfront wage concessions." Pete Love, National's chairman, felt that the JSC simply had "shot the first man over the trenches" bearing bad but truthful news about the need for an independent board of directors, not reopening the coke plant, buying foreign slabs, and firing Redline. Troubled by the delay, Love still insisted that the deal close by year's end, or else National would harvest the mill.

While the JSC wrestled with who should be the deal's "quarterback," it also had interviewed management consulting firms, including Arthur D. Little, McKinsey and Company, and Booz, Allen and Hamilton, in order to find one to perform the feasibility study. Eventually, the JSC decided on McKinsey, the world's largest consultant, because the firm seemed to have the most experience with clients in the steel industry and with "end markets" relevant to Weirton, including food packers and car makers. In its lavish presentation to the JSC, the consultant stressed its recent representation of the French and Belgian national steel industries and its development of a computerized proprietary model of world steel production. McKinsey offered to complete a study within three to four months that would detail Weirton's long-term viability under a variety of market scenarios.

■

With Lowenstein gone, the JSC scurried to find a replacement. There was no time for rounds of interviews to explore candidates' philosophies. For the most part, the problem fell to union attorney David Robertson who had two ideas.

First, he thought of calling in Skadden, Arps, Meagher and Flom, Wall Street's largest merger-and-acquisition law firm to do the deal. But that firm, it turned out, had represented a banking subsidiary of National Steel, and conflict of interest problems would surface again.

Robertson also phoned a boyhood friend who worked in Manhattan as a money manager. He recommended Willkie Farr & Gallagher, a venerable two-hundred-member firm in his office building to which Wendell Willkie, the 1940 Republican presidential challenger to Franklin Roosevelt, had belonged. At Willkie Farr, members of the committee met with Kenneth Bialkin, the firm's leading moneymaker, chairman of the American Bar Association's Corporate Banking and Business Law Section, and counsel to a host of household names in finance from American Express to Ivan Boesky. Bialkin made a quick and penetrating analysis of the prospective deal, said that an investment bank would have to be called in, and predicted that the deal was too complex to be done by the end of the year. Bialkin's easy mastery of the details and low-key style—"He didn't try to sell us," recalled David Robertson—appealed to the committee. On May 19, the committee announced that Bialkin would be "the primary lead counsel providing services to the project." Actually, Bialkin only had made it rain for his firm. No one from Weirton would see him again, and he soon would be forgotten and replaced by his partner, Harvey Sperry, fifty-two.

A short, compact man with a helmet of thick gray hair, slightly simian features, and knowing eyes, Sperry was a logical man for the job. In a firm that increasingly serviced the finance industry, he "worked for clients who still made things," manufacturers such as Kerr Glass, for whom he served as general counsel and sat on the board. And he had done his share of deals, more than forty acquisitions since joining the firm in 1957.

An upbeat, aggressive native of Coalville, Iowa, population twenty-five hundred, Sperry retained a rural charm that allowed him to blend better with the West Virginians than Lowenstein had. He was not particularly well liked in his firm, especially by younger lawyers who thought that his toughness slipped into callousness and cruelty. They also marveled that he had married his partner's wife, and continued to go to the office as if nothing had happened. But no one denied his intelligence or productivity.

Sperry relished the Weirton assignment, especially "the idea of representing these employees and helping them do something about their own problems." In his view, the attitudes of Weirton workers contrasted powerfully with those of others hurting in the rust belt. "It seemed like here were these people not just laying back and complaining about what the world was doing to them." So impressed was Sperry, who had never worked with unions, with the self-help qualities of the Weirton workers, that he proposed to David Robertson that the new ESOP use individual employment contracts rather than engage in collective bargaining between the union and management. Robertson replied, "Harvey, watch my lips. You're talking with the union's attorney, do you know what you've suggested to me? Go to the rest room, wash your mouth out with soap, and don't let me hear you say that again."

Robertson liked Sperry, admired his "small, extremely influential client base," and saw him as "just one tough, tough son of a bitch," but also extremely smooth. In fact, he reminded Robertson of Don Ebbert, National's fiendishly clever labor lawyer who had created the ISU.

From the first, Sperry related well to the union. He played up his boyhood on an Iowa farm, and the fact that part of his family came from West Virginia. Unlike Lowenstein, he knew better than to put all his cards on the table. He developed positions with subtlety. Also, unlike Lowenstein, Sperry never had "done an ESOP." But like his predecessor, Sperry favored a traditionally managed company, which he felt would have more appeal to lenders than would a workers' democracy.

Early in his visits to Weirton, he began talking to employees about the desirability of "being workers by day and owners by night." He presented preserving the division between labor and management as a check and balance on the powers of both. In relatively conservative Weirton, Sperry's message won a receptive hearing.

Sperry also understood that the local top management team, which formed a faction on the JSC, wanted to stay in Weirton after the buyout as the leadership of a stand-alone Fortune 500 corporation. Like Lowenstein, he felt that they weren't up to the task, and that Jack Redline, particularly, had to go.

Though counsel to the whole JSC, Sperry moved closer to the ISU, while staying aloof from management's inner circle. At the time, the community was starved for information from the JSC, and when Sperry had a piece of news, he gave it to a union member to release. Also, he began dropping hints that the local management was not competent, particularly Redline, whom Sperry feared would put friends from Weirton on the board of the new company, damaging its profile as a national corporation and its ability to raise funds. Sperry also questioned Redline's ability to lead. "I thought Jack was sick. I thought he was on his way towards Alzheimer's or something. He just didn't have it all." The fact that Redline was not around the JSC to defend himself or to prove his skills during the transition obviously did not help the once-popular executive.

As spring turned to summer in 1982, the buyout process continued to stall. On the one hand, virtually everyone in town was waiting for the results of the McKinsey study, which would spell out whether a new enterprise would be feasible in the first place; and if so, what concessions would be expected of the employee-owners. On the other, labor politics started to intrude in the process. The triennial elections for ISU president, executive committee, and stewards were about to begin.

In the late 1970s and early 1980s, labor politics shifted its focus from "more" to a binary system, as union leaders were asked to respond yes or no to concessions. Obviously, "no" was the more macho and for a time popular choice as an affirmation of union power, though in some situations it implied a death wish. While saying yes to management and concessions might prolong the life of some jobs, it was seen by many American workers as being weak and collaborationist.

At Weirton, the ISU leadership on the JSC quickly divided into "negative" and "positive" factions. Led by Mike Hrabovsky, Chris Graziani, and John Pastoric, the negative voices reflexively said no to almost everything proposed by National Steel or local management. The subtext of these militants' positions, barely spoken at this time but looming larger and larger, was that a shutdown was more in their interest than a new company. This irony was grounded in the fact that they were older workers with long years of service who were close to receiving their pensions. They expected that National, hated though it was, could honor its retirement commitments, while they weren't sure if the new company would even offer pensions. Moreover, they knew that if the mill shut down, other handsome benefits would kick in, including ten weeks of severance pay plus the vaunted $400 monthly supplement. Plus, the "no" faction had been highly impressed by the opinion of equally militant autoworkers at Hyatt Clark whose angry message Mike Hrabovsky understood to mean that "at Hyatt Clark the union took on management as partners and it's hurting us. If you [Weirton union members] are going to set up an ESOP, do it on your own. And if you can't do it on your own, close the place down, do not go into an ESOP with management."

On the other side were truly old codgers, seen by Hrabovsky as quislings. Chief among them was Dick Mort, chairman of the tin mill who had been a founding member of the union executive committee, and had served ever since. In late 1981, Mort and a since retired union committee member named Bob Conley had made an unauthorized visit to Bill Doepken, management's counsel. Astute, Mort and Conley had seen the writing on the wall. National Steel was not keeping pace with its environmental consent decree commitments; nor was it modernizing the mill.

The ISU successfully had resisted concessionary bargaining during 1980 contract negotiations. A year later, according to Doepken, who recalled the clandestine meeting, the senior union leaders offered him a plan: They would try to sell economic concessions to the workers, provided that the savings could be escrowed for funding the upgrading of the facility. Enthusiastic about the offer, Doepken reported it to his superiors in divisional management, who likewise approved, and conveyed it to National president Jim Haas and chairman Pete

Love. Haas liked the idea, but Love did not—he was trying to downsize, not modernize steel capacity—and it died.

The negative clique in the ISU, led by Hrabovsky, not only abhorred concessions but also reviled those who helped management. Of Dick Mort, Hrabovsky offered: "As long as they have people like him around, Judy Jordon over in Steubenville is a saint. She's the madam who runs the house of ill repute over there." In Hrabovsky's view Mort was not an exception, since management

> always made sure that they controlled a certain number of votes on the executive committee. If they needed something all they had to do was make their phone calls. . . . Living in a small town, you are going to have friends in management, and I knew things were coming down, and guess who presented them. Someone on our committee or our union president would come up with a brainstorm of an idea that we should do this. Hell, I knew it was going to happen five months ago because management told me it was going to happen. But yet when you went around the room, it was Aye, Aye, Aye, Mike Hrabovsky nay, Chris Graziani nay, John Pastoric nay. The vote was always lopsided. And that way they took care of these people. They always gave them a few extra crumbs.

For its favorite union leaders, Hrabovsky explained that the company provided:

> a couple of extra grievances granted, a new water fountain, or nice lunch room facilities, those kind of things. They always made sure that that man looked like a gem, and they made sure that that man got credit for the little things they did in the plant so his reelection chance was always greater.

Though Red Arango was friendly with Hrabovsky and his heart was with the more militant unionists, whom he allowed to set the tone for JSC meetings, the ISU president continued to stumble through pro-ESOP speeches in the community. Hrabovsky confronted Arango. "I said, 'Red, they're using you. And when they get done with you, they're gonna toss you aside like a used rubber.' I said, 'If you don't wise up and open your eyes and see what they're doing to you, I'm going to run against you.' Well, Red and I had a falling out then."

In addition to Arango and Hrabovsky, nine other candidates signed up to run for union president in the spring of 1982. Under the ISU bylaws any active member of the union could run for the office. Usually candidates emerged from the leadership. Red Arango—who had never held a stewardship, had been a local football hero, and had won the top office in 1980—was an exception though he had the strong support from the popular previous president, Sam Bakich.

In 1982 the only member of the union executive committee to challenge Arango, besides Hrabovsky, was Walter Bish, thirty-six, a former conductor on the mill's railroad who had become a steward in 1976. An owlish man, with a West Virginia twang and a head for business and horses, he had been reticent about running in 1982. He "liked Red, but I didn't think he was really a union leader." In addition Bish felt that Arango "listened to the wrong faction in the union . . . I just didn't feel that going into this ESOP process that he should be the one leading us." Similarly Bish believed that Hrabovsky, who was "very, very radical," would make a poor president. Initially, Bish encouraged other union leaders to run, including Bob Conley, the former executive committee member who had served on the body for twenty years, Conley's son Eddie, a young but equally cunning labor politician serving as a steward in the Strip Steel division, and Ben Wade, a massive former scarfer on the executive committee whose size and bearded hillbilly looks gave away nothing in the macho department to Arango and Hrabovsky, but whose views were more conciliatory. After striking out with all of them, Bish threw his hat into the ring.

A union politician for twenty years, Hrabovsky had paid little attention to Bish before except to notice that the younger man sometimes read the *Racing Forum* at union meetings. Arango did not like Bish, whom he viewed as pro-company. Consistent with the overall industry practice, there was a clause in the 1980 ISU contract that compels management and labor, in the name of remaining competitive with foreign suppliers, at least to talk together about reducing crew sizes and eliminating work rules. Arango believed that Bish "wanted to give jobs away."

Ordinarily free of issues, union elections at Weirton resembled high school popularity contests. There were no slates, caucuses, platforms, speeches, debates. In this milieu, Red Arango was the favorite. In addition to being a famous local athlete, Arango, a former welder, had been assigned to jobs in all areas of the mill, an advantage over Hrabovsky, whose profile was highest in Steel Works One where he had worked as a crane man and steward. Bish had no fame as an athlete—in the words of a close friend, "He was a nerd who played in the high school band"—but his old job as a conductor on the mill railroad also had allowed him to circulate throughout the plant complex and to build relationships outside his home division.

Perhaps because 1982 was a unique and perilous time, issues for once spilled into the election. Hrabovsky ran a tough campaign scoring management for being inflexible, insisting on a role for the union in business decision making, blasting the one-to-five ratio of foreman to workers as too high, and demanding fewer supervisors. Hrabovsky did not focus on the potential ESOP, dismissing it as a plot by National to elude its environmental and modernization obligations.

Like many of the relatively younger workers, Bish viewed employee ownership as the only chance to keep working in Weirton. As a campaigner, he took a moderately pro-ESOP line. In order to be acceptable, according to Bish, the employee-owned company would have to keep pensions at present levels, honor retirees' rights to health and life insurance, and put laid-off employees back to work (even if they had been off so long they had lost recall rights) before hiring new people.

In fact, it was an ingenious platform. Weirton included numerous families with members at every level in the workforce, from new employees (most of whom were laid off) to mid-career workers to retirees. Bish's campaign version of an ESOP was aimed at protecting each group.

Arango ran a relatively traditional popularity-oriented campaign, though his duties as cochairman of the JSC may have cut into the time he spent on it. Miles Dean noticed that when Arango had a commitment to speak publicly outside the mill, Bish was in the mill campaigning.

The campaign also affected work within the JSC. According to Bill Doepken, at Weirton, unlike at other steel companies, "every grievance is a political grievance." At plants with USW representation, periodically a union staff person—not an elected official—would review the grievances filed and make decisions about which to arbitrate and which were "garbage." The shop steward was insulated from the decision and could not be blamed for it.

At Weirton, no international union staffers weeded out bad grievances. Stewards and committeemen could not drop them because, as Doepken put it: "Every grievance is a vote." Hrabovsky, according to Doepken, began bringing his constituents' grievances to the JSC. If management refused to discuss them, Hrabovsky walked out. "Mike Hrabovsky," said Doepken, was "a real tub of shit."

In the balloting of June 22, 1982, Red Arango polled 1,611 votes to 1,147 for Bish and 536 for Hrabovsky. Hrabovsky, who called his finish a "sloppy third," edged out newsletter gadfly J. J. Varlas by only 18 votes, a surprising showing for Varlas, since clerks have little status in other mill areas.

Because no candidate received a majority, a runoff was held three days later between Bish and Arango, the latter the obvious favorite given his 500-vote margin in the primary and the fact that most of Hrabovsky's supporters would be expected to switch to the incumbent. But with a larger turnout than in the primary, Bish outpolled Arango by 2,715 to 1,641 and won five of six divisions. Arango, who narrowly carried Steel Works One, his home production area, had as good an explanation as any: "People wanted a change." In fact, it was in the average hourly's interest to pick someone clearly in favor of an ESOP in order to preserve jobs, who was bright enough to master financial complexities, and articulate enough to communicate them to the workforce.

Other factors also worked in Bish's favor. In late June, National Steel closed more of its coking operations at Weirton, resulting in the loss of two hundred jobs, which Arango appeared powerless to stop. On the crucial final day before the runoff, Arango had to be occupied with a parade and media event, involving local and national political leaders, called the "Save Our Valley Rally," which featured Senator Byrd and congressmen from West Virginia and Ohio, who were introducing "stretch-out" legislation to extend Weirton's compliance date with 1980 environmental consent decrees from the coming September until 1987. People in the crowd carried signs reading, "Give us time" and "You can't eat Clean Air," and filled out form letters asking Congress to vote for delayed environmental relief. As Arango hobnobbed with politicians and made a forgettable speech, Bish campaigned hard in the plant.

Unlike the union leadership, top management at Weirton was unified in its enthusiasm for the proposed ESOP. The National Labor Relations Act (NLRA) forbade management from intervening in any way in a union election, a particularly important rule in a company-dominated community such as Weirton. But Weirton management liked Bish, whom Redline called "a good, smart guy. We did what we could to get Bish elected. Wherever we went we had a good word to say about Bish." After "Bish won," said Mike Hrabovsky, "everything was full steam ahead."

The ISU leadership also turned over almost completely in the 1982 election. Sixteen of eighteen ISU committee members failed to return. The average age of the group dropped from fifty to forty-three. The new younger members had a clearer pro-ESOP orientation.

Mike Hrabovsky's defeat was typical. After winning his stewardship, Hrabovsky found himself in a contest for a Steel Works One committee post with John "Skip" Spadafora, thirty-four, an operator on the continuous caster. A slim, studious-looking man with long curly hair, trimmed beard, and an easy smile, Spadafora had never run for union office, but handily beat Hrabovsky.

In many ways, Spadafora was the prototype of a new union leader both at Weirton, and nationally. His grandfather, a miner, had had his arm shot off while picketing during a strike, but neither his father (an insurance man) nor Spadafora had any interest in doing blue-collar work. After high school, he served with the army in Vietnam in the Finance Corps, where he became financially adept, and in Germany where he became fluent in the language in six months. (Later, the company would send him as a labor member of delegations to Germany to review steel-making technology.) After his discharge from the service, Spadafora returned to Weirton and found that the best-paying jobs in the region were in the mill, and started working at the continuous caster. While rising to the "top of the sequence" in caster jobs, he made progress toward a college degree, and became certified to sell insurance and real estate. After work, he went to an office in his home, wrote policies, and sold houses. This led to a number of fat years. "Jesus," he recalled in an interview, "my income was tremendous with the real estate and what I was making in the mill. As soon as I came home from the mill I would line up appointments." He not only listed real estate but invested in a number of homes in Weirton. After Pete Love's announcement on March 2, the bottom fell out of the local real estate market, and the properties became impossible to sell. Spadafora went through a "gloomy period," during which he saw that "people started moving out of here. I won't have anybody to sell insurance to. Kids grow up and can't stay in the valley. Real estate could be totally gone.

"I felt I've got to find what's going on. That's how I got involved in the union. I used my business background to convince my constituents that they needed someone in there who understood the terminology of the whole process. My background was my platform."

Also, the campaign brought out a sharp contrast with Hrabovsky's personality. "Mike was a good person and good steward, but he didn't believe anybody. He had a negative approach toward everything. People didn't want anybody negative in there. They wanted somebody positive; and if nothing else I'm a positive individual." Throughout the mill the electorate "supported the idea of change by ousting a lot of the older people."

All of Hrabovsky's allies on the committee, including Glenn Ohler in Steel Works One and John Pastoric and Chris Graziani of the sheet mill, also were defeated. Graziani, a scrappy twenty-three-year former warehouseman, maintains that "management got rid of that committee. They put out rumors that Red Arango, Mike [Hrabovsky], and John Pastoric, and myself were anti-ESOP. If we was anti-ESOP, then why did we vote to spend five hundred thousand to fund the McKinsey study? The people in the mill were afraid. Once the company starts puttin' out rumors there's no way to stop them. They started havin' these breakfast clubs for wives. A guy would come home and his wife would tell him he better vote ESOP or he's gonna lose his job. They said we were a bunch of dissidents. We really got shot down."

8   America's Mill

"Our future lies in cans, not can'ts."
—PARADE PLACARD, JULY 3, 1982

In mid-1982, the Weirton division's communications drive intensified. A twenty-four-hour hot line manned alternately by labor and management began processing concerns from the workforce. When a caller's question could not be answered immediately, it would be relayed to someone who had knowledge of the issue, who later would write back to the employee. Often, the hot line, which handled more than a hundred calls per day, would serve as a valve to release rising pressure in the mill. In the first five hundred calls, employees raged against shutting down the plant, hiring management's children for upcoming summer jobs, the number of foreign cars being driven to work, and the use of paper clips made in Taiwan, while raising tough questions about ESOP architecture and pension law.

After Walter Bish and the new ISU executive committee were installed, the in-plant meeting drive also took off. Unlike his predecessor, Bish had a penchant for detail and a calming, moderate manner that made him a superior communicator. As Chuck Lafferty, who headed the communications effort, put it: "The union suddenly had a touch of class in Walter Bish. Bish appeared to be an open, interested, very bright man." Weirton also strived to capture national media attention. The public relations department under Chuck Cronin constantly released information to the networks and wire services. By making "America's Mill," a nationally known Cinderella story, Cronin, Lafferty, and others hoped to make it all the more difficult for National to shut down the operation or convert it to a small-scale finishing operation.

The effort began to bear fruit at the town's Independence Day celebration on July 3 when workers and their families paraded through a downpour carrying signs reading, "Hungry? Eat your Toyota," "Our future lies in cans, not can'ts," "Save my Daddy's Job," and "Reagan Where Are You?" The event was covered by the CBS evening news as well as by the *New York Times* and the *Washington Post*, which featured "The Town That Refuses to Die" and interviewed division president Jack Redline, who spoke bravely if predictably: "I'm very confident the ESOP plan will work. We have the best workers in the industry, and we have put our destiny in our own hands. It is up to us to make it work."

But Walter Bish, the president-elect of the ISU and incoming cochairman of the Joint Study Committee, seemed most adept with the crowd and with the media. The bearded, baby-faced, studiously bespectacled union leader with an Appalachian drawl got off the day's best quip: "I always said to my wife that I wanted to go into business for myself, but I never thought I'd start by buying a steel mill."

Not everyone was delighted by the mill's celebrity status. Staughton Lynd told Peter Pitegoff of the Industrial Cooperative Association, which was furnishing the Rank and File Committee with

research, that "Weirton is big news . . . the place is lousy with TV reporters and movie makers." Indeed, two documentary film crews had
begun shooting films for and against the proposed ESOP. The positive movie, under the direction of Chuck Lafferty, would be called
On Our Own Again. The more critical and radical film about the
buyout, which largely focused on Lynd and the Rank and File Committee, was being shot by a French film crew and was called *The
Great Weirton Steal.*

For months, the Weirton community had been preoccupied with a
team from McKinsey, who had headquartered themselves with computers in a makeshift situation room in the General Office. From
there, they roamed the mill interviewing workers and bosses, gathered data, and queried customers. In many ways, the destiny of Weirton as a company and community was in the hands of this cluster
of fresh-faced well-dressed consultants all but one of whom were
younger than thirty-five. If they found that the spin-off from National was not feasible, then banks would not support the new venture. If they said that a stand-alone company could make it, but only
with deep wage cuts that lowered the standard of living, then perhaps the employees would be less attracted by the idea, preferring
retirement, pensions, and migration.

From the first, the McKinsey study was shrouded in secrecy. Without authorization, someone distributed notes of the May 24, 1982,
presentation of McKinsey to the Joint Study Committee, which
forced the JSC to print a "Special Edition" of its newsletter on
June 4th in order to "help dispel any rumors resulting from unofficial
publications of the study and place the results of their work to date
in a more accurate perspective." The JSC also distributed an "interim
progress review" of McKinsey's work.

On the key issues, the interim report was not clarifying. "At this
point," according to McKinsey, "it is premature to reach a conclusion on the feasibility of an independent Weirton." Despite customer
satisfaction with Weirton's "good quality and excellent technical service," the consultant believed it would "be difficult to gain much
sales volume in the short term," due to competition from other steel
makers and products such as plastics. Worse, McKinsey forecast a
$330 million cash flow shortfall if the independent company contin-

ued to function on a "business as usual basis." In all, it was a fairly
gloomy picture. McKinsey promised subsequently to identify cost reductions needed to reduce the shortfall. It did not say that these
would have to come out of paychecks, which some in the community
thought was less than candid.

Not surprisingly, the consulting firm became highly controversial.
While complaining that McKinsey spent too much time talking with
management, many ISU committee members wanted nothing to do
with team members at least until after the union elections. In general,
however, the McKinsey team received a high degree of local scrutiny.
Michael Chesick, a young member of the group who had principal
responsibility for computer modeling, found Weirton highly insular.
"Pittsburgh could have been Tokyo. Weirton is a one-horse town
and the horse is the steel plant. Everybody was really concerned
about the viability of the mill. I have never been in an environment
where we had more goodwill, but more inspection of what we were
doing."

Over the next few months, McKinsey continued to refine its data.
On July 14, 1982, at meetings in Steubenville open to workers, Ron
Bancroft, a ramrod-straight former naval officer and Rhodes scholar
who had headed Defense Secretary Melvin Laird's staff and now led
the McKinsey "engagement," voiced a bit more optimism. He foresaw a "reasonable but not terrific" ten-year outlook for markets
served by Weirton, and believed that the independent company
would be able to ship steel at the relatively healthy level of 2 million
tons per year for a decade. Nonetheless, Bancroft warned that the
operation "would expect cost reductions on a significant basis."
Again, he declined to identify where these reductions would come
from, offering that that would be revealed in the team's final report
due on July 26. He did, however, speak in terms of "sacrifices," and
warned that "we are not here to tell you what you want to hear but
what makes good business sense."

A number of workers at the meeting bristled with questions about
whether from behind the scenes National was orchestrating the situation to get employee concessions rather than to sell them the plant.
Harvey Sperry, the New York lawyer who had been retained to negotiate against National and had begun feeling out his opponent, an-

swered the crowd that this was not the case, and that there would be a sale.

Another employee in the audience wanted to know if the workers would be given the opportunity to vote on the terms of the buyout. Outgoing ISU president Red Arango, who was on the panel, replied that a vote was not expected. On one hand, he spoke murkily about achieving a "consensus." On the other, he made it seem that whether or not one went to work for the spun-off mill would be an individual choice: "I don't want three to four thousand employees to tell me what decision I will make."

The news that there might not be a vote came as a shock. From the first, a referendum on the new ESOP had been anticipated as a check and balance on the power of the small group of consultants and JSC members who where steering the process.

Almost immediately, the Rank and File Committee capitalized on the issue and began pressing to hold an eventual ballot on the buyout as part of its general theme of a democratic ESOP, where employees immediately would be able to vote their shares. At meetings during this period Steve Bauman, the white cochairman of the Rank and File Committee, passed out materials showing that 73 percent of the ESOPs in a University of Michigan study never allowed their employees to vote their stock. Bauman would ask: "Are we supposed to supply both labor and capital and still have no control?" Around this time, Bauman and others in the Rank and File began receiving anonymous phone threats. But in the mill, he recalled, "people were still listening to us."

The McKinsey report, which contained strong medicine, made workers more receptive to the radicals' message. However, even before its release on July 26, the forty-page document produced sparks on the Joint Study Committee.

McKinsey's most controversial finding was that employees after the buyout would have to give up 32 percent of their wages and benefits in order for the new company to make a go of it. Before news of the cut was announced, the team of lawyers at Willkie Farr & Gallagher in New York phoned Carl Valdiserri, the management cochairman of the Joint Study Committee, and suggested that even 32 percent was not enough—another 10 percent should be added, bringing the total concession per employee to 42 percent. The lawyers' position focused on attracting lenders. Harvey Sperry, according to Valdiserri, said, "We'll finance this thing a lot easier if we show that forty-two percent. The cash flow is fatter; the profits are better. We'll be able to peddle the paper."

Valdiserri believed that the "thirty-two percent allowed us to stay profitable even in the worst of scenarios, but that it required the maximum sacrifice that could be asked of employees, including himself. "When Sperry asked for more, I just blew up, I lost it. I shouldn't have but I did."

Bill Doepken, Carl Valdiserri, and Jack Redline believed, probably correctly, that 42 percent would not be tolerated by the employees and would have stopped the deal. Though they felt increasingly uneasy with Sperry, and saw their positions under attack by him, they decided not to go public with his effort to expand the cuts. "Sperry would've been fired," felt Bill Doepken, "and Weirton would've become a finishing mill with fifteen hundred employees." Doepken, Valdiserri, and Redline also were convinced that the process could not withstand another Lowenstein-type disaster; nor could they imagine National tolerating more delay in order to enable the JSC to find a new law firm. "Sperry," said Doepken, "was among the most evil men I've ever met. But firing him would have cratered the deal."

The 10 percent add-on was carefully kept from the JSC's labor component, because of its explosive nature. McKinsey, recalled Valdiserri, also was "incensed." They said, "You've paid us all this money. We've done all this detailed market research and analysis of your competition. What did you hire us for if you were just going to pick a number out of the air?"

Before the July 26th release date, Sperry relented, and McKinsey's figure was held at 32 percent. But, ironically, a serious breach had opened between Sperry, who always had been a counsel to management, and Weirton's management. Subsequently, Sperry cemented an alliance with labor, which never knew he had tried to reduce their livelihood by an additional 10 percent.

While it was the document that blessed setting up a new Fortune 500 corporation, the McKinsey report contained numerous hurdles. In order for Weirton to continue as a fully integrated producer with the ability to make raw steel, roll, coat, and finish it, the company would have to spend more than a billion dollars in a decade on new equipment and environmental compliance. McKinsey contemplated that the independent company would rebuild and operate the coke battery, add a second continuous caster by the mid-1980s, have full finishing facilities in the tin and sheet mills, run a substantial research and development facility, including the materials utilization division, which it would have to win through negotiations against National, and add capabilities in marketing, sales, finance, and information services.

McKinsey believed that there were three ways to pay for all of this: issue stock funded out of personal contributions; pledge vested pension benefits as collateral for credit; and use compensation reductions to build an equity base. The management consultant considered the first two options "too risky." Also, as it pointed out, using retirement benefits to secure loans would not divide the risk fairly among employees. In actuality, it would focus on heavily vested employees who were closest to retirement, rather than on those who still had the most work years remaining in the mill and thus the greatest interest in its long-term survival.

The best option, according to McKinsey, was the compensation reduction of 32 percent. If the company succeeded, the consultant believed that the cuts would be temporary and the lost compensation eventually would be restored to the employees through renegotiated wage contracts, profit sharing, and stock price rises. Even if the new company plunged into bankruptcy, the employees still would not lose their pensions or personal assets.

Neither McKinsey nor the JSC considered two other options being debated in the rust belt at the time. One involved raising funds by selling stock to members of the local community, in addition to employees, which had been the method that failed in Youngstown due to the intransigence of U.S. Steel. The other strategy involved a public condemnation and seizure of the mill by eminent domain, and then reopening it as a socialized entity on the order of the Tennessee Valley Authority (TVA). The idea, championed by unemployed Pittsburgh Steel workers and their colorful magazine, *The Mill Hunk Herald*, remains untried.

Though it went largely unnoticed and unpublicized by the media, the McKinsey report made clear that the 32 percent cut could be expanded. Geared to make Weirton, historically one of the highest-cost producers in the industry, into the lowest-cost producer, the figure was *relative* to wages at other major steelmakers. In other words, if the United Steelworkers union gave up major concessions in its upcoming negotiations with other companies, then in McKinsey's view the amount of those cuts would have to be added to the 32 percent at Weirton to keep the new independent company competitive.

According to Ron Bancroft, McKinsey's team leader, the toughest internal struggle before the release of the report was not over whether to expand the reductions to 42 percent, but whether to drop it to about 20 percent. The leader of this movement was Lazard Frères, the New York investment banking house, which began exercising influence over the deal even before it was formally retained in the fall.

Bancroft believed that the 32 percent figure was suitably conservative and pegged to giving the embryonic company "about an eighty percent chance of success," which was what the assignment from the Joint Study Committee had requested. Like the management leaders of the JSC, Carl Valdiserri and Bill Doepken, Bancroft saw no reason to bring an investment bank into the deal. At the time, the three believed that the assets of the Weirton division, including the physical plant, equipment, land, and accounts receivable, could more than secure the necessary credit to fund the buyout.

Typically, investment bankers gather a group of creditors to finance a deal when the buyer's collateral is not sufficient to secure it. During the 1970s and 1980s, investment bankers made possible leveraged buyouts in which relatively small companies targeted and absorbed much larger corporations.

An investment bank did not work cheaply. Ordinarily its fee, according to the "Lehman formula" recognized on Wall Street, was about 1 percent of the total money raised to finance the transaction. Some critics of commercial financing argued that investment bankers saddled nascent companies with more debt than necessary in order to get the most out of their percentage take.

From the first, Willkie Farr believed that an investment bank would be important. Before his early disappearance from the Weirton project, Kenneth Bialkin registered this opinion, which Harvey Sperry, who succeeded to the position of lead lawyer and negotiator, consistently advanced. Willkie Farr's clients included several leading Wall Street firms such as Shearson American Express, and Lazard Frères. Independent Steel Workers' union counsel David Robertson, whom Sperry cultivated, and who grew close to Sperry, also from an early date favored hiring an investment bank. Shearson and Lazard Frères interviewed for the position as did Pittsburgh's Mellon Bank, Oppenheimer and Company, Merrill Lynch, and other firms.

West Virginia governor Jay Rockefeller attempted to be of help by referring the JSC to high-ranking officials at the Chase Manhattan Bank in New York, which in turn gave advice on the relative merits of the Wall Street investment banks. David Robertson recalled being told that Lazard Frères was the "place to go if you had cancer. Well, we thought that Weirton had cancer." In particular, the Chase official recommended that the JSC should work with Felix Rohatyn, a senior partner at Lazard, who had presided over the New York Municipal Assistance Corporation (MAC) when it raised $10 billion in the 1970s and restructured the city financially in order to avert bankruptcy. The Chase official also warned Robertson that Rohatyn "was an unguided missile," and that Lazard, if retained, would attempt to completely control the deal.

Members of the JSC met with Rohatyn at the firm's austere headquarters in Rockefeller Center. The off–Wall Street location, the lack of frills, and Rohatyn's proposed national economic policy, which included a key role for industry, as well as his close ties to the Democratic Party in a time of raging Reaganism, impressed the group from the rust belt. They decided to retain Lazard, and understood that Rohatyn would head the firm's team. Coming out of the meeting, Bill Doepken jokingly bet Walter Bish that the JSC would never see Rohatyn again, much as Kenneth Bialkin had quickly disappeared after Willkie Farr was hired. In fact, Doepken was right.

9 Secrecy

"One day we are going to have to burst the 100 percent employee ownership bubble. But for now, we should let this perception continue."

—DAVID ROBERTSON

Local leaders at Weirton tried to put a positive spin on the McKinsey report. Outgoing ISU president Red Arango called it a "good deal." Jack Redline said he "would hate to see the alternative," and added that according to McKinsey's proposed scheme of cuts "everyone will be treated equally, including myself." Union president-elect Walter Bish saw the document as a "glimmer of hope on the horizon," and pleaded with his constituents to "weigh the facts."

But, the report was wildly unpopular with the workers and gave new life to the Rank and File Committee. For one thing, McKinsey forecast a leaner Weirton with only about seven thousand employees. The glory days of the forties and fifties when the majority of the Panhandle's workers as well as droves of hoopies could find economic solidity in Weirton clearly had ended. While McKinsey urged job reductions in all sectors of the workforce, it stressed that the "area most clearly overstaffed based on ratio comparisons with other companies is the salaried area. These comparisons suggest that Weirton Steel has approximately 400 more salaried employees than the average steel company of its size."

Even more paradoxical and controversial was the fact that while the report advocated a "comprehensive communications effort to inform the employees on the reductions and risks associated with the ESOP," McKinsey withheld a soon-to-become notorious "confidential appendix" from the document released to the Weirton workforce. Not even the Joint Study Committee would receive a copy, though one was provided to Willkie Farr & Gallagher.

The appendix, which included information about Weirton's production costs, the likely sales price, and McKinsey's proprietary computer model of global steel operations, began to loom large in the public mind because the main body of the report offered scant justification for utilizing the 32 percent figure as opposed to, say, 27 percent or 35 percent. Could the confidential appendix justify 32 percent with precision?

On July 27, 1982, Tony Gilliam, Ed Mixon, Steve Bauman, and a handful of others associated with the Rank and File Committee sent a certified letter to their "Brothers" at ISU headquarters stating that "as a member of the Independent Steelworkers Union, as an employee (or laid-off employee with recall rights) at Weirton Steel, and as a potential investor in the new employee-owned steel company, I respectfully request the opportunity to inspect and copy any or all parts of the complete text of the feasibility report by McKinsey and Company."

Newly installed union president Walter Bish rejected the Rank and File's request, publicly stating that the appendix contained "strategic information," which if released would damage the company. Bish, however, added that he had not read the appendix. The Rank and File began a petition drive in the plant to get the report released, garnering about five hundred signatures. For the moment, the focus of the Rank and File Committee switched from gaining a seat at the negotiating table to full disclosure. "These were" said Staughton Lynd, "steelworkers whose primary concern was to find out what was going on."

Despite the forecasted white-collar cuts, local divisional management strongly backed McKinsey. Bill Doepken immediately sent copies to the West Virginia, Ohio, and Pennsylvania congressional delegations, terming the report the "cornerstone to the building of a successful ESOP."

At a press conference on August 5, 1982, Doepken said: "It boils down to two choices. It's either jobs or no jobs, a new company or a shutdown. If you prolong the process, it only creates more problems." The 32 percent employee concession "is the money that's gonna swing the deal. We asked McKinsey to be as conservative as possible. We didn't want a pie-in-the-sky outlook." The attorney also took a moment to refute a recent *Time* magazine story depicting Weirton as "homespun socialism." "This is just like any other acquisition," insisted Doepken. "But it may turn out to be a wonderful experiment."

Doepken saw four steps on the path to corporate stand-alone status. First, there would have to be yet another study—one more critical in some ways than McKinsey's—that assessed National and Weirton's pension liabilities. Then, the employees would have to accept the 32 percent slash. Third, the ESOP would need to line up lenders; and finally, negotiations with National would spin off a new employee-owned company with reasonable assets, resources, and prospects. The closing, he hoped, would take place before the end of the year, though the absolute deadline would be July 31, 1983, when the collective bargaining agreement between National and the ISU would expire. After that, the workers no longer would have work or a negotiating partner, the situation would turn chaotic, and potential lenders would flee. As a practical matter, Weirton had about ten months to seal the deal. But the period also could be much shorter. Word had leaked about Redline's interest in attempting to buy the mill. In a small meeting at Willkie Farr in New York on August 12, David Robertson spoke of fears that the divisional president, perhaps with the backing of a major Weirton customer such as Worthington Industries, would close a deal first with National.

The group, which included Sperry, two other Willkie Farr lawyers, and Jack Curtis, believed that there were two ways for an independent ESOP to get start-up financing: through commercial lenders, or using National as a "backstop," which would take back paper. Both had disadvantages. Sperry said National would attach strings to its money, impinging on full independence, and lenders could want equity, so they could make money on the risk. On balance, he favored the gathering of lenders by an investment bank. Jack Curtis wondered if the JSC should use more than one investment bank. "No," Sperry said, "they'll be at each other's throat." Possible investment banks mentioned included Lazard Frères, Mellon, Bear Stearns, and Shearson American Express.

The group at Willkie Farr also discussed what Robertson called "structural decisions" affecting the deal. For one thing, the employees were "getting the idea that the quid pro quo for the thirty-two percent [concession] is one hundred percent employee ownership." Eventually, the investment banking community would want less than total employee ownership, as Robertson noted. "One day we are going to have to burst the hundred percent employee ownership bubble. But for now, we should let this perception continue."

Raising a related point, Sperry argued that traditional ESOPs stumble because of cash-out clauses that force them to buy the stock of their retirees. The largely passive cost, also know as the repurchase liability, could hinder a company's competitiveness, which was why Sperry wanted employees to have the "right" to market their shares, and the company eventually to have the ability to sell stock to raise capital. The downside of a public marketing was that it would water down and eventually eliminate employee control.

During the countless public meetings about the ESOP that occurred in 1982 there was little if any mention of eventually selling shares outside and none that found its way into news reports. The bubble was not burst, at least for a time, which is not to say that no one perceived the problem. A Rank and File Committee memo reflects concern that if the stock went public, the employees could lose control, and could make quick money by selling, a situation that spelled the demise of ESOPs at Vermont Asbestos and the Chicago Northwest Railroad. The public market would work against jobs in the community, but fighting it would "be tough."

Before dealing with stock, the Joint Study Committee had to buy the company, which required money. The JSC overcame management's qualms and decided to audition investment bankers. At a dinner on August 25, Tom Bryan, Sperry's partner, told the ISU lawyer that Willkie Farr wanted Lazard Frères in as the investment bank, but did not want word to get back to New York that the law firm preferred Lazard over Shearson American Express, a client on whose board Kenneth Bialkin sat. Bryan asked Robertson to steer the process toward Lazard.

Nonetheless, Bear Stearns made an appearance in Weirton, led by one of its general partners, Tom Sturges, a young former schoolteacher who told the group that his bank, which specialized in leveraged buyouts, had fought Frank Lorenzo over Continental Air Lines, managed over $2.7 billion in corporate underwritings in 1981, and recently had doubled its personnel. Led by pit boss Ace Greenberg, perhaps the quintessential eighties trader, Bear Stearns also had participated in the only public offering to date by an ESOP.

The next day Shearson American Express came to Weirton and touted itself to the JSC as "the best-managed firm on Wall Street." When Craig Petrella, a savvy computer operator and member of the Salary Non-Exempt (SNE) component of the ISU, questioned Shearson about the fairness of the one point rake-off in the Lehman formula, Sperry bruited: "Don't fuck around with the one percent. Focus on raising the money"—at least making a good show for his firm's client, whom he knew would not get the business.

Lazard Frères came on board in early September, and as Bill Doepken had predicted, Felix Rohatyn was not evident. Eugene Keilin, forty, a lean, dark, bushy-haired man given to elegant suits but known as "labor's man on Wall Street," led. The son of a Texas civil liberties lawyer who represented mainly poor and black clients in the forties, fifties, and sixties, Keilin himself had practiced law for a few years in the early 1970s before joining New York City's Budget Office and soon becoming its general counsel. When the city faced bankruptcy in 1975, Keilin, as *Fortune* magazine put it, was at the "vortex" of the crisis. Keilin's work won the attention of Felix Rohatyn, chairman of the Municipal Assistance Corporation (MAC), who hired the young lawyer to be its second executive director. During Keilin's tenure, people called the state agency "Big Mac," and as Rohatyn recalled, "It really took over the rescue of the city." MAC issued billions of dollars in bonds to refinance New York's debt, reformed accounting practices, and involved itself in the herculean task of bringing the budget into balance. The main lesson that Keilin learned from the crisis "was the benefit in the end of dealing with problems of that kind through cooperation rather than confrontation." Initially the unions blamed the banks for high-interest loans, and the banks blamed the unions for the number of jobs, high wages, and pensions. "The cause was always somebody else and the cure was always that somebody else should pay."

Keilin brought people to the table and had them listening "to the same set of facts." Eventually a plan of "rough justice" emerged that apportioned sacrifice according to "contribution to the problem" and "the ability to absorb hardship." Moreover, the participants came to believe that "it was a good plan, that it was likely to succeed. Therefore you weren't just pitching pennies in a well. You were making sacrifices to produce a result that you'd be happy with." In most respects MAC succeeded. The city survived, the unions eventually got their jobs and concessions back, and the banks, which made loans and gave interest rate concessions, avoided large liabilities, and saw their investments ripen.

After MAC, Rohatyn hired Keilin at Lazard Frères to help other ailing cities, including Detroit and Cleveland. In 1981 Keilin began advising the United Steelworkers union on its alternatives during the collapse of basic industry. A man of known probity, Keilin was not troubled at first by a conflict of interest between his USW ties and his work for Weirton represented by the ISU, but later would be.

At Weirton, Keilin was assisted by Josh Gotbaum, another young Ivy League lawyer turned investment banker. Only thirty, Gotbaum, who had worked the Carter White House on industrial policy issues, including the Chrysler loan guarantees, was the son of Victor Got-

baum, chief of District Council 37 of the New York municipal workers, who had played a key role in the MAC negotiations during
Keilin's tenure. A stocky man with a thick mustache, Josh Gotbaum
wore a peace symbol ring and carried a laptop computer, which he
flipped open at a moment's notice to crunch numbers. Both he and
Keilin gravitated toward the labor side of the Joint Study Committee, as Sperry had known they would. Indeed, Sperry's choice of Lazard, as opposed to a traditional management-oriented merchant
bank, was a stroke of political brilliance. Keilin, viewed organized labor as a positive, reforming factor in society. "If unions didn't exist,"
he told *Fortune*, "they would have to be invented."

The Lazard team found the Weirton process unusual in two ways.
First, the lawyer (Sperry) had picked the investment banker, when ordinarily the banker picked the lawyer. Second, the three-to-one
labor-to-management advantage on the Joint Study Committee was
odd. Within Lazard's experience, usually the sides were even.

In Keilin's view the imbalance on the JSC led to activism in meetings by the ISU leaders, especially Bish and Spadafora, who became
integrally involved in the processing of the financial data with Gotbaum. On the other hand, the outnumbered managers struck the investment bankers as passive and gave Keilin the sense that they were
making moves outside of meetings. The unionists and consultants
complained that the managers exercised power by controlling and
sometimes blocking the flow of information vital to formulating negotiating positions, and that the salaried group seemed more interested in securing jobs in the new corporation than in its well-being.
The same charge, felt Keilin, impressed by the results of the recent
ISU elections, could not be leveled against the union leadership,
which historically had a high turnover rate. The Lazard bankers reasoned that ISU members were more concerned with fashioning an effective new company, because they eventually would return to work
in the mill as other union candidates rose to beat them.

In most ways the accusation that the divisional management withheld information lacked accuracy. At that point, National, rather
than local executives, still controlled Weirton's marketing and data
processing functions, so the JSC's knowledge gaps were attributable
to the parent corporation.

However, the divisional leadership clearly wanted to manage the new corporation. Jack Redline campaigned openly for the chief executive's spot. Upper management at Weirton increasingly was perceived as self-seeking, and at the same time blamed for continued layoffs, which it was powerless to avoid. In an effort to shore up its image, the white-collar group added a new member, Ken Hunt, to the JSC in August. A third-generation Weirton employee, Hunt had worked his way up from blast furnace foreman to vice president of operations, and had taught himself metallurgy along the way. His grandfather, who began work in 1917, had designed plants on the Weirton site for E. T. Weir. Possibly the most popular boss in the plant, Hunt saw his role on the JSC as keeping union politics out of the process while attempting to give the salaried workforce more of a voice. But Hunt understood that the JSC would not steer the process. "We were like a city council. We ratified policy." Policy, in his view, came down from the consultants.

Hunt's appointment was announced in the first issue of the *Independent Weirton Journal*, subtitled "A Labor Management Publication." The print organ of the JSC, it used the symbol of worker and management hands shaking over the slogan "We Can Do It." The first issue also carried a message of conciliation from Jay Rockefeller, who cautioned that "during this long and difficult process, there will sometimes be the temptation to look back and focus on why, but we have to instead look ahead and focus on how." Because of community concern about the growing power of the consultants, the paper listed the tasks that "primarily" would occupy the lawyers and investment bankers:

1. Value division assets;
2. Design an ESOP plan from a financial/tax standpoint;
3. Negotiate the terms of sale;
4. Obtain substantial additional financing for the new company.

The goals were daunting. As Keilin knew, banks regarded the steel industry and especially integrated makers as cripples "to which they would not make loans as a matter of policy." But New York also had been an "unlendable mess."

In fact, the consultants accorded to themselves far broader powers than had been made known to the Weirton workforce. They would not merely design the ESOP, which was a financial vehicle, but also would shape the structure and power arrangements of the new company, its officers, and board of directors. This is not to say that the JSC members were putty to the New Yorkers. Sometimes the ISU or management members would balk at going along with the outsiders' plans. But, with few exceptions, the JSC members weighed rather than brought ideas to the process.

Loaded with ideas, the Rank and File Committee lacked seats in the JSC, upper management, or in the union leadership. Like other essentially powerless reform groups, it chose the judicial route, filing its first lawsuit, a federal case in the Northern District Court of West Virginia, in July on behalf of John Gregory, a young laid-off ISU member. Gregory had been denied the right to vote in the union's 1982 election, when he was turned away by Red Arango. Through his case, which was handled by Southeastern Ohio Legal Services, Jim McNamara, Staughton Lynd, and a liberal New York labor law firm, the Rank and File sought to guarantee voting rights to all laid-off labor, not only in future union elections, but also in any referendum "concerning the future buyout of the Weirton Steel Division." Because more than three thousand workers were laid off, they could bulk large in steering Weirton's destiny, and empowering the Rank and File, if the court awarded them voting clout.

10 Divide and Conquer

"This takes a combination of sticks and carrots."
—GENE KEILIN

Effectively coupling litigation to public education, the dissidents began a new series of meetings in Steubenville. The flier for one asked: "Who is the 'We' in 'We can do it?' "

Obviously "We" doesn't mean everybody. Right now decisions are being made which will determine who is going to work and who is not. The I.S.U. is determining who can vote and who can't. In 1980 approximately 10,000 people were members in good standing of the I.S.U. and were eligible to vote. Today, according to I.S.U. interpretations of the By-Laws, less than 6,800 members will be allowed to vote. More than 3,000 former members of I.S.U., many just recently laid-off, will not be allowed to vote whether it be for Union elections or for approval of an ESOP.

This question of who has the right to vote is crucial for all employees of Weirton Steel whether working or laid-off. If certain employees can be denied the right to vote now, what is going to prevent all employees from being denied the right to vote in the future?

After Arango's defeat and replacement by Bish as president of the ISU and cochair of the Joint Study Committee, the Rank and File Committee (RFC) intensified its petition drive to force a vote on the 32 percent wage and benefits cut. On August 26, 1982, the JSC and ISU reversed their earlier stands and announced that there would be a ballot on the proposed concession. Though it had won its first victory, the RFC remained galled by the lack of disclosure of the McKinsey appendix, which the group insisted included "all of the cost data and calculations [McKinsey] used to make their proposals." In leaflets on the issue, the RFC carried a new slogan coined by Steve Bauman: "If we don't ask, we won't find out. If we don't speak up, we won't be heard."

On August 31, 1982, Tony Gilliam, the black leader of the RFC, personally confronted Carl Valdiserri and Walter Bish, cochairs of the JSC, who firmly but politely rejected Gilliam's request to examine the document (which by then Valdiserri had seen, but Bish had not), on the basis that it contained proprietary McKinsey and Weirton data.

Three weeks later, Gilliam and Bauman served a petition with five hundred signatures of Weirton steelworkers on the ISU headquarters, demanding that their "Brothers" in the union leadership provide the confidential appendix. After another refusal, the RFC started a new federal case. Called *Bauman v. Bish*, it included various ISU members, Willie McKenzie, and the Rank and File Committee as plaintiffs, and raised claims under the Labor Management Reporting and Disclosure Act (LMRDA) as well as securities and pension law violations. Sometimes known as "labor's bill of rights," the LMRDA basically stands for allowing free speech in union political activities, including officers' elections. In a somewhat novel construction,

Staughton Lynd and Jim McNamara told the court that "without access to and dissemination of the data and factual information upon which the authors of the [McKinsey] Feasibility Report relied, neither the plaintiffs nor the other members of the ISU can cast an informed vote on the proposed thirty-two percent reduction."

The case opened a chasm between the RFC and the new ISU president, who previously had attended some RFC open meetings in Steubenville and had reversed the union's stand on disenfranchising laid-off workers. The plaintiffs accused Bish of bad faith for breaching his "fiduciary duty of trust" to his members by not allowing the information to flow, and in an uglier vein, for "failing to hold the ISU's money solely for the benefit of the ISU and its members," and for acting "on behalf of an adverse party." In essence, the RFC had charged Bish with raising the members' money for a feasibility study, but then protecting the consultant's interest and National Steel's market and cost information over labor's right to know. Believing that the vote on concessions could come as early as December, the RFC asked the court for immediate relief in the form of an injunction mandating disclosure.

Bish, however, urged the court to maintain confidentiality, since "the disclosure of such sensitive information could trigger both the failure of our enterprise and the additional unemployment of thousands of people." He added that the JSC would try at a later date with the permission of McKinsey to reveal some of the information in the appendix, excluding the cost data. The ISU's lawyer, David Robertson, slammed the Rank and File for "asking us to give up our competitive position to satisfy their curiosity."

In an out-of-court interview, Steve Bauman questioned the secrecy. "The Big Eight [steelmakers] have had unified prices and negotiations for the past ten, fifteen years and we don't feel it's affected the competitive stand of steel pricing. The information was just not that damaging to begin with." In addition, the Rank and File had had a number of academic economists look over the release portions of the McKinsey report and each had reached the conclusion that 32 percent was too hefty to be justified. New friction was added to the already rough relations on the Joint Study Committee when the management members, led by Carl Valdiserri, urged in vain that the appendix also not be shown to Lazard Frères. However, once Lazard got the document, it privately agreed with the Rank and File position that the cuts were too large, and Jack Irwin, the division's best internal accountant, concurred. With concessions of this size, Lazard felt that even incompetent management could run the ESOP company for a time without sinking it. However, Lazard preferred strong new management that could attract investors and give the venture long-term stability.

Harvey Sperry, who privately admired Staughton Lynd as a foe as much as he disdained local management, concurred with the RFC stance on allowing laid-off employees to vote. Sperry sensed that out-of-work blue-collar labor would favor the ESOP simply because the alternative meant that mill jobs never would survive. Like the ISU, the JSC decided that laid-off employees could vote in an eventual ESOP referendum.

In late summer, Weirton's situation darkened. The mill hit a seventy-seven-year workforce low with seventy-eight hundred active employees, and thirty-one hundred laid off. In back-channel communications with David Robertson, a Mellon Bank senior official doubted that lenders would put up the billion dollars needed to promote steel productivity in the Ohio Valley over the next decade. Moreover, even if banks came up with the cash they would be asking to be repaid in five to eight years. "That billion," the banker said, "scares the hell out of us."

The federal credit avenue quickly turned into a dead end. Craig Fuller, who had received the Weirton delegation in the Reagan White House, gave Robertson the news that the $3 million Economic Development Administration (EDA) application would yield only $100,000, not even seed money in a project of this magnitude.

In July, the City of Weirton had applied for a $20 million Urban Development Action Grant (UDAG). It planned to shift the money to the new steel company for rebuilding coke batteries on Brown's Island. With the backing of Senate majority leader Robert Byrd, who had pumped so much federal funding and patronage into his poor state, the plan seemed destined for success. But in September, Byrd had to tell his constituents that the Department of Housing and Urban Development was blocking the grant because the city lacked the amount of low-income public housing needed to quality.

On August 16, 1982, the actuarial firm of Towers, Perrin, Forster & Crosby, under contract to the Joint Study Committee, released a startling report. As applied to its Weirton division, the National Steel pension fund had assets of $350 million. Liabilities would range from $452 million if Weirton continued in operation to a whopping $770 million if Weirton closed due to heavy "shutdown" benefits that would kick in. National's red zone ranged from $102 million if Weirton lived, to $420 million if it died. The numbers shook Panhandle households like a cancer scare. The pension fund could go belly-up, and with it, retirement security.

The pension deficit potentially placed Weirton in the big leagues of American business disaster. Chrysler had had $1.2 billion in unfunded liabilities during its crisis, but these had been matched by equivalent federal loan guarantees. International Harvester's exposure was a billion dollars and it went into bankruptcy. Bethlehem Steel, with $420 million in unfunded liabilities, was a tottering giant; and Braniff, with $138 million, had recently died.

But because Weirton was a division of National, the cloud had a silver lining that the Rank and File Committee and Rockefeller's aide Miles Dean detected at roughly the same time. National could not afford to kill Weirton, because the $420 million liability would kill National. Almost giddily, the usually somber Dean told United Press International that the cost of purchasing the mill from its parent "could be nothing." The following day, Bill Doepken informed the media that Dean's view that the mill could be swapped for assumption of pension debt was premature and wrong. In fact, Dean was on the right track, but the card was not yet ready to be played.

Another problem was leadership. Paralyzed by the weight of its task, and by too many consultants, the JSC stalled in its efforts to mobilize for the takeover negotiations. On August 24, Miles Dean called David Robertson to warn that "you and Bill [Doepken] are going to start looking at the structure of the organization. It's going to become critical soon." By organization, Dean meant the top jobs in the new company, a matter on everyone's mind.

Two days later Robertson met in his office with Doepken. The management lawyer insisted that the "new organization is set," and included Jack Redline as CEO, Carl Valdiserri as executive vice president, Ken Hunt as vice president of Operations, Doepken as General Counsel, and John Madigan as vice president of Industrial Relations. The divisional leadership proposed to reinstate itself with one exception; it would demote Gene West, the present chief financial officer and go outside for a replacement. Robertson made no comment.

On September 2, Sperry confronted Robertson by phone about the "necessity" of replacing top local management, including the popular Redline. "You, David Robertson, are not going to be able to be home free on the issue of who killed Cock Robin." Not ready to endorse a coup, and knowing Redline's emotional value to the community, Robertson wanted to keep him "for an appropriate role," though not the top position. "If he won't stay unless he's CEO, so be it." Robertson had begun to weigh other possible candidates, including an official of Wickes Steel, a specialty producer in southern California.

Meanwhile Redline stumped hard. He made pro-ESOP speeches at West Virginia Northern Community College and at the Weirton Knights of Columbus, where he told a mainly white-collar crowd that the biggest problem was in trying to inform the employees about the benefits of ownership. Redline claimed Weirton had a better shot at survival as ESOP than other steel companies, because it had "only fifteen percent free-loaders versus forty percent in the industry." Unimpressed, the state's largest newspaper, the *Charleston Gazette*, headlined, "ESOP Doomed," and urged seeking a traditional buyer.

In the Joint Study Committee, in early September, cochairman Carl Valdiserri continued to fail to see the need for an investment banker. Even after Lazard had been retained, he didn't want its team to review McKinsey's numbers, or even to come into JSC meetings. But outnumbered by the union, he relented.

On September 13, Bish, Robertson, Doepken, and Valdiserri traveled to Willkie Farr in New York to complain to Harvey Sperry about his firm's "productivity" as the deal's quarterback. McKinsey had offered to assume the position for an extra $20,000 per month. Carl Valdiserri requested clear role definitions from the consultants especially since, with Lazard on board, the need existed to avoid functional overlaps and duplicate billings.

Sperry, whom Robertson perceived as doing "a lot of denying and side-stepping," justified the impasse by saying that "normally the client tells us what they want." Under these circumstances, the client was "amorphous," and neither the roles of management nor the union had become clarified. "A lot of feathers," he said, "have to be put on this bird before it flies." In his view, the JSC had to develop items for negotiations, and a business plan for at least the first three years of operations, and above all Weirton employees had to commit to the 32 percent cut before the negotiations began.

Bish and Robertson insisted that the details of the transaction would have to be worked out before the employees voted on the cuts. While capitulating on this point, Sperry successfully deflected Carl Valdiserri's renewed assertions that the JSC did not need an investment banker, and that McKinsey's information should not be shared with Lazard, to whom it was provided the following day.

When the group moved on to the question of how the board of directors would be selected, Valdiserri contended that lending banks should have representation. But the consultants rejected the notion as out of keeping with industry practice. While all present believed that the company and union should have seats, Lazard's Gotbaum achieved consensus around the idea that "outside" independent directors should predominate, who "need to be people with lots of experience with running businesses in bad times."

Both the exchange of information and quarterback controversies continued to simmer. Robertson found Sperry's responses to charges about how little had been done to prepare for negotiations "glib," and wondered, "Who is going to whip this team of jackasses into shape—a CEO, a board, Willkie Farr, Lazard Frères, or McKinsey?" In any event, the rough sense of the meeting was that Willkie Farr would put the deal together while Lazard got the financing.

Afterwards Robertson met with Keilin and Gotbaum, who estimated that Weirton probably would be borrowing $150 million to $200 million to swing the deal and support initial operations. Gotbaum believed that preliminary negotiations with National could begin as early as October 1. Keilin did not see Willkie Farr as the sole quarterback, but anticipated that Weirton's negotiating effort would involve a "collective leadership" including himself, Sperry, two from the union, and two from management. "Trust," according to Keilin, would evolve, "through mutual self-interest."

Back in Weirton on September 15, Robertson took a call from Sperry who told him that Lazard was hoping to make $2 million to $3 million from the deal, based upon its share of the price. Sperry, however, wanted to find a way that Lazard could be "incentivized to get the lowest purchase price." After the call, Robertson expressed his worry in a memo that once the JSC ratified the deal, "it could lose any control over the structure of the company."

Walter Bish and Skip Spadafora began looking at labor-related costs and cuts that would reduce the purchase price and which the ISU could swallow. For instance, the union leadership endorsed no longer giving steel-industry wages to groundskeepers, window washers, and mail truckers who had been receiving them since National's salad days. Also health care costs could be trimmed by eliminating the Weirton dispensary and contracting out services to local hospitals on a bid basis.

Bish authorized Robertson to continue his informal confidential meetings with Mellon Bank. On September 16, the union's lawyer reviewed the New York sessions with the bank's deputy chairman, who agreed that McKinsey was strictly a management consultant, not an appropriate quarterback, and from then on should be consulted only on an as-needed basis, but also confirmed that Lazard's fees had to be incentivized downward. Robertson revealed qualms about the extent and quality of the information that the JSC was receiving from Weirton management, which was still under National's control. If the deal fell through or was poorly made and jeopardized the resulting company, who would be held liable? Members of the JSC? He wondered whether they should get directors' and officers' insurance.

Dealing with the same question, Willkie Farr decided to incorporate the JSC, which placed a protective "veil" around the management and labor leaders. Oddly, the first president of the JSC corporation, and hence of the embryonic company, was one of Harvey Sperry's law partners, Tom Bryan.

In mid-September, Bish, with a good grasp of detail and a clear way of conveying it, assured his membership that the union would not agree to a 32 percent cut, until it knew precisely what its members, as equitable owners, would receive in return in terms of properties, patents, and pension rights. Packaged by Chuck Lafferty, Bish's message went through the plant's print and electronic media. But the concession's size made approval uncertain. John Robinson, an old-line steel boss and Weirton vice president, told Lafferty: "Fuck these people in the mill. When they vote no, we'll come in and buy this place and those who voted no won't have a job."

A week after the New York trip Robertson and Bish teleconferenced with Lazard and Willkie Farr. Keilin perceived a power struggle at National between Love and G. Watts Humphrey, the son of Weir's cofounder, who was less than pleased about the chairman's flight from steel. From a negotiator's perch, the fact that the opposite side rumbled internally was a hopeful sign, as was a piece of intelligence that Keilin had snared in conversation with Gene West, the Weirton comptroller whose ties were close to National's leadership. According to Keilin, West believed that National "at some point will give up and eat a big loss." Cautioning against optimism, Robertson injected that "West may be parroting the party line."

The call also made plain that the rift between the consultants and divisional management would not heal. Keilin registered that Weirton management's loyalty was "at best divided," and reported that he had warned Jack Redline that there could be "no surprises" from management to the union. Local management had the ability to create disastrous surprises in the form of withheld critical information, such as a bid to buy Weirton, or an emigration of highly skilled technical personnel to other National divisions. Such a brain drain could render the ESOP unbankable. Redline pledged no surprises, but the bad feeling persisted. Keilin termed Carl Valdiserri "hard working, but stupid," and also "treacherous. . . . He must be convinced that it's in his own interest to pay attention to the god damn workers." To Keilin, Redline was "vague, almost not there."

Sperry rated Redline higher than Valdiserri, and disputed Keilin's assessment of the latter. "He's not stupid," but "cognizant of what he does," and the group would have to "keep an eye on him."

Robertson worried that "we are being told what they want us to know when they want us to know it." Believing it critical to "keep management moving in the same direction" as the union, Keilin said that "this takes a combination of sticks and carrots, or pity and terror. How do we keep Carl on the program?"

Claiming that he did "not like the tune management is playing Weirton," Sperry had made some covert contracts with National, and believed that the parent company's clout could push the local leaders toward his objectives. "I propose," he said, "a pincer movement."

1 1 Propaganda

"This relationship includes openness, honesty, and communications, both upward and downward."

—CHUCK LAFFERTY

As September ended, the JSC's Valdiserri and Madigan began defining the myriad issues that would land on the negotiating table, such as whether Weirton or National would get or pay for patents, trademarks, pending grievances, lawsuits, workers' compensation claims, rights of way, research and development, raw materials, inventory, insurance, MUD, retiree costs, health care, mobile equipment, real estate leases, Conrail yards, and vendors' contracts. Knowing that all the work and negotiations would be an existential exercise unless the employees voted for concessions, the JSC adopted a full-scale "Communications Philosophy" and program. Largely created by Lafferty, it remains unequaled as a corporate propaganda effort, and like the unaffiliated union, gave Weirton a potent survival edge not found in the rest of the rust belt. High-minded, the philosophy

> recognizes ESOP as a concept—a multi-faceted way relating the Company and the employee to each other. ESOP is not simply an employee benefits plan, but rather a broad program through which employees become a part-owner and take upon themselves the responsibility of ownership.
>
> In essence a new relationship has to be developed with employees, one in which considerable information is provided so that the employee can have an effect on the performance and growth of his/her company. This relationship includes openness, honesty, and communications, both upward and downward. Weirton Steel believes it has the responsibility to communicate both the good and the bad, to provide more information about the Company and to *listen* to the employees, their ideas and criticisms.
>
> The Company believes that it is important for each employee of Weirton Steel to recognize that ESOP is a long-term program that will supplement an employee's retirement and contribute to the growth of his/her personal estate.
>
> [I]t is important to emphasize that all employees must gain by feeling that they are a part of the company and each has an opportunity to participate; and it is only then that understanding of ESOP will become something real.

The plan provided for small joint white-collar and blue-collar teams "to go into the mill and conduct a series of meetings with employee groups to answer questions, sell the ESOP concept and show labor/management cooperation." A four-person unit, the initial team consisted of the cochairs of the JSC, the vice president of Operations (Ken Hunt), and a representative of the IGU. As the four worked their way through the plant they "would pick up the manager and union chairman of the area they were in."

The JSC wanted to cover all the hourly and salary employees before the anticipated vote on the ESOP concessions, which could occur, it was thought, as early as December. Logistics required three meetings a day for thirty-seven straight days, with some sessions beginning as early as 6 A.M. and others catering to night turns starting up after 11 P.M. As a result, in addition to the core team, other squads had to be cobbled from JSC members, stewards, superintendents, and staff managers, all of whom received a two-day training from the Communications Department on mastering and presenting facts about the proposed ESOP. Scheduled to coincide with the beginning or end of a shift, and set in lunch rooms, locker rooms, garages, and other relatively open machine-free mill areas, each in-plant meeting reached about seventy-five employees.

In order to supplement the program and keep employees up-to-date, weekly video programs, hosted by well-prepared workers, also played on monitors in the strip mill, tin mill, coke plant, blast furnaces, boiler house, BOP (basic oxygen plant) shop, blooming mill, and in salaried centers. An external distribution system under Charles Cronin ensured that all laid-off employees received JSC print material by mail, and that copies were delivered to service organizations (Rotary, Kiwanis, Jaycees, Moose, Elks, Lions, Odd Fellows, etc.), to the mill's three credit unions, to the region's federal, state, and local political leaders, to area radio, TV, and newspapers, to all local churches, and especially to customers.

Based on an outline prepared by Lafferty, the JSC was asked to spend $5,000 on a seventeen-minute film. The "objective," according to the treatment, "would be motivational and informational, and will record the heritage and spirit of the men and women of Weirton Steel," through a "positive, grab-your-socks" approach. Lafferty hoped to use the film to complement the often droning talking heads at in-plant, business, and civic group meetings, to present it to influential bodies such as the Congressional Steel Caucus, and to see its footage shown on regional and national television. Recognizing the project's importance, the JSC pored over the treatment, which began with a shot of a "Silent Youngstown Sheet and Tube Plant—no music, only wind"—segued into a review of the American steel crisis, built to National's March 2, 1982, announcement, and captured local reactions including Jack Redline's MacArthuresque: "I will remain." Using a montage of antique stills, the narrator provided a capsule history of Weirton, emphasizing "the pride of the people," then cut to a basic explanation of an ESOP, a piece on the JSC at work, a sermon on the uncertain future, including shots of local children, and finished with a parade float carrying a "WE CAN DO IT" banner. Impressed, the JSC appropriated the funds, but scratched Lafferty's title, "A Different Beat," after David Robertson termed it "bullshit," and then decided instead on "On Our Own."

The JSC approved a half-dozen thirty-second commercials for television and radio stations in the tristate area, as well as a handful of forty-five-second "speak-out messages," which would run for free, plus an hour-long TV "round table" for the week before the vote. Cronin's public relations department also identified a raft of radio call-in shows whose hosts had agreed to use mill figures as guests.

Having accessed billboards in Weirton and nearby communities, the communications group proposed two initial signs. The JSC approved the first: Ken Hunt and Walter Bish shaking hands above the pervasive "We Can Do It" slogan. But it balked at the second, a photo of a child asking Walter Bish, who wore a hard hat, "What's 32%?" Bish replied; "Your future." Robertson scored the message: "You'll destroy his credibility with his members." The lawyer worried about the effect of having Bish vouch for the 32 percent "before all questions are answered."

A week later the ISU, which had reviewed the communications plan with its steward body, objected in writing to the sign and to the excessively upbeat nature of the propaganda, which it termed "premature. Succinctly stated, too many questions about the ESOP are left unanswered at this time for the ISU to participate in the purposes of a communications philosophy which has clearly been designed to propagandize only the positive aspects of an ESOP." The union questioned utilizing television and radio round tables and call-in shows, anticipating "participation by the Rank and File Committee or other employee groups who claim to represent a diverged or minority viewpoint."

In lieu of the 32 percent billboard, the JSC posted a huge, slick photograph of E. T. Weir on a *Life* magazine cover from 1937. The big red-block-lettered title of the magazine became the first word in the phrase: "Life Goes on with ESOP." The ISU was not delighted by the choice of Weir, whom David Robertson called "one of the most ruthless union-busting industrialists of the nineteen thirties."

Even so, most of the ISU's reservations about the communications campaign soon evaporated. Affected by the crisis of survival and the calm sway of Walter Bish, union leaders dedicated themselves to the frequent meetings and media events that marked the period. Like their management counterparts on the JSC, they spent long hours manning the ESOP message center (EMC). The phone bank processed thousands of questions, rumors, and comments. Each week representative calls were transcribed and circulated on the JSC.

In time the EMC became an electronic vox populi. Callers dealt with the proposed ESOP but got other things off their chests. For instance, in the early fall of 1982, when members of the JSC, including Carl Valdiserri and Walter Bish, began stating that the full 32 percent, if approved, did not need to come completely from wages, but could be extracted from other perks such as vacations, it caused a message storm. One caller protested: "I can't work fifty-two weeks a year without a vacation and not become a babbling idiot." Another growled: "I see you want to cut vacations down to a week for hourly. You people have to be nuts! I'm not going to work all these years and not take a vacation. Maybe you guys don't have pressure up there, but we do down here in the mill." The Brown's Island coke operation cuts drew heated comments. "I think," said one caller, "it's a disgrace what has happened to the men in the coke plant and you're telling us about bringing in people to take over ESOP! You'd better clean your main office out. You better start cleaning some of your management out and then take care of the men in the mill, and then we'll talk about ESOP."

So many callers phoned in complaints about Jack Redline that it looked like an orchestrated campaign. Some lauded the recent installation of Hunt on the JSC. One caller said, "He can walk through any part of the mill and any man can walk up to him and talk to him because they have respect for him." Employees asked questions about safety and about the intricacies of their own pensions or seniority. The EMC listened as workers accused bosses of having mistresses as secretaries, and named alleged thieves in the mill. Occasionally, callers would perform a useful corrective function by pointing out an inaccuracy in a JSC publication or speech.

1 2 A Lawyer's Dream

"I'm the surgeon. I've done this all my life . . ."
—HARVEY SPERRY

In early fall 1982, all of Weirton was on edge because the negotiations with National were about to begin. Neither a member of management nor labor, Miles Dean, who had become the impartial "reasonable man" of the committee, was concerned because the JSC still had not outlined for its chief consultants, Willkie Farr and Lazard Frères, "who the fuck is to do what." As a high official in a poor state, Dean became upset by the realization that Lazard expected seven-figure compensation. Perhaps not cognizant of the rift that the consultants had widened between management and labor, Dean suggested that Robertson, Doepken, Valdiserri, and Redline

136

needed to get together to define the outsiders' roles. "So long as you don't," he warned, "everyone will suck the tit."

National threw the first curve in the negotiations by announcing that it would be represented by Elliott Goldstein from Atlanta rather than by the Pittsburgh law firm of Thorp, Reed & Armstrong. Goldstein, chairman of the American Bar Association's Corporate Section, was qualified, but Thorp Reed virtually was family, having stood with Weir at the beginning, assisted with the transactions that put National together, fought with Roosevelt, defeated the USW, and designed the ISU.

National declined to explain its choice, which was economically and emotionally devastating to the old-line Pittsburgh firm, but JSC speculations centered on two theories. First, Thorp Reed was so well known in Weirton that some believed its lawyers' moves would be predictable. Also, it was felt that the firm was too close to Weirton people, and information would leak out of its offices during negotiations. As Harvey Sperry sensed, "There was a direct pipeline from that firm right into Doepken or Robertson, either one." James Haas, National president, according to Sperry, "was very clear that he wanted special counsel for that deal."

National chose Goldstein on Lowenstein's recommendation. Born in 1915, Goldstein, a senior partner in Atlanta's Powell, Goldstein, Frazier & Murphy, one of the South's leading firms, had had an illustrious career as a transactional lawyer, including serving on the New York Stock Exchange's Advisory Committee and as a special counsel to the House of Representatives' Committee on Official Conduct. A lean, courteous man with a hint of a drawl, he quickly sized up Weirton and its weakness, a "conflict between the younger employees and the older employees." The younger employers, whom he knew had gained control of the union leadership and thus of the JSC, needed the mill to order to have a future with work in Weirton. He sensed that they would favor making the purchase, even with substantial liabilities, in order to keep the place going. Mainly concerned with retirement security, the older employees "would much rather shut the place down and get their pension from National." A deal would "never have been possible if there had not been in effect a revolution in the union. A younger group of people came into control of the union, became officers and kicked out an older group who were more reactionary, less inclined to give anything, and more inclined to just stand on the union contract."

However, some old-guard elements remained both in the union and to a much greater extent in management. Therefore, Goldstein saw his opponents Sperry and Keilin as having to deal with a "matrix of four different types of constituents," young and old groups of blue-collar and white-collar workers. But Goldstein had his own problems. Ordinarily, he believed any major deal could be made in thirty days or at the outside in forty-five. But Weirton symbolized a new type of transaction that was tough to quantify, because many of the critical costs such as health, pensions, and environmental compliance were "off the books," open-ended, and continuing. The balance sheet was of limited use, really just a starting point. Even ordinary assets resisted pricing. Untold millions of dollars in irregularly stored spare parts were scattered in the plant. Virtual mountains of precious coke, destined for Weirton, lay on islands in the middle of Lake Erie, and were susceptible to measurement only by "eyeballing." But above all, Goldstein knew that National had to deal to survive. His client "had no recourse but to go into bankruptcy."

The negotiations began in Pittsburgh on September 29 when representatives of the JSC, Willkie Farr, and Lazard Frères met with National Steel officials, Goldstein, and members of his firm. Cumbersome and unproductive, the initial sessions basically laid the groundwork for future meetings. However, Harvey Sperry saw his role as "a corporate lawyer's dream. The sky was the limit." But Sperry was not pleased about negotiating in front of a group of his JSC clients, who had insisted on being brought along. "I'm the surgeon. I've done this all my life and I've got to have a group from Weirton standing there? That was wild. . . . They went to the first meeting. After that we scheduled meetings that they didn't really know about."

Soon Sperry and Keilin got Goldstein and his partners alone. Sperry took a hard line on establishing a price. "Our objective was to pay them nothing and maybe to get them to loan us some money. The reason National was doing this deal was to avoid the $800 million plus shutdown costs. Why in the hell should we pay anything? We were doing them a favor. That was our philosophy."

Elliott Goldstein would have known how to deal with "Kenny" Bialkin, the top gun at Willkie Farr, and Goldstein's friend and fellow patrician in the profession. But it was hard to get a handle on Sperry. Unlike most who advertise in national lawyers' directories, Sperry did not lard his entries with academic honors, elite clients, or famous deals, though he had completed more than forty major transactions. You could find out these things, but you would have to ask. You could not easily find out what Sperry cared about either, though David Robertson soon learned that he regarded Weirton as "his child," and that he would do virtually anything to win for it. Sperry did not simply represent companies, he bonded with them, and he did not play by rules.

A cardinal principle that lawyers must abide by or face discipline such as disbarment involves avoiding contacts with opposing parties outside the presence of their lawyers. Yet such unusual communications now became the norm.

"What generally happened in our negotiations," recalled Goldstein, "was that I would take the position that this was it, and couldn't do any more. Then Harvey Sperry would go to Pittsburgh and talk to them [National chairman Love or President Haas] directly and they would give in." While not within the ground rules of the negotiations, Goldstein let it occur, because the National executives seemed to know what they were doing. "I wasn't going to go screaming at them, you can't do this to me. I just assumed that they had their own agenda."

Sperry utilized his contacts with National to ferret out the parent company's views about Jack Redline, and was surprised to learn that they preferred not to have him run the spin-off. Also, National did not want a management group buyout to spoil the ESOP. Similarly, Sperry's interventions with National helped to prevent it from raiding Weirton for key personnel or stripping it of equipment, and to encourage it to keep the JSC managers in line.

National wanted the deal done quickly. Weirton was desperate to preserve its jobs. In October 1982, American unemployment peaked at a postwar high of 10.1 percent, the first double-digit rate since the Great Depression.

Gene Keilin, Sperry's partner on the Weirton side of the table, complemented him. Less overtly aggressive, Keilin absorbed reams of detail before acting, while Sperry shot from the hip. Holding different views on the nature of the eventual ESOP, the pair sometimes clashed in front of the JSC, though they generally got along. Sperry sought a new, lean, traditionally managed company that would focus on profits and appeal to the financial community. Keilin wanted the corporate charter to reflect profits in conjunction with maximizing the number of jobs. Sperry saw no reason for union representatives on the eventual board to be employees. Keilin expected them to be hourly workers from the plant. Keilin had strong feelings about keeping the plant 100 percent employee-owned, but worried about having sufficient cash to buy back shares. Sperry favored eventually going public.

In mid-October, the JSC released an optimistic schedule, which included beginning negotiations with banks on November 15, reaching an agreement in principle with National on December 15, and obtaining worker approval for the buyout terms and the wage and benefit cuts by December 20, 1982. Both sides were in a rush. Weirton feared a brain drain if the process stalled. National, which recently had announced a 10 percent cut on all nonunion salaries, including thirteen hundred employees at Weirton, feared mass retirements and pension costs.

Questions swirled concerning the mill's price. While book value equaled $320 million, market value probably had dropped below $100 million, and there were those huge off-the-books costs such as pensions and severance in a shutdown.

It appeared that National would not roll over. Reports in the media indicated that the parent wanted to retain its General Office complex in Weirton, one of the region's most valuable real estate parcels, as well as the Materials Utilization Division (MUD), one of the keys to Weirton's competitiveness.

The Rank and File Committee seemed to be on a roll, with its victory in the fight for laid-off employees to vote, and its innovative federal lawsuit over the McKinsey document, which had the potential to stop the deal cold. On October 15, a frustrated caller to the ESOP message center asked whether it would be possible "to put on the ballot whether or not we prefer the Rank and File Committee to represent the mill and I think you'll find with as radical a group as those, most people don't. Is it possible to eliminate them?"

In a historical referendum four days later, the members of the ISU inadvertently took an important step toward eliminating the Rank and File. After much prodding by Walter Bish, David Robertson, and the union's new, younger leadership, the blue-collar membership voted by 1,600 to 1,228 in favor of contractual changes resulting in a restructured seniority pattern more conducive to advancement by racial minorities and replacing a cumbersome, nearly incomprehensible four-tier seniority system that almost invariably had favored whites with a simpler unified method of computing seniority. The referendum ended a race discrimination class action that had been going on since 1972. The new consent decree contained payouts to aggrieved blacks from a trust set up by National, gave minority employees greater opportunities to go into trade and craft jobs, and provided them with easier access to entry-level plant management positions. Despite a solitary protest by Willie McKenzie, the consent decree went a long way toward removing the racial edge from the embryonic ESOP. By giving minorities hope that the new company would be more fair, the vote also reduced the need for minorities to have a standard bearer in the Rank and File Committee.

1
3

Hard Ball

> "What will the money derived from our concessions be
> used for? To buy machinery to eliminate jobs?"
>
> —STEVE BAUMAN

On October 22, 1982, Robertson and the JSC consultants met for
dinner and lingered past dawn. Josh Gotbaum raised three strategic
points. First, the union had to convince National and the Weirton
management that the ISU could pull out of the deal. Second, it was
important to avoid the natural tendency to get embroiled in "due
process" financial audits, which could create a time bind, and a last-
moment take-it-or-leave-it crisis. Third, Lazard's information held
that without a commitment from Weirton employees to take the

142

32 percent cuts by December 15, 1982, National Steel's board of directors was poised to shut down Weirton's primary iron- and steel-making operations.

Gotbaum rekindled the charge that local management was withholding data from the JSC on wages and benefits costs, in order to control the timing of the deal. He cautioned that Lazard, as an investment banker generally servicing management, could not go public with its pro-purge views. Privately, however, he maintained that none of the present "troika" of Redline, Valdiserri, and Doepken should stay. In addition, as a political matter, he sensed that the union membership would need to see a management turnover before they would ratify the concessions. As the discussion shifted to the details needed to accomplish the coup, Gotbaum suggested that among the independent directors on the future board of directors there could be at least "one killer" who could initiate the housecleaning of top management. The group considered that Sperry and Keilin could serve as such directors.

It concerned Robertson that the management killers were not necessarily pro-jobs. Tom Bryan said that no hourly employee with under ten years of seniority would ever work in the new Weirton. Taking issue with the McKinsey projection of seven thousand jobs at Weirton by the end of 1989, Gotbaum countered that "there could be five thousand jobs here." Robertson realized that the publicly bandied-about figure of nine thousand "is crazy," and worried that the investment banker's view of leanness reflected the thinking of Ian McGregor, the former Lazard partner who after becoming CEO of British Steel had sliced its workforce from 240,000 to 100,000.

The inner circle of Lazard Frères, Willkie Farr, and David Robertson (sometimes with Walter Bish) soon eliminated Jack Curtis from its discussions, and began to take up the question of who would be Weirton's CEO. Gotbaum recalled from his Carter White House days that George Stimson, the former Weirton president and National Steel chairman, had been impressive in dealings with the administration. Sperry and Keilin asked about Stimson's reputation with the ISU and the community. Robertson replied that it was high, as Stimson stood for "the old Weirton and prosperous times; and whether it was true or not [Stimson] had convinced the working stiff that he and his family had a special place in their hearts for Weirton."

Sperry, however, worried that Stimson still backed Redline. Consequently, the Willkie Farr lawyer made inquiries among his high contacts at National, who reported that Stimson now opposed Redline's remaining in the Weirton leadership. Now seriously considering Stimson as a CEO candidate or at least as a future Weirton director, Keilin and Sperry made an appointment to meet with him privately in Pittsburgh.

The meeting, according to Sperry, was a "net negative." Stimson not only disappointed them by looking and acting like a man in his sixties, but he praised Carl Valdiserri, who by now was the inner circle's bête noire; and Stimson's candidacy was over. Sperry began moving toward finding a CEO from the outside, whom he thought would be installed in March 1983.

Sperry also met with National's president James Haas, and alerted him to Weirton's poor labor relations, which could jeopardize the buyout referendum. Noting that no divisional executive was indispensable, Haas offered to eliminate certain Weirton managers now. But the offer concerned inner circle members who fretted over who could push the deal in the community if Redline lost his job. There was no satisfactory answer.

The inner group also searched for a strategy to blunt the Rank and File, which continued to score points in the local and national media with its suit over the confidential McKinsey appendix. Staughton Lynd and Peter Pitegoff of the Industrial Cooperative Association took to the Op-Ed page of the *New York Times* on the day before the trial. In a piece entitled "Workers Can Be Choosers," they characterized the situation as one in which:

> Your employer threatens to shut down the plant. You are given a choice: buy your job through employee ownership or lose it. More and more, this "choice" is forced upon workers as conglomerates shift investment away from industries with low return to more lucrative investment opportunities here and abroad.

Workers at Weirton would do well to examine other recent experiences in worker ownership before they make their decision. That experience is mixed. Worker buy-outs have saved jobs, but some of these jobs have lasted only a short time while others have reduced wages and benefits, relaxed work rules and threatened the security of pension plans. Therefore, buy-out negotiations should be treated like any other concession bargaining. Workers must measure the cost of proposed givebacks against the value of the jobs to be saved.

Like G.M. at Hyatt Clark, National Steel has much to gain from an employee purchase of the Weirton mill. And, in exchange for concessions, the steelworkers have a chance to save their jobs. But until they obtain sufficient information to weigh the value of those jobs against the cost of the concessions, they would do well to look very cautiously at this gift horse.

In a last-ditch effort to avert the trial, Lynd wrote to David Robertson proposing a meeting to "seek common ground" on the matter. The ISU attorney declined to discuss settlement. Proceedings began in a crammed federal courtroom in Parkersburg, West Virginia, on October 28, 1982, with District Judge Charles Haden II presiding.

Staughton Lynd argued that as it stood, the McKinsey report provided findings without foundations, especially on the concessions, and that the recommended $1 billion investment was not linked to any specific costs. The union, Lynd claimed, had violated its duty to provide information adequate to enable its members to cast an informed vote.

In Parkersburg, Harvey Sperry's litigation partner astonished the union members by engaging in deep meditation to prepare himself for court, then slammed the Rank and File leaders as "self-appointed ambassadors without portfolio" who had brought an expensive, "frivolous" lawsuit.

At trial, Lynd's examination of Rank and File cochair Tony Gilliam was flattened by evidentiary objections, which Judge Haden generally sustained. Lynd asked Gilliam, "Why are you concerned with the possible transfer of the pension plan from National Steel to an employee-owned company?" The Rank and File cochair responded: "It is my feeling, based on the information that I have and what I understand about ESOP, that my pension would be much more secure under National Steel than under a new employee-owned company." Gilliam viewed National as "an established corporation with numerous assets of value." At best, he thought that the new ESOP would be "somewhat insecure in terms of success."

Lynd asked, "Is there a reason why you want information concerning the thirty-two percent reduction in compensation now?" "Yes," said Gilliam. "So that I may have an opportunity to study it and go over with others to try to educate myself enough about it so that I will be able to make an intelligent vote and my coworkers at Weirton Steel will also be able to make an intelligent vote when it is put to us on the issue of wage and benefits reduction."

Steady, sincere, obviously overworked and fatigued by JSC efforts, which he viewed as the best hope to keep jobs for ISU members, Walter Bish made a strong witness for the defense. Lynd failed to shake him, by pointing out the ISU leader wanted to avoid releasing a document that he had not even read.

Somewhat surprisingly, the Joint Study Committee lawyers promised that well in advance of the vote all Weirton employees would receive a deluxe "disclosure document" on the order of a shareholders' prospectus, which would be replete with information on the proposed buyout and ESOP structure, save for the confidential cost data and McKinsey's world steel model. Naturally, the adequacy of the proposed disclosure could not be weighed by the court. But Judge Haden had not heard enough from Lynd and the Rank and File to order disclosure through an injunction at that moment. In essence he based his ruling on social policy rather than law.

[T]he public interest lies in the concern that perhaps all of us have, and that is to save the employment and save an entity which employs anywhere from 7,500 to 11,000 people in and about the states of West Virginia and Ohio and Pennsylvania. It is the largest single employer in the state of West Virginia in the private sector currently. Perhaps by some arrangement it will remain so, and that I think is the fond hope of everyone.

But the impact on the economy of West Virginia, on the individuals sitting in this room, whether they be management or hourly employees, is going to be something that will be very severe, even if the thing happens to be a success.

This court does not want to do anything at this time to jeopardize the overall public interest in this matter and to jeopardize the individual interest in seeing to the success of it.

While denying the injunction, the court did not dismiss the case altogether, choosing instead to determine later the merits of whether the union breached its fiduciary duty to its membership and the related question of the adequacy of the disclosure. As for the JSC, it had achieved its first clear victory over the Rank and File.

Relations between the two groups grew nastier. The JSC redbaited and scapegoated the Rank and File, blaming it for the expense of court and accusing it of disloyalty to the idea of corporate independence.

The Rank and File lashed back with attempts to depose David Robertson under oath. Taking a lawyer's deposition generally is considered an extreme hardball litigation tactic. In any event, Robertson later won a protective order preventing the questioning.

After the injunction hearing, the Rank and File attempted to put a positive spin on the loss, by distributing a leaflet titled "What Happened in Court?" Maintaining that: "Our worst fears were confirmed," it targeted Bish for special derision. "Our union President is doing nothing to protect our interests." It pointed out that Bish never took notes at critical meetings on the buyout, and had neither read the Towers pension report nor the McKinsey appendix. "He's made himself nothing more than a mouthpiece for the bankers. Whatever they tell him, he turns around and tells us."

The Rank and File took a Luddite antiautomation stance, ripping Bish, the union, and the JSC for never investigating alternatives to the five thousand to six thousand job levels forecast by the consultants. "Are we being asked to take cuts to buy machines that will eventually replace our jobs. . . . If the ISU doesn't provide real answers, then we will go back to court." Meeting the press following the hearing, Steve Bauman insisted, "We are not done yet."

Concerned by the public relations and legal firepower exhibited by the RFC, the JSC wondered if the dissidents had access to outside funding. According to the local rumor mill, the United Steelworkers covertly gave support to the RFC, which seemed unlikely given Lynd's many go-rounds with the international union's leadership. Nonetheless, the worries prompted Robertson, Bish, Valdiserri, and Doepken to lunch with Governor Rockefeller and Miles Dean. Sufficiently concerned, the governor told Dean to call Paul Rusen Jr., the USW's chief organizer in Wheeling (coincidentally the son of Paul Rusen, who tried to organize Weirton after World War II), and to warn him in the strongest terms to stay clear of the Rank and File. Also, Rockefeller promised to convey the matter personally to his friend, National chairman Love, who had close ties to the Steelworkers at the highest levels.

During November, the inner circle of the JSC continued to monitor the likelihood of a management coup and takeover. Jack Redline's profile remained high in the mill and town. The "Turkey Day Special" of the *Varlas Newsletter*, which nominated for "assholes of the year" those employees who tied green ribbons on the antennae of their foreign cars, had kind words for Redline. "Someday, we'll tell our grandchildren that he saved the whole upper Ohio Valley with the help of the best steelworkers in the world." The divisional president had continued to make statesmanlike pro-ESOP speeches, which prompted Robertson to tell Sperry over the phone that Redline "does not seem like a guy who is thinking about doing this some other way."

On November 26, 1982, Robertson, Valdiserri, Doepken, Bish, and Dominic Tonacchio, a street-smart older member of the ISU executive committee and JSC from the tin mill, spoke with Sperry, some of his partners, and Gene Keilin at Willkie, Farr & Gallagher. Sperry and Keilin had been meeting with National and reported a major mutual concern from the early negotiating rounds: more retirements. If they occurred, National's liabilities would skyrocket, while Weirton would suffer a skill and brain drain. The consultants proposed attempting to negotiate a retirement package based on "lock and freeze," and "work to get" pension contributions. In essence, these buzzwords meant that if an employee had worked for, say, twenty years at Weirton under National, and then worked five more years at the independent Weirton ESOP before retiring, National would pick up 80 percent of his retirement costs, and the new company would absorb 20 percent. The idea, though new in American business, met with approval. If Keilin and Sperry could sell it at the table, then the concerns of both sides could be allayed.

The inner circle also discussed the issue of having an eventual public offering of the stock, which Sperry favored. Local management was warming to it, as Robertson noted, as a way to protect themselves from numerical domination by the unionized workers, whom the executives assumed would have more stock.

Three days later, Keilin and Sperry met with Redline over the course of four hours. The consultants, who found Redline calm and collected, informed him that he could be a candidate for CEO of the independent company. They planned to initiate a broad search. Redline told the New Yorkers that he did not think that the spun-off mill could make it without him, and that if he did not get his "shot," he wanted his "dignity."

Redline revealed his view that the outside directors should include the president of the Bank of Weirton, the CEO of a local trucking company, and bank presidents from Pittsburgh. Keilin replied that there was "no way" that such a group would suffice in a national company, but concluded that Redline knew steel and might be all right as the chief operating officer. Sperry saw him possibly as a consultant. Keilin at least wanted Redline to have a visible role in the start-up, though not as CEO, but perhaps as chairman of the executive committee, an essentially honorary position. Both left Redline with the notion that he would be considered among others for the top executive spot. Redline, who resented the search, believed that the mill would reject the ESOP without his designation as CEO.

Others shared Redline's view that the ESOP should provide local empowerment. Louis Kelso wrote a scathing letter to Jay Rockefeller on November 30, 1982, terming the Weirton plan a "failure. It will delight those who are emotionally and ideologically opposed to the entire concept of employee ownership. . . . The proposals before the Joint Study Committee have no chance of success."

In response to the Bauman case, the ISU began implementing more disclosure by mailing to its members the Towers Perrin pension study and a Touche Ross audit of operations, both of which had not been generally available before. Staughton Lynd filed papers with the court, insisting that the figures disclosed by the union showed that compensation at Weirton would have to be cut only about 9 percent (as opposed to 32 percent) to ensure competitiveness with the rest of the industry. Lynd reargued the need to depose both Bish and Robertson (who objected, based on the attorney-client privilege) in order to get at the truth and to prepare for trial.

For Weirton, government matters were moving in the right direction. Senator Byrd lobbied his colleagues hard for an eighteen-month "stretch-out" of compliance with the federal Clean Water Act, which would delay costs of $30–$35 million by the mill. On December 4, Byrd achieved another environmental "victory" by announcing that the EPA had granted approval under the Clean Air Act for Weirton's first "bubble," which permitted it to aggregate overall emissions for agency approval instead of forcing it to focus on smokestacks. This particular bubble, the largest in West Virginia, enabled Weirton to clean up 2,600 tons of ground dust on its roads, yards, and parking lots, in lieu of installing pollution-control equipment at the cast house, blooming mill, and basic oxygen furnace. Byrd estimated the savings at $30 million. The next day, the company filed for a second bubble covering sinter operations.

Financially, Weirton got a big break on December 13, when Governor Rockefeller announced that the state had reappraised the mill's property value, reducing it from $290 million to $163 million, which would almost halve the annual $5.4 million tax bill. As an added plus, the dropped valuation would hurt National's negotiating posture, as Weirton could argue that the parent company now had less to offer and should be paid accordingly.

But as the clock wound down the shutdown issue also loomed large. Sometimes, to avoid huge liquidation sums, other companies had been forced to keep money-losing plants open. For instance, Kaiser Steel continued operating in order to avoid a $350 million liability for pension, medical coverage, and severance costs. Rather than pay $200 million to close the *New York Daily News*, the Chicago Tribune Company had kept printing the money-losing tabloid. But USX, the leader in steel, chose to bite the bullet. With an approximate shutdown cost of $70,000 per employee, it had absorbed $415 million in costs by abandoning sixteen facilities.

On December 16, 1982, *Parade* magazine, the nation's largest-circulation Sunday supplement, featured Weirton in a cover story entitled "Why They Fight to Save a Way of Life." The article focused on steelworkers hoping that the mill would survive so that their families could stay in the Panhandle, and on Jack Redline, whom *Parade* portrayed as a rags-to-riches hands-on boss and logical first CEO for the job. Redline was willing to make sacrifices, including 30 percent of his compensation plus all of his perks, including the company home. Besides a brief mention of the struggle over whether laid-off workers would get to vote on the buyout, the *Parade* piece made no reference to the controversies wracking Weirton.

Recently, friction had come from the Ministerial Association, a group of clergy from the Panhandle and adjacent areas, who had made their pulpits available to management and ISU members of the Joint Study Committee. But now the ministers had begun to object to speakers touting Sperry's line that future ESOP worker-owners would be "employees in the daytime and stockholders at night," which struck them as perpetuating the powerlessness of the local people. The Rank and File had won favor with a few of the ministers who wondered whether the workers were getting the best possible deal.

Lynd continued to build his case against the proposed wage and benefit cuts. He received analysis and support from Sam Rosenberger, a leading labor economist at Roosevelt University in Chicago, who reviewed McKinsey's figures with alarm, because the consultant had failed to factor in worker productivity increases or consider that Weirton could survive even without becoming the lowest cost producer in the industry. Rosenberger worried that an excessive Weirton wage reduction could be used as a basis by the rest of the industry to demand unjustifiably large concessions from USW workers, and concluded that a rational figure was closer to 10 percent than to 32 percent.

As a result, Lynd, who feared control of the buyout process by "outside financial interests," publicly stated that the wage cuts would affect the entire industry, and that those considering taking them should "feel some responsibility to other steelworkers." But the argument fell flat in Weirton, as David Robertson hastened to point out: "It's an independent union and . . . there's no feeling of solidarity" with workers at other plants.

Still sticking with 32 percent, Ron Bancroft of McKinsey tried to persuade employees that the concession would have "no downside if the economy is good," because it would come back to workers in the form of "bonuses." The notion that Weirton had to be *the* lowest-cost major producer also receded, as Bancroft began speaking in terms of its being in the bottom third. Nor would the new company, according to Redline, have to be a star on Wall Street in terms of profitability. The divisional president made clear that if he were in charge Weirton could survive with as low as a 12 percent return on investment, which paled in comparison to the glamorous gains of the period. Meanwhile, the JSC actively publicized the amount spent litigating against the Rank and File Committee, which in 1982 exceeded $57,000.

As for National, at the end of 1982 its plight worsened with that of the rest of the steel industry, which now yielded 22 percent of the market to imports, up five and a half points in two years. During the first nine months of 1982, National lost $186 million, though its steel division lost $305 million versus an operating profit of $130 million during the first three quarters of 1981. Though still a massive company with net tangible assets of $1.125 billion and working capital of $221 million, its increasingly precarious condition whet its desire to unload the losing steel operation in Weirton before year's end. National announced that it was willing to receive from Weirton an amount "substantially below the net book value of the assets sold." Even so, the intricacies of the deal, and the problems on both sides, had erased Love's original timetable with its hoped-for 1982 closing.

In late December, David Robertson reported optimistically to the Independent Steel Workers Union executive committee. First, he dashed rumors that laid-off worker-stockholders in an ESOP would not qualify for unemployment insurance. Then he explained that Judge Haden had quashed the Rank and File subpoenas to him and Walter Bish in the Bauman case.

In New York, negotiations between Weirton and National had stalled, according to Robertson. As Sperry and Keilin tried "to keep National on the hook" for pensions and retirees' insurance costs, National demanded cash up front for current and fixed assets, to which Weirton objected, needing the funds for operations. Nonetheless, Lazard already had started compiling potential CEO and board of director lists for the new company. The ISU officials speculated about who would be the union representatives on the independent company's board.

However, because the Rank and File Committee had quietly dropped a new bomb, such discussions became academic. Indeed, it now seemed unclear, including to those on the ISU executive committee who comprised the bulk of the JSC, if they had the authority to hold discussions, or any authority at all.

Earlier, the union had conceded in the suit brought by John Gregory that laid-off steelworkers would vote on any concessions and ESOP issues. But Gregory, a black ten-year employee from Steubenville, and his RFC lawyers took the matter to the edge.

In a complaint to the U.S. Department of Labor they insisted that the summer 1982 ISU election that installed Walter Bish and the young, practical, and conciliatory executive board also had to be voided because workers on laid-off status had not been able to vote, though it was not clear that many had tried. The case threatened to erase all that the ISU and JSC had done. Moreover, because of the uncertainty in the Weirton community about the status of the deal, and the widespread disgust with the proposed 32 percent concession at the time, the candidacies of Arango, Hrabovsky, Pastoric, and other old-line confrontational types could have been attractive if the election were rerun.

Gregory, a lean, quiet millwright with a record free of disciplinary or attendance problems, had a sympathetic case. Laid off from his job in the coke plant on May 7, 1982, he had filed a grievance with the union charging that nineteen millwrights with less seniority had been retained. The matter might not have gone further but for the fact that while Gregory was in the ISU filling out the severance papers, he asked whether he could vote in the upcoming union election. When officials told him he could not because he was laid off and not "a dues-paying member," Gregory took out a ten-dollar-bill and tried to pay his dues, which was refused.

On the day of the election, he showed up at the union hall again and attempted to vote. The union's office manager went through the charade of telling Gregory to go to the registration table to see if his name was on the voters' list. Naturally, it wasn't, and Gregory was denied a ballot.

Another way that Weirton differed from other communities facing shutdowns was that it attempted to deal with every problem, never running out of hope or energy, and David Robertson in particular was endlessly resourceful. In Washington in December, Robertson prodded Paul Fasser, the EEOC's appointed master for the Weirton race discrimination case, for the names of individuals who could advise the union on dealing with the Department of Labor. Fasser put Robertson in touch with a number of former Labor undersecretaries now in private practice in Washington. They advised the union attorney not to try to beat the charges against the ISU, but to delay implementation. The Department of Labor under Reagan's appointed secretary, Raymond Donovan, they felt, would be amenable to delay, especially when threatened with a suit that could drag the matter over three or four years.

In early 1983, the 32 percent figure continued to jeopardize the process. The union executive committee sensed that Lazard, which had promised to meet with the membership on the issue, was stalling. Jack Irwin, the divisional auditor, was told by Josh Gotbaum, that Gene Keilin, the lead investment banker, had been warned by his supervisors that he "had to do the deal" with National or else he was "through at Lazard Frères." Keilin was especially concerned about the union election complaint lodged with Labor.

In January 1983, the ESOP message center became a magnet for complaints against the local leadership. One caller vented his anger against the division's Management Club. "Why," he asked, "do you think management is so much better than the employees? Why do employees carry their food in paper bags, while you're served in a private dining room? Japan would laugh." Another caller targeted Redline. "The saying now among the union is get behind Jack, so he can shit all over us again."

The message center also served as a vehicle for whistle-blowers, named and anonymous. For example, a worker on a tandem mill nailed a boss for switching to an inferior lubricant in order to receive a payoff from the new supplier.

Campaigning for the future top executive positions had begun in earnest. On February 3, Jack Redline made the prediction that an "agreement in principal" between National and Weirton was only two to three weeks away. His ally, executive vice president Carl Valdiserri, fleshed out the expected details including protected pensions for retired and active employees and a financial safety net extended by National to prevent the new company from failing during its early years, plus guaranteed contracts through which National would provide necessary quantities of new and semifinished materials to the new company. Recalling the nurturing separation between General Motors and Hyatt Clark, the safety net and potential contracts also went a long way toward calming fears that the fledgling company would fail fast and then be bought out of bankruptcy by National. Valdiserri also claimed that National would convey all the necessary patents, proprietary processes, and trademarks to the new Weirton.

The union still had to tangle with the Department of Labor. On February 13 and 14 Walter Bish, David Robertson, and Miles Dean negotiated with the department in Washington for eighteen hours. The union's goal was to achieve a "treaty" with labor rather than try to carry the point that the last election results should stand. Internally, the union knew it had illegally disenfranchised its laid-off workers, and saw no reason to get involved in a lawsuit with the government.

Fortunately, Labor generously agreed to give the ISU a timetable for the election rerun. By June 15, 1983, the ISU was bound to draft revised bylaws, providing voting rights to those on layoff status. By November 1 the ISU pledged to furnish lists of all eligible voters to the department. Nominations were to be completed by December 31, 1983, and the new election would be held on or before January 31, 1984. No one in management or labor at Weirton believed that the deal with National would not be closed in 1983. In order to get the timetable treaty with Labor, the ISU had to waive all its defenses of the prior election. More important, the union officers had to win approval from the stewards, which would not be easy because all their elections also would be invalidated and subjected to reruns within the year.

A natural tension existed between the stewards and the executive committee elite. Both groups received the controversial sixth day of pay, but the stewards actually put in a five-day work week in the mill, while the committee had the freedom to devote full time to union business. Executive committee members who lost reelections were said to "go back to work."

On February 15, the day after returning from Washington, Walter Bish convened an emergency meeting of all the Weirton stewards, in which he and David Robertson initially responded to angry questions of the "Can they really do this to us?" variety. Some stewards wanted to know if noncompliance would lead to decertification of the union. Robertson said no, but warned that if the stewards rejected the timetable, the Department of Labor would sue and win, a costly result that also would take control of redrafting the bylaws and running the election away from the ISU and would give it to the government. Soft-spoken but firm, Walter Bish insisted, "We're going to agree" [to the treaty]. "It gives us the ability to reconstruct our bylaws the way we want them and to protect the integrity of the union." Carl Ferguson, a tough welding steward, wanted to know: "If I'm here illegally, how can I ratify anything?" Robertson jumped in: "It's been litigated many times—you can." Another steward suggested foxing the Labor Department, by rewriting the union's bylaws to redefine the stewards as nonofficers, thereby preventing them from being subjected to a rerun. Robertson said it wouldn't work.

Someone called the question, and the timetable treaty was approved by 48 to 9. A motion to reconsider failed by 41 to 11. What Robertson had neglected to mention was that the situation was unprecedented. No arguably invalid union leadership ever had comprised the majority of a labor management committee such as the JSC, which with its hired guns was negotiating for the purchase of a billion-dollar company. If these union leaders were tossed out in the rerun, would the sale stick? Too complex to answer, the questions could go either way in court.

On February 18, discouraging news leaked out of the negotiating sessions with National, which showed that they had failed to progress as far as had been hoped. The threshold question of the price remained unresolved, as was the major headache of who would pay for retiree health care benefits, as well as which company would own the Steubenville plant. A deal appeared months, rather than weeks, away.

The public relations arm of the JSC continued to keep the pressure on by raising funds in February with a bowling tournament, the "ESOP Ball," and most ambitiously with a telethon, the first ever held on behalf of a commercial venture. The eleven-hour cable show, which featured rock groups, country and western bands, sports stars, an auction of Pittsburgh Steeler regalia, and pitches from Walter Bish, Jack Redline, and John Madigan, netted about $150,000. Although the good feeling was palpable, the calls that clogged the ESOP message center in late February reflected frustration with the process and especially with ISU leadership, which according to one caller were a "bunch of cake eaters," a local slur for rich snobs. Another caller blasted the labor leaders for their sixth day of pay and for the salaries of Walter Bish ($75,000) and ISU office manager Sam Cadile ($50,000). "We can't do it," complained one voice on the tape, "if y'uns stay in the union hall."

In mid-February, the *New York Times* analyzed the Weirton situation. Steel industry reporter William Serrin noted that if the deal failed, then National would operate only a skeletal finishing mill with about fifteen hundred employees, meaning that workers would need twenty-eight years of prior service to remain employed. Another discouraging note was that a National source told the *Times* that the parent company intended to retain its research facilities in Weirton. Serrin also aired the confidential appendix controversy, allowing Lynd to grumble in print that "What I love about this is that there are 11,000 workers in West Virginia whose destiny is at stake and the three copies of this information are in New York City." The *Times* ran a picture of Redline in shirtsleeves at a center of a clutch of hourly workers who appeared to be listening to him intently. Described in the article as a "convivial man for whom many Weirton workers and community residents have a genuine fondness—his presence seems a major reason why the proposal has gone this far— [Redline] said the company, unlike some other major businesses, would be content with a profit rate below twenty percent on investment." Indeed Redline took the occasion to undercut his earlier position on ROI, suggesting that even 8 percent would suffice. "We don't need all the frills that a large company has," said Redline, who was sending a message to Wall Street that Weirton, if it became his to run, would not cut labor costs to the bone and become a profitable star among public companies; indeed, perhaps it would not go public at all.

On March 2, 1983, the Weirton community marked a year since National's announcement, and a year without a deal. The Rank and File Committee exploited the occasion. In a pamphlet passed out at the plant gates, Steve Bauman quoted Hannibal, "We will either find a way or make one," then listed the Rank and File achievements. "We got the union to concede voting rights. We got the union election declared illegal." Bauman added, "We are supposed to be owners not just on paper," and wondered "what we'll be voting on. Will we be able to vote our stock? When? Who will control management? How? What will the money derived from our concessions be used for? To buy machinery to eliminate jobs?" As usual Bauman attacked the McKinsey number and its secret basis, which remained a political liability for the JSC and the union. Now the RFC also reported that Lazard Frères only saw the need for a 19 percent cut. Somehow the dissidents had penetrated the JSC's secrecy to get the figure.

Equally important, in early March the United Steelworkers union leadership voted by 169 to 63 to ratify a new concession package covering 260,000 workers, which gave steelmakers back about $2 billion, including $1.25 billion in wages and benefits. The pact included a raft of incentives to get older workers to retire but none of the agreements that the USW had sought against plant closings. In Weirton apprehension mounted that the $1.25 billion, amounting to a 9 percent cut for United Steelworkers, would be added to the proposed 32 percent cuts.

All factions began analyzing the question. The following day Jack Redline announced that the USW concessions would not affect the negotiations with National. The Rank and File Committee drew the same conclusion, contrasting the USW's 9 percent figure with JSC's bulging 32 percent proposed cut as a basis for arguing that the international union was doing a better job of representing its members. After all, the Big Steel companies had gone into their contract renegotiation talks seeking 30 percent.

At the March 10, 1983, executive committee meeting, Walter Bish and David Robertson related recent discussions with Sperry and Keilin. Atypically, Robertson seemed somewhat confused and his report contained contradictions. "We are," he said, "within days of it happening or not." But Keilin also had told him there were open issues, so it could be "back to square one." Robertson had requested Rockefeller's intervention, to push National Steel, and in fact, the governor had phoned Love that morning. Then Robertson received a call from Sperry indicating that "We're at a make it or break it stage."

The next day, the steward body met and Robertson passed out the new United Steelworkers contract, and indicated that Lazard was looking at it in the context of the 32 percent number. One steward argued that the McKinsey report was inaccurate. Another suggested voting down the 32 percent number now. Robertson persuaded the body to wait for Lazard to "give us the answer."

The stewards wanted to know the next step. Robertson said he hoped it would be an "agreement in principle," outlining the basic terms of the transaction. It would not include important details or governance issues such as who would sit on the board of directors or be the CEO, or whether pass-through voting would be allowed.

On March 12, 1983, at 6:20 P.M., Lazard alerted the media that Weirton and National negotiators had reached a nonbinding agreement in principle. In fact, they had signed it a half hour before on the hood of a car at the Pittsburgh airport. The next day, the JSC endorsed the document in a statement to employees calling it a plan for "a strong long-range, independent Weirton Steel for us, our families and our communities."

The draft pact, which National also endorsed publicly, outlined the eventual purchase in eight key sections. The first resolved the thorniest point—the purchase price and how to pay it. The new company would give National $66 million, which amounted to only 22 percent of the facility's depreciated book value. Expected to complete payments in fifteen years, Weirton would not have to make payments on principal until the sixth year. Moreover, no interest would be due until the spin-off achieved a net worth of $100 million, at which time it would kick in at 10 percent, then a favorable rate. If the new company did especially well in terms of reaching certain profit thresholds,

National reserved the right to accelerate payments of principal. But most important, National acceded to a Lazard request to subordinate its payment position to new creditors. The fact that that banks would be paid before National, as Lazard knew, would facilitate lining up loans for the enterprise.

The second decision settled current assets: Weirton acquired all receivables, steel inventory, and raw materials at a price to be determined but equal to or less than market value. A quarter of this amount, probably around $75 million, was to be due at the closing, with the remainder stretched over twenty-eight years with interest at 10 percent or less. Of that amount, $40 million would be paid over five years beginning in 1988.

Third, it addressed retirements, establishing that pensions received from National would never drop in value after the transfer date. Also, anyone employed at Weirton would be vested under National's plan regardless if he had worked the requisite ten years. As had been hoped, any future service at Weirton after the transfer would be added to the time under National, and the two companies would pro rate the payments. A special pension safety net provided that National would give a $400 monthly supplement to each employee in the event of a shutdown during the first five years.

Fourth, National remained obligated for benefits, including life insurance and health care, for all employees who retired before the closing, as well as all benefit claims before the transfer.

Fifth, the negotiators decided that National would defend or pay grievances and lawsuits started before the closing.

Sixth, they defined the property to be included. Weirton won the entire physical plant save for National's Research and Development Center and the Williams Country Club. For two years National would lease the Steubenville plant to Weirton, and then would sell it to the new company. Weirton would acquire all patents and trademarks pertaining to its products.

Seventh, the sides arrived at scheduling arrangements that provided that the closing would not occur until May 1, 1983; and that during the first six months of independent operations Weirton and National would divide customers and orders on a "historical basis."

Eighth, a new symbiotic system specified contracts through which

National would ship Weirton iron pellets and coal, while Weirton would provide National with high-grade slabs of raw steel.

The employees tentatively agreed to take responsibility for the division's current and long-term liabilities, estimated at $85 million, but the payments would fall due years after the buyout when it was felt that the new company would be able to handle them. In essence, under the agreement in principal, the employees would put up $75 million in front money for $200 million in working capital. Getting bank loans, as Carl Valdiserri was quick to point out, would not be a problem with collateral having a book value of $300 million.

In some respects, including overall purchase price, the deal was vague. The *Wall Street Journal* calculated the mill's price at $181 million, while the *Weirton Daily Times* and *Pittsburgh Press* figured it $85 million higher. To the extent it was understood, the deal seemed popular in Weirton, where the steward body and the mill's superintendents approved it on March 14. Theirs of course were straw votes. The ISU and IGU employees later would vote officially. But Robert Crandall, an industrial analyst at the Brookings Institution, called the deal "a giveaway" because building a comparable facility would cost $9 billion.

Both sides were upbeat in the wake of the agreement in principle. Calling the Weirton negotiators "tough and professional," National's Pete Love insisted that his company "did not get all it wanted," but hinted that National had foisted $75 million in debt onto the Weirton employees. Josh Gotbaum believed that the agreement would "enable the birth of a very important new American institution." David Robertson called it "the ultimate experiment in capitalism." According to press accounts at the time, the community expected the company to be a hundred-percent-employee-owned, rather than a public, company.

Three steps remained: settling the concessions, choosing Weirton's leadership, and formal voting by the unions pertaining to the new company. Local management, which hoped to run Weirton, and Wall Street still liked 32 percent. Carl Valdiserri termed the figure "not carved into stone but pretty firm," adding that "salaried workers already have taken cuts totaling seventeen percent." David Healy, a Drexel, Burnham, Lambert vice president, agreed. "I think the only thing that makes [the deal] feasible is the thirty-two percent pay cut the workers will be taking. Otherwise the plant probably won't make any funds. With the cut, there will probably be enough money left over to pay back National for the purchase and raise money to modernize."

Yet the concession could ruin the referendum. Walter Bish insisted that if the union voted down the terms, "there would be no second chance. Lenders would be scared off."

Nevertheless, the festive but nervous mood prevailed at a crowded press confidence at the General Office following the release of the agreement in principle. Bish's soothing influence was apparent when he explained the key safety net and pension provisions:

> We were able to negotiate what is known as "work to get." Future service with the new Weirton will be added to the years of service with National to "work toward" a retirement. For example, a 26-year employee with National who goes with the new company can work 4 more years and be eligible for a 30-year regular retirement with National paying 26/30th and the new company paying 4/30th. Without the work to get National would only be required to lock and freeze the 26 years and would not begin paying a pension until the employee reached age 62.

Bish, who also outlined the security afforded by the five-year safety net, was followed by Redline, whose remarks were more exuberant. "The sequence of our Weirton Steel situation since March 2, 1982, summarized, might run like this: surprised, organized, energized, legalized, and soon, we anticipate—finalized. We are strongly optimistic about the agreement in principle on the proposed employee buyout of the Weirton plant. It is a good, workable package. . . ."

Redline offered reasons behind his confidence.

> First, we in Weirton have never known anything but steel. It's been our lifetime occupation with a tradition of generation after generation working in our plant. We know how to make steel and we intend to continue to do those things that we know how best to do.
>
> Second, our mission in life is to service the customer as we are ac-

customed to doing, satisfy our stockholders which will be us—the employees; and support our community, county and state which have been supportive of us in this long and arduous experience in obtaining an agreement with National.

Third, we will spend the bucks where they are needed to keep this plant modern and competitive within, as I see it, a contracted market. Those that survive in the recent onslaught of the marketplace will realize a fair return of their investment.

Not everyone was as positive. In addition to the referendum, lawsuits could queer the deal. As the Rank and File Committee pointed out, both the Bauman and Gregory cases, standing for full financial disclosure and letting the laid-off workers vote, remained alive. Indeed the disclosure document that the JSC had promised to Judge Haden had not been produced, and while laid-off ISU members had won the general right to vote in future union elections, their status in the upcoming ESOP ratification referendum was still unclear. "What," asked the Rank and File, "is the significance of the McKinsey Study now? When will the actual vote be? The dates keep getting pushed back. WHERE IS THE DISCLOSURE DOCUMENT?"

At the March 16 union executive committee meeting the ISU leaders seemed confused about whether they had agreed to let laid-off employees vote in the referendum. The unresolved status of the wage cut issue also dismayed them. Robertson indicated that Josh Gotbaum and Lazard were "committed to getting it done this week."

Weirton continued as a focus of national media attention. On March 18, the *Wall Street Journal* carried an editorial entitled "Karl Marx in West Virginia," which called the proposed ESOP "an important experiment for companies and workers that have lost their historical strength," but saw no reason for giving it "special tax breaks." Luis Granados, the executive director of the ESOP Association, while basically favorable about the company's chances, cautioned the new owners about the problem of buying back stock from any employees leaving the company. "Weirton Steel," warned Granados, "had better be able to come up with the cash to buy it back."

On March 18, the ISU reconvened to weigh ESOP governance, particularly who would fill the two union seats on the board of directors, a matter that could arise quickly. The committeemen knew that these directorships were to be prestigious, powerful, and backed by generous stipends. Craig Petrella, an SNE clerk, wanted the seats filled by "card-carrying union members." Eddie Conley, the politically savvy young committeeman from the strip steel mill, agreed and suggested that the board members be picked by "a popularity vote." Another SNE clerk, Steve Karnopakis, who had worked with Chuck Lafferty on the communications campaign, demurred: "We'd be the joke of the valley." He favored picking "outsiders" with at least the appearance of objectivity.

Fearing that a maverick union director could obstruct the board, Skip Spadafora urged, "We shouldn't risk a union seat to popular election." Echoing the point, Walter Bish said, "My thoughts were that the executive committee [of the ISU] would select the two and put [them] into the prospectus," which was his term for the forthcoming disclosure document.

With the question unresolved, the group began to debate credentials. A number of members wanted at least one of the two to be someone from the mill, an employee whom Don Murray, a rigger (basically a carpentry-construction position) who had served as president of the local Lions Club, described as an "upstanding citizen who already has business sense." But Tony Julian, another ISU committeeman, objected that "no matter who you get from the mill, they won't be on the same basis as the independents," those directors who would comprise the bulk of the board. Dominic Tonacchio, a tough immigrant who had risen to the top labor position in the tin mill warned against "underestimating a lot of people from the mill."

Robertson shifted the conversation by asking what they thought about who should get the independent seats. A consensus arose that these directors should have no past or present affiliation with National. Ed Martin, a blast furnace committeeman, also wanted no one who held "outside contracts with Weirton Steel." Don Murray argued against seating any "Redline puppet." He added, "We want Harvey's hit man," meaning the independent whom Sperry hoped would purge top management.

On March 24, Jack Redline focused the region's attention on himself by announcing his future provisional resignation. In effect, Redline said he would retire from National as an executive if not chosen as Weirton's CEO. "I certainly want the job, think I can do the job and have the qualifications, [but] I don't want to impede the process of forming a search for the best possible chief executive officer." Redline made clear that if he did not become CEO, he would not be back in National competing against Weirton. Calling working for Weirton the greatest experience of his life, Redline pledged to remain in the community even if not chosen, and to be available to advise the new company.

Praising Redline's "unselfish gesture," Walter Bish said, "This shows he truly wants the ESOP to work." The local media were filled with testimonials to Redline, some likening him to E. T. Weir, and quoted the hopes of local people that he would become the CEO. For example, Mal Graham, who had headed the ISU during Redline's first presidency, declared, "I'm retired but I still am concerned about Weirton Steel, and its future. In my book, Redline is the number one man to head the new employee-owned company. He's the guy to do it, I have all the faith in the world in this guy, and we can't get along without him. With Jack Redline I don't need a written contract—all I need is a handshake."

As a campaign tactic Redline's gesture of burning his bridges to National had worked. Now, other top divisional managers were watched to see if they would act in kind. When questioned about the matter, Carl Valdiserri, the executive vice president whose roots in Weirton were not as deep as Redline's, offered no comment.

The state now gave the ESOP another boost by reducing its business and occupation tax by $450,000. Calling it a "substantial tax break for five years for a worthy purpose," Governor Rockefeller said that "all West Virginia is rooting for" the independent company, and added that the "We Can Do It" ESOP motto had been adopted as an unofficial state slogan. "The legislation is an insurance policy [for Weirton] to remain in business."

14 Shots from Left and Right

"If there is going to be one domestic steel company alive, we intend it to be Weirton."

—WALTER BISH

At the end of March, the ISU invited Jimmy Zarello, the president of the UAW local at Hyatt Clark, to address the stewards. According to Zarello, the bloom was off the rose at the New Jersey ESOP, whose former GM factory produced rear-wheel-drive bearings, at a time when GM and the rest of the auto industry trended toward front-wheel drive. Zarello complained about the pseudo-equality of the white collar–blue collar "partnership." On employee ownership he warned: "If I could do it again, I would go alone without manage-

166

ment by giving equity only to hourly workers." He lamented having had "to take the board of directors to court to get salary information." Viewing his role on the Hyatt board as being more of a union representative than a true director, he urged the stewards to resist tokenism on the Weirton board, and once on it to fight for significant input. "You have to get as much control as you can in exchange for each of your concessions." He told them to hold out for participatory provisions in any upcoming collective bargaining agreements under the ESOP, as well as the right to hire and fire management. Zarello cautioned against the union putting its faith in the "outside" independent directors who, he predicted, would be retired business leaders sympathetic to management.

At Hyatt, he stated, the board allowed management to raise their own salaries while freezing hourly wages. In order not to lose ground, "strict discipline" was enforced among the labor directors. "Under no circumstances, do the three union members [of the board] ever enter the [board] room divided. Ten years down the road, we want the board of directors to be all union." The experience of co-existing with an ESOP had tempered even Zarello's militancy about job growth. He explained to the Weirton stewards that it was "not in anyone's interest to load the plant with employees. This dilutes profit sharing."

At the time, no one, including Zarello, could predict whether Hyatt Clark, with its archaic product and dependence on GM, would survive for ten years, or whether it would quickly go the way of Rath. However, as Walter Bish insisted, "if there is going to be one domestic steel company alive, we intend it to be Weirton."

Those in charge of designing the new company had little use for Zarello's or Lynd's ideas of labor control. "This is not socialism," Gene Keilin said. "It's worker capitalism." They intended to operate traditionally, to attract investors, but exploit all the tax breaks available with employee ownership. Such ESOPs, according to Keilin, "will be repeated many times or will be outlawed."

Refraining from using workplace democracy as a carrot, Keilin and Sperry pushed the process with notions of eventual high stock values and enhanced employee net worth. At the end of March, Lazard Frères finally dealt with the nagging concession issue by recommending numbers lower than McKinsey's. Instead of 32 percent, Lazard proposed that ISU and IGU members take cuts of 18.38 percent, while salaried employees, who already had suffered the National management slash of 17 percent, now would give up about 8 percent more. For the most part, people in Weirton who were realistic about the need to stake out a competitive market position were relieved and pleased with Lazard's figures. Others, mainly older employees with twenty-five to forty years in the mill, were less than satisfied.

Mike Hrabovsky, the single remaining steward in the blooming mill, an operation soon to made obsolete by continuous casting, understood what he had heard from Zarello as "union busting pure and simple." Like Zarello he saw no reason to go into a "partnership with management" and deemed participatory techniques such as quality circles, where labor and bosses got together to suggest improvements, as "circle jerks." To those who would listen, Hrabovsky would say: "Beware the wolf in sheep's clothing that calls himself an ESOP." Cynical and churlish, Hrabovsky had reached the "top of his sequence" as a crane operator, but nonetheless believed he had "really wasted my life in the mill," as had his father, who retired after thirty-seven years at Weirton. "There wasn't a day he didn't come home and complain about being treated unfairly."

Hrabovsky hated the relentless pro-ESOP communications machinery at Weirton, which "brainwashed" people and "could make Hitler look like some kind of virgin." The picture of E. T. Weir on billboard's around town appalled him. "People forget why Weir's picture was on the front of *Life* magazine in 1936. He managed to keep unions out of Weirton."

To Hrabovsky, Lazard and the other consultants, as in *The Godfather*, were "making us offers we can't refuse." He believed that the ISU with new leadership like Bish and Spadafora, who replaced him on the executive committee, had plunged into greed. "Spadafora's the chairman of the [Steelworks One] division now. He told me that he envisions the older people being offered the early retirements, the younger people being laid off, and the people that are left becoming very wealthy. If that's what unionism is all about, then I'm in the wrong game."

Infuriated, Hrabovsky crossed a line that could have gotten him impeached as a steward. Without authorization, he secretly began contacting other unions, and asking them to enter into the Weirton situation. "I felt that if I could convince some of the stronger unions to come and help us, maybe we could have a fighting chance." First, he phoned the archenemy United Steelworkers union. Ten minutes later, then USW president Lloyd McBride returned the call from Pittsburgh. "He asked me what I wanted. I said that we were in the process of setting up an ESOP in Weirton and I felt that it was wrong. They wanted the people in Weirton to take major pay cuts and major concessions and benefits cuts and I said I didn't feel that it was right, that the working man would have to go backwards when so many people fought and gave their lives to get the steelworker where he was today. I tried to explain to him that this was the beginning of something that I felt was coming, that once they got their foothold and accomplished what they set out to do in Weirton, that he was next in line. And he very politely told me that he wouldn't touch Weirton with a ten-foot pole."

Hrabovsky then phoned the United Mine Workers local in Billy's Bottom, West Virginia, which gave him UMW president Richard Trumka's number in Washington. Trumka was out campaigning and Hrabovsky's call was taken by a UMW staffer. "Their answer to me was, well, we are mineworkers, you are a steelworker, so we don't think we can help you."

Hrabovsky, who assumed, probably correctly, that he would be brushed off by other unions, decided to take a different tack. After battling with Red Arango for the union presidency, the two had mended fences. Critical of the agreement in principle, Arango bragged that if he, instead of Bish, still held the union presidency, he could have bought the mill from National for $50,000.

For a year the specter of "shutdown pay" had threatened to derail the deal. Employees with more than twenty years of service had the contractual right to receive their pensions plus a $400 monthly "sweetener" until the onset of Social Security if the mill closed. Many senior workers, Arango and Hrabovsky among them, favored getting their pensions and sweeteners rather than taking chances with the new ESOP. The problem involved having the mill officially declared shut down or abandoned by National, which then would have to pick up the heavy costs. Courts also had delivered shutdown rulings, triggering deluxe benefits, when all or most of a plant was idled. In order for Arango and Hrabovsky to prevail, National could close Weirton, or operate a tiny finishing operation, but could not transfer an intact, integrated facility to the employees.

The pair started looking for a lawyer. They did not consider the RFC and Staughton Lynd because the cultural gap was too wide. "I thought he was some kind of nut," said Hrabovsky. "He looked like he was smoking something to me." Nor did they think lawyers in Weirton would move to quash the transaction. Arango thought he knew a lawyer in Maryland, but when the two drove to see him, he turned out to be a professor rather than an attorney.

Hrabovsky determined that the only way would be to hire a major lawyer from out of town, which would require real money. With Arango and a nucleus of others who previously had been ISU leaders, he formed a group called the Committee of Concerned Steel Workers (CSW). Its initial meeting at Weirton's small Kosciusko Hall, named for a Polish hero of the American Revolution, unexpectedly drew an overflow crowd of four hundred and had to be moved to the larger community center. Asking for $500 apiece, the CSW quickly collected more than $40,000 and retained leading Ohio labor attorney Eugene Green, who once had fired Staughton Lynd. The Concerned Steel Workers' choice of counsel probably ensured that the two dissident groups would never come together.

Naming 170 members of the CSW as plaintiffs, Green, a raspy, thick-set two-hundred-pounder, whose elegant suits were all that physically distinguished him from his clients, filed an aggressive federal lawsuit in Wheeling intended to halt the transaction. In addition, in the suit and a parallel charge to the National Labor Relations Board, the Concerned Steel Workers argued that the Joint Study Committee had negotiated over pension funds without proper authority in violation of the federal Employee Retirement Income Security Act (ERISA).

As the Rank and File Committee had taken on the embryonic ESOP and its leadership from an antiauthoritarian leftist position, so the CSW attacked from the right, trying to get every possible penny for its members without regard for the collective well-being of the workforce or the community. Not only would the CSW suit, if successful, stop the ESOP plan in its tracks, but it also stood a chance of bankrupting National.

Publicly, Hrabovsky took the position that the CSW did not oppose the ESOP, but merely wanted workers' contractual rights honored. Privately, he knew that success spelled an end to steel making in Weirton. Even the good-natured, but mush-minded Arango sensed that the mill would close if the CSW won, though he baselessly hoped that the city of Weirton or state of West Virginia would step in to run the operation.

The suit, which also sought $50 million in punitive damages, aroused strong feelings in the region including suspicions about the loyalty of senior workers. The fact that so many had signed the CSW petition and made donations also raised questions about how the ESOP would fare in a referendum. As tensions mounted between young and old, the mood turned ugly. When Mike Hrabovsky drove back from court in Wheeling with his wife and daughter, someone blasted their car full of buckshot, fortunately harming no one.

The local leadership and its consultants seemed taken aback by the CSW. David Robertson said it would be "premature" to comment on the lawsuit. Instead the JSC stressed Lazard's revised numbers, and the fact that the disclosure document, which had been catalyzed by the Rank and File suit, and was nearing completion, would contain the new board of directors.

Even though his numbers had been sliced, McKinsey's Ron Bancroft told *Metal Producing* magazine that the ESOP would make Weirton workers secure. "After six years and under the worst [market] case the average employee's share will be worth $50,000, and possibly as much as ninety or $100,000." Campaigning hard, Jack Redline assured the Rotary Club that soon it would be like the old days in Weirton. "I think we'll do famously. If the company does two and a half million tons [of production] as it once did, we'll have a workforce of ten to eleven thousand." National, he convinced them, would not back out at the last minute, because of its fears of shutdown costs. To wide acclaim, Bill Doepken announced that the stock shares in the ESOP would be divided equally, allaying worries of management domination.

In April the CSW continued holding public meetings. Eugene Green maintained that the JSC's negotiations had been conducted under a "coercive cloud," that the Joint Study Committee, by name and charter had authority only to study ESOP feasibility, and the JSC broke the cardinal rules of American labor by conducting collective bargaining not at contract time, and by allowing local management to help formulate worker demands. "When the JSC negotiated on pensions," insisted Green, "collective bargaining took place." Red Arango spoke against the agreement in principle with National. "In the mill everybody's scared, everybody's against it. It would be voted down, if they voted today." Arango also used the forum to announce his candidacy for president in the next union election.

The pro-ESOP forces held responsive mass meetings at St. John's Arena in Steubenville and the Millsopp Community Center in Weirton, where the leadership explained that the JSC had done nothing wrong by trying to save thousands of jobs, and that the financial sacrifices now had been reduced. Representative calls to the ESOP message center for April reflected divisions in the community. One urged: "Don't take rights away from old-timers"; another, "Hang Arango." However, the April 18, 1983, issue of *Fortune* predicted that the union would vote overwhelmingly pro-ESOP.

Robertson, for one, continued to act as if the buyout would occur. Never ceasing to learn, he amassed and read materials on corporate reorganization, while tapping available experts' brains. He conducted an ongoing dialogue with William F. Whyte of Cornell's School of Labor Relations, probably the leading guru on how unions should function in the new cooperative (as opposed to confrontational) workplace of the late twentieth century. In mid-April, Robertson asked Whyte to recommend names to fill the labor seats on the board of directors at Weirton. Whyte advised that "because the company has a very paternalistic reputation, it's important that you have on the board people with a commitment to active decision making and with some practical and theoretical background along this line." Whyte's choices included Chris Mueller of Local 46 of the United

Food and Commercial Workers, a "key figure in developing the very active and far-reaching participation program with Rath Packing," as well as Lyle Taylor, formerly the union president at Rath, but now the CEO, and Jim Zarello of the autoworkers at Hyatt Clark. Additionally, Whyte favored Professor Robert Cole of the University of Michigan, a specialist on Japanese employee involvement programs, Joe Blasi, head of the Kibbutz Studies program at Harvard, and Corey Rosen, the executive director of the National Center for Employee Ownership (NCEO), the most participative of the mainline ESOP organizations. Robertson filed away the suggestions, none of which struck him as right for Weirton.

On April 23, Harvey Sperry brought an emergency to the Joint Study Committee. National's president, James Haas, had alerted him that the critical pension safety net provision in the agreement in principle did not reflect National's position. "Somebody," said Haas, "fucked up." In his view, Elliott Goldstein, during negotiations with Sperry and Keilin had gone too far. Under the agreement, if the safety net kicked in within the first five years of the ESOP, National would have to pay a minimum of $350 million in accelerated pension and severance costs, enough to bring the parent corporation's net worth below a billion dollars, and create a serious incident of default with its creditors.

In conversations with Robertson, Sperry, by now at war with the division's management, accused them of subtly bringing the issue to the corporation's attention, "by making feelers as to the future of National." On this occasion, Robertson defended Doepken and Valdiserri, the supposed culprits. "I don't think," he told Sperry, "this issue is being raised to tank the deal." The Joint Study Committee quickly took a hard line that the agreement in principle was not open to reinterpretation, and could not be scrapped, because it already had been pitched and well received in Weirton.

National worried that once independent, Weirton would work for four years, and then threaten a shutdown to extort funds from it, say $100 million, or go through with a shutdown and get all the pension and severance money. According to Bill Doepken, National feared that the ISU would control the Weirton board within four years, and that the union would "want to collect the four hundreds."

Doepken, who had close ties to National, proposed an approach to preserve the safety net. First, it would be necessary to ensure National that there would be no "blackmail," and that it would be liable for the safety net only if the shutdown would have been implemented "by reasonably prudent businessmen." Also, National would need confidence that labor strife would not close the fledgling company during the five-year period, so Doepken proposed offering a six-year no-strike clause. Along the same lines, Doepken believed that profit sharing should hinge on compliance with the labor agreement. To further calm National, Doepken said Weirton could show National that independent rather than union directors would control the ESOP's board. Finally, to allay National's concerns that labor costs could sink Weirton, Doepken mentioned that the proposed charter of the new corporation did not need to state that its object was to preserve jobs, a matter that previously had won a favorable reception in Weirton.

On this make-or-break occasion, Doepken, Valdiserri, Bish, and Robertson joined Sperry and Keilin on the Weirton negotiating team. Elliott Goldstein was not on the National side of the table. National's president Haas led his delegation.

Weirton at the outset took a tough stand with Sperry, saying that without the safety net the deal was off. Sperry also conveyed that the consultants already had selected the Weirton board, and that National had nothing to fear from mill demagogues. Not satisfied, National retorted that if the deal fell through it had an "operations plan" ready that could take over Weirton, harvest it, and deal with a strike.

To some extent Weirton softened its position. While insisting it already had won the safety net, it proposed "further discussions" to define and clarify it.

National continued posturing. If the buyout collapsed it would move to decertify the ISU, bring in the USW, cut crew sizes, and change the pensions. Bill Doepken snapped that "no one can run Weirton if the deal goes south. There will be mass retirements, and sabotage." The impasse lasted for two days, with the Weirton team trying to convince National of the extremely slim chance that the safety net would be needed, based on promises to fill a majority of the board seats with independent directors who would be made known to National before the referendum and who would pick the CEO. In addition, the ISU, which for once was represented directly by its president in the negotiations, would have to approve a six-year no-strike contract. Profit sharing would be tied to the approval of the collective bargaining agreement. Based on these representations, National achieved an adequate comfort level. In order to preserve the safety net, the Weirton team had doled out four of Doepken's five points. But it had not given up the charter objective of preserving jobs. Still obsessed with shutdown costs, National made it plain that it would decline to make the deal if the Committee of Concerned Steel Workers won its lawsuit.

At the end of April, the Arango, Bauman, and Gregory court cases all were consolidated before Federal Judge Robert Maxwell, a well-regarded jurist who unlike Judge Haden had a reputation for being somewhat pro-plaintiff. In their filings to Judge Maxwell, Steve Bauman and the Rank and File Committee continued to hammer the point home that ISU members still had not had access to "documents necessary to conduct an informed vote." The Rank and File told the court that workplace fairness "requires that all those affected by decisions which will affect their lives have an opportunity to participate in the decision-making process. If informed democratic decision making occurs at Weirton, it will be seen by the entire nation as a successful experiment in economic democracy." The Rank and File raised doubts as to whether the Joint Study Committee's insistence on secrecy had been a sham on the community and the court. How could a confidential appendix issue used to justify an initial cut of 32 percent for hourly employees now support a reduction of 18.38 percent? No information, complained the Rank and File, allowed one "to figure out exactly where this 13.62 percent savings in costs comes from."

In hearings that began on April 28, Walter Bish, who swore that the JSC had not "negotiated away or changed" pension rights at the bargaining table with National, again held firm under cross-examination. Carl Valdiserri likewise testified emphatically that the JSC's disclosure document, still in preparation by JSC consultants, would answer all the court, community, and employee questions about the buyout, the cuts, and proposed future organization, without compromising confidential information. Bish said that employees would have adequate time, at least three weeks, to digest the material before voting. From the bench Judge Maxwell came down particularly hard on the Concerned Steel Workers, asking caustically whether they wished to see "the Northern Panhandle collapse." In declining to impose injunctions, Maxwell, however, continued to allow the cases to proceed to a full resolution on their merits. In order not to stall the buyout process Maxwell ruled directly from the bench rather than making the factions wait for a written decision.

The court's opinion had four chief grounds, which the JSC immediately publicized throughout the Panhandle. First, the plaintiffs had not managed to prove that, without an injunction, they would suffer irreparable damages. Second, in balancing the dangers triggered by the suits, the court found that far greater harm would come to the defendants—the ISU, JSC, and National—than to the plaintiffs if he ordered an injunction, particularly because the institutional defendants' roles twined with the public interest.

Third, the court sensed no violation of federal pension law or the Labor Management Relations Act by the union. Finally, Maxwell ruled the negotiations between the JSC and National to be "collectively and singularly valid and lawful."

The JSC also asked the court to dismiss totally the suit on disclosure of the McKinsey appendix. Through Staughton Lynd, and its other attorneys, the Rank and File shot back its response, which included the record of prior Judge Haden's statement the previous November that, "when the union membership is presented with a proposal it should be presented with all aspects of that proposal, except something that might be absolutely privileged. . . . Other than that, I think every aspect of what turns out to be the proposal, should be distributed to the union membership so they can cast an informed vote on what the proposal is. I would construe 411(a)(1) [of the Labor Management Relations Act] to provide that right." The Rank and File asked the court not to dismiss but instead to review the disclosure document for completeness before ruling. Judge Maxwell bought the argument, and denied the JSC's motion.

At its executive committee meeting on May 4, 1983, the ISU continued pondering the potential labor members to the board. Nick Petrovich, the chairman of Steel Works One, suggested that in order to be considered, a candidate would need to know "labor law, ERISA, and Weirton, and have a union background." Although nearing retirement, Petrovich's influence had grown because he had shown himself to be effective in preventing older workers from defecting to the Arango-Hrabovsky CSW camp and in keeping them pro-ESOP.

A big, open-faced man, with a full head of thick graying hair, and a raunchy sense of humor, Petrovich had led one of the few overt moments of labor militancy on the Joint Study Committee. After the coke plant closing, National refused to pay legitimate shutdown benefits to employees, some of whom had long seniority. These workers began "bumping" others out of jobs throughout the mill. To Petrovich, the situation "was a plague. They [National] were giving us a hand job." As a result, he led a labor walkout from the JSC.

Calling Petrovich at the union headquarters, Sperry told him he "was ruining the deal." Petrovich grunted, "So what, maybe it should all be shut down." Within twenty-four hours, Sperry called back and said, "You got it." National declared the coke plant shut down, released the benefits, and the crisis eased.

In early May 1983, it was unclear whether the union would get two or three seats on the board. Petrovich urged the executive committee to hold out for three. One of six brothers who had worked in the mill, as well as the father and son of Weirton Steel workers, Petrovich believed that the ISU and the company "got in trouble with the EEOC, because of families helping themselves and not minorities." Now he recommended Paul Fasser for a union seat on the board of directors. Fasser had been the court-appointed master in the marathon race-discrimination case against the company and the union, which had done so much to improve opportunities for minorities. Emil Morelli, a pipefitter and executive committeeman from the Strip Steel division, seconded the motion, which passed unanimously.

But no one knew if the vote would have any effect, as the executive committee remained unsure about the proper selection procedure for choosing the union's directors. Walter Bish, Petrovich, and Tony Julian wanted the committee to pick the names, with approval from the steward body. Tom Gaudio, the tin mill secretary, objected. A wiry man in his thirties, with a fashionable "punk" brush cut, hip clothes, and an easy smile, Gaudio said: "I think you have to give the men in the mill a say-so." The son of a former president of a now defunct USW local near Mingo, West Virginia, the center of the state's worst labor strife, Gaudio jokingly referred to himself as "a socialist," though his family branded him "a scab" for working at Weirton. In the ISU and JSC, he argued forcefully for future equal stock and profit sharing distributions in the ESOP. He also wanted to see "cultural" changes in the new company, including the erasure of blue-collar and white-collar distinctions, such as the management dining rooms, parking spaces, and special white hard hats, which kept people from teaming effectively. Unable to resolve the formal mechanics of picking a director, the committee nonetheless took another recommendation. Eddie Conley moved to put the union president on the board. Skip Spadafora warned that "with Walter it's okay, but with someone else it might not be." Bish abstained from the subsequent vote, which passed unanimously.

Fielding the Team

"We were looking for razor blades in the mashed potatoes."

—DAVID ROBERTSON

On May 9, Lazard completed the draft of a "private placement memorandum" for banks in order to attract $80 million in notes due in 1990, and a $70 million revolving credit line. According to the document, "As a result of substantially reduced costs—an average cut of $8.00 per hour—and other cost savings, Weirton should enjoy profitable operations and strong cash flows, even in weak markets." The phrase "very weak markets" was crossed out. The memorandum profiled a conservative company, not the classless entity anticipated by

Tom Gaudio and the Rank and File. Lazard gave assurances that it would pick the majority of the board—the independent directors—who then would win JSC approval. "Profitability and business judgment," asserted Lazard, "will continue to guide the firm's operations." *In Search of Excellence*, by Tom Peters and Robert Waterman, the landmark study of successful American businesses, showed that winning companies avoided overdiversification and "stuck to their knitting." Lazard foresaw that the independent Weirton would adopt such a strategy by continuing to focus on its historical strong suit—tin mill products—which made good sense at that moment in the industry.

Weirton's primary competitors have been United States Steel and Bethlehem Steel, each of which has historically held about a 30% market share. National Steel's Midwest Division is also a significant producer. National's practice has been to allocate orders first to its Midwest Division, as a result of that division's heretofore lower costs. These and other competitors have reduced T.M.P. production and capacity in recent years in response to reduced demand. For example, Bethlehem Steel has recently announced plans to close its Burns Harbor, Indiana, tin mill, which currently produces about 312,000 tons of T.M.P annually. Kaiser Steel plans to shut down the finishing facility at Fontana, California, where primary operations were suspended in November, 1983. Imports have not played a significant factor; from 1976 to 1981 exports exceeded imports in every year but one.

In short, not only were competitors ceding the market to it, but Weirton no longer would have to play stepchild within National.

Lazard touched on the delicate upcoming leadership problem. "Divisional president John Redline will be a candidate for CEO, but the selection of CEO will be reserved for the new board of directors. The recruiting firm of Heidrich & Struggles has been retained to develop other CEO candidates." Lazard hopefully predicted that the board would be picked in May with the closing to follow in June.

Lazard also forecast labor peace, since "relations between the Division and the ISU have historically been peaceful. The ISU has never engaged in a strike." Further, "The ISU would pledge not to strike for six years as part of their contract with the new management. The new ISU contract unlike the USWA contract will provide for no general wage increases, nor any cost-of-living increases for the term of the agreement. As a result, over the life of the agreement Weirton's cost advantage compared to its competitors will most probably be increased."

Lazard projected that employees and company would own all of the stock. At the outset, the company, it said, could retain "five to ten percent for bonus and incentive plans." At Lazard's request, the consulting arm of the British Steel Corporation had reviewed a proposed capital spending plan for Weirton and pronounced it sound.

While Lazard's memo could give banks confidence, the buyout still wasn't in gear. On May 12, National's Love threatened weakly that the vote at Weirton would be before June 30, 1983, or else National would "have second thoughts." Actually, Love's demand made sense because the contract between the ISU and National was slated to expire on July 31, 1983. National had no interest in beginning labor negotiations with the union, much less making another pact with it. But if the present collective bargaining agreement expired, the result could be Weirton's first strike at the worst possible time.

The lawsuits, which Love described as "brought by fringe groups losing support," surely had slowed the process. Plus, the disclosure document wasn't done. Walter Bish had insisted on the ISU members having at least three weeks to study it before voting. Now, in a new wrinkle in their lawsuit, the Rank and File Committee also asked Judge Maxwell to give it a week to screen the disclosure document for defects before it was distributed to ISU members.

The JSC leaders also were scratching their heads trying to come up with a way to provide Weirton's salaried employees with some ratification role or voice in the buyout. Feeling disenfranchised due to the ISU majority on the JSC, white-collar employees, unlike the union workers, had no upcoming referendum on whether a contract would be modified to allow the ESOP. They would face concessions without a choice, and had already taken a major cut.

Love continued to "lose patience." He wanted Weirton's high costs off his books, which he believed would give him the chance to show his directors the 20 percent return on investment that was his goal for the highly diversified National Intergroup.

Nevertheless, in mid-May, National reluctantly pushed back the voting deadline until July 15, 1983. As employees remained uncertain about whether to retire, the JSC extracted an agreement from National that played as a taped message by Don Murray, the vice chairman of Steel Works Two, to callers to the ESOP message center. Anyone "eligible for retirement as of April 30, 1983, shall be entitled to apply for a pension until five (5) days after the vote on the union contracts or July 15, 1983, whichever comes earlier."

The Concerned Steel Workers continued to press the point that the pension situation of workers staying with Weirton remained uncertain. The Rank and File hammered the ISU for giving the impression to its members that in the Gregory case the question of laid-off workers being allowed to vote had been resolved, when in fact "it was alive and well in Judge Maxwell's courtroom." On May 25, Walter Bish made the grim admission to the media that "if the employees were asked to vote today, they would say no." Later, he lamented that "we've been sued for everything we've done so far," and expressed frustration about getting the disclosure document into shape for distribution. The original draft had run to more than seven hundred pages.

In late May and early June the Weirton communications drive went back into high gear. At the Fort Steuben Mall, the merchants held a special "ESOP" week rally and promotion. The Serbian Club of Weirton sponsored a pro-ESOP "Chicken Blast." Local television stations carried ESOP roundtables where ISU and management leaders insisted that the consultants were "interacting with the Joint Study Committee, not dominating it," and that the lawsuits were simply "nuisances that cost money."

In addition, the panelists posed and answered such questions as: What do we get under the safety net? Why don't we get severance when the sale occurs? How much will my wages be cut? Under ESOP who runs Weirton? (Answer: You, the employees, own Weirton, but you don't run it on a day-to-day basis.) Will my pension change under ESOP? (Answer: For most people it will improve. Under no circumstances will it be less than accrued benefits prior to ESOP.)

In the second week of June, the PR included an ESOP polka party at the Weirton Knights of Columbus, an ESOP golf outing at a Weirton Country Club, and an ESOP banquet sponsored by the Weirton

Chamber of Commerse, which featured Senator Russell Long, who spoke of Weirton as the culmination of all that he had worked for in Congress, viewed its chances optimistically, and paraphrased Mae West—"too much of a good thing is simply marvelous." Weirton's annual carnival and fireworks party, called the International Food Festival, likewise was ESOP-themed and fifty thousand people turned out to see Pittsburgh Steeler great Franco Harris receive a key to the city, congratulate the local people for their courage, and urge them to press ahead with their "new beginning."

In mid-June, National requested the ISU to extend the collective bargaining agreement, due to expire on July 31, until November 30, 1983. Walter Bish convened a meeting of the stewards, who wisely agreed to the request. The expiration date of the pension agreement remained December 31, 1983. The stewards' vote prevented the labor situation from becoming chaotic, and also calmed customers. Bish and the JSC continued to expect the referendum to be held in July. National rattled sabers by warning that there would be only one referendum.

July arrived without a scheduled referendum. But Judge Maxwell dismissed the Concerned Steel Workers case by ruling that the proposed buyout would not violate pension or severance rights. Arango vowed to appeal the claim to the Supreme Court if necessary. But the CSW seemed to lose steam. Lead lawyer, Eugene Green, was mortally ill, and other attorneys in the case confused the workers with futile notions of broadening the case to include age and/or ethnic discrimination (Arango had a Spanish surname).

In mid-July, Arnold Levine, a sociologist at West Virginia University, released an opinion poll of seven hundred Weirton employees, which showed 94 percent willing to take some concessions in order to keep the plant open. The study also tracked support in segments of the workforce for the proposed ESOP as it was understood at the time. Overall 78 percent favored it, including 80 percent of management, 89 percent of clerical, 73 percent of hourly workers, and a whopping 92 percent of those who were laid off, which sent a signal to the ISU leadership that blocking their votes made little sense.

Other survey data reflected that 78 percent of management, but only 38 percent of blue-collar workers, had confidence in Jack Redline. The message was clear. The biggest block in the plant, the blue-collar hourly workforce, was the least pro-ESOP and the most anti-Redline. As for the laid-off workers, they wanted a new company because they wanted to work. "If they [the JSC] were smart," said Arnold Levine, "they'd let the laid-off employees vote."

Levine, who made the study without grants because he viewed the situation as "the most important domestic story in the country," also polled employees on whom they held responsible for the crisis at Weirton, and found that 79 percent blamed National, while the rest divided responsibility between Weirton Steel management and the federal government. Seventy-four percent of those polled rated the agreement in principle "fair to very fair." Nevertheless, 61 percent were considering early retirement. Levine found to no one's surprise that the dissatisfaction with the proposed ESOP rose with the age of the subjects. Unfortunately for the senior employees, at least those in the Concerned Steel Workers, their luck with the National Labor Relations Board was no better than with the bench. On July 17, the NLRB dismissed Red Arango's petition, and ruled out unfair labor practices by stating that Weirton management did not dominate or interfere with the ISU by serving with it on the Joint Study Committee. The NLRB also found no harm in the ISU's role in negotiating a concessions package in preparation for the buyout. It likewise declared that there would be no conflict of interest for ISU officials to serve on the ESOP's board.

However, the first group of directors chosen were the six independents who in turn would choose the CEO. Lazard made the recommendations with input from Willkie Farr and McKinsey. Then the nominees were passed along to a subcommittee of the JSC which reviewed their credentials and included Robertson, Petrovich, Doepken, Miles Dean, and Eugene West.

By no means extensive, vetting by the group meant looking for antiunion attitudes among the candidates, which Robertson called "razor blades in the mashed potatoes." Finding none, the credentials subcommittee sent the names to the full JSC, where they sailed through. Near the top rungs of American business, the six white males would please creditors and not offend the union.

Herbert Elish, forty-nine, was the senior vice president of the International Paper Company, a major integrated producer with $4.5 billion in sales. Previously a vice president of Citibank, Elish, a lawyer, had preceded Gene Keilin as executive director of the Municipal Assistance Corporation in New York, and had been his boss. The two had remained close.

Lawrence Isaacs, sixty-two, the vice-chairman of Susquehanna University, had served as chief financial officer of Federated Department Stores, an $8 billion business, and Allis Chalmers. With eleven years as an accountant at Price Waterhouse, and prior service as the vice president and controller of RCA, he obviously had been chosen for a financial background, thought necessary to steer the board through the thickets of ESOP accounting and taxation.

Gordon Hurlburt, fifty-eight, was president of the Power Systems division of Westinghouse, which at the time annually sold $3 billion worth of heavy equipment for electrical generation. His manufacturing background and connections to the Pittsburgh industrial sector had made him attractive.

F. James Rechin, fifty-nine, served as vice president and general manager of TRW's Aircraft Components Group, a half-billion-dollar venture. He specialized in developing employee-participation programs.

Richard Schubert, forty-six, the youngest independent director, then was president of the American Red Cross, but had been vice-chairman of Bethlehem Steel, the nation's number two producer, and an undersecretary of labor under Nixon and Ford. While his expertise encompassed the relations among labor, management, and government, it was hoped that the Bethlehem experience could help Weirton avoid some of "Big Steel's" mistakes.

Philip Smith, fifty-seven, an Australian-born engineer, had worked at Inland Steel before serving for eleven years as CEO of Copperweld Steel, a specialty producer, which he had turned around in the 1970s. While the product lines at Copperweld—steel tubing, bimetallic products, and robotics—bore little resemblance to those at Weirton, it was hoped that Smith's strong hands-on management style would be infectious.

The new directors received rave reviews. "New Board Said Exceptional" was the headline in the *Weirton Daily Times*. Walter Bish told his membership that they "were a very select group and we feel very comfortable with them." David Robertson took pains to point out that the $20,000 director's fee "is not an incentive to people of such stature with such distinguished careers." The fact that blue-chip directors would sign on with the new venture gave it the appearance of substance and stability. Paradoxically, at the same time, the deal almost blew apart.

In July, Sperry realized that he and Keilin had negotiated the agreement in principle with National Steel Corporation rather than with the National Intergroup, the holding company, which clearly was interested in getting out of steel by selling out, or turning the steel division into a joint venture. Enraged, Sperry called Elliott Goldstein, insisting that he come back to the table.

> I told Elliott that we were going to have to get a guarantee from National Intergroup because we weren't going to be dealing with any god damn subsidiary on the kind of issues we were dealing with. We went to the mat with them, which meant we were telling them that if National Intergroup couldn't guarantee the deal there was not going to be any deal. Because our client was not going to sign up with a subsidiary. No way. Because you can't control what a subsidiary does with their capital. You've got to be at the top of the heap with respect to warranties, representations, and with respect to pension obligations. We already had accrued about two million in unpaid billables in this god damn trade. Keilin and Gotbaum were sitting on the edge of their seats and I was telling Haas and Goldstein no deal unless Intergroup guarantees it.

During days of fifteen-hour sessions Sperry remained firm, saying, "Fellows, our deal is not with whatever you decide to put into a subsidiary, it's with you." The lawyer wanted the signatures of both National Steel and National Intergroup. "Were they not going to do the deal without that? No way." Sperry knew his opponent, which capitulated. As it turned out, the move was meaningful because National Intergroup put its steel division on the trading block, first trying to sell it to USX (which the Justice Department blocked on antitrust grounds), and eventually shifted it into a joint venture with Nippon

Kokan (NKK) Steel of Japan. Whether National Steel would have survived as a stand-alone is an open question. Its principal rival, LTV, went into Chapter 11. As either a joint venture or a victim of bankruptcy, its fulfillment of contract obligations would have become questionable. While Sperry's panic play made his opponents "think we're nuts," in time it proved to be the right move.

As everyone in Weirton knew, the first job facing the independent directors involved picking the new CEO from a list compiled by Heidrich & Struggles, the New York head-hunting firm. The last cut included four names, one of which was Jack Redline. The headhunter, insisting that confidentiality is critical to its operations, declined to comment regarding its selections or to identify them.

In the summer of 1983, the "Let's Back Jack" movement and petition drive intensified. One widely publicized signature in support of the divisional chairman, which embarrassed the officially neutral but de facto anti-Redline union, was that of Walter Bish's wife. Sperry and Keilin, who met with the new directors during the candidate interview and selection processes, also continued to oppose Redline.

Sperry's dismissive view of Redline was not based solely on the lawyer's low regard for the steel man's skills. Indeed, Sperry, who was not always consistent in his appraisal, sometimes worried that Redline, if jettisoned, would latch onto a Weirton rival, such as nearby Wheeling-Pittsburgh Steel when it emerged from bankruptcy.

Every major deal embraces some unspoken and probably unenforceable but nevertheless critical understandings. In Sperry's sidebars with National's top brass, they insisted that they did not want to sell to a Weirton contingent headed by Redline, whom they viewed as an old-style steel boss ill-equipped to run a novel employee-owned company. To make the deal fly, Sperry agreed to push Redline out.

From friends within National, Redline learned about Sperry's unauthorized meetings with National's top echelon and considered suing Sperry for exceeding his authority as a JSC negotiator, but decided against it. Also, beginning in the spring of 1983 Redline received calls from Jim Haas and George Angevine, respectively National's president and vice-chairman, who alerted him that they "had heard you're not going to get the CEO's job," and offered him a platinum parachute severance worth a half million dollars more than his regular pension if he would step aside. National even drafted a statement for Redline's signature, indicating that "due to ill health" Redline would not be a candidate for CEO. He refused to sign it, yelling, "Jesus Christ, I'm not sick." He told his wife, who liked living in Weirton, "I'm not going to throw the sponge in. I'm going to see this thing through."

For his final interview with the new board, the headhunter, Sperry, and Keilin, Redline prepared an elaborate book-length document, encompassing detailed financial, capital, sales, and marketing plans for the new Weirton, in addition to an organizational review, an analysis of the labor contract, and a statement of his "corporate philosophy." Aware that he was seen as something of a traditional autocrat, Redline laced this document and his presentation with the lingo of employee involvement and quality-based decision making. Having campaigned among Weirton's product buyers and doubtless become their favorite for the job, Redline urged the directors to "contact and consider the concerns of the customers [whose] perception of our leadership will directly affect our future and profits over the next several years."

Two candidates in the final four remain a deep secret, but Harvey Sperry described them as a high-level executive of Inland Steel, the Chicago-based integrated producer, who headed a seven thousand to eight thousand worker division; and a "real businessman." The latter lacked direct steel experience, though the enterprise he had founded now included a steel operation run by "people below him." While this candidate to Sperry "was a guy who had respect, a good guy," the lawyer favored the candidacy of Robert Loughead, the fifty-three-year-old president of Copperweld Steel in Warren, Ohio.

While the press boosted Redline as the favorite for the job, he knew that the odds had shifted against him. Normally affable, he faced the final panel with the halting diffidence of a practically beaten man. "Jack's presentation," said Sperry, "was terrible."

Loughead, on the other hand, exuded self-assurance. During the previous spring's American Iron and Steel Institute's (AISI) conference in New York, he had met privately with Sperry and Keilin and knew their expectations. Moreover, for Loughead the final interview presented no do-or-die situation. As he walked from the hotel to the session he thought, "I have a good job, and this is very interesting, and if they're interested in me, I'd certainly like to do this; but I didn't feel any pressure, and it certainly wasn't a pressured situation. We were just talking around a large table."

Loughead, according to Sperry, gave a "fantastic presentation, the best I've ever seen. He takes off his jacket, sits there in his shirtsleeves at the head of the table, and proceeds to tell us how an employee participates." Physically prepossessing with broad shoulders, big expressive hands, and a wide, fleshy, malleable face capable of switching a room's mood from friendly to serious, Loughead, a CPA, impressed his judges with an easy grasp of financials. He subtly turned the tables by asking each future board member "what would cause you to want to be a director of Weirton Steel Corporation," despite already "being involved in so many other important pursuits?" The question prompted a round of sincere responses "as we went around the table and that was kind of interesting," Loughead remembered. "I got to hear what their interests were, and why they wanted to become directors. I thought it went well."

On July 27, Weirton named Loughead as its president and chief executive officer. National followed suit by slotting him as the interim divisional president at Weirton pending the buyout. Redline, who announced his retirement effective the following day, was furious and felt betrayed. Unavailable to the press for comment, he promptly left Weirton and never set foot in the town again. To him, Loughead was a "bean counter" without a primary steel-making background or ties to the community, who had no business taking the helm of the new company.

Meeting the press, Loughead projected toughness and cautious optimism. He admitted that "nothing is risk free," that his background in producing stainless alloy bars at Copperweld had nothing to do with the tinplate market in which Weirton would sink or swim, and that Copperweld with twenty-five hundred workers, and sales of about $340 million, was a smaller, less complex operation. For Loughead, Weirton amounted to a step up financially and in prestige, for which he was grateful. At Copperweld, as executive vice president and president of the steel division his last salary had been

$180,000. Now he would make $250,000 plus a probable $100,000 in bonuses.

Locally he won points by mentioning that he had family members in nearby Wellsboro, West Virginia, and that some relatives, now retired, had held hourly jobs at Weirton, including an uncle who logged forty years as a locomotive engineer and two cousins, a craneman in the sheet mill and a fireman. He spoke admiringly of the "spirit and dedication of this whole community and the people in the company," and was particularly taken with "candlelight prayer vigils, bake sales, breakfasts, and all sorts of things. They really meant it when they said we can do it."

The Rank and File Committee griped that the full board, including labor directors, had not picked Loughead, which seemed a harbinger of things to come. Also research by the RFC disclosed that Copperweld really was a subsidiary of Paris-based Imetal, and had been losing money and with it shareholder equity. But the dissidents declined to attack publicly, happy at least about the passage of the autocratic old guard. Moreover, Loughead's dedication to worker involvement predated his candidacy for the Weirton job. At Copperweld, he had installed about twenty employee-participation teams. He practiced techniques termed "management by walking around," and "coffee and conversation." In other words "we [management] will provide the coffee and you [employees] provide the conversation." As it involved management's going into every department and talking to the workforce, "you'd better be prepared to answer questions. Because if you go out there and shy away from dealing with real tough issues and hard questions, you're really practicing management by walking away and you'd be better off to stay in the office—you won't do nearly as much harm." At Weirton, he called the worker an "untapped resource," who "has to have input," while warning that employee participation "only works if top management is committed." At Copperweld, he had had good relations with the United Steelworkers. Now he took to noting that "singleness of purpose" at Weirton had to be achieved, because once the stock was distributed "eighty percent of the shareholders would belong to the union."

Beginning his full-time duties on August 8, 1983, Loughead received a taped anonymous phone message from a longtime worker, recorded by the ESOP message center, which also sent it to the Joint Study Committee and the ISU stewards:

Dear Mr. President: Welcome to Weirton and God Bless You. I come to Weirton in 1929 and went to work for 40 cents an hour. I was proud to be in the Weirton Steel family. I raised a large family and have several grandchildren. My grandchildren have left Weirton. There's no place here for them. Management sons and favorite friends wear the white hats and passed over men with many years of faithful service. When Tom Millsopp left us, big management took over. Big salaries, too many white hats, private clubs, private dining rooms, private secretaries with special privileges. Men with 20 years were pushed aside. A lot of steel and hard work was wasted. This loss hurts. Some heads must fall. Give the working man a chance. The ISU is only a front. With God's help and your knowledge and your understanding and the sweat of the working men of Weirton, we can and will do it! Thank you.

A few days before Loughead took over, Sperry and Keilin made a power play by lobbying the ISU members of the Joint Study Committee to increase the number of independent directors on the new company's board from six to eight, and convincing them to give the extra seats to the pair. "The union," as David Robertson recalled, "then went to management and said we would like these people in as the other two independent directors. There was nothing that management could do about it because of the votes on the JSC." Still reeling from Redline's rejection, the remaining executives on the JSC disliked the ploy. "They didn't see Harvey and Gene as allies," said Robertson. "They were right."

Sperry and Keilin both wanted David Roberton to take one of the union seats. Walter Bish, who already had one, also sought his trusted counsel beside him on the board, but Robertson hesitated. "I didn't think I had any contribution to make. I didn't understand what went on in a boardroom." Eventually, Robertson agreed to become a director provided that a third union seat would be added to attract an experienced labor statesman. The JSC allowed the change, and to be fair provided management with an additional seat.

Within a week, the prospective board had grown from ten to fourteen, with eight independents, three union, and three management members, or, it should be said, three potential management members, because Loughead, who automatically would hold one seat, had the option to appoint the other two. However, it soon became clear that he would not put executives on the board, choosing to serve as management's sole voice.

Based on Robertson's research, the ISU started talking to an array of labor notables. The union contacted Douglas Frazier, the president of the United Auto Workers, who sat on Chrysler's board. But Frazier said he would need the approval of his fellow AFL-CIO chieftain, Lloyd McBride, president of the archnemesis USW, and the ISU lost interest. The union talked to Wayne Horowitz, the well-regarded former director of the Federal Mediation Service. But, Horowitz, according to Robertson, "oversold" himself during an interview with the ISU. Robertson and some of the sports-conscious unionists also became attracted to Marvin Miller, the lead negotiator for baseball players during their strike in the early 1980s. Robertson came to view Miller as "probably too confrontational for what we were trying to achieve here." Also, Robertson recalled, "Sperry got so pissed off when [Miller's] name was suggested," mainly because former baseball commissioner Bowie Kuhn was a partner in Willkie Farr, which counted professional baseball among its clients. Though initially fascinated by the overture, Miller drew back, saying "he just didn't know that much about the steel industry." Miller, however, recommended Irving Bluestone, a former United Auto Workers official, whom he called the "brains" of the UAW on profit sharing, health care, and employee participation. Frazier also had mentioned Bluestone to Robertson, who now included him in the search.

The union approached Bluestone through Josh Gotbaum, whose father had known the former United Auto Workers vice president in labor circles. The ISU sent a delegation to Detroit to meet Bluestone, then teaching in the Labor Studies graduate program at Wayne State University, before inviting him to address the stewards at Weirton.

A short, kindly, intense intellectual with a hint of a Brooklyn accent, the former UAW leader had suffered through the Depression in a single-parent family, then studied German literature at City College of New York in its heyday and in Berne, Switzerland. Returning to New York before World War II, he found himself jobless, sold household goods door-to-door, worked as a volunteer picket for the International Ladies' Garment Workers' Union (ILGWU), and ended up on an assembly line in a General Motors plant in New Jersey, where he became chairman of the bargaining committee. After the war, Walter Reuther, the UAW president, tapped Bluestone for his staff. Over the next three decades, he held a succession of union jobs, including director of the General Motors Department, where he supervised contractual relations, and vice president.

Somewhat of a maverick, in the 1960s as an assistant to Walter Reuther he became "highly supportive of getting involved in employee ownership possibilities, especially where a company would go out of business or intended to go out of business and perhaps the employees would take it over." He also became very interested in "the joint action process between union and management and became a strong advocate of that in the UAW." Not surprisingly, for Bluestone, "it was kind of a lonely period." While holding the extremely unusual notion in the union movement "that labor contracts represent an infringement upon the unfettered right of management to manage," Bluestone also relentlessly criticized the Frederick Taylor scientific management process in which "workers were told what to do. They weren't allowed to think." As a result, managers "were missing greater opportunities for themselves in not using the brain power, the knowledge, experience, and creativity of the workforce. But perhaps even more importantly, they were demeaning to employees, who outside the workplace were treated with due respect given to rational qualified adults. But at work, they were treated simply as robots." To Bluestone, employee participation "was an expansion of the basic goal of industrial unionism, and worker ownership was part and parcel of that."

He became an early proponent of quality circles, small joint labor-management teams focused on improving the job and the product. The notion had tough sledding initially, especially at GM. In the early 1970s, Bluestone vocalized an especially offbeat idea for an industrial unionist. "I became terribly worried about the quality of the cars that were coming out because post–World War II, they could produce anything they damned well pleased and could sell it. They dominated the economy of the world. In 1972, I wrote a bulletin notice and sent it out to all GM local unions, asking them to post this notice on all union bulletin boards, throughout their facilities, thousands of them. What it said was, quality equals employment security. I pointed out that if the engineering is right, if the tools are proper, if the worker has enough time to do the job, everybody can put out a good quality product. We want to do that. This is an obligation, a responsibility of us as workers. Quality sells, therefore that equals job security. Bad quality doesn't sell and you're out of a job. A couple of weeks after these bulletin notices went out, I got a call from GM, telling me, demanding, that we take the bulletin notices down, because quality is their business, not ours. What they really objected to was that I questioned whether the engineering was proper, I questioned whether they had the right tools, whether we were giving the people enough time to do the job. Of course, I didn't have the bulletin notices taken down."

Belatedly, the car companies came around to his views in favor of more shop floor involvement in decision making. In negotiations, he pressed GM to form the Joint National Committee to Improve the Quality of Work Life, a board-based blue-collar and white-collar experiment, subsequently known simply as QWL.

In the 1980s, Bluestone testified to the Senate on worker alienation, emerging trends in collective bargaining, union democracy, effective utilization of labor, and humanizing the American factory, an "endless treadmill" where the "butt of [the] system is the worker." When Bluestone laid out his notions on employee involvement to the stewards at Weirton, he perceived a "general negative reaction." National had tried to impose some of the same ideas, "but instead of involving the union they did it as a management operation, did it unilaterally and in such a fashion that all they did was antagonize people because they [National] portrayed this as something that management got gain out of." Nevertheless, Bluestone later received a call from "Walter or from Dave, to the effect that they had voted to ask me to serve on the board. I was delighted."

First, however, he toured the entire plant, and then phoned the United Steelworkers and set up a meeting with its president, Lloyd

McBride. "If there was going to be any ill-will toward the UAW by reason of this, I wanted to know it." Not objecting, McBride and his aides told Bluestone that "if it [the Weirton ESOP] could work out, it would be very helpful to them," as a future model for saving jobs.

Bluestone agreed to the board seat at Weirton, as the union announced on August 12, 1983. His term was two years. Walter Bish could serve until the union's federally sanctioned election of January 1984. If Bish, who had already announced he would run again, won, he would get a new term on the board. Only David Robertson initially landed a full three-year term.

After accepting the seat, Bluestone became a key adviser to Bish, especially on issues of union governance and modernization. Bluestone also saw the ISU executive committee as anarchical and factionalized, and counseled changes to make power less equal among the divisional labor chieftains and more hierarchical with the union president at the top.

16 Democracy

> "Sure we could have held out for a little more representation and maybe a little clearer explanation, but I felt in principle it was the only way that this place was going to survive in some semblance of what Weirton had been."
>
> —FATHER CHARLES SCHNEIDER

For over a year, a well-publicized key tenet of fairness in the proposed ESOP involved the equal distribution of stock shares to employees regardless of rank. One day during the summer of 1983, Skip Spadafora, the young continuous caster operator with the financial background, who served on the ISU executive committee and JSC, nosed through volumes of the Internal Revenue Code in the General

Office law library, found a passage that attracted his attention, and took it home, studying for another three hours.

Spadafora also did something that lawyers should do, but often neglect—he uncrated the annually updated installments to the statute books called "pocket parts," and analyzed them in conjunction with the main body of the law. "I looked and looked and finally said, 'I'll be damned, they [the consultants] are horseshitting us. We're paying these guys all of this money and they don't even know what's going on.' "

His analysis showed that the Internal Revenue Service did not require equal stock distribution in qualified ESOP plans. Moreover, unequal allocation from a tax standpoint "ultimately was more favorable to the corporation and therefore more favorable to all of us." Naturally, highly paid employees such as Spadafora also would acquire the most equity in the new company through uneven distribution. Next, Spadafora laid out his proof to the JSC and the whole steward body. "I felt good about doing it [but] everything went into an uproar at this point. Things were starting to deteriorate."

Harvey Sperry, whose firm then assessed the situation, recalled acidly, "We found out it would only cost Weirton about twenty million dollars in lost tax deductions if we went per capita," that is, by equal allocation. To Sperry and others, the ESOP's competitive edge as well as its big attraction to lenders—tax advantages—never should be squandered. Blaming Jack Curtis for the error, Sperry drove the San Francisco lawyer and his partners out of the process. "They became," said Sperry, "superfluous." After more research, Lazard Frères, with the endorsement of Willkie Farr & Gallagher, sent a confidential memo to the Joint Study Committee retracting their earlier opinion favoring equal allocation:

> We originally recommended that each year every employee should receive an equal amount of the total stock allocated. We did so because a percentage concession to make Weirton successful would be at least as difficult for the lowest-paid person as for the highest-paid person and because everybody's sacrifice is necessary to make Weirton work.
>
> Unfortunately, as we have studied Weirton's finances and devel-

oped a financial structure for the new company, we have come to the conclusion that Weirton Steel, as a business, simply cannot afford the price that the tax laws place on equal allocation.

While equal allocation is permitted under the Internal Revenue Code, it would deny Weirton Steel, and thereby its employees/stockholders, millions of dollars each year. This result occurs because of the rules for calculating the tax benefits available to an ESOP.

Under the Internal Revenue Code, Weirton is allowed to deduct from its income tax an ESOP contribution equal to 25% of employee's wages. If allocation is based on compensation, the maximum possible deduction for all employees would come to about $45 million per year. Furthermore, each dollar deducted is added to Weirton's net worth.

Under equal allocation, Weirton's contribution to the ESOP trust would be the same for each employee. Since the 25% test would still apply, however, each employee's share must meet that test, too. As a result, under equal allocation, Weirton could contribute no more than 25% of the wage of the lowest paid participant. If the lowest paid employee earned $12,000 after the concession, for example, Weirton could contribute only 25%, or $3,000. For all 7,100 employees, this would limit the tax deduction and the ESOP contribution to $21 million—less than half the maximum possible deduction.

Over the years, the price Weirton would pay in lost tax deductions and lower equity would come to millions of dollars. For example, under the Lazard Frères & Co. projections, at the end of 1987, Weirton's net worth would be about $285 million. Under equal allocation, however, net worth is estimated at almost $30 million less. If Weirton Steel does better than Lazard's base case projections, the cost of equal allocation would be greater still. Under more optimistic projections, equal allocation would cut Weirton's net worth in 1987 almost $50 million.

Equal allocation would reduce the benefits of profit sharing as well. By limiting net worth, equal allocation could delay the start of profit sharing; by increasing Weirton's tax liability, it would reduce profit sharing in amount, perhaps by millions of dollars. It would also delay the allocation of stock to individual accounts.

For all these reasons, therefore, we think Weirton should allocate stock in proportion to compensation. The alternative is just too costly.

The consultants went on to question whether Weirton could afford to buy back stock from people "on demand" as the IRS required in ESOPs owned wholly by employees. The result would take out of the company valuable funds needed for capital expansion. According to Lazard, Weirton's employees faced a serious choice: "Permit Weirton stock to be bought by and sold to the public, like the stock of other major companies such as General Motors or IBM" (which meant that the company's control would shift to outside owners, and worth would be set by market forces), or "limit distribution to keep the stock in control of Weirton and its employees."

As Lazard stated, "This is not an easy choice. It would determine the company's future ownership and direction." As a result, Lazard recommended that the pivotal decision ultimately "not be decided by the Board [of the new company], but instead by a majority vote of all participants in the ESOP (including Weirton retirees) on a one man, one vote, basis." While the referendum could occur at "any time," Lazard predicted its occurrence near the end of the five-year safety net period. For the time being, stock ownership under the bylaws would be restricted to employees. But now, even before the sale from National the consultants revealed that they ultimately would prefer the public market option.

By contrast, Lazard and the other consultants favored pass-through voting on an egalitarian basis, which exceeded the Internal Revenue Code's requirement for ESOPs.

> We think pass-through voting should be provided even when the law does not require it. Specifically, we recommend that there be full pass-through voting, for both allocated and unallocated shares, on major corporate transactions. Furthermore, there should be full pass-through voting for directors after five years if stock distribution is delayed or limited.

Employees with large paychecks obviously would receive the most shares and thus the most votes. "This is the normal practice in corporate ownership." However, even the consultants wanted to prevent a "minority of employees from imposing its views on the majority." Therefore, during the first five years of operation, they favored "super-majority" approvals of at least two-thirds of the shares for "all major corporate transactions." For certain structural policy issues, which under law did not require stockholder ballots, such as amendments to the ESOP plan, or whether the ESOP could sell stock to an outside party, the consultants advocated decision making on a "one-man one-vote basis" irrespective of shareholdings.

As with many other Joint Study Committee documents, the consultants' memo, after about a month, found its way to the Rank and File Committee. Staughton Lynd deplored the "casual substitution of allocation of stock by compensation for equal allocation because of tax reasons." In an "urgent" letter to Peter Pitegoff, head of the Industrial Cooperative Association (ICA), and to Deborah Groban Olson, a Michigan attorney specializing in employee ownership issues, he wondered:

> Is there anything illegal in the proposed structure? If there is not anything illegal (and I do not see anything on the basis of my limited experience), what is your opinion of the package? It appears to me to combine some of the least democratic ESOP options:
>
> (1) Allocation of stock on the basis of compensation.
>
> (2) Public ownership of stock, sold in the name of early distribution of stock.

A week later Pitegoff stated: "As far as I can see, there is nothing illegal about the proposed structure." Due to a lack of financial projections, Pitegoff, unable to give an opinion on the tax loss triggered by shareholder equality, locked onto the public market question. At a minimum, the ICA chief believed that the new company, in order to preserve local control, should explore issuing different types of stock, targeting the public market with nonvoting preferred shares, while distributing common voting stock to the employees. "Admittedly," added Pitegoff, "the scheme is untested and would require an IRS ruling. But it is arguably consistent with the intent of ESOP legislation."

Pitegoff approved of the consultants' recommendation to allow all shareholder voting to be on a pass-through basis. "This is preferable and more democratic than unchecked voting by the ESOP trustee." But Pitegoff did not buy the consultants' argument that West Virginia state corporate laws on most issues required voting on a per share rather than per capita (one-man one-vote) basis. He pointed out that two ESOPs—Rath Packing and The Solar Center of California—implemented per capita voting despite "similar state law constraints," and that Jack Curtis of Ludwig & Curtis "played a role in structuring those ESOPs, and should be able to explain why that method is not being discussed at Weirton." However, Pitegoff did not know that Curtis had been pushed out of the inner circle at Weirton, and no longer had clout.

On August 25, 1983, Groban Olson likewise took a dim view of the consultants' plans. While conceding that distributing stock on the basis of pay is both legal and common in ESOPs, she disputed the argument that the major tax deduction would be lost if Weirton distributed stock equally. "Nowhere in the ESOP literature have I ever seen any statement that the tax savings is tied to the individual allocation as opposed to the total contribution to the ESOP during the employer's tax year."

Groban Olson predicted the public market issue could become as destructive and difficult to stop as a runaway locomotive.

If the company goes public the employees will lose control of it. If the company is successful and goes public they will lose control of it faster, but they will also make money as at Vermont Asbestos Group and Chicago Northwestern Railroad. If the goal of the buyout is for the community and the employees to gain control over job security in the Weirton area, public ownership will defeat that purpose unless the employees structure their ownership so that they retain a controlling interest in the collective hands of the active employees. The plan to distribute stock to employees early and have the company go public will make it almost impossible to retain such control in employee hands. Only if the employees own their stock through a closed trust (one that pays out only cash, not stock) or through a cooperative, can they retain control over it over any extended period.

Fighting this proposal may be difficult. Many of the employees will see the distribution and going public as a way to recoup in a few years the pay cuts they are taking now as part of their investment in the company. You will need to play on the community spirit that has grown up around the Weirton buyout to point out that the distribution and going public plan is not in the long-range interests of the community, although it may be in the best interests of some of the employees and of some outside investors or involved financial institutions. Any investors who have taken any kind of equity as security will want a public market as soon as possible.

Groban Olson termed the voting rights section of the consultants' report "a real sham."

The "major corporate issues" left for the employees to vote on are so major that they will almost never come up. Does West Virginia corporate law require voting by stockholders on any such issues? Does the corporate charter? If not, then the employees have no issues for which this so-called voting "pass through" exists.

In the interim, on August 19, 1983, the Joint Study Committee published the long-awaited "disclosure document," mailed it to the workforce, and filed it in Judge Maxwell's court. Prepared by Willkie Farr, the single-spaced eighty-six-page oversized booklet, dense with financial data and projections, looked like a corporate prospectus but supplied much more detail because its objective was to educate employees lacking investment experience. Because of the complexity of information that needed to be communicated and the limited time, the task was difficult, and in some cases the lawyers' drafting failed to clarify key matters. For example, on stock distribution from ESOP accounts, they wrote:

The ESOP provides that, after July 1, 1988, the ESOP will, on a Participant's request, make annual distributions of the total amount allocated to each Participant's ESOP account (through the last preceding allocation Date) (excluding any amounts allocated to his account within the two years prior to distribution unless he has participated in the ESOP for five full years). Distributions will be permitted only to the extent that the fair market value of Weirton Common Stock distributed to all Participants at such time will not, when subtracted from Weirton's Adjusted New Worth (as defined in the ESOP), reduce such net worth below $250 million.

However, despite turgid lapses, the disclosure document generally spelled out the facts necessary to make an informed decision—as the federal court found. Skip Spadafora likened the comprehensiveness of the document to the Prego spaghetti sauce commercial where the announcer says no matter what anyone wants in a sauce—"It's in there." Spadafora believed that the disclosure document likewise provided every detail that a voter would need to know. "It's in there," he would say, smiling.

Truly a unique piece of work, the disclosure document was written by lawyers who had no models or rules to follow. In the future, as the privatization of history proceeds, and the seminal papers of the modern corporate age are assembled in volumes—much as national historical materials, including the Declaration of Independence, Bill of Rights, and Gettysburg Address are compiled—it would not be surprising to find the Weirton disclosure document among the new source materials.

On August 23, 1983, union stewards and supervisors brought their copies of the document to a meeting in the General Office's amphitheater, where Walter Bish announced that the key ballots on Weirton's future would occur on September 23. They would have a month to study the booklet that explained that Weirton's fate pivoted on the word "if."

> The acquisition will be completed only if: (i) the Division's employees represented by the Independent Steelworkers Union (the "ISU") approve amendments to their current contracts with National, approve the Weirton ESOP and approve new contracts with Weirton; (ii) Weirton completes arrangements for financing to pay the purchase price; (iii) the courts determine that National is not required to pay shutdown pensions and severance on account of the sale of the Division; and (iv) certain other conditions specified in the sales contract are satisfied.

For the first time, the disclosure document established the true purchase price: $194.2 million, which was higher than the $181 million previously announced, but the wage and benefit cuts would be less steep. It was explained that the delays in releasing the booklet were the result of the search for financing, the selection of the board, and the creation of a new corporate structure. The disclosure document indicated that the trust would use a $120 million credit line, and that banks had been found, with Citibank as the lead lender. Stock, as the document made clear, would not be allocated per capita, but to employees according to their compensation. Not only would Weirton workers have to vote for the buyout, but National would not go through with it unless all the court cases and their appeals went its way.

The document settled the question of who would be allowed to vote on September 23. Because the ISU had come to its senses, both active and laid-off employees with recall rights would be given ballots.

At the meeting with stewards and foremen, Bish said the deal "offers a future to the employees, this town, and this valley which is far brighter than what anyone could have imagined some seventeen months ago." Bish called the proposal "very profitable to the employees. It was the best deal we could have received." But he cautioned: "It's just a one-shot deal."

Speaking next, an enthusiastic Loughead reminded those assembled that "Weirton Steel won't be confined to the limitations of the National Steel marketing plan. It's a new beginning for the employees and for me. ESOPs are the wave of the future." The incoming CEO said that he and Bish would be spearheading a new in-plant meeting drive to deal with questions from the disclosure document, and to get out the vote in favor of the buyout.

Already functioning as Loughead's trusted number two, Carl Valdiserri threw in that there would be a major recall of the mill's construction workers from layoff if the vote went well. Weirton, explained Valdiserri, would need about four hundred fifty workers to make capital improvements, such as relining a blast furnace and installing pollution controls.

The disclosure document answered other questions pending for over a year. It clearly revealed the estimated fees of the outside consultants:

McKinsey & Company, Inc.	$ 515,000.00
Lazard Frères & Co.	2,350,000.00
Ludwig & Curtis	110,000.00
Willkie Farr & Gallagher	2,150,000.00
Towers, Perrin, Forster & Crosby	65,000.00
Heidrich & Struggles, Inc.	178,000.00
	$5,368,000.00

Only about $1.2 million of the amount, which was staggering by West Virginia standards, had been raised. The remainder would become the responsibility of the new company.

The report gave a positive rationale for the different sizes of wage and benefits cuts to be taken by the hourly, salary, guard, and clerical employees: "Instead of each taking the same $7.87 per hour cut, it was more equitable and appropriate for a reduction by each employee group in proportion to its own average compensation. Thus more highly compensated employees would take a larger per hour cut."

The disclosure document announced that the independent Weirton would try to deal with labor costs in a new way. During the inflationary 1970s, annualized cost of living adjustments (COLA) in the USW contracts (which were copied by the ISU) helped to price American steelworkers out of the world market. Now, according to the disclosure document the COLAs would be dropped in favor of a liberal profit sharing matrix that would apply after the new company hit a net worth of $100 million, when a bonus equal to a third of net earnings would be distributed to employees. After the company's net worth reached $250 million, profit sharing at a whopping 50 percent level would begin.

The profit sharing provisions proved popular among the workforce because the disclosure document's financial forecasts made the $100 million and $250 million plateaus appear feasible. Year-end balance sheet projections predicted that "total shareholders equity" would climb to $115 million by the end of 1985 and to $277 million by the end of 1988, based on predictions of shipments shooting from 1.5 million tons to almost 2 million tons by 1988. Profit sharing applied to both the salary and hourly ranks but was especially critical to the latter, whose wages would be frozen during the first six years of the ESOP, unlike the executive employees for whom "future levels of compensation, related benefits and other terms of employment . . . will be matters within the discretion of Weirton's Board of Directors. Accordingly, Weirton's Board of Directors may decide, depending upon future events not currently ascertainable, that levels of compensation applicable to non-represented employees may be increased or decreased in appropriate cases or under appropriate circumstances."

The disclosure document included other belt-tightening measures on which the employees would vote on September 23: reducing the number of paid holidays from eleven to five, modifying insurance benefits, and eliminating the one-hour meal allowance as well as various lucrative overtime computation schemes. But the bottom line was the expectation of keeping and even expanding the workforce, which Carl Valdiserri promised the stewards and supervisors that they would see immediately. Moreover, management alluded that a favorable vote would mean that the union could bid on work that previously had been contracted out.

In effect, the campaign was on for the upcoming vote. During the first week in September, the JSC and the Weirton Women's Club invited more than six hundred employees' spouses to breakfast meetings on the referendum. Expanded teams of union and management leaders trained in the nuances of the disclosure document operated phone hot lines to provide immediate answers. Robert Loughead guested on a televised call-in show, appeared at in-plant meetings four to five times daily, often with Walter Bish, and on several occasions spoke to audiences of hundreds of employees and their families at St. John's Arena.

From the first, Loughead showed himself to be more than a cheerleader. Frank about Weirton's problems, he spoke of immediate needs to get advertising and marketing programs up and running, since these functions had always been handled by National. He pointed out issues in the proposed deal that still needed to be clarified, such as which company would control the resources and personnel of MUD, and the fact that National's promise to allocate orders to Weirton on a historical basis was "being adhered to in a less than perfect fashion." Loughead saw the "unique" situation in terms of "many opportunities and many problems, but nothing insurmountable with good planning, creativity, and hard work." He hoped to create a national "model of employee participation." Perhaps the toughest questions he took involved his absent predecessor. He answered honestly that he had had no contact with Jack Redline since the announcement of Loughead's installation as CEO. Nevertheless, he assured crowds that Redline had "no desire to do us harm."

Going all out for the referendum, the ISU bought full-page ads in the Weirton, Steubenville, and Wheeling papers, with bold print explanations of why a "yes" vote was needed. The union hired a fleet of buses to get its members, active and laid-off, to the polls, and rented twenty-five automated voting machines. The ISU officers agreed to form a phone bank to notify the laid-off employees individually of the situation. Some of these workers had been absent so long that no union leaders recognized them, but the ISU agreed to admit anyone with some form of valid identification to a polling station.

Before the vote, it became clear that much of the Rank and File's agenda had been absorbed into the process, including reduced wage cuts, pass-through voting, enfranchisement of laid-off workers, disclosure in minute detail about the ESOP, its structure, and finances, and the removal of old-line management as exemplified by Jack Redline. Nonetheless, the Rank and File continued its attack at public meetings, now not well attended, and by passing out position papers entitled "Vote NO Until You Know," and "Oh Say Can You See?" which argued that disclosure to the workforce remained inadequate. The dissidents stressed that the workforce was being asked to vote based on a summary of the new labor contract with its no-strike clause, six-year freeze on wages, and no COLAs, while the actual proposed contract was never presented. The RFC challenged language that appeared in the disclosure document, usually on the grounds of vagueness. For instance, it raised questions about a clause asserting that "management rights provisions *shall not be* a subject of arbitration." "Does this mean," asked the Rank and File, "that management will be given powers that cannot even be arbitrated?"

The Rank and File noted wiggle room in the disclosure document's summary on seniority, which stated that the present agreement with National would be duplicated "subject to several modifications." The dissidents objected: "Surely we must know what the modifications are on this—the most important thing there is to a steel-worker!"

To the Rank and File, the "most dangerous clause of all" in the disclosure document was one that mentioned that if the United Steelworkers decided to grant additional concessions not contained in their master agreement with Big Steel, then Weirton labor and management would be "obligated to meet to bargain," in order to preserve their competitive position. "This means," insisted the Rank and File, "that FUTURE CONCESSIONS ARE *BUILT INTO* YOUR CONTRACT!"

The Rank and File gibed Loughead for periodic public pronouncements that he wanted to make the new company "leaner." To the Rank and File, this signaled "NO HOPE FOR LAID-OFF EMPLOYEES."

On September 21, the Rank and File went into court again, asking Judge Maxwell to postpone the union vote and delay the sale since the employees had not been given a full text of the new contract, and because the disclosure document still shrouded the McKinsey appendix and failed to explain the 18.38 percent concession. The RFC took the position that only a 10 percent cut could be justified.

Robert Loughead implored the court to allow the vote to proceed as planned on Friday, September 23. He pointed out that the wage and benefit concessions, if approved by the electorate, were scheduled to go into effect on Sunday, September 25. Every day of delaying the concessions would cost Weirton $130,000. The Rank and File's hoped-for postponement of forty-five days would cost about $6 million. Loughead underscored that these weren't just savings to the mill, but would harm the employees directly since it would be "necessary for the new company to overcome those losses before it can commence employee profit sharing." In addition, capital plans dependent on cash flow would be stalled.

Advising the court that he previously had told customers that the vote would occur on September 23, Loughead warned that a postponement would diminish "our credibility in the marketplace. If the vote is delayed, I believe that our potential customers will be little interested in any explanation that we may be able to offer. Instead, they will lose confidence in our future and our stability as a reliable source of supply, and they will take their orders elsewhere."

Loughead also cited an obscure portion of the disclosure document in which National agreed to allow the division to spend money to re-line a blast furnace before the buyout but only after an affirmative vote. Loughead cautioned that "the two blast furnaces currently operating are now at the end of their useful lives. Should those furnaces fail without the division's being able to bring the newly relined furnace on-line, a substantial disruption of the division's steel making operations would result because we would lose one-half of our hot metal production capability." Moreover, according to the new president, "the reline project means jobs," as up to 130 employees would be recalled from layoff to do the work. On the other hand, if the vote was blocked by the Rank and File, Loughead foresaw losing key employees to other companies or early retirement.

After apprising the court of all the arrangements—voting machines, buses, ballots, literature, etc.—which would be wasted by a postponement, Walter Bish argued that delay surely would result in a lower turnout if the referendum ever were rescheduled, as well as a skewed perception in the community. Calling it "likely that a large number of employees would interpret the delay as indicating that there is some serious flaw in the proposed transaction or in the disclosure document," Bish insisted that "this will lend undeserved credibility to the handful of persons who for whatever reasons have sought to prevent or delay the acquisition of the division by the employees, and would no doubt be unfairly exploited by that small group of dissidents in the interim before the rescheduled vote." Bish chastised the Rank and File for unnecessarily "imposing on the court at the very last moment," and for seeking "to sow doubt concerning the proposed transaction throughout the Weirton community."

Lynd and the Rank and File Committee took the unusual step of calling the Joint Study Committee's lawyer, Anthony Phillips of Willkie Farr, as a witness and demanding that he produce the confidential McKinsey appendix on the spot. Phillips refused to turn over the disputed document voluntarily, despite arguments from Lynd that the employees would be voting shortly and still had no clear rationale for the concessions that they were asked to approve. Phillips said that the only full copy of the appendix was with his firm; even Lazard had received only a digest of it. Still declining to release the appendix publicly, Judge Maxwell ordered Phillips to submit a copy into the record "under seal" so that the Court of Appeals could determine if Maxwell had erred, but no party could see the sensitive material. "In conclusion," ruled Maxwell, "the court finds nothing wrong with a procedure whereby a union and an employer jointly retain an expert firm to accumulate confidential data, analyze it, and report to both groups via a [disclosure] document that focuses on the conclusions drawn without revealing all of the underlying information."

Phillips stressed that Weirton's fate should be settled by its employees rather than by a lawsuit. "All that [the Rank and File] say is that they have certain contrary arguments to and criticisms of the proposed transaction. Those arguments should be presented by plaintiffs, if at all, to the union members and not to this court."

Finding that harm of delaying the referendum far outweighed the harm of holding it, Judge Maxwell denied the Rank and File's motion for an injunction. The vote would occur.

After the hearing, Steve Bauman announced that the Rank and File would appeal to a higher court, but conceded that this would be impossible before the vote. "If the worker," said Bauman, "is going to have trust in the system, he needs to be given the reasons why he was asked to take these deductions." Bauman deplored that "the information can be given to a Manhattan law firm, but not to the workers of Weirton, West Virginia." He added that the Rank and File did not oppose establishing an ESOP, but merely wanted the best deal for the workers. Angered, Walter Bish lashed back in an interview: "They want to stop the vote for some reason and are trying to undermine all efforts by the Joint Study Committee and ISU officials. . . . It is unfortunate that a few dissidents have caused the expense and time it took for us to go down there and defend ourselves. It is clear for some reason unknown to us they want the project to fail. . . . Whatever their intent it was not for the betterment of the community or fellow workers."

Now speaking virtually around the clock, Bish and members of the JSC explained the three issues on the ballot, each of which had to receive a majority vote of the unionized employees for the deal to go through. First, the workers would vote on a union contract with the new Weirton Steel Corporation, freezing wages for six years, barring strikes, and eliminating cost-of-living increases (COLAs) but instituting profit sharing. Second, they would decide on amendments to the existing labor contract with National to clarify that the buyout would not trigger pensions and shutdown pay. Third, they would be asked to approve the purchase of the division by an employee stock ownership plan, which would make Weirton the nation's largest ESOP. Keenly aware that management employees were not under contract and had no vote, and that the union would resolve the question for the entire workforce, Bish urged a large turnout and majority. "This is a decision they are making on their futures. I would be disappointed if people sit back and don't exercise the right to vote, that they would take it so lightly."

In the days before the election, flags and ribbons hung throughout the Panhandle. Workers sported campaign buttons reading, "Yes, Yes, Yes." Billboards sprouted depicting a pair of hands cradling a clutch of homes and smokestack factories, like so many Monopoly pieces, beside the caption: "*Your* future is in *your* hands." The union's sixty-four officers phoned twenty-three hundred laid-off employees to remind them to vote. All of the region's newspapers editorialized in favor of an affirmative vote. "There is," wrote the *Wheeling Intelligencer*, "no choice, really, in the matter of balloting today on whether there will be an Employee Stock Ownership Plan at Weirton Steel. That is, there really is no question but to vote 'yes' for those whose desire it is to preserve a chance of future prosperity for the mammoth complex which is the heart and soul of Weirton and environs."

Religious leaders rallied the community. The Catholic churches of Weirton, whose parishes included most of the workforce, came up with the slogan "Believe in Weirton, Jesus does." These churches also developed a special ESOP prayer, which it printed on cards and passed out in the community.

> O God our Father, we praise you and give you thanks for the many blessings you have poured out upon us.
>
> We are now in the midst of economic uncertainty and look to you for strength and guidance.
>
> Strengthen our hearts that we may face the days ahead with hope and confidence.
>
> Help us join with our brothers and sisters of the valley, that united

in Christ and guided by the Holy Spirit, we may find a just and lasting solution to the problems which confront us.

Amen

Prior to the referendum the Catholic churches also put a full-page message in the local papers.

The people of the upper Ohio Valley, particularly the employees of Weirton Steel, are being asked to make a decision affecting our lives and the lives of many others in our valley. The Catholic Church has traditionally spoken out in favor of the rights and dignity of all workers, both labor and management.

Pope John Paul II, in his encyclical of September 15, 1981, entitled *On Human Work*, states a number of principles concerning workers and the workplace. He affirms the primary importance of the worker over the means of production and further encourages worker ownership of those means. These statements follow in the great tradition of Catholic Church teachings on work and the workplace developed over the past 90 years. The Weirton Steel ESOP appears to be very much in line with these teachings.

Each of us has a stake in the upcoming vote. We are being asked to determine our community's future. We are being asked to make a sacrifice on behalf of that future. In light of the Catholic Church's teachings and of the hope that Weirton remain a vibrant community, prayer and a spirit of cooperation is necessary in all walks of life. We must pray that barriers and prejudices between labor and management, millworker and non-millworker and any other groups be overcome.

We, therefore, feel that it is our responsibility to encourage full and prayerful consideration of the proposed Employment Stock Ownership Plan (ESOP) for the Weirton Steel Company.

Mindful of all these needs, we as a Catholic community restate our concern and prayers for ESOP and ask that all of us give it our fullest consideration. With God's help and our own sincere efforts "We Can Do It."

The local religious activism occurred during a period when the National Conference of Bishops was preparing the pastoral letter "Economic Justice for All," the goal of which was to apply the Church's teachings to the national economy. A leader in the movement was Father Charles Schneider of Saint Joseph the Worker, the largest parish in the Panhandle.

A slight, relaxed man in wire-rim glasses who had a wise smile and an ever-present cigarette, Schneider had been a priest for twenty-five years. Before that he had worked as an industrial engineer at a huge Montgomery Ward catalog center in Albany, New York, where he felt weighed down by "the unhappiness of the employees and their inability to take risks." After becoming a priest, he was assigned to dwindling coal-mining parishes in Appalachia. "Prior to coming to Weirton, I had been exposed to out-migration in every community I'd ever been in. Weirton seemed different. When I came [here], I said, my what a delightful change. Young people are here. Everybody seems to be working. There doesn't seem to be the big economic depression that I experienced everywhere else I had ever been. This was not Appalachia."

In 1982 following National's announcement, he saw his mission as two-fold. First, he wanted to avoid another Youngstown-type shutdown of basic industry. Second, he knew from experience that once again he would face "out-migration," because the eventual company would have to be lean and competitive, and would not employ at the same levels as in the past. From the outset, he cast his lot with the ESOP. "The Popes going back to the nineteen thirties have talked about the only way capitalism will be acceptable versus communism—the worker has to have a piece of the action. He has to somehow share the ups and downs."

After the bishop in Wheeling designated Father Schneider as his personal liaison in Weirton regarding the ESOP issues, the priest began trying to unify disparate local churches around the buyout. "This was really the first time in the history of this community that they ever got together for anything—they were always in competition, perhaps due to their differing ethnic complexions." For instance, Father Schneider's church was heavily Italian, including, he said, smiling, many postwar immigrants who had fought for Mussolini, while Sacred Heart of Mary included "anyone who's Polish in town."

All the churches began saying the ESOP prayer every day. In the Fourth of July parade, they bought a float with the banner "With God's Help—We Can Do It." One gap in the unity involved the Steubenville parish in which some of the clergy, taking its cue from the Rank and File Committee, "just smelled a rat." Father Schneider did not attempt to change the anti-ESOP view among clergy in Steubenville. "I just ignored it." As for the Rank and File, "I just did not feel they were credible. They weren't. One meeting was held over here at the high school, another one was held at the K of C. I went. I said I think before you make these facilities available in the future you better find out what this is all about. They were saying that they are doing it in the name of the Catholic Church, but I didn't feel that they had all their marbles. I felt the overwhelming thrust of the Catholic Church has been in the direction of ESOP. That was it."

He recognized that the ESOP presented in the disclosure document was not perfect. "Sure we could have held out for a little more representation and maybe a little clearer explanation, but I felt in principle it was the only way that this place was going to survive in some semblance of what Weirton had been."

During the grim winter of 1982–1983, when employment hit historical lows in Weirton, Schneider helped form a coalition with most of the community's other non-evangelical churches. "We felt that the best thing as church people we can do is to help the unemployed people in Weirton." Families that previously had had well-paid wage earners, who now were laid off, were struggling and sometimes losing their homes and hungry. Schneider found them too proud to take handouts directly, so at Christmas the churches began sending bags of groceries and other donations home with the children. The economic problems had husbands and wives "at each other's throats and miserable," so the churches held a dance and provided child care to "give them a night out." Perhaps above all the Ecumenical Coalition, as it became known, started Change Incorporated, a nonprofit agency dedicated to finding jobs around the country for those laid off without enough seniority to have a likely shot at a position in the ESOP. The Change office subscribed to newspapers from about sixty metropolitan areas, installed a WATS line so that people could respond quickly to want ads, and translated résumés out of steel industry jargon into general market terms so that, for example, mill-wrights and riggers could apply for skilled machinist and construction positions.

"Shipping people out of Weirton was tough [but] we were realistic that Weirton was never going to have ten or thirteen thousand employees again." Because closely tied extended families had been part of the way of life in the Panhandle, the churches counseled that out-migration did not spell the end of relationships. "We would tell them, yes, your Susie or Tom is in Houston or Raleigh, North Carolina, but you are not losing them forever in the sense that there are telephones and good roadways now and you can go back and forth."

To Father Schneider, Weirton had a better chance than the defeated steel communities in Pittsburgh's "Mon" (for Monongahela) Valley. "I think maybe everybody there was doing their own thing and there wasn't any coalition or cohesiveness. Here, the church played a very important role behind the scenes. As I look back, we were all fighting for the very existence of our parish and community. If they closed the mill down and didn't go ESOP all these huge complexes would be empty," he said, waving at the cluster of buildings associated with the church. "We have sixteen years of education right here in this two-block area counting the community college, which is not Catholic, but that doesn't matter. It's survival."

On the day before the vote, rallies and services were held at churches in the Ecumenical Coalition. By evening, the participants had funneled into a candlelight vigil of more than a thousand people on Penco Road, not far from the General Office, where the crowd chanted "We Can Do It," and "We Will Do It." In the evening chill Father Schneider told the group, "It has been raining in the Ohio Valley for the past eighteen months. Ever since National made the announcement a cloud has been hanging over the community. Now God's help has been received." Robert Loughead said in his speech that "the community is on the eve of a most important day, and seeks guidance from God for that effort." Jay Rockefeller said, "It's an historic occasion for American industry and labor, and an important one. I want to be here when the vote is counted. It's important to the state and its families. Everyone has something at stake."

The next morning it became clear that the turnout would be heavy.

USA Today predicted a landslide. For fifteen hours, the unionized employees voted in the gymnasium at the Millsopp Community Center. When it was over, they had approved the three ballot questions by about a seven-to-one margin. On the question "Whether to ratify the new Weirton Steel labor contract," the employees voted yes: 6,136 to 872. On the second issue, which involved amending the existing contracts to prevent pensions and shutdown benefits, the vote was slightly closer: 5,942 to 1,036. By the widest margin, 6,203 to 744, the unionized workers adopted the ESOP concept as defined in the disclosure document.

When the results were announced, horns honked, sirens blared, thousands of green balloons filled the sky, "We Did It" banners unfurled, and an impromptu parade of pickups, police cruisers, and tow trucks wove through town. At the community center the leaders and consultants spoke to a crowd in a victory mood, and more than a hundred members of local and national media. Bish promised Loughead a new era of cooperation between the ISU and management "to make this steel facility the finest in the world." Loughead pledged: "We are going to have a successful operation. I just don't think you can have anything with respect to so many committed and dedicated people without it spelling success. I am," he added, "looking forward to being here a long time. . . . We are facing facts. Everyone has to pull his own weight. Sustained efficient performance by the team is our objective. We recognize the need for change in some of the affairs of our company. We must do things differently than in prior years . . . create and apply new remedies to old problems. The status quo is gone."

Not flanked as usual by David Robertson, whose mother had died the day before, Walter Bish stood beside Irving Bluestone, his fellow member of the board of directors, who had flown in from Detroit. To Bish, his membership's vote "not only will save jobs and the community, as was our intent, but [it] gives us an opportunity to be owners of a Fortune 300 Company, share in profits and be stockholders. That's quite an accomplishment."

Bish declared that the ESOP would herald a new period of employee involvement. "That's one of the basic ideas of an ESOP, more worker participation, giving the worker in the mill direct input into the way the company is run. Of course, we realize management is needed to operate and manage the new company, but feel one of the primary aspects of making the ESOP work is having that worker actually participate in his job."

"In the past," Bluestone interjected, "management had the attitude—a worker is hired from the neck down."

"We want," chimed in Bish, "the whole worker under the ESOP and one of the most important parts of the worker is going to be his mind and ideas."

When asked why he thought Weirton had attracted national and international attention, Bish said, "You pick up a paper and see factory closings and unemployment rising, and here it shows a factory has been given an alternative to closing. . . . We have been given a chance here and are doing something about it. Hopefully in the last eighteen months a deal was constructed with the help of consultants and legal advisors that our people can be proud of and is something we can make work and operate."

As for the delay, "It was justifiable. We went into this very objectively. I don't think we left any stone unturned. It wasn't something we rushed through just to have a vote and be on our own. We have taken all the necessary precautions and of course it took time."

Jay Rockefeller congratulated the people of Weirton. "I doubt there is anywhere in the state which is so totally together and so totally united in a common purpose."

Not yet viable, the ESOP still had to survive the final decisions of a Federal Court of Appeals. However, on Sunday, September 25, the new compensation reductions began and were placed in an interest-bearing escrow account. The average production or maintenance worker would receive a biweekly pay check about $150 to $175 lighter than from National. If the court ruled against National, and the deal failed to close, the workers would get their money back. The average hourly cut amounted to $4.88, which was down from $7.97 based on McKinsey's original 32 percent slice. Over six years, even the reduced cuts would save the company about $140 million. Weirton was poised to become not only the nation's largest entirely employee-owned company, but also its tenth-largest steelmaker (just behind Ford's Rouge River Company). National fell from fourth to seventh.

Not everyone in Weirton was delighted about the ESOP structure, the cut, or the performance of the Joint Study Committee. "They've put the whole thing in the hands of a Manhattan law firm," said Steve Bauman, which is something like handing your kids over to cannibals." The Rank and File also took strong exception to the fact that the independents on the board, all of whom had been chosen by Lazard, would pick their own successors after five years, and that failure of the ESOP and default on the loan agreement with Citibank would lead to breaking up of the assets; while success would provide incentives for employees to sell their shares and end local control. Staughton Lynd continued to call the 18 percent wage cut "unexplained and unjustifiable." He scored the deal's terms "as just terrible. Worker ownership Wall Street Style." Corey Rosen, leader of the liberal National Center for Employee Ownership (NCEO), who had followed the deal closely, conceded: "There was pressure from the investment bankers to do it in the least democratic way and to go public as quickly as possible [but] for a company of its size, with a handful of exceptions, Weirton is the most democratic of the large ESOPs."

Despite their view, Lynd, Bauman, and the Rank and File chose not to appeal their court case, figuring that their complaint on the confidential material had been weakened by the distribution of the disclosure document and the overwhelming popular vote. However, at the end of September, Red Arango and the Concerned Steel Workers announced that they would take their shutdown pay issue to the Fourth Circuit Court of Appeals in Richmond. "If they didn't," said David Robertson, "frankly, we would be shocked." National indicated that it would apply to the court for an emergency expedited review.

17   On Our Own

"Now I'll go back to my office and jump up and down."
—ROBERT LOUGHEAD

After the referendum, the ISU leadership's sense of triumph mingled with frustration over the fact that another vote for union officers, in accordance with the Department of Labor's requirement, fast approached. On September 28, 1983, a union contingent including Ed Conley, Tom Gaudio, Craig Petrella, and Ed Martin met in Pittsburgh with representatives of the Department of Labor, which took a surprisingly hard line. The government insisted that candidacy for the union's executive committee be opened to all ISU members, not simply stewards; that nominations for the rerun election be opened to all members including those laid off; and that laid-off members, including even those whose recall rights had expired, be permitted to vote. Labor, however, allowed the ISU to limit the vote to those who had paid dues. The department also chilled the ISU group by indicating that it now wanted to scrutinize stewards' elections, since the stewards were "officers" of the union under the current bylaws.

The following day the executive committee met and decided not to accept the department's position, but to negotiate against it. Ben Wade said, "We don't want laid-off to run [for office] or the executive committee to be nominated at large." Ed Martin, who had met with Labor added: "This union is as good as there is, and I can't agree to a change. Let's make a final proposal, and tell them to sue us." Calm as usual, Walter Bish stated that the "rerun should be with old nominations. We can let the laid-off vote, and clean up the union bylaws." While no final decision was made, the executive committee reached a consensus for the union attorneys to come up with a proposal to the Labor Department "as close to what we have now as possible."

In New York, the Willkie Farr attorneys also took steps to design the future. In October, they completed the critical subscription and stock purchase agreement for the ESOP, in which the trustee would obtain 6.5 million shares at the closing, for which he would sign a $300,000,000 promissory note that tracked the interest rate of the Citicorp loan, and required payments in the maximum amount allowed by the IRS. Indeed, the overall plan was structured to shelter every penny. The principal would be paid off over ten years in annual installments of $30 million each. In November, Loughead told *Iron Age* that with labor cost reductions of $120 million, he expected an operating profit of $88 million with a net profit of $8 million in the upcoming year. He broadly hinted that the coke batteries would not be restored. "That's a big item. The price tag is $75 million." What to do with the numerous employees in the coking "progression" was still an unsolved problem. Loughead seemed to be of two minds. Aware that "this is an employee-owned company and the essence of this transaction was jobs," he nonetheless sometimes advocated trimming operations to impart efficiency. "When you're talking about what facilities you're going to operate, and what levels you're going to operate, I think you have to take the same things into account whether you're employee-owned or not employee-owned."

Echoed by local management, remarks about efficiency and streamlining received a cool response on the mill floor. In perhaps related incidents, in November a pipe bomb was discovered at the continuous caster, and at the blast furnace three hundred cable tags were vandalized.

The union also continued to spar with the Department of Labor. In December the executive committee was in a refractory mood. Nick Petrovich wanted the department's charges redefined with more specificity. Ed Conley maintained that "we can't agree to another election without membership approval." In other words, there would have to be a time-consuming referendum to decide whether to rerun the election. Skip Spadafora said "I won't run," if the election were to be held under Labor's decision to open committee voting to the full membership. Conley, without resistance, urged that the union meet again with the department.

On December 30, 1983, the Fourth Circuit Court of Appeals in Richmond, Virginia, affirmed Judge Maxwell's rulings that employee buyout of the Weirton division would not trigger shutdown pensions and severance benefits. No further obstacles remained in the way of the deal with National.

It was not the most auspicious time for starting an ESOP. *The Nation* called Weirton "a shaky, unprofitable firm facing cut throat competition in a stagnant market." Only a month earlier, Rath Packing, an earlier hope of the ESOP movement and especially its democratic wing, had filed for bankruptcy.

Toward the end of the year, Irving Bluestone gave Walter Bish two key pieces of advice. A stickler for stabilizing the union's role and power, Bluestone noticed that there were no set provisions for picking the future labor representatives to the board. He urged Bish to get the union bylaws changed so that the ISU president would automatically be placed on the board of directors, and so that written provisions would define the method for choosing the other two labor directors. Bluestone believed that such steps would make the union seats less potentially open to demagogues or to legal challenges.

The retired UAW official also was concerned about the staffing of the ESOP administrative committee, a five-member group, including two ISU representatives, which would exercise day-to-day oversight and interpretation of the complex workings of the relationship between the trust and the employee-owners. Since many of the functions of the group would be "technical and complex," Bluestone warned that "frequent changes in the ISU appointees . . . could be disruptive, requiring a relearning process each time a change in personnel occurs." Therefore, he argued in favor of long-term "continuity of participation." Equally important, he believed, the selection should be "as nonpolitical as possible."

On January 12, 1984, the new corporation finally closed the deal with National in an official signing ceremony at the Millsopp Community Center. The wall-to-wall crowd of executives in suits and workers in "world's largest ESOP" T-shirts mixed in front of a marble cake baked to feed a thousand and inscribed with "On Our Own Again."

With a flourish, Loughead stroked the papers transferring assets from National, and then signed the $120 million loan agreement with Citicorp and its support banks, Ameritrust of Ohio, Comerica of Detroit, and Pittsburgh National. Finally, beaming, he cut the first slice of cake, and shyly presented it to Walter Bish's wife as if she were the bride of the ESOP.

Taking the microphone, Pete Love lauded Weirton's negotiators. "They were tough bargainers, but I think we came out with an agreement we all can live with and will be good for both of us to prosper and succeed in the future." His joke that it "will be tougher than hell to compete against the Weirton Steel Corporation, but we will still beat them" did not go over well. Love explained that National simply hadn't had the cash flow to support Weirton, and now wished it well. He did not foresee other steel divestitures in National's future. While toasting "a very great day," Love noted "a feeling of melancholy on the part of National" as he remembered the dominant role of Weir and Weirton in founding the corporation.

"Now," said Walter Bish, "comes the hard part. Hopefully in the future we will look back and say we got our start from National Steel." The union "wants to make this the finest steel company in the world." The band struck up "We're On Our Own," a song recently recorded in Nashville and played on Ohio Valley stations.

That Weirton pride came shining through
We always knew what we had to do.
We're on our own; we're on our way . . .
Though it's been rough—we've been together every day . . .
The future's now; tomorrow's here.
Our course is set; our goals are clear.
Now we can grow because we know
We're on our own; we're on our way.
So tell the world that Weirton Steel is here to stay.
So tell the world that Weirton made it.
We're on our own; we're on our way.

Loughead kindled hope by telling the crowd, "I really think eventually a great many laid-off people from Weirton will one day again work here." He predicted that the company would soon be in the black, or else he would be fired.

Under ESOP Weirton has the unique opportunity to expand employee involvement in quality, cost control, safety, productivity— matters which influence performance and profitability. Because employees have a proprietary interest in the company, they are challenged to use their energy, imagination and initiative to help in solving problems. We anticipate an enthusiastic response to challenge. We are poised for success.

"Now," said Loughead, "I'll go back to my office and jump up and down."

Most of the nation's press gave Weirton a fighting chance at success. In its editorial entitled "When Labor Owns the Mill," the *New York Times* assured that "Weirton employees are not inheriting a rust bucket."

PART TWO

Gain

18 Changing the Culture

"Drive out fear so that everyone can work effectively for the company."

—W. Edwards Deming

For all its convoluted drama, the buyout had been a straightforward deal. The new company came away with a top ten steel mill complex with an excellent reputation for $66 million, roughly a fifth of its book value. It paid $300 million for raw materials and inventory, all at market or below market prices. The terms were favorably stretched out over decades, and National Intergroup was kind enough to hold much of the paper, thus limiting Weirton's exposure to banks. National would not even take interest until the net worth

227

of the new Weirton hit $100 million. Most crucially, National placed a safety net under Weirton, promising to cover the spin-off's pension and shutdown costs if Weirton failed during its first five years. Also, National agreed to pay a pro-rata share of benefits to those who would retire from Weirton.

In exchange, National escaped three-quarters of a billion dollars in shutdown and severance costs that would have come due if it closed Weirton. On balance, Weirton won the deal. National merely had stayed alive.

Perhaps the first surprise came in early February when it became public knowledge that National Intergroup was trying to sell the assets of its steel division to USX. The announcement caught Loughead and the rest of Weirton, which had heard Love say the opposite at the signing ceremony, off guard, and stimulated a round of wondering if National had other hidden items in its agenda. However, the wisdom of Harvey Sperry's last-minute move in the negotiations to make Intergroup the guarantor for National Steel immediately became clear. No one could say what security Weirton would have had if its deal strictly had been with National Steel, which then was swallowed by USX or another giant.

Economically the picture at Weirton began to brighten. For its first quarter as an independent company, Weirton recorded a profit of $9.6 million on sales of $283 million. In the first quarter in 1982 and 1983, the division had posted losses of $14 million. The biggest factor in terms of getting into the black was the wage and benefit cut, but the company also had added ninety-three new customers.

The quarter was the best recorded by any major steel company. Inland, the only competitor in the black, earned $2 million in profits. LTV lost more than $30 million, while nearby Wheeling-Pittsburgh lost $4.9 million. Weirton's management corps of 1,260 was down 300 since the formation of the ESOP. Moreover, the operating rate was up from 60 percent to 85 percent of capacity, and the mill was even beginning to attract attention from the mainline labor movement. In April, the representatives of a United Steelworkers local visited the ISU to inquire about the possibility of their plant becoming an ESOP. After the ISU provided some basic information, David Robertson offered to be a consultant to the USW local at $750 per day plus expenses. Nothing came of it, though Robertson soon found his expertise in demand, mainly by smaller nonunion businesses.

Things were going well enough in Weirton that in a referendum on April 27, 1984, the ISU voted by a two-to-one margin to dissolve its strike fund and distribute the $2.2 million kitty to the individual members based on how much each had put in. With a six-year no-strike clause in the collective bargaining agreement, most members saw no reason simply to let the money earn interest. The ISU also voted to drop its monthly dues by two dollars.

Cantankerous as ever, the ISU snubbed a motion by their leadership to bring the union's bylaws into compliance with a Department of Labor directive. The measure would have done away with the executive committee in favor of a six-person board of governors elected by the members at large. Defeated narrowly (1,436 to 1,372) it also would have cut the number of shop stewards in relation to the downsized workforce. Not only had the union failed to change its bylaws and structure, it also had resisted federal efforts to get it to rerun the 1982 officers elections enabling the laid-off employees to vote. Dissatisfied, the department began prosecuting a suit against the union in Judge Maxwell's court.

Though structurally the union remained the same, the content of its deliberations changed markedly during the first year of the ESOP. Where in the past under National the executive committee had stressed traditional union concerns such as grievances, arbitrations, pensions, layoffs, and health benefits, now the ISU leadership increasingly focused on strategic business questions facing the corporation from an ownership standpoint. The committees generally invited a member of management to its meetings to review progress on the company's capital plan, organization, marketing, or customer relations.

In the wake of the buyout, Loughead, Bish, and Bluestone aggressively pushed employee involvement, an idea whose track record under National had been spotty, as it had been in much of unionized American heavy industry.

In contrast to the standard factory fascism spawned by Frederick Taylor, which viewed workers as trained apes, the employee involvement school held that blue-collar ideas and input enhanced work culture, quality, and efficiency. The theme had been popular early in the twentieth century. The U.S. War Labor Board actually ordered major defense contractors during the First World War to set up "shop councils" comprised of management and labor representatives who met regularly on productivity issues. In keeping with the effort, the government printed posters captioned "The shot that will win the war," showing Uncle Sam, a worker with a lunchbox, and a boss in a top hat all joyfully riding a bomb. But in the 1920s, companies including Weirton twisted employee representation plans into union-blocking devices. Despite the urging of Philip Murray, president of the CIO, and Walter Reuther of the United Auto Workers, the U.S. War Production Board failed to support the renewing of industrial councils during World War II.

While the idea became passé in domestic industry, it continued to develop abroad. In Japan, workers willingly participated without pay in "quality circles," especially in the largest unionized corporations such as Matsushita Electronics, where they exhibited extraordinary loyalty and clung to an "Employee's Creed: Progress and development can be realized only through the combined efforts and cooperation of each member of our company. Each of us, therefore, shall keep this idea consistently in mind as we devote ourselves to the continuous improvements of our company." Matsushita also hewed to six other "spiritual values":

1. National Service through Industry.
2. Fairness.
3. Harmony and Cooperation.
4. Struggle for Betterment.
5. Courtesy and Humility.
6. Adjustment and Assimilation.

In general, Japanese unions do not see themselves as management's adversaries, and labor leaders place their first loyalty to the company over the union. Moreover, Japanese unions have a sense of security not shared by their U.S. counterparts. After studying both systems, one Japanese labor economist, Harou Shemada of Keio University in

Tokyo, observed: "If American unions give in to American management they run the risk of being destroyed, because management always wants to destroy them."

In postwar West Germany, where industrial unions also were
weak but secure, employee involvement was nurtured by the government. As mandated by the Co-determination Act of 1951, all coal,
iron, and steel companies with more than a thousand workers had to
place equal numbers of labor and stockholder representatives on supervisory boards which in turn appointed management boards responsible for operations. The supervisory boards served as platforms
for extensive dialogue between owners and labor, and gave the latter
an unrestricted view of corporate finance.

The Works Constitution Act of 1952 went further, ordering every
West German business with more than five on the payroll to establish
a Works Council. On a range of key employment issues, including
hours, breaks, fairness, safety, vacancies, and firings, the company
had to consult with the council, which had veto power, though the
employer could take unresolvable disputes to a state labor court.

Sweden, which also has a Co-determination Act mandating union
representation on boards of companies with more than twenty-five
employees, has pushed plant-floor democracy the hardest. Nearly au-
tonomous work teams of employees plan their tasks democratically.
When disputes arise on the teams, the unions, which play larger day-
to-day roles than in Germany and Japan, step in to settle them.

In the 1970s and 1980s, employee involvement began resurfacing
in the United States, especially at the nonunion work sites of companies including Digital Equipment, Procter and Gamble, and TRW.
Occasionally, as at the Honda Plant in Ohio, the Nissan Plant in
Tennessee, and the Johnson and Johnson facility in New Mexico,
management used the concept to stifle union-organizing drives, a
particular slap at the United Auto Workers Union, which long has
pushed worker participation, calling it "jointness," as a corrective to
numbing assembly line existence.

Today, in domestic companies, employee involvement goes under
a number of names, including Quality Circle (QC), Quality of Work
Life (QWL), Employee Participation Circle (EPC), Labor Management Action Group (LMAG), Program for Employee Participation

(PEP), Quality Awareness Team (QAT), etc. Functionally they differ widely, as *Business Week* reported, ranging from "problem-solving teams," which discuss possible improvement to "self-managing teams" of up to fifteen cross-trained employees who rotate from job to job, produce an entire product, and handle scheduling and ordering. Such units are seldom found in unionized shops.

Indeed, segments of organized labor have replaced Taylorist managers as employee participation's main detractors. As John Bradel, the president of United Paperworkers local in Pennsylvania, put it: "What the company wants is for us to work like the Japanese. Everybody go out and do jumping jacks in the morning and kiss each other when they go home at night. That's not going to work in this country."

Again, Weirton was favored by having an unaffiliated union. Though the ISU had resisted Quality of Work Life (QWL) groups under National, now it opened the door to a new Employee Participation Group (EPG) program, whose eight-member steering committee included four from management and four from the union. Its first task involved advertising and selecting "facilitators" to train and assist the EPGs, which hopefully would spread throughout the mill. Since facilitators would not make more money than in the mill, and sometimes less, the heavy response—113 applicants—was surprising.

But perhaps it was not surprising, given the high level of altruism in the company, and that so many deeply wanted Weirton to function in a new way. Also, the position had a different feel—it was not really white collar or blue collar. One in this position would have a foot in both camps and later ostensibly could work in either. Probably for some applicants the job simply seemed like a respite from the mill within the clean walls of the General Office complex.

After a month of interviewing, the steering committee chose the initial four: Joe Copenhaver, a foreman in the mason department with a master's degree in psychology; David Turkaly, a former counselor at the West Virginia Penitentiary; Robert Harris, a plant guard and former coke battery foreman with a masters in counseling; and Darlene McKinley, an accounts payable freight clerk. In Weirton, which never had had a female member in upper management or on the union executive committee, McKinley would become the first high-profile woman in the post-ESOP workforce.

Tough but not harsh-looking, with broad shoulders, a corona of red curls, and a warm beaming smile, McKinley, forty-two, and her husband, Jim, a feeder on the continuous annealing line in the tin mill, were on vacation in Florida on March 2, 1982, traveling between Disney World and the Dodgers spring training camp, when the oil light went out in their rental car. They pulled into a gas station, where the mechanic found nothing wrong. McKinley had a premonition to call home and learned, from a friend, of National's fateful announcement about quitting Weirton. Back in the car, Jim was worried, and wanted to go home rather than drop more trip money. "How can you have a good time? How can you think about that? You might not even have a paycheck next week."

Darlene replied, "They didn't tell me that. They just said National wouldn't put any more money in the mill." She didn't know whether a buyout would be good or bad. She convinced him to stay on vacation but the moment froze in her memory like the time she learned about the Kennedy assassination. Also, she would continue to think about the weirdness of the oil light. In truth she was scared. Weirton Steel was a constant in her life. She grew up in a house near the mill. Her father, a preacher, had worked in the strip mill. Plagued by ulcers, sometimes he had called home for Maalox, and the girl had brought it. After the triple truck garage door rose, she had handed the medicine to her father, looked in at all the complex lines, mills, and cranes, and wished for the day when she could take a place beside him in the mill. However, at the time, Weirton opened few jobs to women. They could either be secretaries or "tin floppers," inspectors of light sheets of metal.

McKinley decided to go to a church college in Nashville, but got homesick and lasted only a year. Returning to Weirton, she first got a job in a furniture store, then applied at the mill, and was hired as a photographic technician for the *Weirton Bulletin*, management's main organ to customers, which came out in a slick magazine format. The *Bulletin* gave her entrée to all areas of the mill, made her a proficient photographer, and allowed her to develop her own pictures of men and machines.

In 1973 she was transferred to accounting, where her feeling for the company grew. Her new boss was Bob McKinley (no relation), the division's treasurer. Newly married and living in a trailer, she wanted to buy a home but lacked the full down payment for a low-interest mortgage. One day, a vice president of the local bank called to tell her that the loan had been approved due to a reference from her "brother" Bob McKinley, who also sat on the bank's board. Now retired from Weirton, and selling insurance in town, Bob McKinley still refers to Darlene as his "sister."

In the mid-seventies, the ISU, led by Craig Petrella, began trying to organize the "salary non-exempt" (SNE) segment of the workforce, including accounting clerks. During meetings, McKinley, who had always felt well treated as an employee, was surprised by the rage of clerical workers who claimed to be doing the work of two or three people for one low salary. After listening to both sides, McKinley thought

> well, wait a minute, if these people want a union and management is telling us how much we are going to lose, and one of those things we are going to lose is money, I don't want a union—why do I have to sit here and take a union. I decided to stand up for what I believe in. And I fought to try to keep the union out. I fought pretty hard, as a matter of fact. I was like a marked girl who should have kept quiet about it. There were times that I got threats not to show up at meetings anymore, because they were talking about how tough they had it.

Using her accounting skills in speeches, she was heckled as the "bean lady" from "the garden of beans." An anonymous handbill went around the plant declaring falsely that the company had bought her a car. It wasn't true, but someone pounded dents in the car anyway, and left a note that warned: "Call her off. We want a union and are going to have a union." McKinley redoubled her efforts, but the union won the election. "That," she recalled "was a tough, tough night for me."

When the vote counting in the mill sales office was over, Ben Wade, the huge scarfer and ISU committeeman, went over to McKinley, put an arm around her, and said, "You fought a good fight, you kept it clean." McKinley sighed, "I'll tell you what. If most of the people want a union, then I'll make the union work."

But at work, antiunion clerks saw her as their leader, and pressed her to head a decertification movement. At the National Labor Relations Board office in Pittsburgh, she learned that a preliminary vote removing the ISU as the bargaining agent would require signatures from a third of the workforce. Back at the job in Weirton, she passed out cards. "I said if there are enough people who are serious about this, we'll do it. If not, I'm not interested in talking about it anymore." After a week, only four clerks would sign the cards to decertify. McKinley then spoke on the issue of a final time. " 'I think,' " she told coworkers, " 'the best thing to do is forget about it, and get in there and make the Independent Steel Workers Union the best union anywhere.' And that's what we started doing—working together instead of fighting against it."

From the first, McKinley liked the idea of employee participation. When National started its small, Quality of Work Life (QWL) program in 1980, she filled out an application to become a facilitator, but wasn't chosen. For her, the most attractive part of National's abandonment was the notion that employee involvement could finally take hold. As a result, she contributed money to pay for the buyout consultants. She and friends held bake sales and garage sales. From the back of a truck, they sold jackets with ESOP patches to pay for the McKinsey study. After the buyout, when the employee involvement idea resurfaced, she nominated herself again for a facilitator's position, and this time won. Leaving her department and friends wasn't easy, but McKinley "felt that there were guys down in the mill that had great ideas. I wanted to watch them work together. I wanted to see those ideas cultivated."

Many in Weirton felt the same way. Not only were there twenty-five applicants for each facilitator's spot, but the sign-up process for the course in participative methods offered by the EPG department looked like a land rush. Registration for the three-day session, which was voluntary, included the majority of mill employees and was so oversubscribed that a two-year waiting list developed.

The EPG program grew popular, not only because it was a break from the mill, but because it got good word-of-mouth for being enjoyable, for allowing people to speak up to management, and for encouraging all to wrestle with actual shop floor, rather than theoretical, problems.

By 1988, nineteen hundred hourly workers, and about eight hundred salaried employees had received EPG certification. Throughout the plant, 115 EPGs were functioning. Training sessions, which included about a dozen employees, often began uneasily. In part, this was a function of the fact that they were held at the General Office, a place where many of the hourly workers had never set foot. The format that brought together management and hourly people, as well as personnel from different plants, was alien in a typically Taylorist domestic factory. It seemed almost Japanese and perhaps slightly un-American. To break the ice, the facilitator tried an ethnic joke: "A foreman at a steel mill had three new employees, a Pole, a black, and a Japanese, and had to give them jobs. He told the Pole, 'You're strong, so go over there and unload trucks.' He told the black: 'You're good in high temperatures, so you go over and work at the blast furnaces.' Then he told the Japanese guy, 'You're smart, so you go over to the stock room, and take care of supplies.' 'I'll come back and check on all of you in a week, and if you're doing okay, you get to keep the jobs.' After a week, the foreman checked on the Pole, who was doing okay loading trucks. Then, he went to the blast furnace where the black also was doing fine.

"But when he went into the stock room something seemed wrong. The lights were off, and there was no activity. The foreman began yelling: 'What the hell is going on in here?' Suddenly, the Japanese guy jumped up from behind the counter and shouted: 'Supplies!' "

The men laughed politely. The subtext of the joke was that the Japanese weren't supermen—they could be as ridiculous as the American steel industry had been. Parenthetically, they also could be competed with, though perhaps it made sense to learn from their methods.

The training began with structured brainstorming. The employees were taught to generate ideas using fish bone diagrams on a flip chart. Then the groups moved into perceptual drills and quizzes of listening and reading comprehension. In addition, they learned to locate and utilize the special skills of individual members, and to delegate tasks in the course of collective problem solving.

The facilitators, who rotated in and out, assuring a fresh, upbeat presenter at all times, instructed the trainees in data gathering and survey taking, analytical methods such as cost benefit and histograms, decision-making measures including conflict management by straw votes, assessment of priorities, and defining of criteria, and the use of planning tools such as milestone charts and worksheets.

The facilitators focused on how to conduct a meeting successfully in the mill environment. They stressed the necessity of building an agenda by consensus, using a recorder (minutes writer) and giving him permission to misspell, defining participants' roles, reaching a second consensus on whether the meeting was productive, and establishing a mechanism for follow-up. The leaders also taught the participants how to package their ideas and make the crucial presentations to upper management.

To some extent, the facilitators attempted to indoctrinate the employees in discussions of the new corporation's labor-saving Mission Statement, which they passed out:

> Weirton Steel will strive to ensure long-term security for its employees. The corporation must provide a quality of work life, capitalize on a reputation for producing high quality products, serve demanding markets and applications while rebuilding and modernizing its facilities and maximizing efforts toward achieving the best possible total costs. Ensuring its Weirton presence and maintaining the ESOP commitment are key objectives.

The EPG movement in some ways had evolved into the third force—neither union nor management—which Staughton Lynd had contemplated for the work environment. The facilitators took pains to assure that EPG was not a threat to the ISU, and distributed the charter of the EPG steering committee, which stated: "While it is the intent of this process to encourage a full range of responses and approaches to solving problems in a cooperative effort that will mutually benefit all employees, it is understood that the committee or employee groups will have no authority to add, detract, or change the terms of the Labor Agreement."

The culture of American heavy industry is such that employees always want to know their roles and what is expected of them. In clear terms, the facilitators outlined the expectations of the three key members in the EPG process—themselves, team leaders, and group members—as it would be played out in the mill. The facilitators explained that they acted as "neutral jurors" in the EPG, suggesting "alternative methods and procedures," protecting "individuals and their ideas from attack," encouraging members to participate, helping the group to find "win/win solutions," calling in technical specialists when necessary, and assisting in presentations to management. The trainees were told that the facilitators would "continually promote the EPG process throughout the company."

EPG leaders usually were the employees who first took the training, and demonstrated an enduring interest. In addition to coordinating agendas, chairing meetings, and conducting follow-ups, they bore the responsibility to keep non-EPG members informed of projects. From an early date, it became apparent that many of those who had run for or lost ISU offices became EPG leaders. Once designated as leaders, they qualified for advanced training, as well as for special attention in the plant media.

The EPG members' responsibilities were delineated in nine points, which instructed employees to:

1. Get to the meeting on time;

2. State opinions and feelings honestly and clearly;

3. Stay on the agenda item;

4. Participate;

5. Avoid communications that disrespect the group (sarcasm, humor, diversions, etc.);

6. Avoid arguing for your own individual judgments; approach the task on the basis of logic;

7. Avoid changing your mind *only* in order to reach agreement

and avoid conflict. Support only solutions with which you are able to agree somewhat at least;

8. Avoid "Conflict Reducing" techniques such as majority vote, averaging, or trading in reaching decisions; and

9. View differences of opinion as helpful rather than as a hindrance in decision making.

During the third day of training, the group was divided into competing teams, and given timed problems to solve in front of the facilitator. Finally, a graduation ceremony was held, with Robert Loughead and Walter Bish passing out diplomas, and then entering into an open-ended dialogue with the workers about the state of the corporation. Since the board of directors always met at Weirton (as opposed to at more expensive hotels and resorts), following monthly board meetings directors also would attend the ceremonies and participate in the discussions. The EPG course was popular as well as transforming. Employees emerged from it with the sense that problems not only could be solved but that the administration would support change.

After individuals took the training they were encouraged to set up Employee Participation Groups in their plant areas. As the EPGs proliferated and took on problems, their efforts were publicized in the plant media.

The teams developed esprit as well as acronyms and nicknames. By the late eighties, the communications department was reporting on scores of EPGs throughout the mill. For instance, SLAB (Solution, Lasting and Beneficial), an EPG in the strip steel plant, was testing new methods of identifying and tagging metal. The Zinc Thinkers, a group on a sheet mill galvanizing line, were completing canted die experiments. AMPS (Always Meeting Problems Swiftly) in the power house planned a mobile trailer carrying all necessary equipment to clean up oil spills. RIPS (Resolvers in the Pipe Shop) organized a portable lifting setup on its trailer. BIT (Better Ideas in Transportation) on the plant railroad helped plan a new track configuration at the blast furnace. WSX (Workers Seeking X-Cellence), an annealing team in the tin mill, analyzed scheduling logistics to eliminate delay time. TOPIC (Team on Producing Ideal Conditions), refrigeration specialists, researched their own poor cleaning efficiency, located a high-pressure sprayer system, and convinced management to requisition it. IMP (Improving Maintenance Problems), a group in the Sheet Works Fuel Department, designed and implemented a backup steam pump that immediately proved successful in stopping work discontinuity when the main unit broke down. The Bee Gees, a team of bearing gang members, addressed the chronic and dangerous problem of lights falling from the roof in the tin mill and achieved a safety-enhancing design change. DREAMS (Diesel Repair, Electrical, and Mechanical Shop) cleared obsolete parts from their space when the company bought new locomotives. The Steel Works Pipe Coverers took the lead in identifying asbestos for encapsulation or removal and won approval for their efforts in a presentation to top management, which included Loughead.

Some of the groups achieved significant savings. In March 1985, the IDEA (Innovatively Developed Electrical Applications) group began wrestling with the problem of a slight spillage from the 54-inch pickler, which dripped into the ventilation system and caused overheated equipment, downtime, and a work hazard. The group cut the leakage with a new airless spray system. Not only was the unwanted flow stanched, but the reclaimed oil was worth about $450,000 to the company.

The Wire Group EPG, another electrical team, came up with the idea to scour the idled Brown's Island coke works for recyclable supplies and equipment. They located a trove of starters, conduits, fittings, and switches, which were put into use in other departments, creating a savings of almost $300,000. The Strip Steel Riggers built a new road to the caster, using mill slag in place of purchased asphalt, for a savings of about $55,000. The Steel Works Crane Repair EPG, with Darlene McKinley as the facilitator, saved about $500,000 by building a 60-ton hot mill crane out of salvaged parts. Faced with constant replacements of transfer car axles in the BOP (basic oxygen plant), the Central Machine Shop EPG analyzed car blueprints, discovered a consistent shear point on the axle, and moved loads away from it. Axles, which cost

$14,000 and had been fracturing at the rate of six to seven per year, now ceased to break.

While on occasion a Weirton worker would make a suggestion during the National era, nothing as extensive as the EPG could have taken hold. In the pre-ESOP mill, management mainly regarded thinking as its prerogative, and broad-based, blue-collar brainstorming would have been deemed by the workers silly if not sissified.

In the mid and late 1980s, Weirton's employee participation program won national notice. President Reagan saw the company as a model for economic development in the third world, and sent Walter Bish on a goodwill tour of Central America and the Caribbean Basin. Forty-seven countries sent delegations to see the Weirton experiment in employee ownership, including fading Communist regimes, both Chinas, South Korea, Albania, and a host of underdeveloped nations in Africa and South America that were looking for economic models.

In wide demand as a speaker, the intense, dynamic Loughead became American heavy industry's leading exponent of employee involvement. At the Harvard Business School's Conference on Worker Ownership in 1985 Loughead stressed:

The starting point must be that of first creating a participative environment, where people want mutual involvement, where ideas can flourish rather than get smothered or ignored. Ideas may be very close to the essence of employee participation. We must look for them and nourish them. Adopt the attitude that "ideas can't wait, something must be done about them." We must create a climate for listening.

Creating that climate—that environment—first requires open, honest communications. And believe me, you aren't communicating if you are talking without listening. People must be told the truth and they must be treated with dignity and respect. We must create the climate before we can cause the change. It can't be done by fiat. It is still a truism, that people must be led, not driven.

And all of the constituencies in a company have to be given the opportunity for involvement at the very beginning. And therein lies a common failure. For example, unions must come into the process at the outset. They have to be involved in every aspect of employee participation and they have to help sell it. If the union is a silent partner, willing to step back and see if the participation process works, it will not work. The union must be an active, equal, interested partner. And this may not be easy for unions. It may place them in an unaccustomed role—attitude changes may be required.

As the keynote speaker at the 1985 ESOP Association Convention in Washington, D.C., Loughead argued that artificial partitions between management and labor be ripped out.

Can the adversarial tradition of mistrust be broken? I think so. For one thing, there is an inherently strong attachment to most of our business enterprises through the worklife experience of today's employees. While that experience can be one of polarization on economic and philosophic issues with each side wielding what some call the "hammer," it can also be one of learning, training and improvement, involving team work, communication and cooperation. In short, the employee can develop a strong sense of attachment to the jobplace and the enterprise furnishing it. Who really knows more about the products made or the services provided than front-line employees? That is why it is not unusual to hear an employee today talk about "my company" or better yet "our company," instead of "just the company." I think when employees talk like this, more than job security is involved.

Unfortunately, the melding of management and union in the employee participation effort hit some snags, especially at the top. Initially, Alan Gould, an innovative engineer and executive, was appointed as manager of the program. The son of a former Weirton division president, Gould was a bitter critic of Taylorist management, and a scholar of American corporate history. A friendly high-energy communicator, Gould believed that "we solve almost no problems in this department. We empower others to seek out and solve their own problems."

Coming from middle management Gould saw his peers as threatened by the process. "This wasn't something middle management agreed upon. This was agreed upon by top management and the union. But we're talking about empowering and that's power sharing. This is where many frontline managers and middle managers get antsy. They will say, if I have so much power and if I share it with you, then I have less power. That's a legitimate question."

Another reason why middle management felt threatened was because their ranks had absorbed so much of the job cutting in industrial America. Hourly employee participation conjured up images of blue-collar "team leaders," functioning without managers, and further slashes of the middle management class. But, Gould made a special effort to encourage these managers to complete the training, participate in the process, and achieve a sense of mutual trust with the workers. In late 1985, the ISU won the opportunity to appoint a comanager in the EPG bureaucracy to work alongside Gould, whose title also became comanager. After Tony Julian lost an election to continue as an ISU committeeman from the tin mill, the union executive committee voted to name him to the EPG position.

Julian, who had taken a strongly cooperationist position before the buyout, seemed a likely choice. Also, like Gould, he correctly perceived his constituency (the union hierarchy) as feeling threatened by employee participation as a new power center in the mill. Julian worked to allay such concerns (sometimes drawing derision from the ISU executive committee), and to bring the union into the process. On paper, it seemed as if Julian and Gould could form a productive partnership, but for four years Gould, the articulate intellectual, and Julian, the street smart organizer, clashed. Finally, in 1989, Julian won and Gould was moved laterally to a newly created engineering position.

Some EPG groups also were ripped for focusing, especially in the early years, on employee comfort issues like additional water coolers and more pleasant lunchrooms. But, the "people issues," as they were called, contributed to the wider sense of dignity in the company, and never made up more than 20 percent of EPG's overall workload. In addition, EPG drew criticism for its cultlike image and almost mystical faith in maxims that divided the world into three types of problems, amenable to six-phase brainstorming and eight-step solutions, when many felt that a commonsense approach would suffice. Indeed, in the early years of corporate independence the major cost-cutting fix occurred outside the EPG fold. After water in the tin mill circulated through equipment, cooling it, it flowed into a reservoir called a lagoon. Periodically, sludge, a solid waste mixture of oils, dirt, and grease picked up from the machinery, had to be pumped out of the lagoon by a boat called a mudcat, loaded into tank trucks, and taken to a landfill. After learning that the trucks were hauling more water than sludge, tin mill employees shelved the mudcat, fitted a crane with a huge clamshell bucket, and began scraping the sludge from the bottom of the lagoon. As a result, cleanings required filling about 150 tankers versus 400 in the past, which saved $900,000 annually.

The EPG department was not without a sense of humor about itself. It put out a paper, *The Participant*, in which one column featuring corporate homilies ("We are what we repeatedly do. Excellence then, is not an act but a habit.") was called "Psychobabble." Also, the facilitators and leaders used a more down-to-earth, less-jargonized approach in the mill than in the training, albeit "following the process," according to Darlene McKinley.

McKinley's role was eminently practical. About once every five weeks she would handle a training session. The rest of the time as a facilitator she dealt on a hands-on basis with problems facing eleven EPG groups in production and maintenance departments including boiler house employees, pipe fitters, riggers, and the bull gang (crane repair). Often the accent was on cost. For instance, when a water blaster in the boiler house failed, the normal course under National would have been to order a new pump head for about $4,000. Instead, McKinley led the EPG group in some troubleshooting, brought the vendor's representative into the process by telephone, and discovered that a control valve was leaking and could be fixed for $300.

At other times, her work involved interfacing between the EPG and management. When her riggers requested a truck and got a Korean War–era jalopy, they called McKinley at home at night and she came to their shop in coveralls, went under the vehicle "which was a disaster," and pried loose a ham-sized chunk of rust. When the riggers' manager told her in his office that he was too busy to see the truck, she said: "I've got it right here," and pulled out the corroded metal. The manager immediately went to inspect the truck, and allowed the riggers to replace it. Shopping for it themselves, they knocked about $7,000 off the price that the company was willing to pay. Moreover, their pride in the new safe vehicle was tangible as they cleaned and maintained it themselves. "The riggers," said McKinley, "are a great bunch of guys. But I knew them well enough to know that the old truck would have found its way into the river. It would have gone up the tin mill hill, and just went out of park, right into the water." The new truck remains in good shape "because the guys have pride in ownership."

As the Employee Participation Group program was intended to improve the culture and spirit of the corporation, Statistical Process Control (SPC) was meant to better the workforce mentally. Managed by a short, stocky chemist named David Shuler, who reviled sloppy management, the SPC program gave employees and customers a rigorous but clear course in practical statistics.

Shuler believed that a company's success was contingent on the pride of its workforce. It had little to do with whether the employees had an ESOP. Hard to find, and harder to define, pride was an elusive commodity in a corporation, but Shuler felt that it came from two sources. One was a tradition of merit with which an employee could identify and which Shuler located in Weirton's rich past. The other was a productive challenge, something that made the workers stretch to attain proficiency, and which translated into satisfaction in the market and personally.

As part of the latter source, SPC was derived from the philosophy of W. Edwards Deming, internationally the most influencial business theoretician of the postwar era. An austere, lean, balding man with piercing eyes, horn-rimmed glasses, and a thin-lipped smile, who looked like a cross between Lenin and Eisenhower, Deming became the apostle of "quality" in a specific, measurable form.

Deming, whose work was derived from that of Walter Shewhart, author of the 1931 classic *Economic Control of Quality of Manu-*

factured Product, served as a consultant to Japanese industry in the early 1950s. Deming made it his point to put the following chain reaction on the "blackboard of every meeting with top management," until it "became engraved in Japan as a way of life."

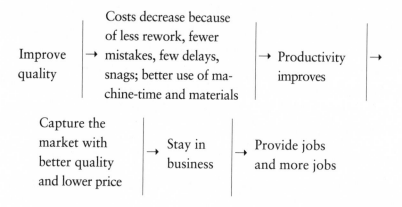

"Deming," according to David Shuler, "turned on a country." At its core, Deming's method involves cutting the waste of time and material to the bone. He despises "inspection," the process whereby a mass of material comes off a production line, and the rejects must be located, given an alternative use or trashed. Deming believes that if data points are carefully plotted and analyzed when the manufacturing process is run in various ways, the causes of the defects can be identified *before* inspection and planned out of the system.

Unfortunately American business in its fat years became addicted to waste and inspection, which Deming sees as the inane equivalent to "planning for defects." His research indicates that from 15 percent to 40 percent of the costs of most American products results from the "waste embedded in it—waste of machine-time, nonproductive use of accompanying burden." Put another way, "Defects are not free. Somebody makes them and gets paid for making them." Moreover, adjusting the scrap or shifting it to another market fails as a solution. "Rework raises costs. No one likes to do repair work. A pile of items set aside for rework grows and grows, and too often, in desperation for downstream parts, they are not repaired at all, but are commandeered and used just as they are."

In 1950, Deming found Japan a defeated country with a negative worth, a dearth of natural resources, and a reputation for cheesy consumer goods. Yet, with management and workers not enthralled to lenders, obligated to shareholders, or afraid of unfriendly take-overs, the Japanese made quality-based transformations in their manufacturing, utility, service, and even government sectors. Each soon provided "repeatable products with minimal variation or waste." As the Japanese adapted to the Deming system, their plants became known for superb organization of equipment, extraordinary house-keeping and cleanliness, minimal inventory and storage (freeing up space for production or growth), maximum utilization of equipment, low downtime, surgically careful spot lubrication (wasting little fluid, limiting part-cleaning costs, and preventing dangerous slopping of floors), and shifts separated by maintenance intervals. Treated as a prophet in Japan, Deming was decorated by the emperor in 1960. In the 1960s, the Japanese Union of Science and Engineering (JUSE) began awarding Deming prizes for outstanding contributions to quality and dependability.

He received similar awards in the United States, and the American Statistical Association also gave out Deming prizes for quality and productively. But domestic industry initially was less receptive to his teachings. Deming deplored America's fetish with short-term profits, archaic antitrust limitations, and underutilization of the workforce. In 1983, he wrote that "the United States may be today the most underdeveloped nation in the world."

Following his Japanese experience, Deming codified his key principles for management as the "Fourteen Points"—not coincidentally the same title that Woodrow Wilson had chosen for a new international order following World War I. Deming fully intended his Fourteen Points to bring about a new world of business.

The Deming points stress that top management must be held responsible, that the cycle of defects, inspection, and waste is archaic, that it is foolish to award to the lowest rather than the best bidder, that the company must vigorously train on the job, and that numerical quotas for work should be eliminated, as should office and plant rah-rah in the form of slogans, posters, and cant, which has become all too common. Some have become famous as business maxims themselves on posters such as "Drive out fear so that everyone can work effectively for the company," and "Break down barriers between departments."

In the early 1980s as American manufacturing slid, and imports, especially from Japan, flooded markets, Deming and his points finally received the domestic spotlight. Attempting to capitalize on the famous figure and his quest for quality, General Motors gave Deming a widely publicized role in the development of the Pontiac Fiero. Intended to fill an open-market niche for an inexpensive sports car, the Fiero was the result of utilizing some Deming techniques—including listening to the workforce's ideas—plus robotics, and sheathing the chassis with a high-quality composite skin. But GM loaded the car with inventoried mechanical parts intended for other models and tried to hit the market too fast. Early Fieros had faulty brake cables, potential fire hazards, and con man sticker prices, not including air conditioning and automatic transmission. Paying for them took the car out of the inexpensive range. As Japan readied to enter the market with such high-quality imports as the Toyota MR-2 and the Mazda Miata, GM discontinued the Fiero. Despite the Fiero fiasco, Deming's luster remained undimmed, especially at Weirton, where Shuler and the SPC staff treated the Fourteen Points as gospel.

Many employees participated in both SPC and EPG, which were seen as complementary. One gave workers a sense of commitment and responsibility, while the other taught sophisticated techniques to be used when they exercised that responsibility. But the two programs also sharply differed. Since Deming found it critical to "eliminate slogans, exhortations, and targets for the workforce," the SPC program had a dry atmosphere that contrasted with the cheerleading, epigrams, and psychobabble of EPG. The SPC groups, which met weekly, had nondescript names such as the Tin Mill Team, the Blast Furnace Capability Team, and the Delivery Performance Team as opposed to the snazzy acronyms of the EPGs. While SPC depended heavily on listening to workers and especially on receiving their empirical data off the production lines, it was more hierarchical and less democratic than EPG. In EPG sessions, employees stepped out of their characteristic jobs definitions to brainstorm and problem-solve. "SPC," said David Shuler, "is a management tool."

In 1985, Shuler wrote that

> The Weirton SPC process believes in and has implemented the concept that the department manager chairs/coordinates the SPC teams in his/her area. SPC teams are comprised of department supervision (including manager, superintendent, general supervisor, turn supervisor), SPC analyst, line operators, support crafts, services, quality control, production planning, and additional support or operating groups which are added on an as-needed basis. The team concept is a dynamic process that provides everyone the opportunity to participate and succeed by "working smarter."

More stratified than EPG, SPC teams also included authority figures. Unlike EPG, which had to make elaborate presentations to top management, SPC sought to have the executive leadership and, if possible, decision makers within the group.

In addition, SPC required more commitment and study than employee involvement programs such as EPG. Shuler likened the difference between employee involvement and commitment to a plate of ham and eggs. "The chicken," he said, "was involved. But the pig is committed."

Unlike EPG, which held classes in the modern spacious classrooms of the General Office, the SPC course took place in the bowels of the old brick mill administration building, where workers in ball caps and T-shirts wrestled with the thorny science of statistics. Like most great teachers, Shuler was somewhat autocratic but infinitely patient, and willing to break from the lesson to work one-on-one with a struggling student. Over four or five days, he sprayed the blackboard with symbols: x (mean), x̄ (grand mean—the average of the averages), s (standard deviation), Σ (sigma—sum of), n̄ (sample size), r (range of values), and r̄ ("r-bar"—the average of the range of values).

Through exercises, some quite demanding, the employees learned the application of Pareto's Principle, that 80 percent of the problems in an industrial process are due to 20 percent of the causes, and the plotting and interpretation of key control charts. Key aids such as x-r charts, for example, graphically reflected a process's variability by using sample means and ranges.

As they absorbed the SPC's mandate to prevent rather than inspect out defects, the students prepared p-charts, showing the rejected fraction of total units inspected, and pn-charts, providing the number of defects per lot. U-charts broke down the problem into the number of defects per unit. Taught that no industrial process ever achieved defect-free perfection, the students learned to recognize the state of being "in statistical control," which meant that only random or chance causes affected the system.

Beginning in 1989, employees also learned to operate small hand-held computers called Datamytes, programmed to perform statistical monitoring and trend analysis. The units, which beeped when fed wrong data, downloaded into PCs and mainframes, or hitched to printers.

Proud of his students, whom he called "the talent," Shuler also voiced displeasure with top management. As Weirton became a nationally prominent Fortune 500 Company, it hired executives from outside the company, instead of promoting from within. Shuler, who when angry looked and sounded like Edward G. Robinson in a tough guy role, argued that the community already possessed a tradition of excellence and sufficient human resources to thrive. Moreover, Deming's message was that if downtrodden Japan could succeed, then any company could flourish with a quality orientation. Shuler saw the new pattern of bringing in outside executives as stifling the ambitions of local managers, destabilizing, and not in keeping with Deming's maxim to "drive out fear."

Nevertheless, observers regarded Weirton's adoption of statistical methods as the most rapid and thoroughgoing in the steel industry. Each year, the effort saved the plant millions of dollars, but the SPC's focus remained on quality for the consumer.

As in all large integrated operations sometimes the "customer" was internal—in other words, a downstream department that would receive an interim product for treatment. Obviously, if the unfinished steel had problems, even the highest-quality processing might not result in a suitable product. As an adjunct to SPC, Shuler initiated another program, "Watch Your Steel in Action," to enable workers to tour the "destination" departments.

The opportunity to see what happened to the steel after they had worked on it fascinated employees. For instance, one afternoon Shuler led a tour of the tin mill for employees assigned to the pickling lines. The two operations were less than a mile apart, but the pickling people, some of whom had thirty years of service, had never set foot in the tin mill, which whirred with steel shooting at a mile a minute through pools of chemicals, climbing tall towers, and plunging into deep cellars. At the end, thirty-ton cranes, resting on rails fifty feet apart, hoisted and stashed the gleaming hot coils.

For an hour and a half the visitors gawked, walked the line, and talked with their tin mill counterparts. The program afforded more than the opportunity to discuss physical characteristics of the product. In addition, employees talked about the optimal times, places, and packaging for delivery of the material to their internal customer as well as the information that should accompany it. Afterwards, those who wanted to continue the dialogue met for a buffet of cold cuts in the mill administration building. Consistent with Deming's injunction to "break down barriers between staff areas," Watch Your Steel in Action instilled a sense of harmony and teamwork throughout the operation.

Using SPC, many departments achieved boosts in quality, some of which amounted to breakthroughs. The chemical and physical qualities of steel vary according to buyers' needs. Looking like volcanic spearfishers, workers cloaked in fireproof suits with visored hoods stood on scaffolds and plunged long lances, which emerged with flaming samples from troughs of molten iron as it flowed from the blast furnaces before being poured into railroad cars for transport to the basic oxygen plant (BOP). These catches were called "runner samples." Others were retrieved by employees who stuck their poles into the smoldering railcars. These were known as "bottle samples."

Both types were taken to the chemistry lab for analysis. Sometimes samples did not accurately reflect the composition of the whole batch, a major problem since the yield would be out of specification for the customer's order and would have to be reprocessed or shunted to another order, resulting in Deming's dread "rework." The BOP SPC team plotted and analyzed the accuracy of runner samples versus bottle samples. It might be expected that the runner samples straight from the blast furnace would be more precise, since bottle samples could pick up impurities from the walls of tank cars. But statistical findings often are counterintuitive, and the bottles proved to be about 11 percent more accurate, which resulted in an effort to steer away from the runners in order to achieve better quality.

At the tin mill, the SPC team looked at the chronic, infuriating, and expensive problem of punch marks, scratches on metal coming off the plater lines. During tin coating, the metal strip passed through a series of plater rolls. When a fine particle of tin or speck of dirt struck a roll, it would scratch the strip repeatedly. Such punch-marked metal had to be sold at a discount or scrapped.

Data gathering first showed that most of the defects came from the number four electroplater. The team analyzed a host of its variables, and found that the plater rolls turned faster than the strip traveled. Narrowing the speed gap by slowing the rolls produced fewer defects. Eventually technicians got the disparity between roll speed and strip speed down to about twenty-five feet per minute, which resulted in a 40 percent drop in punch marks and a million dollars in annual savings.

As environmental enforcement increased, Weirton had difficulty disposing of spent drums of oil and lubricants. Prior to the 1980s, the company sold the drums to reconditioners, but when federal regulations stiffened they could not accept containers with more than an inch of residue. Weirton found that instead of receiving cash, it now had to pay up to $115 to get rid of each drum. Not surprisingly, spent drums began stacking up in the mill. The Labs and Materials SPC worked out an economically feasible plan for disposal. After making a study, it purchased and modified existing equipment to plunge and crush the barrels over a holding tank, which collected the oil and grease. Safely mixed with kerosene, the fluid was used as fuel at the blast furnace. The smashed drums became scrap for the BOP. Instead of a net loss and storage problem, the company got rid of 5,000 drums and saved $50,000.

The Deming system insisted on providing statistically proven quality throughout a business, in expensive and inexpensive operations and in cheap and costly products in order to stimulate an overall approach, as Shuler explained, of giving the customer his due. "The Chevette owner wants and deserves quality as much as the Lincoln owner. True quality is priceless. From a stick of bubble gum to a mansion, you pay for quality, you deserve quality, you have the right to it."

Sometimes with no particular expectation of a monetary gain, SPC deliberately would look into a low-cost problem. For instance, the mill paid a penalty fee, called "demurrage," of .08 cent per day to suppliers of bottled gases such as oxygen, nitrogen, and acetylene for holding a canister for more than thirty days. SPC found widespread demurrage, and a lack of awareness and accountability by supervision, resulting in space problems and gross excess inventories. The collected data, which showed utilization of only about a third of the canisters within thirty days, led to radical changes in ordering, a new color coding system for empties, and a predicted annual savings of between $48,000 and $53,000.

Like Deming, Shuler refused to blame Japan and other importers for the plight of American manufacturing. "The real threat to quality comes not from the outside but from within. Internal differences and noninvolvement destroy quality faster than any outside threats. If we know what's wrong and permit it to continue, we've forfeited our rights without even a whimper. One doesn't have to look too long or too hard to attach responsibility."

It would have been ridiculous for Weirton to go through the processes and formulas of EPG and SPC in order to implement obvious solutions to problems. Through most of its history Weirton had been a division of National rather than a stand-alone company. Before the buyout, the divisional mentality at Weirton had not involved watching costs closely, since these could be passed along to the parent corporation. After Weirton became independent, the realization dawned that serious savings could be won by trimming inefficient and wasteful practices handed down from the National days. In 1985, Loughead created a third reform agent called the Operations Improvement Program (OIP), which in some ways was the most dramatic of all.

Organized with help from McKinsey, OIP sought to recoup for employees their wage cuts through profit sharing. The program, which had a "Core Group" of managers and union leaders from the six plant divisions, requested all employees to alert them of any possible changes conducive to a 25 percent savings or increase in output. Headed by Lou Kondus, a cost analyst based in the General Office, OIP publicized that it would present worthy ideas at special sessions of the seven top executives, including Loughead, and made it known that Core Group recommendations generally would be approved.

Without training responsibilities, OIP functioned like a hyperactive think tank. It received about five hundred suggestions. Kondus steered the group through the ocean of information, recommended half the ideas to top management, and saw all but one implemented. The son of a Weirton Steel bricklayer, Kondus, a fifty-year-old man with thirty years of service, had begun work in the mill as a laborer while commuting sixty miles a day to earn his college degree in accounting. He liked the idea of wiping away distinctions between blue-collar and white-collar employees. He had visited a nine-hundred-employee Cummins Engine plant in New York, which, although not employee-owned, "really impressed me. It had flexibility, no job categories, and a good atmosphere. It wasn't like a traditional adversarial plant."

While Weirton was "all I've known," he wanted to see change. He asked salary and hourly employees: "If this was your house, what would you do different? You work with tools and supplies every day, what do you see that just doesn't seem right? Let's try to save money, give us some quick hits." Kondus and the Core Group sent out notices stating: "We want to hear from your radicals; we want to hear from your so-called troublemakers. Get *everybody* in these groups. A lot of good ideas come from people down there [in the mill] that are perceived as being troublemakers."

Simple and lucrative suggestions poured in. A worker showed how to save a half-million dollars in electric bills, by adopting a logical process of phasing the mill's most power-draining operations. Another employee, a weigh master on the mill railroad, discovered that hopper cars carrying washed coal did not drain completely before reaching the scales. The company paid for water as well as coal. Tests showed that scale weight generally could be reduced by about 2 percent for a yearly savings of $200,000.

Another employee pointed out that duel tandem trucks were not licensed at sufficient vehicle weights to carry their fully loaded capacities. After receiving the proper licenses, hauling capacity jumped by 30 percent per vehicle. A company truck driver demonstrated the substantial fuel savings that could be gained by finding indoor space, with oil heaters, to house vehicles in the winter rather than having them idle outside all week in order to avoid starter problems.

A water treatment supervisor complained that the boiler house used caustic soda at $165 per ton, when lime at $82 would work as well. Instead of continuing to stockpile obsolete spare parts, the company decided to hold a "fire sale." It freed other space by placing its huge inventory of bearings, at no charge, with a nearby bearing company. It dealt with a wasteful system of making parts for equipment within the mill, in which welders cut "burn outs" from steel to specified sizes, then shipped them to be fabricated at the central machine shop. Unfortunately, the physical chemistry of the burnouts was not controlled. Parts made from the wrong grades of steel wore out quickly. Brought together by OIP, the welders and machinists agreed that only grades tough enough for part making would be used. From 1985 to 1988, the period of its most intensive activity, OIP saved about $10 million per year. In 1987, Kondus, who felt privileged and "rounded" by the opportunity to make corrections across the company, said he had "seen more ideas generated in the last five years than I saw in the previous twenty-five."

Kondus viewed OIP as a "quick-fix cost-reduction program that can get you where you want to get quick, but not as a way you'd want to go to make a permanent change in work life. EPG's the way you'd want to go. But EPG is a long-drawn-out affair. I've seen EPG projects that take a year to get accomplished, because you're getting everybody to change their theory of working through groups, brainstorming, fishboning, and all the bullshit that goes with it. In OIP, we had ideas we knew would work and just went straight to executive management."

OIP had two less-known functions. It identified local management employees who had high potential but were stalled in their careers. The old, conservative, divisional bosses had sometimes tended to place creative people "in the penalty box." Now OIP brought them to the attention of top management, which shifted them to slots where they could contribute and grow.

The OIP leadership delved into another vestige from the past—

graft. In Big Steel's heyday, stealing and corruption were part of mill life. Employees loaded up on loot and supplies, and furnished their deer camps with tools from the job. In the ESOP, with the wage and cost cutting, such excess became unacceptable. Among other things, OIP looked into a ring of high bosses, including a vice president charged anonymously on a tape from the ESOP message center with taking kickbacks from a vendor in return for buying for the hot mill inferior oil that burned bearings. The charges proved true. Given the option of resignation or prosecution, the bosses quit. While rarely discussed, the matter was widely known, and had a deterrent effect. The fact that the leader of the oil scandal had a reputation as a tyrant made the forced ouster popular. In addition, purchasing was centralized to prevent future localized economic scams.

19 Hoopy Christmas

"They are the heroes of the industrial world."
—Jay Rockefeller

During the Loughead years it became apparent that the change in corporate culture, the cost-cutting moves, and the well-designed buy-out deal with National all had begun to mesh. In 1984, Weirton registered $41 of profit on every ton, and a 6.2 percent return on sales. Both were the best in the industry. The return on sales figures also topped the average of 5.6 percent in the Fortune 500, in which Weirton placed 289. Steel shipments reached 2.1 million tons, a gain of 17 percent over the previous year, and gross sales exceeded $1.1 billion. With healthy earnings of $60 million, the company was on target to start one-third profit sharing in 1986, when the accumulated earnings would clear the trigger figure of $100 million. In an industry at depression levels of employment, Weirton was not only preserving jobs but adding them as overall employment rose from 7,270 in late 1983 to 7,859 in late 1984. Now in the U.S. Senate, Jay Rockefeller called Weirton workers "the heroes of the industrial world."

The company quickly built a national sales organization by snatching some of National's most able steel sellers. Sales representatives reported that they liked working for Weirton because buyers rooted for the fledgling ESOP, as a Cinderella against the big boys. As had happened so often in the past, the company got a boost in 1986 when the United Steelworkers went on strike and customers of idled mills switched to Weirton.

Loughead proved to be a vigorous and inspiring leader. Speaking at the first annual shareholders' meeting, attended by twenty-three-hundred employee-owners, he insisted that: "We can build Weirton Steel into a company that is as deep and rich in character as the people who own it."

As president, he stressed and expanded the communications blitz of the buyout days. A believer in "face-to-face management," he continued the Joint Study Committee practice of "in-plant" meetings with workers in the operation's far-flung departments. These offered the chance to "talk about the state of the business, to listen, and answer questions. I do this once a week, joined by the president of our union. These sessions give us firsthand information on employee concerns. An added feature is that I particularly enjoy [them]."

The administration also started a new monthly newspaper, *Independent Weirton*, with a joint union-management editorial board. As Loughead noted, "The paper goes beyond the usual perception of a plant newspaper in that we do not 'sanitize' its content. There is a balance of good and bad in terms of how we were doing in all areas of the business."

Independent Weirton carried some soft features about whose son was a star quarterback, but its articles were useful, well-researched pieces on operations, organization, markets, and problems. It also tracked the steel industry as well as the progress of other ESOPs. It accurately predicted and analyzed the faults of Rath due to an outmoded plant, and the fall of Hyatt Clark because General Motors ceased to order tailored bearings. The paper constantly alerted Weirton employees to the twin necessities of modernization and attempting to diversity by developing new products and signing up new customers.

Not only did Loughead preserve the ESOP message center's twenty-four-hour hot line, but he had messages transcribed and brought to his attention, and ordered that every question should be answered in writing. Perhaps, above all, the new company dedicated itself to television. The Internal Communications department under Chuck Lafferty produced "News and Views," a fast-moving show with Lafferty as anchor, featuring "Steel Watch" on key developments in the company and industry, interviews with workers onsite, and the "Customer Corner," a review of how steel buyers viewed Weirton's product quality, service, and delivery, which at times focused on below par performance and served as a wake-up call. Lafferty always closed with: "Thanks for watching and make it a safe workday." Well received by the employees, "News and Views" played on sixty monitors throughout the mill. Internal Communications also regularly produced videos, especially on financial and ESOP administrative issues, which workers watched at work and could take home. The company blanketed the Northern Panhandle with billboard campaigns around slogans such as "Quality People Make Quality Steels" and "Working Together Works." Loughead, who wholeheartedly subscribed to Lee Iacocca's axiom that "The ability to communicate is everything," presided over the best-informed and most heavily propagandized working community in America.

With a favorable balance sheet and strong order book, Loughead tried to take the corporation in new directions. Instead of wringing his hands about foreign producers, he decided to do business with them, buying steel slabs from Germany and coke from Japan. Louhead retained the world's largest steel company, Nippon, to assist and consult with Weirton about basic oxygen continuous casting techniques with an emphasis on "clean steel" free of subsurface inclusions of dirt particles, which cause failures in cans, such as pinholes, weak welds, and cracked flanges. Weirton already had the best quality rate in American industry with one failure per thousand cans produced. But Nippon was ten times better with one reject out of ten thousand. Termed a "witch hunt for dirt," the joint effort exposed the West Virginians to a variety of Japanese production and sampling methods, such as shrouding the process and using new refractories (heat-resistant vessel-lining bricks), which resulted in Weirton's being able to reduce defects in canning stock by half.

Most radically, Weirton asked the Department of Energy for a $65 million grant to commercialize the Kohle-Reduction process invented by Korf Engineering of West Germany. K-R, as it was known, uses coal as opposed to coke in steel making. By eliminating dirty coke plants, K-R represented a major step for the environment. As K-R technology was compatible with West Virginia coal, it was good news for the economically devastated deep-mining region. Also as more and more coke came from overseas, the new method could reduce foreign dependence. Loughead declared, "The K-R process is the way to keep American coal in American steel." The cost of the installation of K-R was about $127 million, so receiving the DOE grant was important. Steel industry analysts were excited. The nation's leading historian of steel, Father William Hogan of Fordham University, wrote that K-R would be far less expensive than rebuilding the nation's coke batteries. John Jacobson of Chase Econometrics called K-R consistent with Weirton's reputation for "continuous casting and saving energy and labor costs. I think Weirton has done extremely well, and better than any steel company in the United States in adjusting to problems in the steel industry."

Weirton, which refused to concede the fight to aluminum for beverage cans, turned loose MUD (the Materials Utilization Division), now renamed Weirtec, and William Saunders on the problem. The research facility came up with a steel product as light and as formable as aluminum but less costly. Weirton aggressively sought new markets, including using the good offices of the State Department to sell about $15 million worth of canning stock to Egypt.

Management made successful overtures to major corporate customers. It struck a deal to become Kodak's sole source of a new high-tech steel embedded with electronics for film cartridges. It leased a portion of the huge Finished Product Warehouse (FPW), a surreal twenty-five-acre world of racks, coils, and forklifts, to Alpo Pet Foods, which agreed to make Weirton its exclusive tinplate supplier.

In May 1985, the corporation pleased buyers by embracing in contracts the quality principle of "Kanban," which is the Japanese term for "just in time" delivery. Customers liked Kanban because it meant that the material would not arrive too late for agricultural canning at harvest time or salmon packing when the fish were running; nor would it arrive too early, necessitating expensive inventory storage. Weirton also keyed the new "just in time" ethic to its transportation system by calculating the time of production and delivery precisely to allow the corporation to maximize use of the cheapest form of freight—river barges—and to limit the more costly and hurried types—trucking and rail.

Weirton successfully penetrated the service center sector of the steel market. Something like supermarkets of steel, service centers stocked and slit a wide array of plates, sheets, coils, beams, and angles, for small-order customers. Melvin Moss, the president of Uniserv's major facility in Ohio, praised the ESOP's products. "Weirton has some of the finest flat-rolled I have seen coming out of a domestic mill in many years. In my opinion, Weirton compares favorably with anything the Europeans or Japanese can throw at them."

In 1986, net worth crossed the $100 million mark and profit sharing began. About $20 million was distributed to employees in individual allotments of between $1,500 and $2,000. Moreover, it appeared that over time the amount lost due to the wage and benefit cuts initiated for the buyout would be more than made up through the annual profit sharing distribution, which, though it occurred in March, was immediately nicknamed "Hoopy Christmas," a reference to the hoopies, backwoods Southerners who flowed into Weirton early in the century to earn company wages.

Things also fell into place for the ISU. Not supplanted by the new activist entities such as the EPG, SPC, and OIP, the union secured seats on the steering boards of each. The ISU also fought for and won the right to appoint facilitators from the hourly ranks who would not lose their union seniority and would keep accruing the rights that went with it.

The union basked in the reflected glory of profit sharing, and in the repeated callbacks of laid-off hourly employees. However, it asked the company to hire a new management consultant to bring about mid-level executive cuts. Rather defensively, Loughead told the Weirton Management Club that the "union didn't run the mill." At an ISU stewards meeting on June 1, 1984, Loughead admitted that he had made the statement, explaining that "there is a concern among the salary [employees] that they will have no say, and that the bargaining unit is running the company. I don't think the bargaining unit even wants to run the company."

Feeling empowered in the Loughead years, the union made a bold move against the Department of Labor. In 1984, the ISU simply reneged on its promise to the department to hold a rerun of the 1982 election. The leadership knew the matter would end up in litigation, and as Eddie Conley expressed it, "If we lose, we lose the structure of our union." In his typically quiet way, Walter Bish calmed the committee, and instructed the lawyers to fight rather than to return to their previously negotiated position.

On March 30, 1984, Secretary of Labor Raymond Donovan filed a legal action against Walter Bish and the ISU in the federal court in the Northern District of West Virginia. For a year, almost nothing happened. As with all the other cases significantly bearing on structural issues at Weirton, the suit was assigned to Judge Maxwell. In 1985, the parties began meeting in his chambers. During discussions, the main sticking point seemed to be the government's insistence on getting rid of the ISU's requirement that in order to be eligible to sit on the executive committee one first had to be elected to a stewardship. However, the department's resolve melted when Judge Maxwell said in chambers that he believed that this eligibility requirement "was not unreasonable." In essence, the department had been signaled that it would lose a trial and face a lengthy appeals process. Backing down, Labor allowed the ISU to hold a new election in July 1985 in accordance with the union's rules rather than rerun the 1982 election with changes.

Probably the truest barometer of worker morale at Weirton is the triennial ISU election process. In 1985, Walter Bish and most of the young committeemen, who had come to power in 1982 favoring an ESOP, won handily. With 2,615 votes out of 4,841, Bish received more support than all five of his challengers combined and avoided a runoff. Embittered, Red Arango, who had vowed revenge during the buyout process, finished next to last with 274 votes, and ceased to be a factor in mill politics.

In the last hurrah of the Rank and File Committee, Steve Bauman made a spirited run for a stewardship in Steel Works One's continuous casting and degassing department against Skip Spadafora, whom he labeled "Mr. D.C." because of Spadafora's frequent trips to Washington on union business. Among other things, Bauman told the voters that the "structural integrity of your pension plan has been completely undermined," and railed against the fact that the company had self-insured its worker compensation plan. "This is hokey," he said. "Your incumbents go around trying to talk you out of making a compensation claim."

Implicitly Bauman's campaign pointed out why the workforce still needed a union when it had an ESOP. The ESOP came with a structural bias against making payouts that would reduce stock value. The union remained necessary to stand up for worker welfare issues that cost money, such as safety in the plant and paying compensation claims.

Also, the ESOP was an extraordinarily complex financial vehicle that affected each employee's security. The union's treasury allowed it to pay for sophisticated independent advice, which would have been beyond the reach of individual members, and which allowed it when necessary to test management strategies relating to employee ownership.

Bauman wrongly predicted that the employees would not receive profit sharing checks, but was right when he foresaw that "management is going to come to you and ask you to sacrifice just one more time." In particular, he predicted pressure on the workforce "to make you believe you have no choice but to go public with the stock." He complained that with wage cuts the hourlies had to "work overtime to maintain the same standard of living as they had had three years ago." While Bauman's handouts were, as he told Staughton Lynd, "eagerly received and read," he did poorly in the election, which he attributed to having "absolutely no taste for conventional politics." Mainly, however, employees were satisfied with the new state of affairs.

Irving Bluestone, the veteran United Auto Worker leader on the board of directors, also took a crack at changing the ISU. He tried to interest the executive committee in the progressive trappings of big unions, such as labor education and expedited grievance procedures, as well as better communications than the typical word of mouth from the stewards. Bluestone argued that *Independent Weirton* did not get the ISU's point across, and urged the union to start its own paper. Intermittently, the ISU put out a lackluster sheet. It attracted little interest. Bluestone could not convince the ISU to adopt a tighter, more hierarchical structure in order to focus power in its president. Nevertheless, he grudgingly admired the unusual former company union. "I see," he told the executive committee, "democracy in depth here which is almost anarchic, but there is almost no sense of direction." Ultimately, Bluestone, like the Labor Department and the Rank and File, was unable to change the ISU.

2 0   Trouble at the Top

"Even if you happen to be on the right track, you'll get
run over if you just sit there."

—ROBERT LOUGHEAD

However, there were some clouds on the Weirton horizon. On-the-
job accidents were rising, as they often did at companies that preferred using large amounts of overtime rather than hiring new
employees, requiring training programs and expensive benefits pack-
ages. Weirton was finding that it had to compete against a new animal, companies such as LTV and Wheeling-Pittsburgh, which had
emerged from bankruptcy with debts trimmed. Senior management
changes at the top, mainly involving getting rid of those left over

from the days of National Steel with liberal severances (only Valdi-serri and Doepken still remained), raised concerns about continuity and loyalty to the community as outsiders were recruited to fill their places.

Also, some workers lamented buying foreign slabs, while others, such as Mike Hrabovsky, dreaded the inevitable coming of a new wave of automation, including totally cast steel, which would eliminate 250 jobs in his department, the blooming mill. But Walter Bish's oft-spoken view that "we have to be market driven" probably reflected the attitudes of most employees, for whom by and large the situation had improved at Weirton since 1982. Certainly few thought much about it at the 1986 annual meeting when Loughead, paraphrasing Will Rogers, said, "Even if you happen to be on the right track, you'll get run over if you just sit there."

In fact, Loughead was in trouble with his board. To the disappointingly sparse crowd of four hundred, neither Loughead nor the company seemed to be sitting still. The previous August, Weirton parlayed its underdog status in Washington with a push from Senators Byrd and Rockefeller to win Department of Energy funding to install the Kohle-Reduction (K-R) process plant, which would make about 330,000 tons of iron per year at Weirton. The company readied a site for clearance close to the extinct coke batteries.

The federal government agreed to contribute $58 million to the project, while Weirton's commitment was estimated at $115 million. For years, the plant would be a "demonstration" facility producing too little iron to be commercially viable, but the company planned, as Loughead said, to "scale it up." He added that "this process or something similar to it eventually will become commercial and blast furnaces will disappear."

In the 1980s, most Big Steel companies had recessive boards who placed corporate destiny in the hands of CEOs, who, like National's Love, rolled the dice on diversification, often with disastrous results. U.S. Steel bet the company on oil. Armco saddled and almost wrecked itself with a plummeting insurance business.

Weirton's board was different. It knew from the start that survival meant staying focused on steel. Also, it prefigured the boards of the nineties by taking an engaged, even activist, stance, and by not according automatic deference to the CEO, whom they had in fact picked.

While the K-R process scored a public relations coup, it resulted in a disaster with the board, which recognized that while the new facility "might revolutionize the steel-making industry," as Irving Bluestone put it, a similar experimental plant had exploded in South Africa (a matter not mentioned in the local media). Above all, the directors saw no reason for Weirton, whose main goal was survival, to become a guinea pig, according to Bluestone "for corporations with more resources. From the standpoint of risk taking and defining new technology within the industry, it was an intriguing idea and it still is. But in the final analysis we recommended and decided we don't have to be on the front burner for something like that."

Loughead probably erred politically in his dealings with the board by not using the opportunity to appoint two additional members from management, his view being that all executive leadership spoke through him. Unfortunately, at crunch times on policy decisions he stood alone when he could have used additional support. Much savvier politically, the union filled and made good use of its three seats, which generally voted together.

Another problem for Loughead and the board was the balance sheet in the annual reports, which seemed a bit fishy on one point— the dollar amount of capital spending. Each year under Loughead the corporation actually broke the amount down further into the portions "committed" and "spent." So the $65 million capitalization figure that Loughead described in his preface in the 1984 Annual Report actually amounted to only $37.5 million spent. More important, modernization lagged behind the goal of $100 million per year over ten years. In 1985, capital spending (committed and spent) equaled only $47.5 million. In 1986 the figure dropped to $46 million. The worry was that the Weirton ESOP would emerge from its crucial decade unable to compete with the rest of the industry's survivors following a brutal technological shakeout. Probably worse was the fact that if Weirton had spent the predicted $100 million allotment, earnings would have been erased and with them profit sharing. Nor under Loughead was the corporation making progress toward trimming labor costs. Instead of approaching the 7,000 or fewer number favored by McKinsey, at the close of the fourth quarter of 1986 the workforce reached its modern peak with a total of 8,467 employees. Yet Loughead assured shareholders, "We are reaching for the future and it is within our grasp."

Like the OIP, the board, under the leadership of Audit Committee chairman Philip Smith, a rigorously moral man who had preceded Loughead as president of Copperweld, took it upon itself to investigate corruption in the company, and push out a few residual managers who were running side deals and scams, and taking bribes from vendors. In general, the board wanted the old National executive manage-ment out, and given attractive severances. All but Carl Valdiserri parachuted.

Valdiserri, who had functioned capably as Redline's right hand, now assumed the number two spot under Loughead. The pair quickly cemented a strong bond. In some ways Loughead, a former accountant lacking production experience in flat-rolled steel making and coating, came to rely on Valdiserri more than had Redline. According to Irving Bluestone, the board came to see Loughead "as kind of a captive of Valdiserri."

In 1986, the board demanded that Loughead hire a chief operating officer. The idea was that the COO would handle manpower reduction, rebuilding, and equipment concerns, while Loughead would become a sort of industrial chancellor, raising money, overseeing marketing, and exercising general leadership.

Once Loughead's chief proponent, Harvey Sperry, the toughest, most powerful, and most influential director, became the CEO's biggest detractor. In fact, they had gotten off on the wrong foot. Shortly after Loughead's installation in late 1983, Sperry and Gene Keilin met with him to offer their (negative) opinions about local management. But Loughead, in Sperry's view, already had "adopted literally as his own" the leftover leaders from the division. "We both walked out of the meeting feeling as if we were little kids who had tattled. It was the darndest thing for a couple of adults."

In 1985, Gene Keilin became an ongoing financial consultant to the USW on rebuilding the steel industry. Seeing possible conflicts of interest down the road between serving as a director at Weirton, with an independent union, and helping the rest of the industry whose workers were represented by the United Steelworkers, Keilin resigned from the board and was promptly replaced by Tom Sturges of Bear Stearns, another New York investment banker in his early forties. Loughead rued Keilin's departure, as a "very, very significant loss." In fact, it probably *was* for the CEO, who might have received an understanding ear from Keilin about his pro-labor policies. As it was, Harvey Sperry lost his only peer on the board in terms of knowledge of the company, its origins, and perhaps above all its politics.

During the buyout period, Sperry and Keilin had sometimes argued bitterly in front of the ISU (they *never* fought in front of National, to whom they presented a tough, creative, and unified front), and some union leaders speculated that the lawyer had had a hand in or at least welcomed Keilin's resignation. There is no evidence for that, but Sperry, who was untroubled by serving simultaneously on the boards of Weirton and Kerr Glass (which kept food in jars instead of cans), saw Keilin's resignation as a necessity. "Great loss, the son of a bitch," he said warmly. "He left to go out and be the Messiah in the steel industry, try to lead everybody else into the cost-production promised land. They [the USW] wouldn't give him the numbers and we couldn't have him going out and buying for the rest of the steel industry when he's on the Weirton board. Hell yes, he was a good guy. He left this Loughead job to me."

Sperry knew that getting rid of the CEO would be difficult:

> See, the trouble with it was we had traditional business guys on the board and Bob was making money. And if you're making money you don't fault the guy. That's normal. But our problem was that we weren't building our management. We knew that without good management this thing was not going to survive, no matter what the hell was done. We were losing faith in the kind of presentations he was doing. We were beginning not to quite believe what he was presenting to us. And we knew the job was too big for one guy to handle and we knew the quality was just not in it. Just too many faults. There were too many instances where Bob's reaction was clearly that of a person who was way over his head. He reacted angrily. In the

board meetings one minute he'd just explode and blow up about this and blow up about that. They were afraid of dealing with the problems, how close he was, how he would react to this. And they were afraid of firing a guy, of letting a guy go who was making money. And then there's always the difficulty of the unknown. They were afraid of the unknown.

In addition, Sperry recalled that Loughead feared Phil Smith, his former superior at Copperweld. Smith said Sperry "was one of the guys who became convinced that he had to go. Phil was one of the guys on the board that Bob disliked the most because he thought Phil was always trying to take the thing over, take it away from him. Bob was paranoid. He was a classic Nixon type, except he didn't have some of Nixon's extraordinary abilities. He really had no long view, he had no short view. He really was a perfect Peter Principle proposition. It was a mistake, for him, and it was a mistake for us."

Loughead might have saved himself if he had brought in a COO. But, he waffled and temporized. "His idea," said Sperry, "was to defer it and defer it. He was going to call this guy. He was going to call that guy. He argued with how much the guy had to be paid, because it was too much. It really opened everybody's eyes."

Early in 1987, "the board," said Sperry, "did the most significant thing that a board could do." It fired the chief executive. According to Sperry, the vote was unanimous, with the union representatives falling into line. Bluestone felt that Loughead had become inaccessible by using Valdiserri as a screen, and more importantly that the CEO had failed to follow through on a study to trim middle management.

In the 1986 Annual Report, Loughead guaranteed that "employee-owners have the inherent right to be well informed." By all accounts, openness and candor had distinguished his dealings with the workforce.

On February 1, 1987, his resignation was announced. Looking saddened and weary, at a press conference, Loughead, fifty-seven, insisted that he simply had decided to "resurrect" long-standing plans for early retirement. His leaving was in fairness to the corporation, which was embarking on a long-term modernization drive that a new

CEO should see through. He had made the decision on his own. No, the board had not forced him to resign; nor had he lost touch.

Nothing could be further from the truth in two respects. First, of all, I was not pushed into anything and secondly, my having lost control of the day-to-day operation, [or] to assume that has occurred, is ludicrous. I am as close to the operations as I ever was and I considered that to be very, very important.

I am not suffering from any deadly disease. I am not in poor health. I'm not depressed over the state of the industry. I have decided I am going to do something different. I don't know exactly what it will be. It might not be anything more than sailing a boat, but it may be something more than that. I'm looking forward to whatever I do next.

Loughead praised the communications and employee involvement programs, and said, "My supreme hope would be that it's said after I leave Weirton that things were better because I was here and that I made a difference." Within a month Carl Valdiserri also had quit.

Loughead's resignation shocked the community, which saw through the well-orchestrated charade about a voluntary retirement. The CEO's demise was questioned and deplored by a wide range of people from Staughton Lynd to Mike Hrabovsky, who said: "Loughead in my opinion was a man's president. I think he would've been very good for this company. The man was honest. That kind of man will never make it in Weirton."

In announcing his resignation, Loughead made clear that he would stay until a successor took the helm. He assured the company that he would be "on the job" and "not a lame duck." Morale, however, continued to drop. One problem was the accurate perception that the economic burden was not being shared equally. A premise of the ESOP was that all wages would be frozen, and this became enshrined in the 1983 and 1986 contracts between the company and the ISU. However, in 1986 and 1987, it became apparent that some executives were receiving raises, which the company felt were necessary to prevent them from leaving.

Another problem, potentially far more explosive, was the fact that the board and top management had begun to talk softly about trying to alter the profit sharing formula, and in particular the provision that would raise it from one-third to 50 percent when net worth hit $250 million, which looked like a certainty by 1989. While the promise of an eventual 50 percent distribution had won many votes in favor of the ESOP in 1983, the directors doubted that the modernization could be financed with half the earnings.

In addition, questions about whether steel was yesterday's product, and could no longer compete, gnawed at the workforce especially after *Independent Weirton* republished a ten-year study from *Metal Working News* breaking down the materials mix in the American car. In 1977 the average car weighed 3,665 pounds. By 1987, it was down to 3,178 and most of the loss came out of carbon steel, which contributed 1,995 pounds in 1977 but only 1,459 in 1987. Conversely, plastics shot from 178 pounds in 1977 to 221.5 pounds ten years later; and a rule of thumb in the industry was that a pound of automotive plastic could compensate for 2 pounds of steel. Similarly, aluminum's 97 pounds in 1977 rose to 196 pounds in 1987.

■

While trying to replace Loughead, the board made overtures to a number of outside steel executives. Twice turned down, they now considered picking one of their own to be the second CEO. Sperry favored Herb Elish, fifty-three, who was somewhat of an unlikely choice. First, before sitting on the board he had had no steel-making experience. A former senior vice president of administration with International Paper Company, he had left that position when passed over for the top spot and moved to the Dreyfus Fund, a New York financial service company, also as a senior vice president. Second, if chosen he would be the first Jew appointed to the top spot of a major eastern steel company.

Not troubled by the lack of steel experience, many members of the board viewed it as a plus. Service in the industry during its years of decline and eclipse by foreign producers was seen as synonymous with sloppy management and hidebound thinking—in short, stupidity. Elish, a bearish man, with dense eyebrows shrouding deep-set eyes, was not stupid. His academic credentials—Phi Beta Kappa at

Williams, followed by Harvard Law School—seemed atypical and glamorous in a world of local engineering and business degrees.

At International Paper, he had run operations domestically and abroad, but equally impressive was his prior service as the first executive director of New York's Municipal Assistance Corporation (MAC), where he preceded Gene Keilin, and his earlier job, as the city's sanitation commissioner. Hence, he knew two key disciplines critical in steel: negotiating with labor (and extracting concessions), and environmental regulation. In addition, his jobs at Dreyfus and Citibank gave him a financial background and connections; and Weirton was about to go into a complicated financial restructuring.

The Jewish issue also was discussed by the board. But the gist was that times had changed and religion wouldn't be an impediment. Indeed, the Duquesne Club, bastion of the regional industrialists, had ceased to discriminate, though some elite country clubs were slower to change.

In particular, Sperry liked Elish because "he seemed so darn comfortable with himself," a refreshing change after the Nixonion insecurity and temper of Loughead. Because Sperry had pushed hard for Loughead, he now recruited David Robertson to help talk up Elish, and the rest of the board fell in line.

In fact, Elish, who *was* comfortable with himself, from the outset seemed different from Loughead. While Elish's goal was to lead a corporation, his ambition was not blind to personal issues. Unlike his predecessor, he did not seek the position without alerting his wife. Elish considered with her all aspects of the move from New York, including their decision to locate in Pittsburgh, rather than Weirton, which they felt was more conducive to her work and would hold better educational opportunities for their small child. The decision not to live in Weirton (where Redline and Loughead, though not Weir, had made homes) was viewed as a slight by locals, who also bandied about the fact that Elish bought a house in Pittsburgh so that he and his family could be among Jewish people and practice their religion. Elish, who had a thick skin, appeared not to be bothered by such remarks.

In other ways Elish's background was dissimilar from that of typical steel managers with basically conformist views. The son of a Russian who emigrated to New York in 1913 and became a successful small businessman, Elish attended public schools and recalled a family "concerned with the world, and what we do with it, political questions. I grew up in a house where, certainly on the weekends, the entire family would gather over dinner and argue about political questions for hours. And first, I'd listen, then I'd participate. It was a wonderful thing. Nobody ever talked about making money, it was something you did because you had to live, but that was not anyone's objective. It was never the marker where you measure success, which is what exists too much today in our society, from my point of view. It was always other things, the kind of person you were, who you helped, what you did, how you participated in society."

At about the age of twelve he began going to Union Square, where political speakers of all stripes would climb on soapboxes and declaim to whoever would listen. Elish was there "not for entertainment, and not for ridiculing them, but to participate. At the time there was an ability in the country to have much more divergent views, than is possible today." Now, he believed, "the range of acceptable discourse has narrowed to a pretty unhealthy level," a change "probably stemming from Joseph McCarthy."

At college in the 1950s he majored in political science. Going to Williams from Brooklyn "was like traveling to another country. It was a difficult four years socially, because there was a fraternity structure that was exclusionary and I became somewhat of a revolutionary in terms of trying to end that system." Not knowing what he wanted to do with his life, but having vague notions of public service, he went to law school, which also enabled him to avoid the post-Korea draft. He "never had a burning ambition to be a lawyer," and it never occurred to him to try to join a major Wall Street firm "which was virtually impossible for a Jew. I'm of the age where working for the government was a start."

He took a job in Washington with the Civil Aeronautics Board (CAB), regulating airlines, worked for a time with USAir's predecessor, Allegheny Airlines, and then practiced administrative law in various private law firms. While shaving in 1969, he decided that he needed to make a break. "I remember very distinctly, saying to myself, if you don't do it you are going to be in front of this mirror for the next thirty years and one day you are going to be sixty-five, and you will not have been able to tell one day from another." Not long afterwards he met a friend in New York mayor Lindsay's administration who helped him land a job as deputy environmental commissioner, which Elish held for six months before becoming sanitation commissioner. The position taught him how to manage a large organization and cope with a public crisis, which included garbage riots. Above all he established a labor relations style that involved dealing with a union "very straight up; I'm not a believer in confrontational relationships. In the long run they are dangerous, and damaging unless you get to a point where after a full explanation of being clear, you've got to do what you've got to do." While at International Paper he was the only person tabbed for the Weirton board of directors by both McKinsey, where he had good friends, and by Lazard Frères, whose Gene Keilin succeeded him at MAC. Passed over for chairman at International Paper he quit, took six months off, "paid a lot of attention to my new baby, and read a lot."

In his next position, a vice presidency at Dreyfus, Elish, who maintains, "If I'm learning something, I'm pretty happy," learned about dealing with "a workforce that was about eighty percent clerical. But the top job at Weirton was clearly a much more interesting thing for me to do than what I was doing. It wasn't money. This is just a very rich experience. The ability to make a difference was very important to me."

At Weirton, Elish tried to smooth the transition by appearing publicly with Loughead at company functions and picnics, which conveyed the message that the former president was not being banished in the Redline vein. Also, Elish tried to cope with fears, based on the twists and turns in his job history, that Weirton was merely a stepping-stone or resting place before he moved on to bigger things. "This," he said sincerely, "is going to be my last job. I intend to work here until I retire."

Despite his direct manner, he initially won more favor with the board than with the workforce. Elish appointed a chief operating officer, Warren Bartel, forty-one, whom Weirton hired away from USX, where Bartel had headed the Geneva steel plant in Provo, Utah, until 1984, and then became general manager of all of that corporation's Pittsburgh-area operations known as the Mon Valley Works. Elish, who gave Bartel the special mission to improve worker safety in addition to his other duties, also filled the two vacant management seats on the board with Bartel and David Gould, the vice president of sheet product sales, a friendly, popular representative of pre-ESOP Weirton (his brother is Alan Gould). The balancing of the management seats between the old and the new was politically astute.

With Elish installed, the company drove the final nail into the coke-free K-R project, notwithstanding that the Department of Energy had already approved the grant. Elish maintained that end-stage negotiations with the German manufacturer did not work out, that "the fact remains that [the process] has not been proven in commercial applications," and that the cost to Weirton to contract and run the plant through its two-year "demonstration" phase would have been more than $100 million.

Elish took a hard look at another contemplated spending project that the corporation had embraced publicly under Loughead, the installation of a second continuous caster at a cost in excess of $300 million. Elish convened a task force at Weirton and retained SMS Concast, a leading American caster builder, as an adviser in April 1988. Concast reported that the existing slab caster could be overhauled to widen all four stands and improve its speed at a cost of $38 million with only six weeks of downtime.

In many ways, Weirton was betting its future on the caster issue. In order to be competitive in the world steel market of the late twentieth century, integrated producers knew that they had to become "a hundred percent cast," and eliminate the extra steps, costs, and impurities inherent in the ignot pouring process. At the time, about half of Weirton's product was cast. Whether the company could step up to total casting with a rebuilt 1960s vintage machine was the burning question. As a result, Elish hired a second consultant, Nippon Steel, which confirmed that the caster could be rehabbed at Concast's approximate price to process all grades and widths of steel up to forty-nine inches, as well as to include a state-of-the-art bending system to reduce crack-causing strains at the liquid/solid interface on the blazing slab.

To Elish, choosing to revamp accorded with his earlier experience in the paper industry. "I had spent a lot of time [being] responsible for old mills. My view about them is to try to find existing facilities that can be fixed or modernized, rather than trying to spend a lot of money putting new equipment in. Normally, you have a competitive problem with an old mill anyway, and one way to deal with it is to get as modern as you can while limiting expenditures. Normally, ripping out the old and putting in the new is something my stomach tells me is not the right answer."

The board loved the savings associated with dropping the new caster. "Herb," said Sperry, "paid for his position over the next ten years." The vice president of engineering under Loughead, who had pushed for replacement, was now forced to resign in disgrace. The board, recalled Irving Bluestone, now felt that it had been "snowed" by the old regime.

The caster rebuild proved popular with much of the workforce, which believed that the savings would allow their profit sharing formula to remain undisturbed. But the administration and board continued to doubt that earnings could fuel the remaining substantial capital projects costing about half a billion dollars, including rebuilding a blast furnace, acquiring environmental emissions controls, and revamping the hot strip mill. Moreover, everyone in the corporation was aware that the National "safety net" would expire in late 1988.

Elish was popular with management, which liked the idea of having Gould and Bartel on the board. Also, unlike Loughead, Elish was a natural decentralizer whose aggressive management policy pushed "decision making downward." With more authority, he believed that "good people tend to get better."

At the fall 1987 annual meeting, Elish told the assembled employee-owners that "your success has exceeded everyone's most optimistic expectations," but warned that the steel industry, though enjoying health after a shakeout, was intrinsically cyclical. It would be important to "manage *our* business so that we can prosper in the good times and survive during the downturns. You have a right to be proud and enjoy your gains, but you have a responsibility to plan ahead in a sober fashion." This led into a discussion of such financial options as an initial public offering (IPO) of the stock and profit sharing modifications. "I am here to tell you [that] we will not be able to finance our investments based on fifty percent profit sharing." The board, he said, had retained Lazard Frères and Bear Stearns to opine on the financial issues.

Elish took angry questions from the floor about profit sharing and assured them that any change in formula would have to be approved by a vote of employees. When workers griped about frozen pay while executives drew raises, Elish explained the increases were tied to management job combinations or increased responsibilities. Later he said that raises also could be applied to "critical skills in great demand in the marketplace." Elish also scotched a rumor that the board of directors had voted themselves a raise, but from the crowd, someone called Elish a "maggot."

Fueled by $3 billion from savings and loans, initial public offerings (IPOs) became a major part of the financial fever of the 1980s. In 1983, at the height of the bull market, 687 companies went public with shares valued at $12.6 billion.

Avidly reported by the financial press and new publications such as *Going Public* and *New Issue Investor*, IPOs typically favored high-tech Silicon Valley outfits, health care start-ups, and new entries into the service economy. Some of the biggest winners included Sun Microsystems, the maker of computer work stations, Microsoft, best known for creating the software for IBM personal computers, U.S. Health Care, and Agency Rent-A-Car. These stocks took off after opening. For instance, U.S. Health Care shot from $8 ½ to $20 in the first six months, a 138 percent gain. The other big winners were brokerage houses that served as underwriters for the offerings such as Merrill Lynch, which raised $2.4 billion in 1983.

Naturally there were losers. Typically, the IPOs were young companies without proven track records, and the market could not love them all—no matter how high-tech or glamorous. For instance, Diasonics, heralded for its work in nuclear magnetic resonance, saw its stock plunge from $22 to less than $9 in six months when General Electric entered the market. Kolff Medical, maker of the artificial heart, slipped from $12¼ to $4½ during the same period.

As investments, IPOs were and are inherently unstable. To say the least, Weirton, an antique steel mill, seemed like a weird offering when contrasted with a welter of shiny science and service ventures. Who would buy new stock in such an old industry?

In the ensuing months, wild rumors swept through the plant relating to National and how it would shortly buy Weirton off the public market. The slur persisted that after Elish had done Wall Street's bidding by selling stock and cutting profit sharing, he would leave. On "News and Views," Chuck Lafferty started a new "rumor of the week" feature, in which a balloon was blown up while he recited the rumor. Then Lafferty would give the facts, and stick the balloon with a pin.

Bish and Elish now teamed up to rekindle the venerable tradition of in-plant meetings. Clearly a skilled communicator, Elish never talked down to workers. Nor, like so many other managers, did he adjust his speech and mannerisms to mimic them. Direct while delivering the bitter medicine about sacrificing to stay competitive, he urged them to keep an open mind.

Walter Bish, on the other hand, became ill at ease. While clearly on the same page as Elish, Bish, who faced an election in the summer of 1988, told the crowds in locker rooms, garages, and lunch areas, to wait and see what Lazard and Bear Stearns had to say. In any event, the union would have the opportunity to vote not to go public or cut their profit shares. Often in the back of these crowds there was grumbling about how the company and the union were in bed. While no early formal opposition to Bish emerged, David Robertson, who had stepped down as the union's lawyer but remained close to the ISU president and on the board, observed in January 1988, "There's a lot of dissatisfaction, now, and if it continues, Walter could take a fall."

In early March, after four months of study, Lazard Frères and Bear Stearns released their findings. To no one's surprise, they recommended a public market for the stock and keeping profit sharing at one-third. The report painted a gloomy picture of a company that had lost its competitive cost advantage, and spent less per ton on modernization than its chief competitors. Fifty percent profit sharing, insisted the investment bankers, would eradicate totally the company's labor cost advantage. Plus, they forecast that within five years it would result in a cash shortfall.

In most public offerings, companies sell stock to raise capital, but not to avoid obligations to repurchase shares from retirees and other employees, which, as Harvey Sperry explained, over the next five years even under the most optimistic scenario would result in a $265 million payout. "We understand," he added, "that a number of employee-owners have expressed some concern about loss of control if Weirton Steel common stock is owned by the public." The investment bankers suggested some ways to retain internal power, such as making key corporate actions dependent on "super majorities," say, 80 percent of shareholders, or giving shares held by employee-owners more votes than those held outside the company. But that would discount the price of stock on the public market, where over time the majority of Weirton shares would flow.

Lazard and Bear Stearns also acted as independent appraisers of the presently untradeable Weirton stock. Ominously, the estimated net price had fallen from $51 to $45 per share between December 31, 1986, and December 31, 1987. Skip Spadafora, a member of the ESOP administrative committee, to whom the appraisers reported, explained the 12 percent plunge as a product of fears of a recession that hadn't yet begun. Though the recession was closer in the spring of 1988, Josh Gotbaum of Lazard announced that the stock could fetch $60 on the open market if profit sharing were reduced. On average, Weirton workers held between five hundred and a thousand shares. People began to tot up their holdings.

Before the ISU campaign season began, Walter Bish endorsed the Lazard and Bear Stearns proposal, which he and Elish touted in every corner of the mill, as Lafferty's communications machine cranked out a blizzard of information about markets, securities, and trading.

The idealogues of the ESOP movement, Louis Kelso and Norman Kurland, feared the worst. On March 4, 1988, Kurland called David Robertson to warn that "we can lose everything, if we don't have a strategy which allows us to keep Weirton one hundred percent employee owned. You are destroying a world-class model of employee ownership. We need a game plan or those in favor of a public sale will win." Kurland cautioned that "money available for capital cannot be used to repurchase." He suggested utilizing "a portion of the money present for investment in your pension plan," not to exceed 10 percent, as well as pledge money in the community, plus only sell-

ing preferred nonvoting stock. Unknown to Kurland, Robertson, like
Bish, already supported the Lazard, Bear Stearns plan. At the end of
the call, Robertson dismissively noted that Kurland was looking for a
consulting job.

As the ISU election of 1988 approached, it appeared that Walter
Bish again would face no real competition. Only one rival presidential candidate, Carl Ferguson, a steward from the welding and sheet
metal shop in Steel Works Two, had substantial experience in mill
politics. While talking tough about not trusting management, Ferguson had little new to say and faded fast.

Heavily favored, Bish ran on his record. "We've gotten everybody
back to work," he would tell his constituents. "Everybody that lost
recall rights has had the opportunity to come back. Even with the reductions and concessions we've had to make, our average wage in
the hourly ranks is still over thirty-two thousand dollars here. We've
protected all of the pensions that we had with National Steel prior to
coming into the new company, and we negotiated that 'work to get,'
which means that a person can still retire with thirty years' service regardless of their age. We've kept our benefit package, including first-
dollar medical coverage, the best health care in the industry. We've
had three profit sharing distributions, and over seventy-five million
dollars has gone back to the members. We've had four stock alloca-
tions. Everybody here owns, on the average, between fifteen and
twenty thousand dollars' worth of stock. Today it is something they
can't get their hands on, but four years ago I was told by people we
would never see the first profit sharing check. Now it's a reality, and
someday people are going to get their hands on that [stock] money.
So when you look back, you can say we've got all three thousand
people back; we've had a decent wage scale, and we've got pensions
intact. Sure it's not a bowl of cherries, we still have problems—it's an
industrial setting. But overall with what we faced, my God, it's been
great for us."

Assembled workers seemed to listen without enthusiasm. A few
wore buttons that said: "Just Say No to Concessions." Bish said he
favored the stock sale, reduction in profit sharing, and getting rid of
the stock repurchase snag. He said he had trusted Lazard Frères during the buyout and trusted them to point the direction now.

He also believed the control issues could be resolved favorably.

The alternatives were simply to leave the present financial structure in place in which case he thought the plant would be able to operate four or five years, and then would collapse for failing to modernize and under the weight of the stock repurchase. Financing the massive retooling with loans would be hazardous because the debt service would choke the operation when the inevitable downward cycle in steel occurred.

The surprise of the campaign was Virgil Thompson, thirty-eight, who forced a runoff with Bish. Thompson, a tin mill craneman for nineteen years who lacked union political experience, staked out a position slightly to the right of Ferguson, and argued that Bish had grown too close to management and that a change was needed.

As Bish ran on his record, Thompson, the son of a Weirton retiree, ran on his résumé. At nineteen, he had served as a platoon leader with the 82nd Airborne in Vietnam. Thompson especially impressed the Weirton community with his education. While working full-time in the plant, he had earned a bachelor's degree in business administration, double-majoring in accounting and management at nearby West Liberty State, and then took a law degree in 1986 from West Virginia University and joined the bar. On paper, Thompson looked well qualified to guide the union members through the company's financial maze. In meetings with the voters, Thompson's business acumen clearly rivaled Bish's and eclipsed Ferguson's. Moreover, Thompson had honed political skills, having run but narrowly lost a race for a seat in the West Virginia House of Delegates as a Republican.

Constantly Bish found himself on the defensive. Workers expressed surprise about the proposals to go public and alter profit sharing. Bish told them these changes had been contemplated "during the ESOP," and that they could find the proof in their old disclosure documents. The answer seemed less than satisfying, as did the incumbent's pleading that they trust the investment bankers and lawyers who had steered them through the buyout, Herb Elish, and himself.

Thompson exploited the situation by pointing out that Lazard and Willkie Farr should not necessarily be relied on since they had a financial interest in the proposed changes, namely underwriting the initial public offering (IPO), and providing the legal mechanisms to sell stock and to change profit sharing. The candidate argued that the union should retain its own independent investment banker and attorney in "due diligence" to evaluate the financial moves. Bish and Elish seemed pained by Thompson's notion, as if he had blasphemed the spirit of unity underlying the ESOP.

The pro-Bish forces struck back by questioning why someone with a law degree still would be running a crane. Thompson replied, "I have nineteen years in the mill and I do not want to just throw away that service. I plan to retire from Weirton with thirty years' service and a full pension."

A more serious accusation against the would-be union leader was that he, like many of the border state's Republicans, favored right-to-work legislation, and by extension the end of the closed union shop at Weirton. Thompson virgorously denied the charge, but never made it go away.

When the race was over, Thompson had slammed Bish in a landslide, receiving 3,649 votes to the incumbent's 2,034. A graceful winner, Thompson called his predecessor "a good president. In all honesty, I don't think I won because Virgil Thompson was a better candidate than Walter Bish. I won because people wanted a change." Stunned by Bish's loss, management seemed fearful of Thompson, who extended an olive branch. "A gap exists between union members and management. That gap needs to be closed."

In defeat Bish reminisced about the buyout crisis. "We were all in the same lifeboat. The union and management were facing the same problem—survival—and we all had to pull together." He lamented the present mood in the mill: "I feel discouraged that we have not really been able to get people to fully realize ownership and the responsibility that goes along with it. I still see mistrust among union and management. We have two facilities here, a steel mill and a rumor mill. We have so many vehicles of communication, yet some people would rather take the easy way and believe rumors." He asked the union members to "keep an open mind. . . . Look at all the recommendations and remember that at this point they are only recommendations. We have to face up to the responsibility of ownership by coming up with the best solutions for the long-term viability of the corporation. It is up to us to make the final decisions.

"Profit sharing is great, but, in my opinion it can't compare to what the value of our stock could be someday. In '82 we were facing a shutdown or massive downsizing. There were thousands on the street. Now, we're making money and it's hard to think of times when that may not be the case. But we have to able to survive when the tough times come again. We have to be able to keep up with our competitors. The world has changed since 1982 and that's why we're faced with another decision."

For weeks, the main question around the mill was: What will Walter do? Few could see a man who had spoken on ESOPs at Cambridge University and served on two Reagan presidential task forces going back to work as a conductor on the company railroad. Also, his lifestyle had changed. "He's used to flying in airplanes and staying in hotels," said Bill Doepken, "he'll never go back into the mill." In early fall 1988, Elish appointed him to a white-collar job. As the new director of government relations, the former union leader's main duty involved lobbying in favor of protectionism for American steel in the form of Voluntary Restraint Agreements (VRAs) to reduce the market shares of foreign producers.

Once again the torch had passed at Weirton. The company now had removed its seminal labor leader as well as its founding president. The replacements had no particular stature in the industry. Inevitable questions arose as to whether Elish and Thompson could work together, and more fundamentally about whether they were substantial leaders or momentary place holders under whom the company would drift.

21 The Class of '88

Virgil Thompson lost no time getting up to speed. The new union president cloistered himself with David Robertson and Rob D'Anniballe, the ISU lawyer who had succeeded Robertson. Also, he relied extensively on Skip Spadafora and Eddie Conley, the two carryover ISU committeemen most knowledgeable about restructuring issues.

Eager to get the changes made, Herb Elish began to press them in the media and at EPG graduations. The highly paid New York consultants came back to Weirton. Elish took the position that half a billion dollars had to be found immediately for modernization to

285

proceed. Otherwise, the corporation could not compete. But rapid capitalization, as everyone in the steel industry knew, was a delicate operation. Stock value would be depressed by a top-heavy debt-equity ratio. Moreover, Weirton's nearby rival, Wheeling-Pittsburgh Steel, had tumbled into bankruptcy when saddled with too much debt over too short a period.

The New York consultants returned to Weirton for a raft of pre-sentations to the board, the workforce, and over the in-plant media. Having Lazard and Wilkie Farr advocate financial restructuring was in itself tricky because their firms had come up with the original plan, which they now deemed inadequate. In part, they overcame the seeming contradiction by using new front men instead of Gene Keilin and Harvey Sperry, who for the moment stayed in the wings.

Josh Gotbaum, Keilin's lieutenant, manfully took responsibility for making miscalculations during the buyout period, which now had to be corrected in order for Weirton to thrive. Willkie Farr was fronted by Jim Testa, a tall, quiet technician in his late thirties who had drafted much of the disclosure document and admitted to owing his partnership to Sperry.

The basic message of the consultants to the company and its work-force was change or die. Unlike Weirton, the steel industry had been trimming employment costs. Between 1983 and 1987, overall em-ployment in the industry fell from 243,000 to 163,000. Bethlehem lost a third of its workforce, while LTV and USX dropped 40 percent and 43 percent respectively. Likewise, since the birth of the ESOP, Weirton not only had failed to live up to its plan to spend $33 dollars per ton shipped on capital improvements (its actual figure was closer to $18) but it fell far behind industry leaders such as National ($35), which seemed ironic in that the parent company had blocked mod-ernizing the West Virginia facility, Bethlehem ($37), Inland ($26), and even bankrupt Wheeling-Pittsburgh ($20). Weirton's edge in profitability was gone. The industry leader in 1984 at $42 per ton, Weirton now ran third behind Wheeling-Pittsburgh and LTV, and had Armco and Bethlehem at its heels.

Nor, to use a phrase coined by human resources managers in the 1980s, had it "rationalized" its workforce, by eliminating work rules or combining jobs through "multicrafting," or eliminating rigid clas-sifications. At the time, the industry, led by USX, was agreeing to multicrafting with the United Steelworkers on a local-by-local basis. National had stunned the steel business by going from more than eighty job categories to less than twenty at its Great Lakes mills.

The investment bankers painted a picture of Weirton as the new dinosaur of the industry. They pointed out that even at the present level, Weirton's profit sharing topped the industry. Bethlehem offered profit sharing within a 10 percent to 20 percent range. National was slightly lower. Bloating to 50 percent, argued Keilin and Gotbaum, amounted to fat that the corporation could not carry. Even if the figure stayed at 33 percent, they argued that Weirton would not have enough cash on hand to pay for modernization.

The investment bankers warned the employees that the amount of capital needed for modernization could not be extracted from traditional lending institutions, which had grown leery of steel's long-term prospects. In other words, E. T. Weir's historical answer to growth—debt—would not work, and 100 percent employee ownership would have to yield. A bitter pill to swallow, Gene Keilin sweetened it with notions of market riches. In the spring of 1988, the Lazard banker educated employees on the concept of price-to-earnings ratio (P/E), and used Bethlehem Steel as an example. Though not as healthy as Weirton, Bethlehem in 1988 enjoyed a 6.7 P/E multiple. Keilin, who had great credibility with the workforce because of his role in the buyout, his identification with labor, and his principled resignation in 1985, estimated Weirton's value in the public market assuming the elimination of the stock repurchase liability and keeping profit sharing at a third: With stock worth $56 to $65 and an average of 750 shares per employee, the typical Weirton worker's holdings would be worth $42,000 to $50,000. Though Keilin cautioned that he based values on the "current market," which "will change," the opposition to going public and to the eventual loss of local control began to melt, as it had at most smaller ESOPs that had smelled money in the market.

In the early fall of 1988, the union checked Keilin's assessment by inviting a trusted local stockbroker to an executive committee meeting. Even after hearing a chilling presentation by a pipefitter suffering asbestosis about the pervasiveness of asbestos in the mill (complete removal estimates were in the $1 billion range), the broker confidently announced, "I'd buy every share you've got at forty-five dollars." Like Keilin, the broker spoke of some urgency to get the shares sold before the economy went sour.

Financial consultants played a key role in Weirton as they did at other companies in the eighties. Typically they provided management with high-level composite data about the steel industry and competitors, the next best thing to inside information. From their lofty positions as outside experts they came up with market and capital strategies, and often with "bitter pills," in the nature of reducing labor costs, jobs, and benefits. Because the ideas originated with outsiders who came and went, these consultants rather than management were seen as the "bad guys." Moreover, if the advisers' ideas were too unpopular to implement, management could back away from them.

On the brink of a potential IPO, investment bankers played a different but related role. They hoped to underwrite the new stock, in other words to buy it from the company, thus guaranteeing it capital, and then selling it to the market at a markup to the highest possible price. Because outside shareholders perceive that stock value is reduced by inefficiency and high labor costs, investment bankers have an interest in marketing tightly run companies in a cost-cutting mode. Sometimes before going public, management will hire an industrial psychologist to quantify the mood of the employees—happy companies also sell—and to determine how open they are to sacrifice.

Embarking on its crusade to go public and alter profit sharing, the company hired David Sirota, a New York psychologist, to conduct an attitudinal survey throughout the corporation. On September 28, 1988, the gentle, bespectacled Sirota appeared at the ISU executive committee meeting to request the union's cooperation with his study. During a somewhat windy presentation, Sirota mentioned that Elish, before coming to Weirton, had commissioned him to gather similar data on labor at the CEO's prior companies. Suddenly Dominic Tonacchio rose and stormed out of the room, ranting against retaining yet another consultant. Others favored resistance to the study in light of the fact that the reports of consultants (with whom the union had cooperated), who had recommended eliminating numerous supervisory personnel, had met with a managerial deaf ear.

Virgil Thompson and Eddie Conley argued that a study of employee morale could prove valuable to the union as it attempted to represent its membership through a tricky transition process. But negative voices drowned them out. A huge, particularly angry committeeman, wearing a baseball cap emblazoned with a "snuffer" logo, and a muscle gym sweatshirt under which he seemed to be smuggling bowling balls, added, "You better believe that Sirota is a Jew like Elish." After an awkward pause, someone called the question. By 8 to 6, the committee voted in favor of participating in the Sirota study.

While many in the community in the early fall of 1988 expected the workforce to reject management's restructuring package, David Robertson took the ISU's executive committee's flip on Sirota as a harbinger of its eventual acceptance of relinquishing 100 percent ownership and 50 percent profit sharing. Robertson felt sure that "much of the negativism had been absorbed in the 'no' vote on Walter." But resistance remained strong as Herb Elish found when he implored the ISU executive committee in October not to hire its own investment banker. Sticking up for Lazard Frères and Bear Stearns, who he said had "great interest in Weirton Steel and a lot of feeling for this place," he decried a lack of communications between labor and management over the previous months and a downturn in morale, vowing to correct both.

Unswayed, the union hired Prudential-Bache Capital Funding, as its analyst and counterpart to Lazard and Bear Stearns. After a brief but intense period of negotiations with management, the ISU won the right for Prudential-Bache to serve as a co-underwriter of the initial public offering. Because the ISU did not want to entice its own Wall Street player to do a deal if not in the employees' interest, Virgil Thompson negotiated a fallback position with Elish. If the IPO did not occur, the company nonetheless would pay Prudential-Bache $150,000.

The company obviously was trying to make the union feel comfortable as its membership moved headlong into the financial fray. Clearly management also felt a necessary degree of comfort with the union's chosen investment bank. However, the company soon made it clear that it would let no outside challenger into the tent.

The union also perceived a need to hire its own lawyer-negotiator (and foil to Sperry) and again went to Wall Street. It quickly engaged Mike Connery of Skadden, Arps, Meagher and Flom, a gigantic firm specializing in mergers, acquisitions, takeovers, and defenses, which happened to be the office that Kenneth Bialkin, the JSC's first lawyer at Willkie Farr, subsequently had joined.

In his late forties, tall and fit, with close-cropped sandy hair and chiseled jaw, Connery cut a coolly impressive figure in an expensive suit at a general ISU membership meeting on a muggy Indian summer night. After an introduction by a profusely sweating Virgil Thompson, Connery explained that he and his firm had the background and experience to do battle with management's Wall Street consultants, and that he saw the unfolding process as "great opportunity" for the employees to "learn about the company."

Thompson also introduced members of the Prudential-Bache team, including George Doty, a tow-headed fresh-faced analyst in his early thirties with slightly popping eyes behind thick glasses, who looked like a young version of Dave Garroway, the television pioneer. From microphones set back in the aisle, the crowd, in a feisty mood, peppered the consultants with questions mainly about control issues. Some speakers criticized Walter Bish's new management position, which a few contended should be subjected to an NLRB probe. Steve Bauman accused the consultants of "having an economic interest in doing the deal whether it was right or wrong." Thompson rose to refute the charges, but the meeting ended on a chaotic note.

Moreover, for reasons that remain unclear, management took a hard line against paying Connery's fees. The two labor directors, David Robertson and Irving Bluestone, prevailed upon Thompson to fire the Wall Street attorney, whom Robertson called a "gun fighter," before he dug into the deal, which created political embarrassment for the union throughout the mill and left the impression, as Sam Cadile, the ISU's office manager and an ex-CIO man, put it: "In dealing with the company, the company holds the aces." The ISU tried to put a good face on the firing of Connery by stating that those who had worked with him on projects in the past had not good things to say. "He just wasn't who he said he was," said Thompson.

Some ISU representatives went back to Wall Street to interview the Sherman and Sterling law firm, which estimated that the process would require 120 work days. The union knew that the company would balk at paying for that number of billable hours.

Much of the executive committee had turned over in Walter Bish's defeat. Indeed, only three members, Skip Spadafora, Eddie Conley, and Dominic Tonacchio, remained from the buyout group. Even younger than their predecessors, the new leaders, who averaged in their mid to late thirties, seemed less impressed with Wall Street talent. One member, Delbert Littleton, a squat, quick-witted bow-hunting enthusiast who wore camouflage overalls, said, "I like the idea of getting out of New York," and convinced the committee to search for a regional lawyer.

Because a former steelworker from a popular Weirton family now practiced law there, the union interviewed the large Columbus, Ohio, firm of Emens, Hurd, Kegler, and Ritter, whose lead partner, Dick Emens, appeared at an executive committee meeting on November, 2, 1988, and brought along the ex-Weirton worker, Mike Zatezalo. Now wearing a tie and balding, he took a ribbing from his former colleagues. "Hey, Zatez," blurted one, "you got a high forehead now." Zatazalo, whose presence had a calming effect, exchanged greetings with familiar faces in the crowd, and then gave the floor to Dick Emens. A tall, rugged Midwesterner, with a common touch, Emens impressed the hourly workers by explaining that he had helped Ohio companies to fend off hostile takeovers. Perceiving his principal role at Weirton as advisory "from the standpoint of protecting shareholder rights," he noted that "the trade-off is control versus basic stock value." In essence, outside buyers would pay less for shares knowing that employees rather than investors held the majority, and could set the course of the company. Of course, the employees, who were also shareholders and relied on their stock as an investment and retirement vehicle, likewise would find their holdings worth less as a result of control.

In addition, Emens cautioned that the union or the Weirton board could get sued by the workforce or shareholders, especially if the stock was improperly priced. "You want to make sure your evaluation is really independent." Delbert Littleton questioned Emens whether his firm had done business with Weirton's management, Lazard Frères, Bear Stearns, or Prudential-Bache. Emens gave the correct answers: no, no, no, and yes—his firm, as it happened, had worked with Prudential-Bache on some oil and gas limited partnerships, and the relationship between the two offices was good.

While his firm sometimes engaged in securities litigation, "which is really war," Emens hoped that his advocacy position on behalf of the union, and against Sperry and the company, "would stop short of a lawsuit."

Dominic Tonacchio, the oldest and most emotional committeeman, bruited: "I want you to kick his [Sperry's] ass." "That's okay," replied Emens.

"I want you to kick his ass," said Dave Elo, a massive steward from the blast furnace and one of the brightest committee members, "if it's necessary."

Tonacchio added: "We want to get everything we can for our people. He's [Sperry's] cunning and conniving. You people have a helluva challenge."

"You'll find out," said Elo, "that Harvey Sperry's a very arrogant individual. But he did a lot for us."

Mike Jacobs, a Steelworks Two committeeman from the powerhouse, warned that it would be equally difficult to satisfy the ISU membership. "We represent seven thousand attorneys."

"Yeah," sniped Gary Anderson, a bearded committeeman, "shit house attorneys."

Tonacchio asked: "Okay, what's the price?" Emens explained that "our hourly rates are lots less than the New York people's. Fees range from $75 to $175 per hour. I can't tell you the total cost today."

"I know," said Eddie Conley, "that if Zatezalo's associated with this firm that it will be a good firm."

"Our main goal," reminded Bob Pearce, a Steel Works Two committeeman from the diesel yard area, "is to keep a full integrated steel mill." Emens said he understood.

In late 1988, mass meetings in Weirton became almost as frequent as during the buyout. Moderate, competent, and easygoing Skip Spadafora spoke at the ISU general meeting on November 14, in favor of ending total ownership by the workforce. After all, of nine thousand ESOPs nationwide "few were one hundred percent employee-owned."

Many ISU members expressed reservations about tampering with profit sharing, a contractual issue, in advance of company-union negotiations on a new labor pact slated to begin the following fall. A speaker from the floor lamented, "When we give up profit sharing we'll be giving away all our clout" [in collective bargaining]. Why are we doing this, Virgil?" Thompson had a ready answer. "With less profit sharing the company is going to be in a better cash position to increase wages." That seemed to quiet some of the grumbling.

Management, led by Elish, also pressed to resolve the profit sharing issue in upcoming negotiations (rather than in labor talks), arguing that stock price and the market's receptivity to the IPO otherwise would be depressed. They wanted to accomplish the financial restructuring in a complete form rather than piecemeal. Plus, the initial phase of the feared repurchase liability would hit in the summer of 1989, unless the restructuring took place first.

Scheduled to begin shortly after the first of the year, the financial negotiations between the company and the ISU were eagerly awaited not just in Weirton but also in the business world, which wanted to see how a union composed of owners would face off against management. Questions arose about whether the ISU leaders would stress traditional labor goals, or take shareholder postures. At fifty-nine, Dominic Tonacchio wondered if "the young kids in the executive committee who have never been in negotiations with the company can handle it. The younger generation doesn't have guts."

The company and the union approached the talks differently. Management and its consultants adopted a close-mouthed and low-profile stance designed not to telegraph its moves. Indeed, Lazard seemed so busy with the RJR Nabisco leveraged buyout that people wondered whether they would even be prepared for the Weirton negotiations. About the RJR Nabisco deal, Josh Gotbaum would smile and say: "The only question is whether Ross Johnson," that company's CEO, "is going to be rich or very rich."

The union, in part stemming from its fiduciary duty to members, and in part due to the confusing nature of its role in an ESOP, went public with its preparations, which led to tactical flaws. Having already indicated its willingness to negotiate on profit sharing prior to collective bargaining, it continued to broadcast its actual positions during meetings with its membership.

The most damaging situation occurred during a session at a local hotel in late November, when the union presented the Prudential-Bache team for questions. Naturally, many employees wanted to know if the IPO would be attractive to investors if profit sharing stayed at 50 percent. Nick Toufexis, a young securities analyst, matter-of-factly opined that the stock still could be marketed successfully. Suddenly, ISU leaders on the dais looked seasick, and Virgil Thompson jerked George Doty out of the room for a talking to. Privately, the union leadership already had backed off 50 percent. When an ashen Doty returned, he rose to announce that it would be "healthier" for profit sharing to remain at a third, though both banks and the market could go along with 50 percent.

Later that day, the union executive committee convened with the realization that they had another political problem with the "man in the mill." Now, said Dave Elo, even "God's not gonna be able to tell him to give up fifty percent. Maybe the banks will go along with it, but that doesn't mean we can survive at that level."

"That Nick guy," said Virgil Thompson, "was full of shit. He didn't go beyond the marketing aspect. They'll do the IPO, and go back to New York, and we'll be left here with this corporation in a recession."

Hearing his ISU colleagues inveigh against maximum profit sharing for the members puzzled Gary Anderson. "Sittin' in here, I get confused if I'm in the company or in the union hall."

Mike Jacobs added: "We got rid of Mike Connery. Now we've got to tell the men that Prudential-Bache's ass is twisted."

Some committee members told Thompson to keep 50 percent profit sharing as a bargaining chip, which would mean not telling the workforce the leadership's true position. "It's not a bargaining chip," muttered Thompson, clearly weakening, and then added, "maybe I shouldn't tell them."

"Tell them!" shouted Elo and Littleton, who carried the point. "This is like sticking your dick in a ringer," sneered Gary Anderson.

News of Prudential-Bache's opinion on marketability at 50 percent infuriated Herb Elish. The board of directors passed a hard-nosed resolution making the key planks of the capital program, including the caster and hot mill rebuilds, contingent on freezing profit sharing at present levels. In other words, the union could have 50 percent with an uncompetitive, moribund mill.

Because the board had taken a collective bargaining issue—profit sharing—out of collective bargaining and placed it in the forthcoming financial restructuring negotiations, the ISU leadership responded in kind. At the December 2, 1988, meeting, Dick Emens asked the union executive committee: "How many collective bargaining issues do you want to get into the agreement?" Immediately, the union leaders began making laundry lists restoring vacations and holidays, adding jobs, and preventing contracting out.

While noting that "there seems to be a lot of sentiment in favor of the public offering," Emens mentioned the possibility of staying private but taking on more debt at favorable ESOP terms to pay for the modernization. But loans, which always had been Weir's way, looked like another frightening fixed loss in the face of a dawning recession. Moreover, it would be difficult to justify paying banks more while simultaneously giving out less to employees in profit sharing.

In his fifties, Lee Sweat, a thoughtful sheet mill steward ruminated on the consequences of selling stock. "Nobody in the mill knows that when they go public, that they're eventually going to lose control. It's just a matter of time. They don't know it but five, ten, fifteen years down the road they're going to lose the company. Are they going to believe that the class of 1988 sold them down the river?"

Delbert Littleton interjected that he had discussed the issue with the men in Steel Works One. "They felt relatively safe with that fifteen-year cushion," although some of the younger men worried that they would end up with stock but out of a job.

Fearing an eventual Japanese buyer or a corporate raider, the union leaders began weighing options to retain local control as long as possible, including placing restrictions on how and when employees could sell stock as well as limits on the extent of their holdings that they could market. Troubled, Dave Elo snapped: "There's guys in the mill planning to use that stock to buy a home."

Lee Sweat dragged deeply on a cigarette. His lean furrowed face bespoke a life of working shifts in the mill, then trying to make a go of it in the restaurant business. "I believe," he said, stubbing out the cigarette, "in the free enterprise system. I think it's wrong for us to tell the employee-owners what to do with their stock. It's up to them. Why put it off? It's going to happen anyway. It's only a matter of time. You might have someone come in and run the place better than it is now. T. Boone Pickens might come in here and throw some of the dead weight out."

"Yeah," said Virgil, "but you might get someone in here who'll set a lower wage rate."

"That's what happened at Oregon Steel," Skip Spadafora said, referring to a small West Coast minimill that had recently conducted a successful IPO on the American Stock Exchange. Oregon Steel was a somewhat chilling example to organized labor. First, it had gotten rid of its union to become an ESOP. Then it ceased to be 100 percent employee owned, and scaled back profit sharing from 35 percent to 20 percent when it went public.

"The people down there [in the Weirton mill] know what they're doing," said Sweat.

"They elected us," said Thompson, "to make a decision."

"I'm making a decision," said Sweat. "I'm leaving it up to them."

Gary Anderson agreed: "There's no way we can tell them, We're taking away your profit sharing, we'll give it back to you in stock value, but you can't have it." Then he seemed confused. "Are we acting as union officers or shareholders?"

In the afternoon, George Doty flew in from New York. Without his customary cigar, he stiffly explained that "It is still the unanimous view of Prudential-Bache that fifty percent profit sharing is within the range of possible scenarios. But there are other options which we think are superior which include a public offering, a reduction in profit sharing, and a second ESOP." The last would raise some capital while pumping a million new shares into employee accounts, thus forestalling outsider control.

While basically satisfied with Doty's "mix," the men were still reeling from Nick Toufexis's public 50 percent opinion, which now was on the mill grapevine. "That last meeting at the Grand Hotel," said Dominic Tonacchio, "went haywire. The rumors are everywhere. Nick was a meatball. I want some background on him. Is he a putz or a top shelf dude on Wall Street? He blew our fuckin' minds."

Doty stood up for his "talented, highly competent, and well-respected" colleague, insisting that Toufexis "had not changed his mind." Then, exasperated and raising his voice, Doty declared, "Look, I want this to stop right now. I'm not going to leave till this is stopped."

"I hope you brought your pajamas," said Littleton.

"Look," said Doty, "I'm just trying not to be a bullshitting New York investment banker."

"Okay," said Tonacchio after a long pause, "it's water over a dam."

"We mishandled ourselves," said Doty.

"It's okay," said Tonacchio. "You're not God. We heard you say 'fuck' in front of women. We don't expect you to be perfect."

The slightly bizarre exchange showed that the ISU had been embarrassed by its investment bank, which ironically had publicly pointed out that the union was too quick to yield a concession. Doty's assurance that Prudential-Bache would take the union's cue sat well with the leadership, which settled on an approach of reduced profit sharing, a secondary ESOP, and an IPO. But a new rift was rapidly developing. Emens and Virgil Thompson took the lead in presenting sophisticated control devices such as weighted shares, different classes of stock, and the use of dividends to entice employees to hold their shares. Occasionally wearing his lawyer hat, Thompson clearly relished mastering and expounding the sophisticated securities issues. But in so doing, he forgot David Robertson's maxim of Weirton politics: "Never get too far ahead of the people."

Though he fought it, Thompson seemed patronizing. "Does everybody in this room feel comfortable talking about the stock market?" Eyes rolled when he began to offer "a caveat." The sharp-tongued Littleton injected: "Maybe I don't like caviar."

On the eve of the negotiations, Thompson's authority began to wane, and the chaos of rival but equal chieftains designed by Don Ebbert reemerged. However, Thompson at least rallied a fragile consensus around attempting to keep a majority of the ownership local as well as maximizing employment in Weirton notwithstanding the pressures from Wall Street. Lee Sweat shook his head: "We're just buying time."

Skip Spadafora said, "No one can be too concerned about losing control after fifteen years." Indeed, with the rapid strides of aluminum, plastics, and advanced ceramics, as well as minimills, no one could assure a strong future for integrated steel making.

Thompson brought the Prudential-Bache team back to talk to the stewards on December 20. Still shaken, and looking younger than his years, George Doty came on strong trying to impress the unionists by telling them that he had done $20 billion worth of corporate financing for giants, including General Electric and Ford. "I'm not wet behind the ears. I have a lot of professional credibility. What we say today is the unanimous judgment of our firm. We're getting to an essential point in decision making. It's clear to us that this company has underspent the industry and underspent the asset here. The caster upgrade and hot strip mill are vital projects that have been too long delayed. Your customers say quality is good, but your competition now is exceeding you on quality. Sooner rather than later [to make capital improvements] is better for everyone in this room. But the company doesn't have the money. A hundred percent of profits will be going out the door for profit sharing and depreciation."

Ted Pryor, Doty's colleague, spoke briefly in favor of going public, adding that "increasing shareholders' liquidity is extremely important." He defined this as giving "access to the wealth," but added that "employee control is essential."

Somewhat vaguely, Doty rejected the possibility of modernizing with loans. "There's only a finite amount of debt that banks will lend."

Some debt, though, could be raised with a second ESOP, which would save taxes and replace lost profit sharing with new stock. Control would be factored into the initial public offering by marketing two classes of stock, with different voting powers, and staggering the terms of directors.

When stewards questioned whether having different classes of stock would lessen value in the market, Doty said, "The discount is negligible, five to ten percent, probably closer to five. No one today views Weirton Steel as a takeover candidate. But the way the world is today is not the way it will be tomorrow. Two classes gives you ample protection, and if someone said to me would you take a five percent discount to have two classes of stock, I'd say all day long."

Mike Zatezalo rose. "Your number one goal is job security. You need to preserve Weirton as a community-based steel company that continues into the future. The big thing is two classes of stock with weighted voting."

Doty and Thompson each spoke of an initial public offering in the $50 million range. Less of a "float," according to Doty, would reduce the attractiveness.

With public stock, the company would have to issue firm rules about the selection of directors, including those filling the union slots on the board. Now a steward, Tom Gaudio, the former radical ISU committeeman from the buyout days, voiced anger: "What business is it of the company who sits in our seats on the board?"

Rob D'Anniballe, the ISU lawyer, termed the matter "a corporate structure item," but failed to appease Gaudio, who insisted, "The steward body or the union membership should select."

"It's a shareholder issue," countered Thompson.

Another note of dissatisfaction came from Lee Sweat who announced, after doing some calculations, that issuing new shares through a second ESOP would drop stock value by a third.

Agreeing, Doty returned to control issues. The public company could require two-thirds voting of shares for mergers, consolidations, major sales of assets, liquidations, and corporate reorganization. The downside was that "if you guys have eighty percent of the stock and you want to go out and do something stupid, you can fuck up this company. We have to go out and persuade the market that you're sensible people as you have been."

"I'll probably take a lot of heat on this," said Skip Spadafora, "but the control issue looks like it will cost $35 to $37 million, or $4,500 per employee. Is it necessary?"

Lee Sweat worried that the old rift between junior and senior employees would reemerge around the issue with the younger workers favoring jobs, while older personnel and retirees would want top prices for their shares. He asked a practical question: "How much would it cost someone to start a proxy fight?"

"Because so much of the stock is held here," Doty conceded, "you could start a proxy fight cheaply. But today there's not enough profit to start a takeover. Ten to fifteen years from now, I don't know."

From the meeting at the union hall, almost all the stewards shuttled downtown to the community center where the general membership had assembled. The crowd pressed Doty on profit sharing. "Yes," he admitted, "fifty percent remained possible," though he would not recommend it. From the floor microphone a worker in the audience called fifty percent, "a sacred thing with me, because it had induced employees to vote for the initial ESOP." Indicating that he favored less than 50 percent, Thompson argued that the difference could be recouped at contract negotiations time.

Men asked Doty what to do with their publicly tradeable stock. After stating that the Securities Exchange Commission forbade him personally from acquiring Weirton shares, Doty cautioned: "If you're asking me would I continue to roll a hundred percent of my net worth into Weirton, I think I'd diversify a little bit."

At this point Thompson left the room to confer with someone outside. "Virgil seems to have abandoned me," joked Doty.

"You're not the only one," shouted someone in the crowd.

A member of the audience wanted to know if the union and company were significantly apart on any points going into the negotiations. Rob D'Anniballe responded, "I don't think you'll find two classes of stock in the company proposal."

As the year ended, the union debated bringing contract negotiations wholesale into the talks. Thompson argued that "if you get a demand list together, there's no reason to go, because the negotiations would collapse." Others felt that without a list the union would lack bargaining power, but no finished strategy evolved.

The control problem also refused to die internally within the ISU. Littleton spoke for many when he announced at the December 29 stewards' meeting, "The control issue changed when I realized I had to pay for it. It used to be: Give me as much control as I can get. Now it's give me as much as I need."

While the union noisily and openly debated policy and moves, the company had the advantage of formulating its positions in private. On December 30, the management sent the ISU a complicated message that it would not go along with two classes of common stock, a vaunted union position affecting control. Developed by Sperry, the company's position held that the Department of Labor regulations

forbade such dual offerings. "Virgil," said Ed Conley, "that's a fuck-
ing bombshell they dropped in here." The union leaders ripped their
hired lawyers for not anticipating the government's objection.

Thompson tried to explain that the company's position and that of
the federal government at least seemed to allow for a second class of
shares called convertible preferred.

After hearing the complex details, Ben Wade said to Thompson:
"It comes across as if you're the attorney and we're the fuckin' pe-
ons, though I'm sure you didn't mean it that way."

"Any other comments?" bristled Thompson. "I don't try to act
like an arrogant asshole." When no one spoke, the union president added: "I don't think were gonna come out of there with an
agreement."

Ike Eisnaugle, a committeeman from the tin mill, sighed. "We're
going in there without a game plan." The mood grew more somber
when the union's staff benefits analyst stated that less profit sharing
would reduce eventual pensions.

By contrast, management, and especially Herb Elish, was upbeat
going into the negotiations. Relaxed and happy as the year ended,
Elish spoke of working ten more years before leaving Weirton in
good shape for a successor. "We'll get a deal," he insisted, equally
sure that the workforce eventually would vote in favor of it, provided
that the communications department could cut the financial complexities "down to two clear pages." All things considered, the CEO
seemed more concerned with the upcoming birthday party of his
four-year-old daughter.

The union's position was murky. It had accepted management's
position that a stock sale was needed to raise capital and that a drop
in profit sharing would make the stock attractive. But how much
stock should be sold, and how much of a reduction in profit sharing
was necessary? The union was clearer about the fact that it would
fight forfeiting voting control of the corporation.

2 2 Going Public

> "It seems pretty fair, but I'm not a numbers guy. Mostly I was concerned with the control issue. I wanted to be sure this place would be here in a generation."
>
> —DOMINIC TONACCHIO

The negotiations began in January about fifty miles south of Weirton at the lodge in Oglebay State Park, a remote setting intended to prevent leaks into the mill. The company footed the bill for the rustic Tudor-style ballroom. The union and management teams along with their respective consultants sat at tables across the cavernous chamber from each other.

"Okay," said Virgil Thompson into a microphone, "we're ready to go."

Seventy-five feet away, flanked by Sturges, Sperry, and Gotbaum, sat Herb Elish, looking comfortable. In his introductory remarks he stressed urgency. "It's time to move forward. We don't have the luxury of delay anymore. These investments are the price of doing business. Our competitors now are one hundred percent cast."

Elish continued to sing the corporate blues of running an old facility lagging behind in quality, facing a new threat from lean, nonunion minimills, while "trying to create a capital structure which will last indefinitely. . . . We're here to do whatever we can to reach an agreement as long as we don't compromise the long-term viability." Then, directing his remarks directly at Thompson, Elish called the process "probably the most important responsibility during your term of office." Nor was it ordinary collective bargaining. "I don't," emphasized Elish, "regard this as a normal labor negotiation."

Though both sides agreed on the key issues of selling on the public market while retaining control at Weirton, the sessions got off to a tense start. The ISU wanted the two classes of stock (the initial issue and those resulting from the new ESOP) both to be common shares. The company wanted the new ESOP to issue preferred shares because of federal regulations. The union, however, feared that if employees held different mixes of the two types of securities, as they inevitably would, friction and political problems would erupt in the mill.

Dick Emens, the lawyer retained by the union, offered his belief that the U.S. Department of Labor surely would make an exception and approve the two classes of common shares. When Harvey Sperry, who felt strongly that the company did not have the time to risk the critical deal to the discretion of federal bureaucrats, pressed Emens on the basis of his belief, the Ohio lawyer blew up and left the room.

Sperry merely smiled, then injected a new item into the negotiations: Not only should profit sharing be slashed, but it should not even kick in until the company had achieved a certain amount of earnings, which he termed the "carve-out" or "base." The union despised this notion, which it called "playing baseball." Mocking it, members of the ISU began showing up in Prudential-Bache baseball caps, and insisting that profit sharing could not dip below 40 percent; that it could return to 50 percent provided that earnings crossed a healthy threshold, and further that there would be no base or carve-out.

While both sides stressed keeping control in the hands of employees as opposed to outside shareholders, management and Sperry voiced concern that a multiplicity of control features in the IPO would dampen market enthusiasm and stock prices. "We have a responsibility not to create a monster," insisted the lawyer.

"You can," added Gotbaum, "get a real haircut in the market if capitalization looks too weird." In other words, the shares would sell at a discount.

Among others in the union, Littleton took a militant line on control, remarking that "nineteen consecutive quarters of profits was what created this market." However, later in an ISU caucus, Doty argued that planning for too much perceived local power in the hands of employee shareholders versus outside stock buyers could be disastrous. "You're rubbing the public investor's nose in the fact that he has no nuts."

While never pulling control off the table, the union began demanding a pension "gross-up," which meant that pensions still would be calculated as if the employees had 50 percent profit sharing, though all by now knew that the figure would be less. The ISU also made work-related demands, including banning contracting out, initiating a no-layoff policy, providing an additional week of vacation pay, and adding an hour lunch break to overtime shifts.

As meetings went late into the night, participants on both sides became increasingly testy—with flare-ups and threatened walkouts. At one point the company stopped paying for food. Yet, watching the negotiations, it always seemed that both sides would reach a deal. For one thing, important safety valves were in place. Communications, for example, never completely broke down, as David Robertson, who had a foot in both camps, carried messages between the company and the union.

Plus, Elish, an experienced labor negotiator, seemed adept at keeping the negotiations on course. Unlike many CEOs, he declined to delegate bargaining with the union to his vice president for human resources, which highlighted the importance of the proceedings. He won respect by announcing that his negotiating policy did not involve taking items off the table when problems arose. Knowing labor well, he weaved an offbeat sexual metaphor into the negotiations. Whenever the discussions finally focused on the make or break details, Elish called it "getting down to the short strokes." The union guys soon also were speaking in terms of short and long strokes. Unlike many self-important steel industry bosses, Elish could absorb tweaks and insults from labor without getting flustered. After a while, the jabs became light-hearted. For instance, when Elish, who had dressed down for the sessions, took off his sweater during a heated discussion, Dominic Tonacchio quipped: "What's the matter, Herbie, you having a touch of menopause?" Elish also knew when to stop the negotiations for a few days to give everyone a face-saving break and to try out ideas in the mill.

But toward the end, the talks foundered. Every item had to be dollarized, then plugged into projections. In a corner, hunkered over his laptop, like a furry creature from *Star Wars,* Josh Gotbaum crunched the numbers, then issued the news, which was often bad. Friction from the shear tedium and from the realization that some labor divisions would profit more than others resulted in raw exchanges and accusations of collusion at the union's caucuses.

On January 13, Thompson and Tonacchio went to Elish's room to get the company's bottom line. The key sticking points remained profit sharing and the base, though now the company was transforming the latter into a cap on dividends, which would be "backed out" of total earnings before the computation of profit sharing.

A few days later, back in the union hall, Tonacchio, whose small office, with walls covered with signed glossies from celebrities such as Bobby Rydell and Joe DiMaggio, looked like the backroom of a 1950s nightclub, recalled the final play of the negotiations after every detail had been dollarized and the two sides were at an impasse.

"Here's how the deal went down. I went into Herb's room and he kicked everyone out except Breneissen [the vice president for human resources]. Then he got off the bed and started pacing up and down. His face turned red. 'Look,' he said, 'I don't need this anymore, this nickel-and-dime bullshit. You want to fuck up this company and put it in the toilet, I'll sell my house in Pittsburgh, and go back to the city. There's a job waiting for me. We know who the troublemakers are. We can hear you screaming all over the fuckin' hotel, and know you guys are almost having fist fights. I got the board of directors on my back. I'm ready to tell my people to go home.'

" 'Look,' " said Tonacchio, " 'I don't give a shit if the mill's here in five years. I'm gonna be sixty. I'm older than you. I'm gonna retire in two years. I'll have enough to fuckin' go back to the city too. I don't give a shit; I could torch this place. So cut the bullshit and sit down. Your face is turnin' all red. Here's the deal: thirty-five percent profit sharing and a thirteen-million-dollar cap.' Herb made like he went in the other room to caucus, but I knew he just went to call Harvey.

"When he came back he was smilin'. He told me he once had been in big negotiations in New York City. The labor guy said to him that he was taking off, leaving. Then two minutes later, he knocked on the door and said, How can I leave? This is my room. So Herb gave me a kibbitz; then he took the deal.

"It seems pretty fair, but I'm not a numbers guy. Mostly I was concerned with the control issue. I wanted to be sure this place would be here in a generation. When I see homeless guys in the soup lines, I think that they had a job one day, and held babies in their arms and gave them dinner. They had dignity. I don't want to see that go."

More complex, the rest of the new deal, agreed upon in principle on January 13, 1991, abolished the company's repurchase obligation, but allowed active employees to sell up to 35 percent of their stock on the open market, while retirees could unload all of their shares. The proposed second ESOP would issue 600,000 shares of convertible preferred shares with the same dividend rights as the earlier common stock. But the preferred securities came with ten votes per share, as a key control feature, though an employee could convert them to common stock at any time for public sale. Ten percent of the preferred shares would be distributed to employees each year, so that all would be allocated within a decade. Retirees could sell the shares back to the company, which would recycle them to other workers. The company calculated that voting control would reside with the employees for fifteen years.

The corporate charter also was amended to perpetuate control. Regardless of how much stock an outside individual or institution acquired, it could never hold more than 5 percent of the vote. Moreover, changing the corporation's ownership or structure would require approval by 80 percent of the shareholders. Issuance of new stock could not proceed without 90 percent of the board of directors' consent. The company promised to give each worker a week's vacation pay or $500, whichever was larger, provided the deal survived the voters.

While pledging to increase wages at the upcoming collective bargaining negotiations, the company nonetheless won most of the shop floor issues that the union had forced the negotiators to handle at Oglebay. The company blocked labor's effort to achieve a no-layoff rule. Management also watered down the ISU's proposed ban on contracting out. The company agreed only to notify the union and discuss any plans to use nonemployees on a project.

Following the negotiations, the financial proposal, which still required ratification, gathered momentum. At his January 16 staff meeting, Elish called the Oglebay agreement "excellent for the company. It's critical that everyone get behind it a hundred percent. Throughout the mill and in the community, I have to talk about this like it's the second coming." Elish had invited Chuck Lafferty, who already had developed plans for radio and TV, in-plant meetings, a phone bank to answer questions, and a new publication called *Straight Forward*, which featured advanced computer graphics in color, and came out on a weekly basis. Distributed by mail to all employees, *Straight Forward* boiled the financial changes down to palatable nuggets. Elish, who wanted a heavy majority in favor of the restructuring, reminded management of the 84 percent pro-ESOP vote in 1983. "If a majority of people," he mused, "vote not to change the profit sharing, then fuck it. It's democracy. Besides, it's Lafferty's problem anyway. Eighty percent," joked the chairman a little ominously, "is his job. Besides, it would be nice to beat the previous vote."

On January 19, the board approved the financial proposal and authorized entering into agreements with vendors to upgrade the continuous caster and revamp the hot mill. The directors warned that they would void the contracts if employees voted against the financial changes, which the ISU stewards ratified two days later.

While union leaders continued to harbor certain misgivings about going public, cutting profit sharing, and seeing control pass to out-side investors after fifteen years, no organized or vocal opposition materialized. However, a Chinese-style "Democracy Wall" campaign emerged around the mill with workers using broadsides to attack the financial plan. Some posters accused management of lying when it maintained that no companies shared profits at 50 percent, and then listed corporations with plans at that rate.

In the tin mill, the ISU president's base, an angry employee named Ken Lucas posted screeds showing that the company variously had claimed that the capital plan would cost $500 million, $600 million, and $650 million, and that estimates on the key equipment purchases for the caster and hot mill also had shifted.

I cannot, nor will I ever support the proposed Financial Plan at the Weirton Steel Company! I cannot support any person, union or Management, who supports the program!

Is there any need for Weirton to become a "World Class" mill? We made a $155 million profit in 1988, is this not enough? After the Capital Spending Plan, if there is one, how much additional profit is projected? Who will benefit? *WHY HAVE THE WORKERS NOT RECEIVED AN ACCURATE, UP-TO-DATE STATEMENT DE-TAILING WHAT EACH PROJECT WILL COST, THE START-ING AND COMPLETION DATE, AND THE EXPECTED PROFIT OF THE PLAN?"*

During the public relations barrage, management explained that capital program prices had risen over time and would jump even higher if the contract costs were not locked in immediately. As the balloting approached, the atmosphere in Weirton became nearly as emotionally charged as it had been in 1983. However, in 1989, the company also enfranchised salaried employee shareholders, so the electoral base had broadened.

In February a new disclosure document, also called the Informa-tion Statement, was mailed to employee and retiree shareholders. Prepared by a financial printer, it physically resembled the landmark document distributed to workers prior to the ESOP. A fourth as long as the 1983 tome, which had buried the notion of outside ownership near the end of its ninety dense pages, the 1989 booklet forthrightly outlined the implications of going public. Likewise, it defined the three crucial votes that employees would cast on whether to (1) amend the corporate charter to permit public stock while using local control measures, and discouraging large accumulations of shares by outsiders; (2) amend the 1989 ESOP to allow employees to sell up to 35 percent of their securities, and (3) amend the profit sharing plan to set a new plateau at 35 percent. Confident of pro votes from management, the board of directors warned the ISU and IGU that if either voted no, it would result in banning their members from participating in the new ESOP, each of whose 600,000 shares not only would have ten times the voting power of the common stock, but also would have a preference and a value of at least five dollars in a liquidation of the business. The new disclosure also promised that because Weirton common stock would trade on a major stock exchange, public information about the company would be expanded, because of Security Exchange Commission rules, and the corporation would become even more open than it had been since splitting from National.

The mailing spelled out that the common stock would be split in order to bring it within the ten- to twenty-dollar range where most major steel shares traded. Designed to make the offering affordable and attractive to small investors, the split was intended to broaden the ownership base, and to prevent concentration and control in the hands of a few. In order to satisfy the workforce, the company promised a dividend, payable within the third quarter of the year, enabled employees to buy additional common stock at a 10 percent discount, and agreed to pay all brokerage fees for those selling shares and to set up a dividend reinvestment plan.

In only one respect did the new disclosure document lack clarity. "The weighted voting preferred stock to be held by the new ESOP as well as certain amendments to the Certificate of Incorporation will permit active employees to maintain control of the company for the foreseeable future." In fact, the computer model utilized by negotiators at Oglebay showed that the majority ownership in employee hands would cease before the turn of the century, and control— despite the ten-to-one voting ratio between the convertible preferred shares distributed through the new ESOP and the regular common stock for sale to outsiders—would pass out of employee hands by the year 2003. In fairness, the point was plainly made at numerous in-plant meetings. Also, 2003 loomed beyond the work horizon of most of the employees though not of their children. While E. T. Weir, an owner obsessed with control, had tried to plan his corporation's destiny in fifty-year blocks, change now occurred more rapidly. In the late twentieth century, planning fifteen years ahead probably was just as ambitious as staking out fifty years had been earlier in the century. In any event, most Weirton workers were at least somewhat aware that they were being asked to make a choice between the long-term future of the mill—someone else's future, really—and the ability to cast their lot with the market.

On March 7, more than a thousand employee shareholders crowded into St. John's Arena in Steubenville. After an animated rock-scored film by the communications department about a sexy female robot who, in the year 3000, still preferred products packed in steel, the audience listened to Elish announce the ballot results. The amendments to the corporate bylaws and the ESOP agreement won 85 percent approval, while reducing profit sharing passed by 79 percent. Elish, who also reported the company's twentieth consecutive profitable quarter, called the vote "an event of historic proportions. . . . Weirton Steel is seven years old this year. It has an extraordinary history and tradition as a leader of our industry through every decade of the twentieth century. . . . How lucky I am to be able to make a contribution to that tradition and to do my part to make sure that it continues well into the next century."

Harvey Sperry termed the company a "world-class mill" with "world-class people." Irving Bluestone, the UAW's wizened godfather of labor management cooperation, congratulated his "sisters and brothers" in the stands, then contrasted Weirton with Hyatt Clark, an ESOP plagued by "a deep animosity between labor and management," failure to modernize, low productivity, employee slowdowns, declining market share, and poor quality. For the numerous college professors and business analysts who complained about America's industrial workers, Bluestone had an answer: "Oh, yeah? What about Weirton?" As a result of their dedication and sacrifice, he foresaw "a new day for Weirton Steel Corporation, with secure jobs and secure incomes for you and your families."

Elish had kind words for Virgil Thompson: "We argued, we negotiated, we worked as hard as we could. Virgil has my highest respect. He's strong-minded, tenacious, very smart, and has the highest integrity. His word is his bond."

"This is a great day for Weirton Steel," said Thompson. "The employees are responsible. Because of you, the future is bright. We credit a teamwork attitude, and with teamwork we can do anything." He introduced and thanked the members of his executive committee, George Doty and Dick Emens, and lauded the efforts and ethics of the CEO. "This ship called Weirton Steel is headed in the right direction because of a captain named Herb Elish."

Elish popped the cork on a bottle of champagne to toast the workforce. "I've been in many corporations. I know that no other group of employees in any other company would have done what you have done. This was an exercise of the democratic process at its best. You got complex information and dealt with it. Now we have a new unity of purpose and closer relationships. This is the best steel company in America." Messages of praise from Jay Rockefeller and major steel buyers were read. Elish, Virgil Thompson, and George Vacheresse of the IGU then cut three huge cakes, one for each passed measure.

Following the party, the corporation entered an SEC-mandated "quiet period." Pending the completion of its prospectus by Lazard Frères, Bear Stearns, and Prudential-Bache, it refrained from publicly discussing financial conditions, projections, and other matters that could be viewed by the government as "touting" or selling without proper filings and could lead to sanctions.

Under close scrutiny by the SEC, the company halted its stream of financial information to employees. As Elish explained, "We can only tell the people here who are stockholders the same thing we tell public stockholders." However, Weirton utilized the quiet period to seek opinions from the employees through the Sirota attitude survey, which the union narrowly had approved in the fall.

To its credit, the company gave Sirota a wide berth. Entitled "A Report on Employee Satisfaction, Attitudes and Intentions, Based on a Survey Conducted During April 1989," and including more than a

hundred questions, the study reached thirty-seven hundred employees at all levels of the organization.

The report probed the business environment—decision making,
communications, safety, compensation, workload, expectations, cooperation, job security, benefits, and recognition. Sirota isolated several core complaints on fairness issues. Only 16 percent of the
subjects agreed with the statement: "I understand how pay is admin-
istered in this company (how salaries are determined, who is entitled
to an increase, etc.)," while 64 percent disagreed, and 20 percent
were "neutral." Similarly, only 7 percent believed that "pay is ad-
ministered fairly in this company," while 74 percent disagreed.

Only 20 percent of ISU employees favorably perceived an "opportunity for advancement," while 55 percent viewed the situation unfavorably. Thirty percent approved the record of promoting from
within the company, while 53 percent objected. Only 15 percent of
the sample supported the statement: "When sacrifices are necessary
to meet business needs, all levels and parts of Weirton Steel share
equally in the sacrifices." Sixty percent disagreed, 25 percent
strongly.

But for the most part, the study reflected positively on Weirton.
Sixty-eight percent of the workforce rated the company favorably
compared to other companies that they knew about, while only 5
percent viewed Weirton unfavorably. For hourly workers, the figures
grew more impressive, with 73 percent comparing Weirton favorably
to other firms, while only 3 percent viewed it negatively. Seventy-one
percent of the employees felt proud to work for Weirton; 5 percent
did not. Seventy-nine percent lauded the company's profitability,
while only 5 percent were unsatisfied. Sixty-three percent termed
Weirton ethical in its business dealings versus 8 percent who found
fault. After the March vote, 60 percent "felt more confidence" in
Weirton versus 6 percent who felt less.

The study also focused on the job site. Sixty-two percent viewed
their immediate supervisors as competent (16 percent did not). Sixty-
seven percent rated their coworkers highly. Only 7 percent gave them
poor marks. A whopping 72 percent of the employees expressed
"satisfaction with the job itself," surely a high-water mark for American steel, while just 8 percent viewed work unfavorably. Sixty-one

percent also felt secure in their jobs. Ninety percent of the respondents felt a mutuality of interests with their employer and agreed with the statement, "The better Weirton Steel performs as a business, the better it is for employees like me." Was this Japan?

Looking for another point of view, in the spring of 1989 I accepted a dinner invitation from Steve Bauman. Other guests included Staughton Lynd and his wife, Alice, and Jim McNamara, the attorney who had assisted Lynd with the Rank and File Committee suits six years before. A slight, spritely long-haired man with a wry wit, McNamara, now based in Columbus, was back in Steubenville to defend the right of "creek dwellers," a group living in shacks hard against the Ohio River.

Still in a job of performing maintenance on the huge ladles that poured hot metal in the BOP shop at Weirton, Bauman lived in a humble frame house on a racially integrated ridge in Steubenville. The sparsely furnished home with pictures of kids on the walls had the cleaned-out feel of a recent divorce. But the former rhetorician of the Rank and File, a husky, curly-haired, friendly, soft-spoken man with Coke bottle lenses in his glasses, proved a gracious host who kept our wineglasses filled and served shrimp on ice followed by roast beef sandwiches.

Lynd wore an old wash-and-wear suit that had been made by Alice, who had recently graduated from the University of Pittsburgh Law School and had joined him in practice. While at Pitt, Alice had developed problems with her hands that made writing difficult, and had received permission to dictate her exams to her husband. Their marriage gave the appearance of a team of equals committed to social justice, whose roles were complementary.

On this evening, Staughton served as the interlocutor while Alice listened attentively, actually aggressively, occasionally interjecting a trenchant opinion. With her, one had the sense of a perceptive Madame Defarge sitting in judgment, writing briefs, and stitching suits for lawyer radicals, while weighing responsibility for the cataclysm that had wrecked America's industrial base and ruined its workforce.

Staughton Lynd seemed surprised and disappointed as he drew out Steve Bauman on the current state of Weirton. Bauman maintained that shop floor relations never had been better at Weirton. His supervisor's door was always open, and the men's suggestions regarding equipment and materials "were usually followed. There's been a big change since ESOP." He felt no discrimination in the workplace due to his previous radical activism.

"To me," said Lynd, "worker ownership is worker control." Didn't Bauman object to governance at Weirton by a CEO and board who had little connection to the shop floor?

"The world is changing so much," said Bauman. "I'm not sure that hourly guys would want to make the decisions of the CEO or the board. The attitude in the mill is that the CEO better be working hard for his money."

It disturbed Lynd that people in Weirton cared so little about other workers. "It's not a one-mill industry." It surprised him that no one in Weirton took notice of the bitter strike then occurring at Eastern Airlines. In Youngstown, workers cared about other workers. He smiled. "Of course, I eat that up."

The men reminisced about the Rank and File Committee, and why it finally collapsed. Lynd said that after it had won voting for laid-off workers, a reduction in the McKinsey cut, and more openness, it had ceased to attract much outside interest. Also, Lynd believed that the group had lost a charismatic leader (and some would say its racial edge) when Tony Gilliam died. Lynd found the timing of the death of such a young man suspicious and wondered if Gilliam had been murdered to silence him. Bauman, who knew Gilliam well, insisted that the evidence pointed to a natural death. Early coronary disease ran in Gilliam's family. "He had bad heredity and ate fatty foods." Lynd remembered the leader's funeral. Roll was called among members of the group. After Gilliam's name was read, his widow said, "Here." It reminded Lynd of the funerals of Sandinista soldiers where the widows say: *"Presente."*

Jim McNamara wanted me to understand that the Rank and File Committee was simply a "situation. It never grew into a movement. It made a big initial noise and just faded out." One reason was the "awesome media blitz" of Weirton Steel, which had whipped up mass support for the ESOP. "All of a sudden, it was whoosh and the publicity was everywhere." So strong was the propaganda in favor of the ESOP and against anyone in its path that Bauman still was surprised that none of the critics had been assaulted. Recently, the same sort of all-pervasive media drive had been waged inside and outside the mill. Signs and bumper stickers with their new slogans: "We can do it, *BETTER*," and "A *Capital* Idea," still blanketed the region. Probably it would have been pointless to fight.

Staughton Lynd had continued as writer, lawyer, teacher, and activist in the service of human values and employee empowerment, which ran counter to the era's ethic of tight competition. In particular, Lynd had refocused his efforts on Youngstown. Small independent companies had begun to operate on a nonunion basis in the shells of steel mills. In Youngstown, Lynd had begun working on behalf of a fledgling union called "Solidarity." A Pittsburgh law firm had not only tried to break the union but sent a lawyer to go after Lynd legally, as well as his assets. "I felt a little paranoid for the first time. They were out to get this dangerous radical." But he had won that round against management. "You can't," he said with a rueful smile, "lose all the time."

23 Survival

"If you sacrifice, you're part of the team."

—MARK GLYPTIS

In May 1989, Weirton filed its registration with the SEC, and issued its prospectus offering the sale of four million post-split shares of common stock for placement on the New York Stock Exchange. Its trading symbol would be "WS." Much was on the line. Would the stock attract investors and raise needed capital? Would the shares perform adequately in the market and become solid investments justifying the employees' sacrifice of profit sharing and total corporate ownership? Or would they fizzle and contribute to low morale?

With the "quiet period" over, a Weirton team headed by Herb

Elish and Virgil Thompson began making presentations around the country to invited groups of institutional investors. Elish stressed Weirton's history as National's flagship, its present status as the largest wholly owned industrial company in America, and its consistent profits between 1984 and 1989. Fully integrated Weirton, he added, had an edge over minimills, which then had trouble finding enough scrap. Plus, Weirton had shed the repurchase liability, embarked on its progressive capital program, and seemed cushioned against the industry's notorious cyclicality. Tinplate, related Elish, accounted for 40 percent of sales, and Weirton had almost a quarter of the national market. The material enjoyed the highest margins of any flat-rolled product, and its demand would "hold up through a recession." In a down economy, "people will eat Campbell's soup." Elish spotlighted the company's Weirtec Research Center, the genius of William Saunders, the presence of four customers with manufacturing facilities on-site, the limited reliance on Detroit, and Weirton's rising profile as a specialty steelmaker. "We try to find the most difficult applications." Plus Weirton would pay a dividend.

The institutional investors enjoyed their complimentary tote bags containing products packed in Weirton steel, as well as the prototypes of microwavable cans, advanced closures, and a super-reflective metal aimed at conserving energy costs in lighting applications. They also received news that Weirton would drive down labor costs, hopefully by cutting about 135 people in 1990–1991. "We think," said Elish, "we have a very special company. It is very different from the rest of the industry."

Richard Riederer, Weirton's young chief financial officer, took the group on a conservative but rosy tour of the company's finances. Between going ESOP in 1984 and 1988, sales had climbed 28 percent from $1.08 billion to $1.38 billion. Sales per employee rose from $137,000 in 1984 to $171,000 in 1988 due to "efficiency, productivity, and commitment." Annual operating cash flow before profit sharing had jumped $100 million from $88 million in 1984 to $188 million in 1988.

Virgil Thompson, law-trained, well-groomed, dark-suited, and articulate, proved to be the type of union leader to whom pension and mutual fund officials could warm. While the company was employee-owned, he explained, the majority of directors were independent, so "the corporation is run like a business." He stressed the employees' voluntary reduction in profit sharing from 50 percent to 35 percent. "In a year when the industry is making record earnings, why would they do that?" He answered his own question: "They knew we had to implement the capital plan. They're all shareholders."

Anticipating concerns about the labor-management contract talks scheduled for fall, Thompson told the audience: "The ISU is in fact independent. We're not part of the USW. We'll look at what the USW does [in negotiations] at Bethlehem, National, Inland, and Armco, look at, but not necessarily do what, they've done. We'll maintain our competitive edge."

Ending on a vote of personal optimism, Thompson said, "I've told employees that I'm not going to sell my stock. I think over the long term it's going to be worth a lot of money."

After the luncheon, Thompson seemed pleased that the offer had attracted so much interest that it could end up being oversubscribed. But he complained of having "political problems at home." Speaking around the country, Thompson necessarily was away from the union hall. Travel by the union president always created envy among those who felt stuck in town. Unable to attend executive committee meetings, Thompson attempted to make up for his absence by participating by speakerphone, which led to clumsy meeting dynamics, with the other union leaders rolling their eyes at the black box. In addition, Thompson was involved with the investment bankers and directors in the delicate task of pricing the stock. One day, by speakerphone, he advised the ISU committeemen that he expected the shares "would go off pre-split around forty," a disappointment. "People who can't hold on may take a hit."

As the time to go public neared, the company sent each employee a "solicitation letter" informing him of the number of shares in his account, and asking how many (if any) he wished to sell, up to his allotted limit. Those who sold faced other choices, such as whether to take cash, which triggered paying taxes. The ESOP administrative committee had selected three tax-deferred vehicles at various risk levels. Without charge, employees could put their proceeds in any or all of the options, which included a Guaranteed Investment Contract

(GIC). Placed with an insurance company or bank and the most secure of the three, the GIC promised a specific rate of return on principal as well as interest. The second diversification option, which was somewhat riskier but potentially gave a greater return, involved a bond mutual fund. Third, and most aggressive, was a stock fund (Fidelity's Magellan), a portfolio of more than a thousand securities, mainly common stock, strategically traded to maximize value. In May, Weirton seemed less like a steel town than a huge investors' conference with financial analysts, fund managers, and members of the ESOP administrative committee lecturing constantly to groups of employees on every wrinkle of the upcoming decision.

In June, the SEC approved Weirton's registration statement, signaling the steelmaker's apparent viability in the market. On June 14, Weirton released 4 million shares, about 23 percent of its outstanding stock, for sale on the New York Stock Exchange, with Lazard Frères, Bear Stearns, and Prudential-Bache serving as comanagers of the offering. The stock opened at $14.50, but enthusiastic investors made it the day's tenth-most-active trade, pushing it to $15.23½ by closing, which elated Elish. "Today represents an important milestone in the history of Weirton Steel Corporation. We are delighted to expand our investor base, giving the public an opportunity to participate in the growing value of our company." Equally ecstatic, Gene Keilin of Lazard, who had negotiated against National, helped design Weirton's governance, sat on the board, and served as an underwriter, believed that the market had responded to the steel company's superb record since the spin-off as well as to Elish's management style. Keilin predicted continued growth for Weirton, including becoming an "acquirer" of other companies.

Most market mavens applauded the IPO, but Charles Bradford, a key steel analyst with Merrill Lynch, voiced skepticism because of the continued strength of the dollar (which depressed exports), an expected increase in steel imports, and his sense of impending economic downturn, which would hit domestic steel hard. "It could be a very serious problem. I don't think [Weirton stock] is a good deal for the investor."

Through the offering, Weirton had shed its repurchase liability, but still would have to go to lenders for half a billion dollars to finance the bulk of the capital program. Moreover, ending total employee ownership signaled a new responsiveness to Wall Street in daily operations, which prompted Louis Kelso to blast the company during the May 1989 ESOP Association Conference in Washington for "betraying the ESOP movement" and creating a "disaster."

In the fall of 1989, negotiations between labor and management produced an agreement to restore the early ESOP wage concessions over three years and provide a thirty-five-cents-per-hour increase in the fourth. Nonetheless, the pact narrowly won workforce approval by about two hundred votes because it included a sweeping new "multicrafting clause," which broke down the barriers between and combined maintenance jobs into new "expanded" categories requiring additional training, and would result in the elimination of about forty positions per year. "Rationalizing the workplace," according to Bill Breneissen, the vice president for human resources, meant new levels of efficiency. "The idea is for a pipefitter to be able to strike an arc and tack weld his own bracket." In the past, a welder and a rigger would have had to assist.

Initially, multicrafting was wildly unpopular, and the union leaders most closely associated with it received threats and slashed tires. Soon, however, the five-week cross-training courses, which led to certifications of expanded ability plus raises with job class promotions and a bonus of $250, were fully subscribed.

Perhaps more than anything, Elish and top management believed and conveyed a belief in education and personal improvement. The corporation trained more than a thousand employees, mostly hourly workers, in the operation of personal computers in order to facilitate its new $16 million Integrated Mill Information System (IMIS). IMIS was meant to provide employees and customers with the capacity to track and record information about orders as they progressed from production through finishing. Under the old system, simply locating steel in the labyrinthine mill sometimes took a day. A user-friendly system that emphasized bar-coding and kept keyboarding to a minimum, IMIS eliminated the manual recording and the costly quantity and delivery errors that went with it. It expedited inventory control for the mill and the customer, and allowed management to plan the workday on a "real time" as opposed to a lead time basis.

Under Elish, Weirton initiated Work Place 2000, an optional program at West Virginia Northern Community College, which enabled employees to take a range of undergraduate computer, math, accounting, and communications courses. Much of the funding for the free credits resulted from worker education legislation engineered by Senator Jay Rockefeller.

For upper management, the corporation structured a three-week course at the University of Pittsburgh Business School on the modern global steel business, a valuable exercise since many of the top team, which Elish had assembled, like him, had come from other companies and industries, and it was as he put it "necessary for us to speak the same language." Before the precious new capital equipment came on-site, Elish also sent the future operators to be trained at the suppliers' plants. This effort included 160 hot mill workers who learned how to operate their new machines at a General Electric facility in Virginia. Favoring employee participation but disappointed in the lack of white-collar commitment at Weirton, Elish now mandated that all managers go through an EPG course.

As EPG, now headed by Walter Bish and Tony Julian, continued to thrive, the corporation publicized its triumphs to the market. The blast furnace EPG devised a new iron sampling rod that could be used over a hundred times, while the traditional rod had to be discarded after a single heat. Another EPG, which looked at the problems of the scarfers' consumption of about seven hundred copper torch tips per month at a cost of $10,000, came up with a reconditioning method that all but stopped purchase of the $130 nozzles.

Guided by Darlene McKinley, the EPG in the basic oxygen plant pondered the performance of the flat, insulated ladle lids that covered the 360-ton heats of molten steel prior to continuous casting. Looking like immense glowing waffles and prone to crane damage, the lids, which each cost $12,000, allowed heat seepage, resulting in the undesirable formation of slag "skulls" in the vat. After compiling data, the BOP group designed a new dome-shaped lid that retained heat, prevented skulls, and prolonged use from about fifty to more than twelve hundred heats with a savings in the millions.

The corporation also involved itself in day care, work hardening, and physical conditioning at its new gym/rehabilitation center, and wellness—a behavioral monitoring and modification program to improve employee diet, stimulate exercise, and decrease smoking, drinking, weight, blood pressure, and cholesterol. Speaking constantly about "changing the culture," Elish, who wanted a new corporate man and woman, began with himself. He took his top managers on retreats. He hired an industrial psychologist to suggest improvements in organizational behavior, beginning with an analysis of the CEO.

The consultant interviewed all who worked with Elish and wrote a report. "It wasn't all that complimentary," Elish recalled. "I was too controlling, too directive." Afterwards, the interviewees and Elish met in a five-hour no-holds-barred session, which he termed "pretty awkward [but] terrific. People finally opened up, and it was a beginning. I was told I was very difficult. I was somebody who always thought he had the right answer. It turns out teams do it better." Elish changed. He became more relaxed and less dominant. He lost weight. He grew intellectually, mastering the details of the steel industry, "a harder business than I thought," and finally put to bed the commonplace among employees that he was simply a generic New York executive who would leave for a better offer. His wife, Eloise Hirsch, owner of a consulting business in Pittsburgh, lectured to Weirton women employees on empowerment tactics.

Under Elish, the major teamwork initiative involved a mass effort to create a "Vision for Success" for the corporation. Elish instructed management to pick four hundred highly motivated employees at all levels in the company and across all disciplines, including sales people brought in from the field, to create a "serious diagonal slice" of the workforce to meet for three days in 1990, mainly in small breakout groups with flip charts, to generate ideas pertaining to corporate values and problems. At the end of the three days, leaders from the workshops met with Elish and members of the executive staff for wordsmithing. After a series of drafts had received comments from the four hundred, the ISU, and the board of directors, the final document, which won approval, read:

WE ARE BOUND TOGETHER
IN THESE COMMON BELIEFS AND VALUES
WE MUST . . .

FOR THE CUSTOMER

- Have a total quality commitment to consistently meet the product, delivery and service expectations of all customers.
- Give customers increased value through processes that eliminate waste, minimize costs and enhance production efficiency.

FOR THE EMPLOYEE

- Reward teamwork, trust, honesty, openness, and candor.
- Ensure a safe workplace.
- Recognize that people are the corporation and provide them with training and information that allows for continuous improvement.
- As employee-owners, obligate ourselves to provide a high level of performance and be accountable for our own actions.
- Respect the dignity, rights and contributions of others.

FOR THE COMPANY

- Continuously invest in new technology and equipment to ensure competitiveness and enhance stockholder value.
- Manage our financial and human resources for long-term profitability.

FOR THE COMMUNITY

- Commit to environmental responsibility.
- Fulfull our responsibility to enhance the quality of community life.

Upper management hoped that the "Vision," like the venerable creed at Polaroid, would serve as a daily litmus for all corporate actions. In sum, only deeds in keeping with the document would be done. "It's not," offered vice president of materials management Tom Evans, "supposed to be just a sign that hangs on the wall."

Imprinted on a big triangular Delta, the Greek letter symbolizing change, the Vision statement, often framed, hung on walls throughout the mill, giving the place the look of a pyramid cult. While some employees, conceded Evans, viewed the Vision "as a bunch of bullshit," many took it seriously, including the four hundred creators, each of whom signed Weirton's 1990 Annual Report.

The hourly workforce especially valued the Vision's accent on safety, which prompted the company to start grass roots workshops in all departments where workers identified the types of accidents occurring and generated lists of preventive steps. Called "action items," these measures became the responsibility of managers who reported back to workers on a monthly basis on the status of implementation. As a result of the workshops, the mill rerouted dangerous roads and railroad tracks, placed railings on platforms, removed storage-choking production areas, bought new safety equipment, including gas analyzers and long-sleeve flame-resistant gloves, conducted days away from work (DAFW) competitions among departments, and improved housekeeping.

The shop areas, historically dingy, dreary, greasy places in American mills, particularly benefited from steam cleaning and new lighting. Previously regarded as a nuisance by many, safety now became a "pride issue," according to Tom Evans. Workers' compensation costs went down, as did "OSHA recordables" (incidents logged by the Labor Department's Occupational Safety and Health Administration). Days away from work incidents per hundred employees dropped from 5.3 in 1989 to 3.9 in 1991. As the economy worsened in the 1990s, the company, said Evans, "hasn't moved one heartbeat away from its safety commitment."

Even before the recession, Wall Street did not like Weirton. In January 1990, after only six months on the market, the stock had fallen from 15⅝ to 10⅜. Institutional investors, holding more than 80 percent of the common stock, were not impressed. In *Business Week*, a portfolio manager stuck with 260,000 shares sneered, "This company is run strictly for the employees."

In 1990, Weirton declared the "Year of the Customer." Management prated the mantras about "total quality" and becoming "world class" heard in most U.S. corporations during the period, but took steps to fold buyers into IMIS, provide them with "just-in-time" delivery, and give them better, cleaner products. But the rebuilding and retooling process led to equipment outages, at times interrupting the product flow from Weirton, which had to purchase slabs, and could not keep up its traditional level of shipments to American National Can, the nation's largest seller of metallic packaging. Even so, there were triumphs—as when Weirton became the first domestic steelmaker to win Campbell Soup's "Select Supplier" award, its highest. Receiving the accolade at Campbell's Camden, New Jersey, headquarters, Elish stood under a boat-sized red-and-white picture of a soup can emblazoned with "Campbell's Soup and Weirton Steel, a Partnership That's M'm! M'm! Good!" and spoke of the Herculean effort to modernize while keeping up quality.

Weirton also fought to revive old and open new product lines. It asserted leadership in the national drive to recycle steel cans (which have an important advantage over aluminum in that the ferrous containers can be separated magnetically from the trash stream), as part of an effort to increase its beverage can market share. By switching from lubricants containing animal fats, Weirton started making "kosher steel," providing an entrée into the substantial domestic food container market whose twenty to thirty million customers include vegetarians, Jews, Muslims, and Seventh-Day Adventists. Plus, there would be a potentially vast worldwide demand. Weirton became the only U.S. mill capable of rolling a super-smooth tinplate product receptive to permanent lamination with a silverized polyester film. Used mainly for office lighting, the extraordinarily reflective material trapped almost no light, eliminated diffusion, and yielded a 50 percent savings over standard fixtures.

Sometimes being first had its drawbacks. The only domestic supplier of Galfan—an advanced "mischmetal" of steel, zinc, and aluminum with superior formability and paintability properties compared to standard galvanized steel, as well as two or three times the corrosion resistance—Weirton found potential automotive, construction, and appliance customers hesitant to switch over to the new alloy fearing that they would be left out in the cold without an alternative source of supply if for any reason Weirton ceased production. Moreover, while its microwavable stock did well in tests, consumer acceptance built slowly because of worries about putting metal into microwave ovens.

Committed to rapid capitalization, the company attempted technical prodigies unseen since the days of Weir. The hot strip mill modernization began with huge insectlike Sikorsky sky crane helicopters dangling I beam frames for new roof towers into place. After ripping out the old equipment for shipment to India, the company redug and reenforced the foundation of the mill, which for two years became a beehive of torch welders, electricians, and riggers. Periodically, massive new machinery arrived on a 148-foot-long, 19-axle, 74-wheel truck weighing 200,000 pounds.

Using new motors that jumped horsepower from 5,500 to 7,000, the mill, which had hundreds of high-speed rolls to move the slab, now added sophisticated automatic roll changers to avert breaks in production. To achieve new efficiencies in uniformity and waste reduction, Weirton installed computerized gauge, width, and "crown" (top surface) controls, whose operators wore cloth booties as they sat before gleaming full-spectrum terminals in glass-enclosed, air-conditioned, elevated, clean-room pulpits that resembled video arcades. The mill's new "walking beam" reheat furnaces handled slabs with sophisticated overhead extractors, an improvement over the old method of merely pushing it through, which had led to scuffs and had expended 50 percent more energy. The state-of-the-art system included programmable crop shears, scale breakers, markers, weighers, and down coilers. It derived fuel savings from hydraulic insulation, and a final cooling conveyor.

Probably the jewel of the system, the reversing, roughing mill, which smashed and flattened the slab, reducing its thickness from nine to two inches, eliminated four conventional mill stands. Billowing smoke poured from the three-story square face of the rougher, before it spat out the long glowing slab clotted with fire. Then the rougher would suck back the slab, blow smoke, and re-emit the flaming tongue at four hundred to twelve hundred feet per minute like a maniacal vision of Moloch.

The new $300 million hot mill also acquired precision temperature controls, X-ray profiling capacity, and the ability to make weld-free coils weighing up to 60,000 pounds, twice the previous limit, which reduced setup time and was a boon to customers. Weirton ripped out much of the existing continuous caster and rebuilt the remainder, increasing its annual capacity from 1.9 million to 3 million tons. Combined with the hot mill and the new disulfurization equipment, the faster caster with its four widened stands yielded higher-quality steel, in a better range of sizes with a cost-per-ton savings of $20, which annualized to $45–$60 million depending on demand. In March 1991, Weirton rolled its last ingot, closed its antiquated blooming mill, and became the second integrated American steelmaker (following National) to become 100 percent continuously cast.

The capital program, which also included mandatory clean air and water controls, did not go off without hitches. Outages lasted longer than expected, a fire wasted $10 million worth of computer equipment, and a typhoon damaged a critical sizing press for slab-width reduction during shipment from Japan. Moreover, the caster, with a potential of 3 million tons, and the hot mill with a 4-million capacity, did not precisely mesh, which signaled that the caster would become the system's bottleneck, and that over time Weirton would be buying slabs.

Some of the early modernization choices raised questions. The decision to forgo rebuilding on-site coking facilities, which made sense at the time, looked worse as the price of coke, especially from Japan, climbed. Revamping rather than replacing the caster, clearly the right call in 1987–1988, now appeared to be a temporary fix. Nucor, the feisty nonunion electric arc producer, surprised the steel-making world in 1990 by successfully bringing on-line an 800,000-ton thin slab caster that eliminated most of the slab reduction applications and costs found in a hot mill. Moreover, as Elish reported to his shareholders in 1990, Nucor had another million-ton capacity thin-slab machine on order. With less than 1 percent of total domestic production, Nucor became the industry's pricing leader, snatching the position held by U.S. Steel for most of the century. In order to remain competitive in steel, America would have to buy five to ten more thin-slab machines by the year 2000. Every major integrated producer, including Weirton, would need one, as numerous others would be built in foreign countries. Preparing for the lapse of Voluntary Restraint Agreements in 1992, Brazil, Korea, and China were building highly modern steel plants notwithstanding the fact that the world already had more than 100 million tons of excess capacity. It was, as Herb Elish found, a very tough business.

In order to survive and meet never-ending capital needs, other integrated domestic makers in the 1990s took foreign partners. LTV formed a sheet steel joint venture with Mitsui and gave an equity stake to Usinor Sacilor, the French giant. USX and Kobe Steel formed a joint venture to produce hot-dipped galvanized at Lorraine, Ohio. Nippon Steel became Inland's largest shareholder with a 13 percent stake. Bethlehem made plans to transfer half its rail and structural business to British Steel. National Steel became a subsidiary of Nippon Kokan (NKK). Armco's venerable Middletown, Ohio, facility gave up a 40 percent share to Kawasaki, which transplanted a hundred Japanese cherry trees to the site. As a protest, Middletown's union put three American pin oak trees in the ground.

Proud of Weirton's status as a fully American integrated steelmaker, workers draped flags around the mill and hung them from the tops of blast furnaces. They showed their spirit in myriad other ways, from taking active roles in steel recycling drives to harassing Pepsi, which started shipping soda in aluminum cans into West Virginia. A concerted phone campaign by employees, which tied up the beverage company's 800-lines for weeks, led to Pepsi's "surrender" and its switch back to steel.

But as the early 1990s recession deepened, demand in the automotive, construction, and appliance sectors weakened for sheet metal products, which made up half of Weirton's output. In 1990, sales fell 10.9 percent to $1.19 billion as sheet shipments dipped by 17 percent. Net income, a mere $314,000 compared with $16 million the year before, failed to reach the profit sharing threshold, so employees received no distribution.

If 1990 was bad, 1991 was a balance sheet disaster. Net sales slipped another 13 percent. Sheet tons plunged 17 percent. Basically holding their own in the recession, tin mill products were off only 1.8 percent. Overall production declined from 2.65 to 2.31 million tons. The company recorded a net loss of $75 million, which again foreclosed profit sharing, but also caused the directors to cancel quarterly dividends in February. By mid-year, the stock price had sunk below $4, and Moody's Investors Service noted the company's long-term debt-equity ratio of 140 percent compared with an industry average of 45 percent, and dropped Weirton's senior note and bond rating from Ba2, which already was less than investment grade, to Ba3.

Despite its newfound leanness and modernized equipment, the

steel industry lost a billion dollars in 1991. Weirton found itself between a rock and a hard place. Its stock was undesirable, and it could not raise debt. Weirton did not want to go into bankruptcy or to dance with a Japanese partner. Moreover, the company was in peril of dropping below $260 million in "tangible net worth," which would breach key covenants with its creditors.

In retrospect the IPO looked like a poor deal. It had neither solved the company's financial needs, nor provided the employees with a sound investment.

Weirton went into a hyper cost-cutting mode. The company identified all possible energy savings, including the reduced use of heaters. As part of its "total quality" effort, management made all departments explain each of their functions in terms of a real benefit to the customer or the corporation. If none was shown, the chore could be axed. Finally, the company entered a period of downsizing that cut the workforce to 6,800 in 1992, down from 8,400 in the Loughead era. Most of the jobs were lost through attrition, though retirements were enticed through the use of enriched pensions and monthly cash sweeteners until Social Security kicked in. In some cases, departments reduced positions by seeking volunteers for furloughs in which special benefits coupled with unemployment would leave the worker with about three-fourths of his working wage. In most respects, Weirton simply kept pace with the industry. Even Inland Steel, the major maker with the best history of labor relations, announced in 1991 that it intended to shed a quarter of its workforce.

Whether called "attrition" or "voluntary cost cutting" the policy bred resentment at Weirton, and in February 1991 picketers carrying signs peacefully circled outside the General Office in the rain. One read, "How can we own a steel mill and still be unemployed? We bought our jobs!!" Another, noting management's practice of contracting out construction work in the hot mill, declared, "We don't want outsiders working in our mill while our employee-owners are *laid off!*"

Virgil Thompson, who faced a reelection campaign for the ISU presidency in 1991, ran on his expertise, which contributed to taking the company public and achieving the popular capital program. But Thompson endlessly had to fend off questions about layoffs and the loss of profit sharing. As in the past, it appeared likely that the union electoral process would become a forum for debating management policies.

Thompson's main competition came from Mark Glyptis, a steward in the pipefitters' department of Steel Works Two. Olive-skinned and mustachioed, with wire-rim glasses, Glyptis, a high school graduate on layoff status at the time of the buyout, contrasted sharply with the law-trained incumbent. While Thompson had had no union experience prior to the presidency, Glyptis had won a reputation as one of the best and most active stewards in the mill. Indeed, he carried a beeper in order to be instantly responsive to worker problems. Additionally, as a pipefitter and insulator, he had led the fight to abate the use of asbestos and to screen employees who had worked with or around the material for lung disease.

While lacking Thompson's academic degrees, Glyptis matched his verbal skills both in speech and writing, though the challenger never made the mistake of getting ahead of his audience. During the campaign, Glyptis, who had been a leader of the headquarters picketing in February, urged an end to contracting out construction jobs, and railed against any layoffs besides purely voluntary ones. He insisted that the company had drifted away from the "spirit" of the ESOP, and urged a return to it. He struck a nerve by arguing that the workers paradoxically had received less information about the company since it had gone public, which in fact was true, because management felt bound by the SEC to release financial material simultaneously to all shareholders, and no longer could inform employees first. Nowhere was the change more pronounced than in *Independent Weirton*. Probably America's best corporate newspaper before the public offering, afterwards it turned tame with predictable rah-rah pieces on "change," photos of retirees, and solicitations from the editorial staff for submissions from employees' about their summer vacations.

Most fundamentally, Glyptis appealed to ISU members' priorities, reminding them that they were employees first and shareholders second, a fact he promised never to forget, even while sitting on the board. "I don't believe," he said again and again, "in maximizing profits at the expense of losing jobs." The victory margin of 3,151 to

1,074 ruled out a runoff. Virgil Thompson, unlike Walter Bish who had landed in management, went back to his crane in the tin mill.

Unlike Bish, who always deferred to his counsel, or Thompson, who never had asserted control over the union executive committee, Glyptis was the first ISU president since before the buyout who possessed natural leadership skills. He constantly told the members, "If you sacrifice, you're part of the team." They in turn wanted to follow him.

Glyptis made no bones about the fact that he didn't trust the top management or the board to look out for the worker. Elish, the dominant executive at the mill since Redline's first term, for the first time had a problem dealing with a strong ISU leader.

Relations between the men got off to a ragged start, but it was not an issue that Elish could address until it became clear that the company would survive. Backed by the board, the CEO made two controversial moves, which worked, but made one serious error.

In late 1991, Weirton issued 500,000 shares of the new nonvoting series of preferred stock to Cleveland Cliffs, a mining firm, for $25 million. The shares, which paid Cliffs, a Fortune 1000 company, annual dividends of $6.25 or roughly 12 percent, were redeemable in twelve years. In the interim, Cliffs would supply Weirton with iron ore pellets at a "competitive price." At first blush, it seemed that Weirton, which during the fat late 1980s had looked to become an acquirer, now had given an outside corporation an equity stake. But, the preferred stock deal in reality was a loan and cash infusion that raised net worth by $25 million and won Weirton breathing space with its banks.

In a second deal, the company sold about 4 million shares of common stock for $15 million to the employees' pension plan. Permissible under federal law since it involved less than 10 percent of the stock, the transaction boosted net worth to over $300 million and raised stock and bond prices. Moody's removed the company from its alert list. During the first half of 1992, Weirton, the second-most-profitable stock in the Pittsburgh portfolio, rose 71 percent and approached $7.

The workforce, which learned of the deals simultaneously with their making (as did the rest of the market), initially raised sharp objections. They wondered why employees could not loan the company money at 12 percent. Elish replied that the need was too immediate for a local solicitation of funds, which would dribble in in small quantities.

Concerns about "dipping into the pension fund" decreased as the stock rose and the already healthy fund made an $8 million profit. The employees earned media credit for saving their company yet another time. Financial stability enabled Weirton to finish the hot mill without running afoul of creditors. Glyptis also quelled union doubts, calling the deals "not something we wanted to do, but we knew it had to be done to raise the company's equity."

Management's error touched on a delicate question of contracting out. Bricmont, an engineering firm hired to work on the hot mill's walking beam furnaces, walked off the job in the midst of a dispute involving cost overruns. Weirton's own construction team finished the work, suggesting that it could have handled it in the first place. But Weirton still lost in excess of $24 million. Worse, there was no insurance because management signed the contract with Bricmont without requiring a performance bond.

In 1992, the rage spilled into a messy shareholders' lawsuit against Elish, top management, and Willkie Farr, the corporation's counsel, for negligence in failing to bid the job properly, neglecting to get the bond, and for releasing Bricmont from liability. According to a fellow board member, Elish viewed the Bricmont deal as a complete failure along all management lines. So angry was director Philip Smith, who felt belatedly and poorly informed about Bricmont, that he insisted on hiring his own defense attorney rather than standing with management in the suit. In particular, Smith declined to be represented by Willkie Farr, or any lawyer of its choosing.

A plain-spoken MIT-educated engineer from Australia, Smith now locked horns with Harvey Sperry, questioning the millions in fees that Weirton had paid to Willkie Farr over the years and alleging a conflict of interest, which became a public sore. Smith and two of three union directors, Mark Glyptis, the ISU president, and Rob D'Anniballe, its counsel, challenged the propriety of Sperry's seat on the board given that his firm represented the Japan Galvanized Iron Sheet Exporters Association, with whom, as D'Anniballe put it, "we bang heads in the market every day." The third union director, David Robertson, supported Sperry as did other board members, including Gordon Hurlburt, a retired Westinghouse manager whom Sperry had eased onto the board at Kerr Glass, and Richard Schubert, an ex-Bethlehem vice-chairman who now headed a charity called the Points of Light Foundation.

Sperry maintained that only his firm's office in Washington lobbied on behalf of the Japanese and that Willkie had erected a Chinese wall to keep lawyers who worked on Weirton from exchanging information with those representing the Japanese. Thus, there could be no undue influence. The two union directors now found it suspicious that Weirton, alone among America's integrated mills, had failed to file antidumping actions against foreign steel producers, especially since Willkie Farr defended such cases for the Japanese. By 10 to 3, the board found no conflict of interest and allowed Willkie's dual relationship to continue. Smith voted with Glyptis and D'Anniballe, but Robertson did not. Now a clamor arose to remove Robertson from the board.

At the spring 1992 annual meeting, shareholders pummeled the CEO with angry questions. Since Elish had known about Willkie Farr's "conflict of interest" did he now plan to resign? No. Would the corporation fire Harvey Sperry for a conflict of interest? No. When asked for an explanation of how the Bricmont problem occurred, Elish skirted the question but admitted that the situation had cost the corporation $24 million, that new administrative safeguards had been installed to avoid similar future debacles, and that no plans existed to hire outside contractors to maintain the hot mill. Queried about giving Bricmont a release, Elish took the position that it was a necessary consideration in order to allow Weirton to take over the project. Elish conceded that he did not know whether another outside contractor then working in the mill had a performance bond. Asked if any board members had interests in or connections to Cleveland Cliffs, Elish gave a flat no. Then he was forced to defend his own compensation package, worth approximately $600,000, and refused to apologize for it.

The meeting was attended by only three hundred shareholders. *Independent Weirton*, now cowed into *Pravda*-like complicity, reported none of the critical exchanges, focusing entirely on the blander business aspects, including the happy news that Standard & Poor's had reaffirmed Weirton's bond rating. Probably the other aspects of the meeting wouldn't have been reported to the workforce had not the ISU's revivified paper *Union Focus* chosen to publish the sharper dialogue. Under Glyptis (of whom Delbert Littleton said: "He's got balls this big," holding up his hands as if to measure a bass) the union became less compromising, not an easy thing in an ESOP.

The ISU's new tack crystallized in the Robertson affair. During Virgil Thompson's tenure, many union leaders questioned David Robertson's continued seating on the board as an ISU delegate. Over the years Robertson's contacts with the union had diminished, as his firm did more and more business for management, including making the cases against injured hourly workers seeking compensation. Littleton argued that the situation cut against the notion of a union director as "a check and balance" on management at board meetings. "Look at it this way," he said. "Robertson's firm's getting a quarter million dollars from management and he's sitting there next to Elish [at the board]. If he doesn't vote right, he's out." But as board meetings were confidential, Robertson's critics could not prove any antiunion stands by the director, who retained a few powerful allies on the executive committee, including Skip Spadafora and Eddie Conley.

Before 1992, the most Robertson's detractors could do was to force the company to reveal his firm's fees at shareholders' meetings. Then the pro-Sperry vote leaked out, as did Robertson's backing at the board of a stock option plan for Weirton vice presidents. Opposed by the other union directors, the lucrative plan failed to carry the board during a tough economic time. The fact that Robertson was rumored to covet the position of vice president for Human Resources at Weirton also made his position seem colored by self-interest.

In 1992, Littleton learned that Robertson had consulted and joined the board of Newell, a West Virginia porcelain factory, which employees had thought was becoming an ESOP, which would give them shares in exchange for wage concessions. In a tragedy that rivaled that of Rath, they learned that they had been given no stock, that the company had not become an ESOP, and that their union had been broken. Compounding the embarrassment was the fact that one of the Weirton employees' federal credit unions had invested in the Newell firm, believing that it was becoming a legitimate employee-owned company.

An informal group of union executive committee members, called the "after five club" because it met after work and outside the presence of their colleagues, termed "double agents" by Littleton because of suspicions that they leaked to management, pondered Robertson's role at Newell. They believed it gave them new ammunition to force him off the board.

The matter came to a vote in a May meeting of the executive committee. In an unprecedented step for an independent director, Philip Smith showed up at the union hall and stated: "If you guys think David Robertson is the best person to represent this union on the board, then you need a lobotomy." Calling Sperry a "no good son of a bitch" who had "betrayed the company," Smith held himself out to be a committed investor holding more than half a million dollars of company stock and bonds while Sperry and Robertson respectively owned only 300 and 500 shares, a fraction of the 2,500 held by the average employee. The easily drawn inference, according to Littleton, was that the controversial directors' main interests involved "taking money out of Weirton," rather than growing with it.

The committee voted 11 to 3 to ask for Robertson's resignation, and moved unanimously to place the issue before the stewards. In *Union Focus*, Glyptis wrote: "There are three primary reasons for removing Mr. Robertson from the board. They are: 1. The appropriateness of Mr. Robertson serving as a Union Director while he and his law firm bill the company for legal services. 2. With the development of his legal practice, it appears that he is 'losing touch' with the concerns of the union. 3. The union has indicated for some time that we would like to fill one of the board seats with an individual who has a strong financial background."

On June 1, 1992, the stewards met. A Robertson partisan, in a surprise move, introduced a motion to table the resignation issue. Not wanting to step into a political hornets' nest, the stewards agreed by a vote of 28 to 11. In a side agreement, the stewards and Robertson pledged to keep the affair out of the media.

Several days later, the *Wheeling Intelligencer* quoted Robertson concerning his fitness for the board seat and his refusal to resign. Believing that the deal had been broken, the stewards took up the matter again in a lengthy session on June 11. Skip Spadafora spoke eloquently in favor of the former ISU attorney calling him the "Father of the ESOP," and the one who "made it happen." But Glyptis got up and said, "No, the employees made it happen. They're the ones who took the twenty percent pay cuts." The stewards voted 28 to 14 for Robertson's resignation, which he declined to give, challenging their authority and taking his fight back to the front page of the *Intelligencer*:

> As a union-nominated director who is a native of Weirton and who has remained in Weirton since the inception of the ESOP, I have a strong sense of responsibility to the employee shareholders and to my hometown community. I firmly believe I have effectively advocated and influenced the decisions of the board of directors which ultimately are in the best interest of not only the unionized shareholders, but other Weirton Steel employee shareholders and our overall community.
>
> I intend to continue to fulfill those duties and obligations and continue to effectively advocate and express the concerns of all Weirton Steel employees to the board during any decision-making process as a corporate director of Weirton Steel.

In the same article, Elish lauded Robertson as an outstanding director and ESOP founder. "It would be a great loss to the company and its shareholders if he ceases to serve." The ISU, which regarded Elish's gesture as meddling in union affairs, then sent a letter to Bill Kieffer, the board's secretary, citing, as its basis to oust Robertson, language in the public offering filings with the SEC that the union executive committee could certify a vacancy among its directors. Kieffer indicated that he would seek a legal opinion from Willkie Farr, which had written the document. The opinion was not received on the day it was due, July 1, 1992; instead, Robertson resigned.

Philip Smith also disturbed the ISU with revelations that the independent and management members of the board met on some issues outside the presence of the union directors. Dispensing with an expensive search to fill the empty seat, the ISU sought recommendations from the International Shareholders Association, a public interest group stressing officer and director accountability. From among the names, the ISU chose Philip Karber, forty-three, a former leading arms control negotiator, analyst, and consultant who had played key roles in developing strategic plans for the Ford Motor Company and the Defense Department. To the union, he seemed an appropriate choice given management's recent announcement that it would embark on a five-year plan to develop new markets, cut costs and, like Inland, reduce its workforce by 25 percent, "mostly," as it said in an official release, "though attrition," and by "instituting a program of enriched retirement benefits" to attract quitters. The market mandated downsizing, according to Elish, who sensed "a difference in incentive because we now have public stockholders who have a clear objective of increased shareholder value and maximizing that over the long term." The cuts, he insisted, would be humane. "Where people don't have alternatives and have essentially made their lives around the company, there is a real obligation." He expressed the "most concern about people in the middle of careers who have kind of narrowed their options and don't have much of a choice."

With Robertson's demise, Smith's power grew. A corporate Cromwell, he became a protector of the realm and flayer of royal prerequisites, all the while assuring everyone that he did not wish to be crowned CEO. The board's best steel engineer, he inspected all aspects of the hot mill renovations. He found the controversial walking beam furnace vented by poorly designed fans, and mired to the height of seven feet in glassy slag that covered its plows and thermocouple. When the project's chief engineer tried to minimize the situation, Smith branded him a "lightweight." Putting on his "wash pants and boots," the salty Australian found rupturing hoses and water in the new hot mill's basements, signs of shoddy plant engineering. The equipment ran too hot, had air leaks, and cracked seals. The electrical contractors were "thieves." The crop shear mulfunctioned. The system was "overautomated" at the "man machine interface," with employees unable to override the computers. "I have never in forty years in the steel industry seen a worse-managed capital project." Support for Smith's position came not only from the Bricmont over-runs but also from the fact that the hot mill, which pre-shutdown had produced 3,000 tons per turn, in 1992, after investing a quarter billion dollars, produced only 2,500 although the board had been promised 4,000. After the Bricmont suit made the *Wall Street Journal*, the stock price began to slip.

As chairman of the board's audit committee, Smith announced plans to formally investigate the overruns, the hot mill performance problems, and Sperry's alleged conflicts. In 1992, it came out that Willkie Farr not only represented the Japan Galvanized Iron Sheet Exporters Association, and the Japan Iron and Steel Exporters Association, but a host of other foreign steel clients, including NKK, which owned most of the hated National's steel operation, Nisshin, a Japanese co-venturer with Wheeling-Pittsburgh, Stelco, a Canadian competitor, and steel companies from Brazil, Taiwan, Mexico, and India. Smith was outraged that Sperry could sit on the board at Weirton, and hear the company's most sensitive and strategic information while his firm also represented competitors. Sperry shocked the board by noting that Elish's predecessor, Robert Loughead, had "waived the conflict." Not satisfied, Smith "tried to reach the former CEO; he was a friend, but he refused to comment on it."

Nevertheless, the board now voted 10 to 3 (Glyptis, Smith, D'Anniballe) to waive the conflict. When the majority moved to make the vote unanimous, the dissenters declined. Sperry also passed out a memo from his firm to the board, on "Multiple Competing Clients." The three-page, typo-laced offering concluded that a law firm was not even required to get the clients' consent "as their interests are only generally adverse . . . and the matters worked on for the clients are not related."

By now the matter had become very public, and *Agents of Influence*, by Pat Choate, a book identifying lobbyists including Willkie Farr, for the Japanese, was a best-seller in the Ohio Valley. Splitting expenses, Smith and the ISU retained a large Michigan law firm, Varnum Riddering Schmidt & Howlett, with a senior partner known for his service to that state's bar on ethical matters, to weigh the Weirton question. Its twenty-nine-page opinion termed the Willkie Farr memo "superficial and incomplete." The Varnum firm's document took the modern view that an intrinsic conflict of interest exists between serving on a corporation's board and serving as its lawyer, because the lawyer may be asked to advise the company on the conduct of its directors, including himself. "This risk of impaired judgment might very well be present in any legal analysis by Mr. Sperry or Willkie Farr of the propriety of any actions undertaken by Mr. Sperry as a director, or by those directors who may be acting in concert with him on any particular matter." The problem already had arisen in the context of the propriety of Sperry's conduct regarding Bricmont.

The Varnum opinion identified an "obvious clash between Mr. Sperry's fiduciary duty to the corporation and his individual interest as a partner in Willkie Farr." Varnum challenged whether Sperry, the director, ethically could hire Willkie as the company's lawyer. "Simply put, as a fiduciary director, Mr. Sperry's interest would be the promotion of competitive bidding and reduction of legal expenses for the corporation; as a partner in Willkie Farr, he would obviously prefer to maintain the status quo, and he may in fact be obligated to his partners to govern his actions accordingly." Nor was the conflict simply economic. In lawsuits, the lawyer-director could be forced to testify, thus defeating the attorney-client privilege, and the company's reliance on what it thought was confidential advice.

In the dual representation of Weirton and the foreign steel interests, Willkie maintained that it had gotten the approval of Loughead. Unimpressed, Varnum argued that the consent only follows when the lawyer completely divulges the extent of his work for the rival and all the "implications of common representation." Varnum found no evidence of such a full disclosure either to Weirton or to the foreign clients.

One must wonder what incentive the Japanese steel producers would have for consenting to representation of an American producer, like Weirton Steel, by their lawyers. Clearly, if the Japanese steel producers consented to this arrangement, they must believe that their interests are not only not prejudiced by Weirton Steel's counsel acting on their behalf, but indeed are advanced. The question for Weirton Steel becomes whether the Corporation wants to be represented by a law firm whom its competitors are so confident will exclusively advance their interests in a competitive economic environment, that they are even willing to consent to its representation of Weirton Steel as well. Likewise, one wonders why the Japanese and Brazilian steel producers would consent to be represented by the Willkie Farr firm when one of its senior partners—and through him, the firm—sits as a fiduciary on the Board of Directors of a competitor, Weirton Steel.

Varnum skeptically treated Sperry's view that a Chinese wall had been set up within his firm to prevent the commingling of information among lawyers to competitor steel clients. Ordinarily, firms raise Chinese walls to protect a former client's confidences, "or in the situation where a lawyer joins the law firm from a government agency or other firm which took a position adverse to an existing firm client. No case has been found where a Chinese wall was held to be effective where the firm was actively serving two existing clients with adverse interests, however." Moreover, if Sperry observed a Chinese wall he could not inform himself sufficiently about the firm's work for the foreign rivals in order to make a full disclosure to Weirton. It was obviously an impossible bind, which Varnum believed necessitated Sperry's resignation from the board or Willkie's removal as counsel.

To Philip Smith, the Chinese wall was "horse pucky." He went public with the memo and with his effort to drive the "scoundrel" Sperry off the board. Smith felt that Willkie's fees in excess of $1 million annually were unwarranted and emblematic of a corporation squandering on outsiders, consultants, and overruns rather than paying dividends and profit sharing.

In August of 1992, Sperry struck back. Bill Kieffer circulated a memo from Willkie Farr arguing that the directors had nothing to fear from the Bricmont lawsuit because under the law of Delaware (Weirton's state of incorporation) they had made "informed decisions." Smith hotly disputed the opinion because "we were misinformed" by management about the project.

Then, a well-orchestrated effort by directors began to remove Smith from the audit committee, which he chaired, and from the nominating committee. While Sperry in Smith's view was the "ring master," he used compliant directors Gordon Hurlburt, Dick Schubert, and Tom Sturges to make and second the necessary motions. Smith's opponents had the votes. Only Glyptis and D'Anniballe supported Smith. Union director Philip Karber was too new to vote.

Smith fought for over two hours. He challenged each of the directors to give him "a ballpark figure" on the total amount of cost overruns in the hot mill. None could. How could they throw him off the audit committee at a time when spending seemed out of control, and the company was about to borrow another $125 million? "Does this mean," said Smith, "that if anyone on the board gets out of line he can be sanctioned?" Glyptis added that "the men in the mill have more confidence in Smith than in anyone else on the board."

Schubert was enraged. "Smith has been terribly divisive. He obviously wants to force the chairman out." Leaving this "loose cannon" in place was "creating terrible morale problems," and threatened future financing.

New independent director David Wang, fifty-nine, a close friend of Elish's who had served alongside him as a vice president at International Paper, was summering in Ireland, but hooked into the meeting by speakerphone. Wang lashed out at Smith. "You are just an evil man. You are an evil person. You are just evil."

After the two union directors made known to Smith that they would not go along with any compromise, Smith played his trump. If they threw him off the audit committee, he would immediately go to the lawyer representing the shareholders suing over Bricmont and reveal everything he knew. The air went out of the board. After a break, Elish moved to table the motion to degrade Smith. Glyptis seconded. There were no negative votes. For the moment, Smith had beaten Sperry in a forum that the lawyer previously had dominated.

Predictably the problems plaguing the board continued to fester. Anger flashed through the mill in 1993 when the foreign companies represented by Willkie Farr won their suit in the International Trade Commission (ITC), which ruled that they did not have to pay damages for steel dumping. Glyptis railed against Sperry. "I believe a majority of our people are infuriated by his being a partner in the firm. We know they represented our competition and represented them quite well. They won all thirty-four suits."

The company's response that Sperry neither had provided nor received information from the Willkie lawyers who handled the suit in the ITC failed to satisfy Glyptis, who charged that Sperry shared in the profits of his partners. The ISU president began a campaign to prevent the lawyer's renomination to the board when his term was scheduled to expire in 1994.

Philip Smith concurred: "Sperry's dual representation is a cancer eating at the corporate body." Cartoons of Sperry with a noose around his neck began to show up around the mill, and one, to the embarrassment of the company, made it into the pages of *Forbes*.

The Bricmont suit also took a toll. As new revelations of high-level incompetence leaked, board and management popularity continued to skid. At the May 1993 annual meeting, Elish narrowly retained his seat as a director, winning only 57 percent of the votes cast, the lowest majority received by anyone up for the board. The vice president of operations, Warren Bartel, the former U.S. Steelman who had never been popular in Weirton, resigned, reportedly over his role in Bricmont.

Desperate to avoid a trial over the furnace scandal, the corporate defendants urged the West Virginia Supreme Court to dismiss the case on technical grounds. Specifically, they claimed that the plaintiff employees lacked standing to sue, since their stock was not held by them personally, but for them by the ESOP trust. The high court did not buy it, and in July 1993 voted 5–0 to allow the suit to go forward. The community braced for the trial. Paradoxically Bricmont failed to strengthen Philip Smith's hand. After he had been subpoenaed to vent his views of the affair at a deposition, his enemies on the board, who perceived that the feisty Australian had played his best card and could do them no more harm, removed him from his position as the audit committee chair.

In the fall of 1993, management and the union continued to bicker. Management favored the North American Free Trade Agreement (NAFTA). Bitterly disappointed in President Clinton, who had proposed the treaty, the ISU opposed it as a scheme to shift heavy industry and jobs across the border.

But the chasm between white collar and blue collar at Weirton widened over management's plan, backed by the board (with the exceptions of Smith and the union directors), to sell about 60 million shares, a hefty block of stock, at a new public offering.

In principal, the union agreed that selling shares made sense. Obviously, it would defray the company's huge debt from the modernization drive, which amounted to about $495 million and cost $1 million per week in interest payments.

But the ISU and Smith knew that such a large offering would end employee control, and urged shareholders to vote against the sale. For the proxy fight, management cranked up the public relations machine. Richard Garan, the company's personable financial spokesman, warned shareholders not to "ignore opinions from our investment bankers, who said that a no vote could so damage a company's reputation in the marketplace that our future ability to sell stock would be destroyed." Calling the vote a "blank check" for management, Mark Glyptis, the ISU president, led rallies and pickets outside the General Office where hundreds waived American flags and placards reading: "What goes around comes around," and "Don't Do It Herb." As Philip Smith had defected from his brethren on the board to fight the sale, Skip Spadafora, the most financially acute of the ISU committeemen, broke with the union. Braving hecklers at meetings, he reminded workers that other steel companies were issuing stock, and that Weirton could not compete without following suit.

While not explicitly rejecting a stock offering, the union maintained that the ESOP dream would die with the end of employee control, and pleaded for a hiatus to consider other alternatives. To Elish the sale was a necessity. "There is no plan B," he asserted. "In the next downturn, which we know will come, there'll be a real question about the company's ability to survive. It is necessary for this to be done now and not at some future time."

But the president's position seemed to weaken. When Elish praised Weirton as a bastion of corporate democracy, Smith publicly attacked the CEO as a dictator who forced workers to watch company propaganda videos. Elish termed the charge "repugnant." But less than a week before the proxy vote to decide the issue, he offered to cut the amount of shares for sale; and when the union challenged him to an eleventh-hour debate, he lamely counterproposed a televised session with reporters as "a more appropriate forum."

In early November 1993, with public emotions running high and proxy votes coming in at 3 to 2 against the sale, the board called off the IPO. Elish attributed the defeat to a low turnout and "a lot of confusion about what the issues were." Jubilant, Glyptis called the results "the first step in the rebirth of Weirton Steel Corporation, a growing, profitable, and competitive ESOP Corporation."

In an end-of-the-year story about employee-owned companies, with the tired title "ESOP Fables," the *Wall Street Journal* had a field day with Weirton. Blasting the company debt, cost overruns, and low morale, the *Journal* quoted a disaffected employee and plaintiff in the Bricmont case who claimed that "the trust factor here is zero." But the *Journal*, which conceded that labor relations were better at Weirton than if there had been no ESOP, failed to mention that other major steel companies were still losing money, and that Weirton's fundamentals were in place. Its prices were rising, its order book was full, and its modernization drive was complete.

In truth, the time was ripe for a renaissance in steel. Pruned production capacity and employment rolls coupled with growing demand from the revived auto industry soon resulted in higher prices. The soft dollar signaled that buyers first would look to domestic sources.

Despite Weirton's strife-torn reputation, investors services began recommending it to their subscribers, deeming it underpriced. In early 1994 the stock hit a five-year high of $11.00 per share. Then disaster struck in the form of the company's worst fire since the Brown's Island coke battery conflagration that killed eighteen in 1973. On April 6, 1994, a leak in a high-pressure hydraulic line generated an oil-based mist at the company's critical number 9 tandem mill, a cold rolling facility. When the mist drifted into contact with the exposed coil of a space heater, the instantaneous combustion produced a twelve-hundred-degree firestorm throughout the area that turned the atmosphere into an orange wall and sent fifty-five-gallon drums shooting upward like popping corn.

Union firefighters headed the battle against the blaze. A vestige of the deluxe National Steel days, the firefighters were expensive, highly trained workers paid mainly to wait. Repeatedly, they led or carried dazed workers suffering from burns and smoke inhalation through obscure passages. Amazingly no one died. It is doubtful that the contracted safety personnel found elsewhere in the industry would have had such mastery over the intricacies of the mill, or been able to respond so fast. In a sense the old Weirton had saved the new. When the time came to repair the fire's wreckage, management deployed union workers instead of contracting out.

Luckily, the adjacent computer faculty escaped damage, but the fire destroyed the number 9 tandem mill, the most modern in the industry, and the processor of about 40 percent of the steel for Weirton's tinplate product line. The day after the fire, a "buy" recommendation by Wall Street steel guru Peter Marcus went unheeded by the market. Weirton, which in the near term would function at only 80 percent, laid off more than two hundred employees, and saw its stock slide two points.

In the late spring and summer of 1994, the fire and its true stories of Forrest Gump–like saves, which Elish called "miraculous," and Glyptis credited to "the man upstairs," exerted a healing pull on management and the union, who agreed to a strategy on debt, and a new conflict-of-interest policy. Jointly, they spurred shareholders to approve selling 20 million shares (compared with 60 million, the proposal rejected in 1993), including 15 million to the public, and 5 million to company vehicles (such as a new ESOP trust from which employees could buy stock at a 15 percent discount), and the pension plan. If approved, the public sale would reduce the debt by about $120 million.

Endorsed unanimously by the ISU stewards, the scheme proposed to add a new "ESOP director," responsible to the interests of worker and retiree shareholders. More important, it tightened requirements for other board members. The novel conflict-of-interest measure banned anyone employed or consulted by the company or union from serving as an independent director. A new age requirement barred independent directors from being elected after age sixty-five. After announcement of the conflict clause, Harvey Sperry revealed that he would not seek another term. Plainly aimed at Philip Smith, the age limit got the same result from the scrappy dissenter. Smith, however, pleaded with the directors and the union not to impose an age ban, which would keep senior or retired industrialists off the board. If they wanted his resignation, he would give it; there was no need to deny the company expertise from others merely because of their years. But his pleas fell on deaf ears in both camps. Without Sperry and Smith, its great founding antagonists, the board hoped to go forward in peace.

The reform package, which embraced a system for evaluating the CEO cribbed from the one utilized by General Motors, left the employees with 53 percent voting control in contrast to the defeated measure that denied them a majority, and required approval by 80 percent of the shareholders because it included bylaws changes. To sweeten the pot, Elish announced that Willkie Farr would cease to serve as general counsel to the corporation. In late May, after a vigorous unified campaign by labor and management, the measures passed by 82.5 percent.

Even the dreaded Bricmont suit ended not with a bang but with a whimper. It settled in July 1994 for $6.25 million, a third of which went to the plaintiff's lawyers. Because the case was a "derivative suit" filed on behalf of the company by unhappy shareholders, and because the sued directors had insurance, the carrier ended up paying the balance to the company treasury, so Weirton Steel, the loser, won about $4 million. The *Pittsburgh Post-Gazette* called the result "bizarre." Philip Smith termed it "a sell-out." Some disgruntled plaintiffs initially contested the legal fees, but later withdrew their objections.

In August 1994 the new shares went public, with Elish calling the sale the "last piece of the puzzle." He and Glyptis, mortal foes a year before, teamed up on a road show to troll for investors in the United States and Europe. "That we could get this [offering] done when we did," said Elish, "is a testament to the company. It was done by putting behind us the differences of the past. We did this together. It's a reason for openness for Weirton Steel. We're ready to take advantage of the wonderful market we have. Business is good and we will be very healthy."

Sharing the podium, Glyptis, who earlier in 1994 had become the first ISU president to win reelection by running unopposed, pronounced the differences between the company and the union "re-solved." He spoke of shareholder value and employment security as reciprocal interests. "A lot of credit goes to the employees on the shop floor. Our production levels are far beyond anyone's expectations. Investors recognized the quality of our workforce. Investors felt confident in Weirton Steel."

By the mid-1990s, Weirton no longer topped the list of American ESOPs. With about 6,000 employees, it barely clung to last place in the top ten. Nor did Weirton lead domestic mills in employee participation, an honor probably won by the L-S Electro-Galvanizing plant, an LTV installation in Cleveland, where cross-trained workers had no job classifications, supervised themselves, hired other workers, made sales calls, dressed like and mingled with management, and won raises based on the mastery of new skills. But without Weirton serving as the example and proving ground, the UAL Corporation (parent of United Airlines) would not have emerged as an ESOP with 76,000 employees; and one would be hard pressed to find a utopian workplace in the grim flats of Cleveland or anywhere else in the rust belt.

In 1994, the predicted turnaround in steel became a reality. The costs had been great. In less than two decades about 350,000 jobs had been lost, and more than 65 million tons of capacity had been shorn. In 1994, the domestic market consumed about 110 million tons, while American steelmakers could produce only 99 million tons. The results were a shortage and sharply rising prices, which would jump $30 per ton at Weirton, Bethlehem, and LTV in January 1995.

Bottom line change was dramatic. The industry that lost $350 million in 1993 made more than $1 billion in 1994. Healthy themselves, domestic automakers, steel's largest customers, would order 10 percent to 15 percent more steel in 1995. Peter Marcus predicted that the strong demand for steel would continue for two decades.

Steel also reclaimed some markets held by plastics, wood, and other materials. Most promising for Weirton was house framing, in which it held 25 percent of the market. It took about forty-one trees or 5,000 pounds of steel to frame a house. More uniform than wood, steel meant no termites, superior electrical grounding, and better resistance to natural disasters such as hurricanes and earthquakes. In 1992 there were 1,000 homes built with steel, in 1993 there were 13,000, in 1994 there were 40,000, and in 1996 there will be about 160,000. Perhaps not surprisingly, Weirton's second IPO performed better than its first.

In January 1995, Herb Elish, sixty-one, announced that he would step down as chairman of the board and chief executive officer at the end of the year. His tumultuous eight-year term would be remembered for returning the corporation to profitability (and profit sharing), emphasizing quality, modernizing the physical plant, and painfully pruning the workforce, all of which contributed to Weirton's competitiveness in the world market. These outweighed the delicate ethical and legal crises that perhaps could have been curtailed before being allowed to fester.

The heir apparent, chief financial officer Richard Riederer, fifty-one, began the transition into the top spot—assuming the duties of president as well as the newly created position of chief operating officer—in early 1995. As CFO, Riederer had distinguished himself as among the most competent managers in the corporation, and had played a pivotal role in the 1994 public offering, during which he forged strong ties with Wall Street.

Against the odds, Weirton had lasted twelve years, and probably will last another dozen, or as long as America still made steel. The future will not necessarily be smooth. As Elish put it, "You have to have a very strong stomach, to rally the people, hear what they believe, listen to it, respond. One thing about steelworkers; when you have a conversation it's not always elegant, but it's always clear." The union had served clear notice that it would go to the mattresses over any layoffs not based on attrition. Yet both sides understood that they would come together whenever corporate survival was threatened. Although the company could not employ armies of the unskilled as in the past, it would continue as the engine and foundation of the local economy. The community would not go to pot.

The players finally had figured out their roles. Management and the board keyed on a company-first brand of competitiveness, inviting employee participation, and had learned the bittersweet lessons of accountability. The union had a tougher time finding its place in a shareholder world, but after a decade it seemed to be stabilizing and ending its days of revolving door leadership. Its scope had grown beyond negotiating contracts and arbitrating grievances, to serving as an unofficial conscience of the corporation, watchdogging conflicts of interest and the lining of pockets, disclosing the facts, and keeping the record. It was a new role for a union, but one that made sense as the era of big labor passed and workers became owners.

Notes

Preface

xi Presidential candidate Clinton's speech in Weirton occurred on July 19, 1992, and was reported in *Independent Weirton*, the newspaper of Weirton Steel in its August 1992 issue.

xii Good analyses of the decline of the Western Pennsylvania steel culture are found in *Homestead: The Glory and Tragedy of an American Steel Town* by Williams Serrin (New York, Times Books, 1992), and *And the Wolf Finally Came: The Decline of the American Steel Industry* by John P. Hoerr (Pittsburgh, University of Pittsburgh Press, 1988).

xii The armed standoff involving steelworkers in Clairton, Pennsylvania, the eventual siege of the Lutheran church where they held out, and the events leading up to the confrontation are described in *Can Workers Have a Voice? The Politics of Deindustrialization in Pittsburgh* by Dale A. Hathaway (University Park, Pennsylvania, Pennsylvania State University Press, 1993).

350

xii I was aided in estimating the number of steelworkers at the height of the industry in Western Pennsylvania by Randolph Harris of the Steel Industry Heritage Corporation, whom I interviewed in August 1994.

1 Black Tuesday

3-5 Staughton Lynd shared his views during a number of interviews including a taped session on November 18, 1987. A good article about Lynd and his transition from historian to lawyer appeared in the *National Law Journal,* September 10, 1979. An excellent interview with Lynd regarding his political views of history and writing history was included in *Visions of History* by MARHO, the Radical Historians Organization (New York, Pantheon, 1984). Lynd also generously allowed me to view all of his documents and correspondence from his involvement with the Rank and File Group in Weirton.

7 The quotations from Walter Adams and Roger Brown appeared in the *NACLA Report on the Americas,* "Steelyard Blues: New Structures in Steel," January–February 1979.

8-9 The plight of National Steel in 1982 was recalled by Howard M. "Pete" Love in an interview at his headquarters on July 12, 1988. I also consulted the annual reports of National Steel and National Intergroup during the 1970s and 1980s.

The state of the steel industry in 1982, including a listing of bankruptcies and closures (1974–82) is reflected in an extensive letter with appendices from J. Bruce Johnston, Chairman of the Coordinating Committee of Steel Companies (the industry's chief negotiator) to Lloyd McBride, International President, United Steelworkers of America, May 28, 1982.

10-11 The career paths of William Doepken and David Roberston were revealed in a series of interviews with both men. A taped session with Doepken occurred on May 10, 1988. Robertson was recorded on December 9, 1987, January 16, 1988, and January 30, 1988. Both men spoke to the seminal role of the late labor lawyer (for National Steel) Donald Ebbert.

11 David Robertson in March 1982 became the ISU's day-to-day record keeper of the Joint Study Committee's activities. These notes (hereafter "JSC notes") became the best record of the early joint management labor effort. Later the JSC would put out a formal newsletter. Robertson's participation with management in February and March is drawn from these notes and his interviews. His notes of March 2, 1988, were especially complete, though I also drew upon the numerous newspaper reports of the crisis in early March, which was covered by the *Weirton Daily Times, Steubenville Herald-Star, Charleston Daily Mail, Pittsburgh Press, Pittsburgh Post-Gazette, Wall Street Journal, Wheeling Intelligencer,* and other papers.

11-18 Senator Jay Rockefeller was interviewed regarding his Weirton experiences on June 2, 1989. Jack Redline was interviewed at his home in Florida on June 23, 1988. Former ISU President Richard "Red" Arango was interviewed in Weirton on July 5, 1988. ISU dissident Mike Hrabovsky was interviewed on July 6, 1988.

2   Weir's World

19   The quotation from E. T. Weir at the head of the chapter as well as the industrialist's views on FDR and the New Deal are drawn from his article, "I Am What Mr. Roosevelt Calls an Economic Royalist," in *Fortune*, October 1936.

20–27   Weir's early life, management methods, love of *David Copperfield*, and unusual views about the Cold War and communism (38–41) were reported in "Ernest Tener Weir: Last of the Great Steel Masters" by John D. Ubinger, in *The Western Pennsylvania Historical Magazine*, July 1975.

The early organization of the National Steel Company is detailed in *The Economic History of the Iron and Steel Industry in the United States*, Vol. 2 (Lexington, Mass. D. C. Heath, 1971), by William Hogan, pp. 575–92. The true genius of Weir's vision of building the components into a harmonious corporation that would be profitable throughout the Depression is found in "National Steel: A Phenomenon" in *Fortune*, June 1932.

A more technical and academic study of how Weir both kept iron control of the company while delegating deeply to managers is found in Ernest Dale's study, *The Great Organizers*, Chapter 4, "Ernest Tener Weir: Iconoclast of Management" (1960).

For insights into the personalities and practices of Weir, Millsopp, and the early corporate leaders, I drew on the knowledge of Charles Cronin, the longtime director of public relations at Weirton Steel.

27   Father Charles Schneider, who educated me about the history of the town's ethnic groups and religions, was interviewed on February 27, 1988.

28–31   For the pre–World War II labor history of Weirton, I largely relied upon *U.S. v. Weirton Steel: Capital, Labor and Government*, an unpublished monograph by J. Carroll Moody. I also drew upon recollections of Bill Doepken.

Much of the early history of the town of Weirton was drawn from the *History of Weirton and Holliday's Cave and Life of J. C. Williams* by Frank A. Pietranton (privately published, Weirton, 1936).

32–34   The nature of the early company union activity and the anti-CIO mood at Weirton is made plain in a publication called "The Weirton Steel Employees Bulletin." I was able to locate issues from the 1930s and early 1940s.

34   The contentious relationship between the ISU and the United Steelworkers in the postwar period is detailed in the USW's journal *Steel Labor*. The September 1950 article, "Murray Confident USA Campaign Will Crack Weirton Iron Curtain," was especially clear about the rancor. I also read the USW organizer reports about Weirton from the 1950s; and its correspondence with the National Labor Relations Board.

35–36   Both David Robertson and Bill Doepken outlined for me the organization of the Independent Steel Workers Union (ISU), including its six divisions and electoral practices.

37–38   The ISU propaganda rhetoric against the USW is from a 1954 Weirton Union flier. The trouncing of the USW by the ISU in that era was reported in the ISU publication, *The Independent News*, "CIO Runs Out," June 15, 1954.

40–41   For information about Thomas Millsopp, Weir's successor, I drew upon the proceedings of the Weirton Chamber of Commerce, January 16, 1966, and a speech to the Weirton Kiwanis on August 8, 1961, by Weirton's then president Charles G. Tournay, as well as accounts of the executive in the *Weirton Daily Times*.

3   The Mill of the Future

42–45   My information about technological and equipment changes at the Weirton Division in the 1950s and 1960s came from National Steel publications. In particular I relied upon "National: A Pace Setter in Steel" by Edmund K. Faltermayer, 1964, and "History and Overview of the National Steel Corporation," by National Intergroup, 1986. The significance of the soaring basic oxygen furnace was reported in the *Pittsburgh Post-Gazette*, April 14, 1967. In his interview, Jack Redline detailed corporate progress during the 1960s and 1970s from his viewpoint as a rising manager.

46   The quotation from Weirton mayor Donal Mentzer "Unity is our strength. . . ." comes from the *Weirton Daily Times*, March 9, 1982.

47   The announcement by the Department of Labor that made a distinction between National's guaranteed pensions and what a new company would provide was reported in the *Wheeling Intelligencer*, March 5, 1992.

47   Red Arango's remark "It's what you wear . . ." is from the *Wheeling Intelligencer*, March 3, 1982.

47   Bill Doepken's quote "Sending Lowenstein . . ." is from his interview, February 18, 1988.

47–51   Allan Lowenstein's Weirton experience was explored in an interview on April 29, 1988. Information about his work at other companies came from various sources. His "resurrection" of Okonite was reported in *Fortune*, June 2, 1980. The better-known Hyatt Clark start-up and eventual failure have been widely reported. However, I drew on the Hyatt Clark Employee Stock Ownership Plan, the coverage in the *Christian Science Monitor*, October 19, 1981, the Industrial Cooperative Association fact sheet on Hyatt Clark (1982), and the *New York Times*, August 11, 1987.

51   State Senator Patrick McCune's comment is from the *Morgantown Dominion Post*, March 3, 1982.

51–52   The response of Governor Rockefeller and Miles Dean to the situation is taken from the interviews of Rockefeller (June 2, 1989), Dean (May 21, 1989), and Doepken (May 10, 1988).

52–53   The civil rights and racial origins of the Rank and File Committee are drawn from interviews with Edward "Skip" Mixon (March 21, 1989) and with Willie McKenzie (March 30, 1989).

53–54   The Rank and File Committee's flier that is quoted was for a meeting, March 9, 1982.

54   Staughton Lynd's remarks "problems . . . language" and "the son . . . City" are drawn from his interview in *Visions of History.*

55   Lynd's remark "would affect . . . up" appeared in the *Wheeling Intelligencer,* March 10, 1982.

4   New Age Economics

56–57   Information about early American unions and their experiences with cooperatives is drawn from *History of the Labor Movement in the United States,* Vol. 1, by Philip S. Foner (New York, International Publisher, 7th ed., 1982).

57–60   The quotations and ideas of Louis Kelso come from *The Capitalist Manifesto* by Kelso and Mortimer J. Adler (New York, Random House, 1958). Kelso's views on expanding the ESOP by idea to other vehicles such as Public Ownership Plans (PUBCOPS) and Residential Ownership Plans (RECOPS) are found in *Democracy and Economic Power Extending the ESOP Revolution,* by Louis O. Kelso and Patricia Hetter Kelso (Cambridge, Ballinger, 1986).

60   Norman Kurland shared his recollections with me in a meeting on May 26, 1989. Also, I attended his speech to the ESOP Association in May, 1989.

60–61   Former Senator Russell Long was interviewed on May 26, 1989. The quotation from Ronald Reagan's radio address, "Our Founding Fathers . . . economy," is found in *Employee Ownership, Revolution or Rip Off,* by Joseph R. Blasi (Cambridge, Ballinger, 1988). This book is an invaluable guide to the history of the ESOP movement, as well as ESOP legislation.

61–62   The negative ESOP experience at Dan River, Inc., was reported in *The Christian Science Monitor,* July 7, 1983. The problems with ESOPs at industrial companies such as Rath Meats and Southbend Lathe were reported in the *Labor Research Review,* Spring 1985.

62–63   The remark of Jack Sheehan, "In most . . . company," was reported in the *Christian Science Monitor,* July 7, 1983. For this chapter, I was educated and informed by a variety of other sources, including position papers by the Industrial Cooperative Association (ICA), materials from the National Center for Employee Ownership (NCEO), as well as by the documents prepared for the 1989 ESOP Association Convention, Washington, D.C., by the ESOP Association. A handbook entitled "A Union Member's Guide to Employee Involvement" by Tom Juravich and Howard Harris, Department of International Relations at Pennsylvania State University, also was instructive.

For background used throughout this chapter I interviewed Luis Granados, Esq., the executive director of the ESOP Association, on July 1, 1988, and read his article, "Employee Stock Ownership Plans: An Analysis of Current Reform Proposal," in the *Journal of Law Reform,* Fall 1980. I attended the speech of Louis Kelso at the 1989 ESOP Association meeting in Washington, D.C., and interviewed him there briefly. Also, I read his article "Karl Marx: The Almost Capitalist," in the *American Bar Association Journal,* March 1957.

Deborah Groban Olson's article, "Union Experiences with Worker Ownership:

Legal and Practical Issues Raised by ESOPs, TRASOPs, Stock Purchases and Co-operatives," in the *Wisconsin Law Review* (1982), was a superior introduction to the ESOP law at the time. In addition, I was able to review certain correspondence between Staughton Lynd and Groban Olson.

An article entitled "Worker Ownership, Participation and Control: Toward a Theoretical Model," by William Foote Whyte and Joseph R. Blasi, in *Policy Sciences*, Vol. 14 (1982), was helpful in terms of analyzing the political ramifications of various ESOP types.

5   The Joint Study Committee

64–69   The quotations by Jack Redline, as well as his reflections of the early days after National Steel's announcement, are drawn from his interview, June 23, 1988. Unless otherwise noted, the quotations from Redline came from this interview.

69–71   William Saunders was interviewed on November 10, 1988. All of his quotations in this chapter come from that interview. In addition, for background on the accomplishments of Saunders and his experimental unit at Weirton, I read Weirtec promotional materials.

71–72   The comments of Carl Valdiserri, who became the management leader of the Joint Study Committee, were provided to me in interviews in 1988 on May 20, June 6, June 20, July 20, August 25, and September 29. The quotations from William Doepken and David Robinson in this chapter also are drawn from their interviews.

74–75   Information pertaining to Joseph Schuchert (Kelso Capital) and his inter-actions with the Joint Study Committee comes from the ISU's Joint Study Com-mittee notes of March 3, March 9, April 7, April 14, and April 22, 1982. The interaction between the JSC and Norman Kurland is reflected in the ISU/JSC notes of March 9 and March 15, 1982.

76–79   Information about the ESOP Association Conference of May 1982 and the interactions between the JSC, Allan Lowenstein, and Jack Curtis is found in David Robertson's records of May 6 and May 7, 1982. In addition, I drew upon the interview with Lowenstein, April 29, 1989.

6   The Rank and File Committee

80–82   The Steubenville meeting of the Rank and File Committee was covered by the *Weirton Daily Times*, March 17, 1982, where the quotations from Tony Gilliam and Willie McKenzie are found. The *Steubenville Herald-Star* of March 17, 1982, also covered the meeting. This article contained quotations from Steve Bauman and Red Arango. Information reflecting the status of rank and file movements in other unions during the 1970s and 1980s came from *Business Week*, April 16, 1984, and August 11, 1986. An article focusing on the rank and file movement in the steel industry appeared in *Business Week* on March 24, 1986. An interesting discussion of the campaign for the presidency of the United

Steelworkers by Edward Sadlowski is contained in *Which Side Are You On? Trying to Be for Labor When It's Flat on Its Back*, by Thomas Geoghegan (New York, Farrar, Straus & Giroux, 1991).

82–85   The Rank and File Committee's meeting of March 22, 1982 was covered by the *Weirton Daily Times* of March 23, 1982, which contained the quoted material. The *Steubenville Herald-Star* of March 25, 1982 criticized the Rank and File Committee in an editorial. Also, I utilized the fliers for these events, which were written by Steve Bauman. The Rank and File Committee meeting on April 12, 1982 at Madonna High School was covered by the *Weirton Daily Times* of April 14, 1982. Also I reviewed Staughton Lynd's handwritten notes of April 1982. J. J. Varlas's caustic remarks were contained in his newsletter of April 1982.

85–86   Information on the ISU's referendum of April 20, 1982, was found in records compiled by Charles Cronin, the director of public relations of the Weirton Steel Division. The comment about Red Arango and his leadership was provided in an interview by Richard Mort on June 27, 1988.

86–88   Chuck Lafferty provided the information pertaining to his early involvement with the process in the spring of 1982 in an interview on February 25, 1988. The results of the May 21, 1982 ISU referendum were supplied in materials by Charles Cronin.

7   Wall Street and Washington

89–92   The contacts between Senator Robert F. Byrd and the Reagan administration about Weirton were covered in the *Weirton Daily Times* of March 8, 1982, and the *Wheeling Intelligencer*, March 10, 1982. The March 11, 1982, trip to the White House by JSC members, as well as issues pertaining to the mill's environmental liabilities, are covered in David Robertson's notes of March 11, 1982. Reflections of Miles Dean about the political process in Washington, as well as about Allan Lowenstein, came from his interview of May 21, 1988. David Robertson's thoughts about the removal of Lowenstein were contained in his interview of December 9, 1987. Allan Lowenstein's explanation for his separation from the Weirton process appeared in *Iron Age*, June 7, 1982.

92–93   The visits by consultants Arthur D. Little and Booz, Allen were reported by the *Weirton Daily Times* on March 18, 1982.

93–98   David Robertson's search for a New York lawyer "quarterback" was recounted in his interview of December 9, 1987. Comments about Harvey Sperry were contained in his interviews of January 16 and January 30, 1988. Sperry's impressions of Weirton were given during an interview on April 28, 1988. During this interview he also opined on Jack Redline. Information about the "positive" and "negative" factions of the union came from the interviews with Mike Hrabovsky (July 6, 1988) and Bill Doepken (May 17, 1988).

98–101   Walter Bish was interviewed and gave his impressions about union politics, including the election of 1982 on October 12, 1988. The results of the union election of June 1982 were reported in the materials of Charles Cronin, the director of public relations of the Weirton Steel Division. Information about the "Save

Our Valley Rally" was drawn from materials compiled by Charles Cronin and David Robertson, including Robertson's draft of a speech delivered by Red Arango.

101–102   John "Skip" Spadafora was interviewed about his entry into union politics and the Joint Study Committee on April 18, 1988. Chris Graziani, an ISU leader who was defeated in the 1982 election, supplied comments in an interview on August 8, 1988.

8   America's Mill

103–104   In order to formulate opinions about the hot line, I read the transcripts and records of the ESOP's message center which were provided by Chuck Lafferty, who also commented about Walter Bish and the new leadership in Lafferty's interview of February 25, 1988. The Weirton Independence Day parade (July 3, 1982) was covered in the *New York Times* on July 4, 1982. Weirton was also covered in the *Washington Post* on July 6, 1982. Walter Bish's quotation at the rally, "I always . . . steel mill," was reported in the *Washington Post* article.

105   The comment on media attention by Staughton Lynd was contained in a letter from Lynd to Peter Pitegoff of the Industrial Cooperative Association, July 10, 1988.

105–107   The experiences of the McKinsey team were conveyed to me in interviews with Ronald Bancroft, who headed the team (August 25, 1989), and with two of the team's members, Michael Chesick and Michael Pearson, on July 1, 1988. The interim report of McKinsey was issued in a Joint Study Committee release on June 4, 1982. The July 14, 1982 Steubenville meetings wherein Ron Bancroft provided information were covered in the records of Charles Cronin and by the *Pittsburgh Post-Gazette* on July 15, 1982. On July 15, 1982, the *Weirton Daily Times* also reported on the Steubenville meetings and reported the remarks of Harvey Sperry and Red Arango.

107   Steve Bauman's remark "Are we . . . control?" appeared in the publication *Labor Notes* on July 21, 1982. Bauman was interviewed about his recollections of the 1982 crises on March 13, 1989.

107–110   Information from Carl Valdiserri about the controversy over the size of the McKinsey proposed cutback was provided in his interview of July 20, 1988. Bill Doepken spoke to this issue on May 10, 1988.

The forty-page McKinsey report was issued on July 26, 1988, and it is summarized in this chapter.

110–111   David Robertson's comments on picking an investment banker and going to Lazard Frères are taken from his interview of January 30, 1988.

9   Secrecy

112–116   The comments of local leaders including Arango, Redline, and Bish on the McKinsey report were taken from an article in the *Steubenville Herald-Star* on January 27, 1982. The Rank and File Committee's demand for disclosure of the

McKinsey appendix was made in a letter to the ISU of July 27, 1982. The remarks of Walter Bish on "strategic information" and Staughton Lynd in response are drawn from court papers in the case of *Bauman v. Bish*. Bill Doepken's remarks on the McKinsey study were reported in the *Weirton Daily Times* of August 5, 1982.

116–119   The information about the meeting with Tom Bryan and the contact with Bear Stearns were reported in the Robertson ISU/JSC notes of August 25, 1982. The contact with Shearson American Express and the Joint Study Committee is recounted in Robertson's notes of August 26, 1992.

Eugene Keilin was profiled in *Fortune* on December 22, 1986. He provided information for this chapter in an interview on May 10, 1988. Joshua Gotbaum, Keilin's subordinate at Lazard, was interviewed on April 6, 1988.

119–120   Kenneth Hunt was interviewed on July 21, 1988. Kenneth Hunt's appointment was carried in the *Independent Weirton Journal*, which was the transitional company's first newspaper. In time it would grow into *Independent Weirton*, the official newspaper of the Weirton Steel Corporation.

10   Divide and Conquer

121–122   The flier of the Rank and File Committee "Who Is the 'We' in We Can Do It?" was used for a meeting of the committee on July 20, 1982. The information pertaining to the confrontation between Tony Gilliam and the JSC leaders was recounted in the court papers of *Bauman v. Bish*, as are the critical comments by Staughton Lynd and Attorney James McNamara pertaining to the McKinsey report.

123   The accusations against Bish for bad faith, and Bish's continued urging of confidentiality also appear in the court records, as does David Robertson's remark "asking us . . . curiosity."

123   Steve Bauman's concerns about confidentiality were reported in the *Wheeling Intelligencer*, October 14, 1982.

124   David Robertson's contact with Mellon Bank about the necessary billion dollars' worth of capitalization required for the new company is embraced in Robertson's notes of September 16, 1982.

124–125   The failed effort to receive substantial EDA financing from the federal government is reflected in a letter of September 10, 1982, from Craig L. Fuller, assistant to President Reagan for cabinet affairs, to William L. Doepken. The likewise unsuccessful bid to get UDAG money from the U.S. Department of Housing and Urban Development (HUD) is seen in Robertson's notes of May 7, 1982, May 18, 1982, and July 30, 1982.

125   The information about the Towers, Perrin Pension Liability Study is found in the documents compiled by Charles Cronin. The matter was covered by the *Weirton Daily Times* on August 18, 1982. Miles Dean's remarks about a possible non-dollar transfer of the mill were carried in the *Wheeling Intelligencer*, July 22, 1982. The telephone call between Miles Dean and David Robertson, "you and Bill . . . soon," is recorded in Robertson's notes of August 24, 1982.

125–126   The discussion between Robertson and Doepken as to possible leadership for the new corporation is recorded in Robertson's notes of August 26, 1982. Harvey Sperry's comments to Robertson about replacing local leadership, including Jack Redline, are recorded in Robertson's notes of September 2, 1982.

126–127   Jack Redline's remarks to the Weirton Knights of Columbus were covered by the *Weirton Daily Times*, September 21, 1982. The New York meetings of September 13 and 14, the remarks of the participants, and the reflections of David Robertson were recorded in his seven-page typed memorandum of September 15, 1982. Also, Robertson handwrote the events of these sessions in his entries of September 13 and 14, 1982.

128–130   The telephone conference from Sperry to Robertson regarding Lazard was noted by Robertson on September 15, 1982. The Robertson-Bish conversation of September 16, 1982, is noted in Robertson's records of that date. The conversation between Chuck Lafferty and John Robinson was recorded in David Robertson's handwritten notes of a telephone call with Lafferty on September 16, 1982. Information about the teleconference among Robertson, Bish, Lazard, and Willkie Farr is from Robertson's notes of September 22, 1982.

11   Propaganda

131–135   Chuck Lafferty was interviewed on February 25, 1988 about the communications effort of the Joint Study Committee. He also provided me with the company's written communications philosophy, which he developed and which is quoted from. Lafferty also supplied numerous treatments and/or scripts for public relations projects. In addition, I watched his movie, "On Our Own," and read its preliminary treatments. The quoted comments and remarks about the proposed film, the billboard campaign, the speak out messages, the roundtables, and the utilization of Walter Bish in the publicity campaign, as well as David Robertson's concerns about maintaining Bish's credibility, are from the Robertson's ISU/JSC notes of September 28, 1982, pertaining to membership communications.

135   The quotations from the ESOP message center (EMC) are taken from the transcriptions of messages that were received.

12   A Lawyer's Dream

136–137   The information in the first paragraph including the quoted material is found in David Robertson's record of a telephone conference with Miles Dean, which he noted on September 30, 1982. Harvey Sperry discussed the choice of special counsel by National during his interview on April 28, 1988.

137–138   The quotations by Elliott Goldstein are taken from his interview of July 20, 1989.

138–139   The Sperry quotations pertaining to the negotiations beginning in Pittsburgh on September 29, 1982, are drawn from his interview of July 20, 1989. The strong feeling that Sperry felt for the companies he represented was described by David Robertson in his interview of January 16, 1988.

139   Double-digit unemployment statistics were reported by United Press International on October 8, 1982.

140–141   National Steel's pay cuts for management are drawn from Charles Cronin's material. The racial restructuring of the seniority system in an ISU referendum was reported in the Cronin materials of October 19, 1982.

13   Hard Ball

142–144   Discussions involving David Robertson and the consultants, including Josh Gotbaum, were recorded in Robertson's notes of October 22, 1982. Harvey Sperry's dealings with National's President James Haas were mentioned in the Sperry interview.

144–147   The Lynd and Pitegoff Op-Ed piece appeared in the *New York Times* on October 27, 1982. Staughton Lynd wrote to Robertson on October 22, 1982, proposing settlement. Quotations from the court proceedings before Judge Haden are taken from court records of the case, which began on October 28, 1982.

147   The Rank and File Committee published Bauman's post-court leaflet on November 5, 1982. The JSC's worries about the Rank and File Committee were reflected in the Robertson ISU/JSC notes of November 18, 1982. A report that the JSC would keep fighting was published in the *Wall Street Journal* on November 9, 1982.

148–149   Varlas commented on Redline in the newsletter of November 23, 1982. The Robertson to Sperry comment on Redline is found in Robertson's notes of November 23, 1982. The meeting at Willkie Farr is covered in Robertson's notes of November 26, 1982. The meeting involving Keilin, Sperry, and Redline and their reflections is covered in Robertson's notes of November 29, 1982. Louis Kelso blasted the Weirton proposed ESOP in a letter to Governor Jay Rockefeller, November 30, 1982.

150   Senator Byrd's efforts to help Weirton with it environmental compliance problems are seen in his letter to Senator George Mitchell of December 2, 1982. Information that Governor Rockefeller gave Weirton a tax break is reflected in Cronin's materials, December 13, 1982.

151–152   The dissatisfaction of the Ministerial Association is shown in the Robertson notes of December 13, 1982. Staughton Lynd received the information from Professor Rosenberger also on December 13, 1982. The economic decline of National and the statistics are taken from the National Steel Prospectus of January 1983.

153–157   Information about the Gregory complaint is taken from the minutes of the ISU and United States Department of Labor records. The announcement of the potential agreement between National and Weirton is found in Cronin's materials, February 3, 1983. The dealings between the ISU and the Department of Labor are covered in the minutes of the ISU executive committee meeting of February 15, 1983, and reported to a lesser extent in the *Steubenville Herald-Star* of February 16, 1983. The ISU stewards' meeting of February 15, 1983, also is covered in union minutes. The *New York Times* reported again in detail on Weirton on February 13, 1983.

158–165   Bauman's quoting Hannibal and raising concerns about automation and voting control were published in a leaflet on March 2, 1983. The activities of the union on March 10 and 11, 1983 are drawn from union records. The Lazard Frères' announcement of March 12, 1983 is reported in Cronin's materials. The draft pact was reported in the Joint Study Committee journal of March 13, 1983. The *Wall Street Journal*'s analysis was published on March 14, 1983. Robert Crandall of the Brookings Institution was quoted in the *Weirton Daily Times* of March 15, 1983, on the deal. *USA Today* also published its analysis on March 14, 1983, in which the quotes by Love, Gotbaum, and Robertson are found. Carl Valdiserri was quoted on it in the *Steubenville Herald-Star* of March 16, 1983. Bish's remarks were delivered at a press conference on March 15, 1983. Jack Redline also gave prepared remarks at this press conference. The editorial about the proposed Weirton deal was in the *Wall Street Journal* of March 18, 1983. Luis Granados commented in the *Weirton Daily Times* on March 19, 1983. Jack Redline's remarks on his prospective retirement appeared in the *Weirton Daily Times* of March 25, 1983, as did Walter Bish's comment.

14   Shots from Left and Right

166–168   James Zarello's remarks were recorded in the minutes of the ISU stewards' meeting of March 29, 1983. Keilin's remarks were reported in the *Pittsburgh Post-Gazette* of March 28, 1993.

168–172   Mike Hrabovsky was interviewed on July 6, 1988. The suit of the Concerned Steel Workers (CSW) was reported in the Cronin materials March 30, 1983. The remarks of Bancroft and Doepken were carried in *Metal Producing* magazine of April 1983. The remarks of Eugene Green and Red Arango were carried in the April 7, 1983, *Steubenville Herald-Star* and the April 8, 1983, *Weirton Daily Times*.

172   The quotation from William F. Whyte is from his letter to David Robertson of April 22, 1983.

173–174   Harvey Sperry's remarks of April 23, 1983, were reported in the ISU/JSC notes of that date by Robertson. Doepken's five points also were covered in these notes.

175–176   The activity in the federal court in Wheeling was reported in the Cronin materials of April 28, 1983, and the *Pittsburgh Press* of the same date. Judge Maxwell's remarks also were drawn from the court records, as were those of Staughton Lynd. The JSC journal also covered the court proceedings.

177–178   The remarks of Nick Petrovich and others at the ISU executive committee were covered in the minutes of May 4, 1983. The early May union executive committee minutes also covered the discussions about whom the union would place on the company's board.

15 Fielding the Team

179–181   The analysis by Lazard Frères appears in its draft of a private placement memorandum, May 9, 1983.

181   Howard Love's remarks were reported in the *Weirton Daily Times* of May 12, 1983.

182   The taped message of Don Murray was found in the records of the ESOP message center. The Rank and File Committee's criticism of the ISU was contained in a leaflet published on May 20, 1983. Bish's pessimism about a vote was carried in the May 25, 1983, *Steubenville Herald-Star.*

182   The TV roundtable remarks were contained in correspondence from Robertson to Bish of June 8, 1983.

183–184   The fund raising events were reported in the JSC journal of June 10, 1983. The extension of the ISU contract was reported in the Cronin materials and the *Steubenville Herald-Star* of June 17, 1983. Judge Maxwell's July ruling was announced in the Cronin materials of July 11, 1983. This also was the release date of the sociological study by Arnold Levine, a WVU sociologist, which I reviewed.

184   Robertson's remark about "razor blades" was made in an interview in January 1988.

184–185   The six initial directors were announced and profiled in the *Wheeling Intelligencer* and the *Weirton Daily Times* on July 14, 1983.

186–191   Harvey Sperry's remarks about going back to the bargaining table came from his interview on April 28, 1988. Sperry also reflected at that time about the CEO selection process, including the rejection of Redline and the selection of Loughead. Loughead was interviewed about the selection process and other issues on February 12, 1988. Redline's views came from his interview on June 23, 1988. The Rank and File Committee's research on Copperweld was drawn from the RFC record of July 29, 1983. The anonymous welcome to President Loughead was found in the archives of the ESOP message center.

191–195   David Robertson recalled the placement of Sperry and Keilin on the board in his interview of January 16, 1988. He also explained the selection of Bluestone. Bluestone provided information in his interview of July 14, 1988. He also supplied his writings on employee participation and his congressional testimony.

16 Democracy

196–204   Skip Spadafora was interviewed on April 18, 1988. Sperry reported on the allocation issue in his interview in April 1988. The Lazard Frères memo initially was prepared on July 5, 1983, for the Joint Study Committee. Staughton Lynd sent it to Deborah Groban Olson and Peter Pitegoff on August 8, 1983. Pitegoff responded in a letter back to Lynd on August 12, 1983. Groban Olson sent her comments to Lynd on August 25, 1983. The speeches in response to the release of the disclosure document were covered in the August 24, 1983, *Weirton Daily Times* and *Wheeling Intelligencer.*

206–207   The public relations drive around the upcoming election was related by Chuck Lafferty in his interview of February 1988.

207–218   The Rank and File Committee issued its leaflet entitled "Oh Say Can You See?" on September 6, 1983. Court proceedings commencing on September 21, 1983, were reported in the Cronin materials and the *Pittsburgh Press*, as well as in the court records. Loughead and Bish were quoted about the vote and the difficulties with the Rank and File Committee in the September 23, 1983, *Weirton Daily Times*. Steve Bauman of the Rank and File Committee also was quoted in this piece. Father Charles Schneider explained activities of the religious community in Weirton during his interview on February 27, 1988. The voting results were reported in all local newspapers. Bish and Bluestone were quoted about the new company in the *Weirton Daily Times* of September 24, 1983, as was Governor Jay Rockefeller. Steve Bauman's cautionary remark appeared in the *Steubenville Herald-Star* of September 26, 1983. The remarks of Staughton Lynd and Corey Rosen appeared in the October 5–11, 1983, issue of *In These Times*.

218   Robertson was quoted on the CSW lawsuit in the *Pittsburgh Press* of September 29, 1983.

17   On Our Own

219–220   The ISU's contacts with the Department of Labor are reported in the union minutes. The draft of the subscription and stock purchase agreement that was completed October 28, 1983, was reviewed.

220–223   Robert Loughead was interviewed by *Iron Age*, November 7, 1983. The ISU's dealings with and comments on the Department of Labor were covered in union minutes. Some D.O.L. records were obtained under the Freedom of Information Act. The *Nation* analyzed Weirton in its December 10, 1983, issue. Bluestone wrote to Walter Bish on December 21, 1983. The ruling of the Fourth Circuit Court of Appeals in Richmond, Virginia, was reported in court documents and in the Cronin materials of December 30, 1983. The proceedings with National on January 12, 1984, were covered in the *Weirton Daily Times*. The lyrics to "We're On Our Own" were supplied by Chuck Lafferty. The *New York Times* reported on the buyout on January 16, 1984.

18   Changing the Culture

227–229   The Weirton transaction was analyzed in the disclosure document prepared by Willkie Farr. National Intergroup's overture to USX was reported in the Cronin compilation. Weirton's financial numbers, as a public corporation, were reported in quarterly reports. The visit of a USW Local to Weirton was covered in a memo from David Robertson of April 18, 1984. The comparison of Weirton's financial gains in the first quarter versus those of other steel companies was covered in *USA Today*, April 23, 1984. The announcement of the union's dissolution of its strike fund was covered in the *Pittsburgh Press* of April 27, 1984.

The situation between the ISU and the Department of Labor is drawn from ISU records, and D.O.L. documents obtained.

229–253   The historical material on Frederick Taylor, employee participation, and the experience in other countries is reported in the manual *A Union Member's Guide to Employee Involvement* by Tom Juravich and Howard Harris (Penn State). *Business Week* surveyed employee participation in its July 10, 1989, issue, which is where John Bradel was quoted. The Weirton employee participation group effort was covered in the publication *Independent Weirton*, including the selection of facilitators and the workings of programs. Also, I interviewed Darlene McKinley on April 26, 1988. I attended and participated in EPG training at Weirton in 1988. The names of the various EPG groups around the mill and their accomplishments were drawn from *Independent Weirton*. The transcripts of Loughead's speeches on employee participation were provided by Charles Cronin. Alan Gould was interviewed in March 1988. Anthony Julian was interviewed on October 6, 1988. I also reviewed the EPG department's documents, including its newsletter, *The Participant*. I interviewed David Shuler in April and May of 1988. Also, I went through SPC training at Weirton and reviewed the materials of the program. In addition, I utilized the videotapes and writings of W. Edwards Deming, especially his book *Out of Crisis* (Cambridge, MIT, 1982). The accomplishments of the SPC programs around the Weirton Mill were covered by *Independent Weirton*. Further, I interviewed John Kirkwood, an outside quality consultant to Weirton, on October 11, 1988.

253–256   I interviewed Lou Kondus, head of the OIP program, on September 19, 1988.

19   Hoopy Christmas

257–264   The financial figures are from Weirton's quarterly and annual reports. Weirton's ranking at 289 is from *Fortune* magazine's annual survey. Loughead spoke to the first annual meeting of the Weirton shareholders of November 2, 1984. In order to analyze *Independent Weirton* I received all copies of the publication from Charles Cronin. Chuck Lafferty provided me with the videotapes of "News and Views," which were produced by the Weirton Internal Communications Department. Weirton's relationship with Nippon Steel was covered in *Independent Weirton*, especially in the October 1984 issue. The K-R process was covered in *Independent Weirton*, especially in the September 1986 issue. The Egypt order was covered in the November 1984 issue of *Independent Weirton*. The ISU/Department of Labor issues, and communications between both, were found in the ISU's records. The election results of the ISU were found in union records, and were also reported in *Independent Weirton*. The K-R process also was covered in the *Pittsburgh Press* on June 18, 1985, especially as it bore upon the U.S. Department of Energy. Information from Steve Bauman's unsuccessful campaign was contained in correspondence from him to Staughton Lynd in June of 1985. Bluestone's remark to the union executive committee comes from ISU minutes.

20   Trouble at the Top

265–267   Safety issues including OSHA incident rates were tracked in *Independent Weirton*. Valdiserri and Doepken describe others' leaving the company in their interviews. The federal government's commitment on the K-R grant was reported on July 26, 1986, in the *Weirton Daily Times*. Bluestone spoke on the K-R process during his interview on July 14, 1988.

267–268 The capital spending figures were extracted from Weirton's annual reports. Employment figures were taken from the annual reports and *Independent Weirton*. Bluestone described his problems with the Loughead-Valdiserri relationship and the Chief Operating Officer issues in his interview on July 14, 1988.

268–272 Eugene Keilin's resignation from the Weirton board and Loughead's comments were reported in the *Weirton Daily Times* of September 27, 1985. Also, Keilin and Sperry discussed the resignation in their interviews. Sperry likewise described the situation between the board and Loughead, as well as Loughead's eventual removal, in Sperry's interview. Loughead's "early retirement" was revealed in the January 24, 1987, *Weirton Daily Times*. Valdiserri's was announced in the February 17, 1987, *Weirton Daily Times*. Mike Hrabovsky commented about Loughead during an interview on January 6, 1988. Loughead's remark paraphrasing Will Rogers about getting run over was made at the company's third annual meeting and reported in *Independent Weirton* in December 1986. The mix of materials in a domestic automobile was reported in the June 1987 *Independent Weirton*.

272–278 Herb Elish was interviewed on February 18, 1988. Sperry was quoted on Elish and the caster decision in his interview on April 28, 1988. Elish's remarks to the shareholders were covered in the November 1987 *Independent Weirton*. Background information on initial public offerings (IPOs) came from *Financial World*, July 10 through 23, 1985; *Fortune*, March 31, 1986; *Enterprise*, June 1983; and *Barron's*, January 23, 1984.

278–279 David Robertson predicted election problems for Walter Bish in an interview in January 1988. Financial studies by Lazard Frères and Bear Stearns were reported in *Independent Weirton* in its February/March issue of 1988. I was present in Weirton for most of the public meetings in 1988 and 1989 wherein these issues were discussed.

284–288 Norman Kurland wrote a cautionary letter to David Robertson on March 4, 1988. Walter Bish was interviewed on October 12, 1988. I interviewed Virgil Thompson on July 28, 1989, and met with him on numerous other occasions. Also, I witnessed much of the campaigning. The election also was reported in the August 1988 issue of *Independent Weirton*.

21 The Class of '88

285–302 The comparative steel industry spending and profitability figures were presented in the "Financial Analysis and Recommendations" of Bear Stearns and Lazard Frères in March 1988. I was present for the meetings in this chapter and recorded the quotations as I heard them.

22 Going Public

302–310 I was present for the negotiations at the Oglebay Lodge. I was permitted to attend the joint negotiations of management and labor in January and February of 1989, and to witness the union's caucuses. The quotations were recorded as I heard them. I read the position papers of the union and management, as well as *Straight Forward*, which was a new publication by the Weirton Internal Communications Department dealing strictly with financial proposals. Similarly, I analyzed the new information statement published by the company in February 1989 in booklet form to deal with financial issues. I attended the March 1989 shareholders meeting.

311–315   All the statistics about employee attitudes were taken from the document entitled "A Report on Employee Satisfaction, Attitudes and Intentions Based on a Survey Conducted During April, 1989," which was prepared for Weirton Steel by Sirota, Alper & Pfau. Remarks from Steve Bauman, Staughton and Alice Lynd, and Jim McNamara came from a dinner meeting on March 13, 1989.

23   Survival

316–319   In 1989 I attended presentations by Elish, Thompson, and the management team to prospective investors. The obligations to the SEC were described in *Independent Weirton*, April 1989. Herbert Elish's remarks and the performance of the stock upon opening were reported in the *Weirton Daily Times* in June 1989.

319–322   I met with Louis Kelso during the May 1989 ESOP convention. I attended the fall 1989 collective bargaining negotiations between management and labor at Weirton. New educational opportunities for workers including the Work Place 2000 program were reviewed in *Independent Weirton*, April 1989. The achievements by the EPG groups were related in the interviews with Tony Julian and Darlene McKinley. The quotation from Charles Bradford, as well as the activity of the Weirton shares on the first day, was carried in the *Pittsburgh Post-Gazette*, June 16, 1989. Gene Keilin assessed the prospects of Weirton during a lunch meeting in September 1989.

322–329   Elish's remarks about "changing the culture" were made in an interview on June 17, 1992. Weirton's Vision statement was printed in the 1990 annual report. Tom Evans was interviewed on August 6, 1992. Safety issues were reported in *Business Briefs*, a publication of Weirton Steel, May 29, 1992. The "Year of the Customer" was reported in the January 1990 edition of *Independent Weirton*. IMIS was reported in the June 1990 *Independent Weirton*. Galfan, "kosher steel," and new equipment also were reported in the company press. Balance sheet and production figures during the 1990s were taken from annual reports. The significance of the updated caster was reported in the *Weirton Daily Times* of October 18, 1990. The securities profile of the company was drawn from *Moody's Industrial Manual*, 1991. Comparisons with other steelmakers during the downturn, as well as technological changes in the industry, and the mini-mill phenomenon during the recession, were reported in *Standard & Poor's Industry Surveys: Steel and Heavy Industry, Basic Analysis*, December 26, 1991. Picketing at Weirton and labor problems were reported in the September 9, 1991, *Business Week*.

330–331   Mark Glyptis was interviewed on July 1, 1992. The Cleveland Cliffs transaction was announced in a Weirton Steel news release on October 1, 1991, and it was covered in the *Weirton Daily Times* and the *American Metal Market* in

October 1991. The results of the 1991 officers election of the ISU were announced by Wallace, Padden & Company—Certified Public Accountants, June 11, 1991. The honor from the Campbell Soup Company was announced in a Weirton Steel news release on February 25, 1992. The trade complaints filed by steel companies were reported in the *Weirton Daily Times* of July 1, 1992. Weirton Steel's workforce cuts of almost 25 percent were announced in the *New York Times*, July 25, 1992.

332–333   The Bricmont matter produced legal papers that I reviewed in the case of *Godich v. Elish*, in the Circuit Court of Hancock County, West Virginia, filed August 7, 1992.

333–334   Microwaivable cans were covered in the *Wall Street Journal* of August 31, 1991. Mark Glyptis was quoted about "maximizing profits ..." in the September 19, 1991, issue of *Business Week*. Glyptis was quoted about "sacrifice" in the same issue. The ISU side of the conflict of interest alleged against Sperry and his firm were reviewed in *Union Focus*, Vol. II, 1992. Delbert Littleton was interviewed on August 3, 1992, regarding Sperry, Robertson, and the union.

334–339   I also reviewed court papers in the lawsuit of *Nixon v. Roberts* (Newell case) filed in Hancock County, West Virginia, January 21, 1992. The Robertson case was reviewed in the July 1992 issue of *Union Focus* and was covered in the *Wheeling-Intelligencer*, July 12, 1992. Philip Smith was interviewed on August 18, 1992. The law firm of Varnum Riddering Schmidt & Howlett issued its ethical report on the Willkie Farr issue on July 20, 1992. Willkie Farr's representation of Japanese companies was reported in *Agents of Influence* by Pat Choate (New York, Alfred A. Knopf, 1990). Votes from board meetings and quotations from board meetings were offered by board members on a not for attribution basis.

339–343   The Willkie Farr controversy and the crude drawing of Sperry being lynched appeared in *Forbes* on August 30, 1993. Warren Bartel's resignation was reported in the *Weirton Daily Times* on September 23, 1993. The West Virginia Supreme Court ruling on Bricmont was reported in the *Weirton Daily Times* on July 23, 1993.

343–344   The effort to sell approximately 60 million shares was reported in the *Weirton Daily Times* on September 2, 1993, and generally through the fall of 1993. Worker protest was reported in the *Weirton Daily Times* of October 29, 1993. The thwarting of the stock sale was reported in the *Pittsburgh Post-Gazette* on Wednesday, November 10, 1993. Also, I reviewed the corporation's "Notice of Special Meeting of Stockholders" for the session, which was to be held on November 11, 1993, but was cancelled. Mark Glyptis's victorious remarks were reported in the *Weirton Daily Times* of November 10, 1993. The *Wall Street Journal* criticized Weirton on September 23, 1993.

344–345   The fire at Weirton was reported in the *Steubenville Herald-Star*, April 10, 1994. The profitability of Weirton was reported in the April 20, 1994, *Weirton Daily Times*.

345–346   The new stock issue, its structural changes for the corporation, and the union's position on this situation were reported in the *Weirton Daily Times*, April 14, 1994.

345–347   Harvey Sperry's decision to leave the Weirton board was reported in the April 12, 1994, *Weirton Daily Times*. ISU politics and Mark Glyptis's reelection as president were reported in the *Weirton Daily Times* of May 3, 1994.

346–347   The reform package at Weirton was announced in a corporate news release of August 2, 1994. The resolution of the Bricmont suit was reported in the *Pittsburgh Post-Gazette* on July 1, 1994, and in the *Weirton Daily Times* of August 4, 1994. Views of management and union on the new stock sale were reported in the *Weirton Daily Times* of August 12, 1994.

347–348   The upturn in the steel market was reported in the *Pittsburgh Post-Gazette* on July 22, 1994, and August 7, 1994. Also, the trend was covered in the *New York Times* on July 22, 1994. Steel's advantages for building were covered in the *Weirton Daily Times* on September 1, 1994.

347–348   For analyses of Weirton Stock, I utilized Paine Webber's *Metal Stock Strategies*, and Salomon Brothers' *Equity Research: Steels*. I spoke during the 1990s with Richard Garan, the Weirton director of investor relations.

348–349   The ESOP at the UAL Corporation was covered in the *Wall Street Journal* of December 23, 1993. Elish's quotation about communications was reported in *Independent Weirton*.

Selected Bibliography

Bensman, David, and Roberta Lynch. *Rusted Dreams: Hard Times in a Steel Community*. New York: McGraw-Hill, 1987.

Blasi, Joseph R. *Employee Ownership: Revolution or Ripoff?* Cambridge, Mass.: Ballinger Publisher Company, 1988.

Boyer, Richard O., and Herbert M. Morais. *Labor's Untold Story*. New York: United Electrical, Radio and Machine Workers of America, 1955.

Brecher, Jeremy. *Strike!* San Francisco: Straight Arrow Books, 1974.

Cohen, Lizabeth. *Making a New Deal: Industrial Workers in Chicago, 1919–1939*. Cambridge, Mass.: Cambridge University Press, 1990.

Deming, W. Edwards. *Out of the Crisis*. Cambridge, Mass.: Massachusetts Institute of Technology, Center for Advanced Engineering Study, 1982.

———. *Quality, Productivity, and Competitive Position*. Cambridge, Mass.: Massachusetts Institute of Technology, Center for Advanced Engineering Study, 1982.

Drucker, Peter F. *Management: Tasks, Responsibilities, Practices.* New York: Harper & Row, 1973.

The ESOP Association. *Employee Stock Ownership Plans.* Washington, D.C.: Twelfth Annual Convention, 1989.

Fitch, John A. *The Steel Workers.* Pittsburgh: University of Pittsburgh Press, 1989.

Fundis, Lois Aleta, ed. *Weirton Steel: An ESOP story, 1982–1985.* Weirton, West Virginia: Mary H. Weir Public Library, 1985.

Galambos, Louis, and Joseph Pratt. *The Rise of the Corporate Commonwealth: United States Business and Public Policy in the 20th Century.* New York: Basic Books, 1988.

Halberstam, David. *The Reckoning.* New York: Avon Books, 1986.

Hareven, Tamara K., and Randolph Langenbach. *Amoskeag: Life and Work in an American Factory-City.* New York: Pantheon Books, 1978.

Harris, Howard, and Tom Juravich. *A Union Member's Guide to Employee Involvement.* State College: Pennsylvania State University. Department of Labor Studies and Industrial Relations, 1987.

Herling, John. Right to Challenge: *People and Power in the Steelworkers Union.* New York: Harper & Row, 1972.

Hoerr, John P. *And the Wolf Finally Came: The Decline of the American Steel Industry.* Pittsburgh: University of Pittsburgh Press, 1988.

Hounshell, David A. *From the American System to Mass Production, 1800–1932.* Baltimore: Johns Hopkins University Press, 1984.

Hutchinson, John. *The Imperfect Union: A History of Corruption in American Trade Unions.* New York: E. P. Dutton & Co., 1972.

Katz, Harry C., Thomas A. Kochan, and Robert B. McKersie. *The Transformation of American Industrial Relations.* New York: Basic Books, 1986.

Kelso, Louis, and Mortimer Adler. *The Capitalist Manifesto.* New York: Random House, 1958.

Kelso, Louis O., and Patricia Hetter Kelso. *Democracy and Economic Power: Extending the ESOP Revolution.* Cambridge, Mass.: Ballinger Publishing Company, 1986.

Labor Research Review, ed. *Workers as Owners.* Chicago: Midwest Center for Labor Research, 1985.

McGannon, Harold, ed. *The Making, Shaping and Treating of Steel, Eighth Edition.* Pittsburgh: Unites States Steel, 1964.

MARHO, The Radical Historians Organization. *Visions of History.* New York: Pantheon Books, 1984.

Mills, C. Wright. *The Power Elite.* Oxford: Oxford University Press, 1956.

O'Dell, Sheri A., ed. *The Rockefeller Years, 1977–1985: Official Papers and Policies.* 3 vols. West Virginia State Government, 1985.

Ouchi, William G. *Theory Z: How American Business Can Meet the Japanese Challenge.* New York: Avon Books, 1981.

Pennsylvania Council on the Arts. *Overtime: Punchin' Out With the "Mill Hunk Herald" Magazine (1979–1989).* Albuquerque: West End Press, 1990.

Perrot, Mark. *Eliza: Remembering a Pittsburgh Steel Mill.* Charlottesville: Howell Press, 1989.

Preis, Art. *Labor's Giant Step: Twenty Years of the CIO.* New York: Pioneer Publishers, 1964.

Preston, Richard. *American Steel: Hot Metal Men and the Resurrection of the Rust Belt.* New York: Prentice Hall Press, 1991.

Reutter, Mark. *Sparrows Point: Making Steel—The Rise and Ruin of American Industrial Might.* New York: Summit Books, 1988.

Serrin, William. *Homestead: The Glory and Tragedy of an American Steel Town.* New York: Times Books, 1992.

Smith, George David. *From Monopoly to Competition: The Transformations of Alcoa, 1888–1986.* Cambridge, Mass.: Cambridge University Press, 1988.

Smith, Lee, ed. The Cuomo Commission on Trade and Competitiveness. *The Cuomo Commission Report.* New York: Simon & Schuster, 1988.

Smith, William Dale. *A Multitude of Men.* New York: Simon & Schuster, 1959.

Strohmeyer, John. *Crisis in Bethlehem: Big Steel's Struggle to Survive.* Bethesda: Adler & Adler, 1986.

Toussaint, M. M. F. *From Ore to Steel.* Dusseldorf: Verlag Stahleisen, 1962.

United Steelworkers of America Education Department. *Then & Now: The Road Between. The Story of the United Steelworkers of America.* Pittsburgh: United Steelworkers of America, 1974.

Zuboff, Shoshana. *In the Age of the Smart Machine: The Future of Work and Power.* New York: Basic Books, 1988.

Index